Inherent Vice

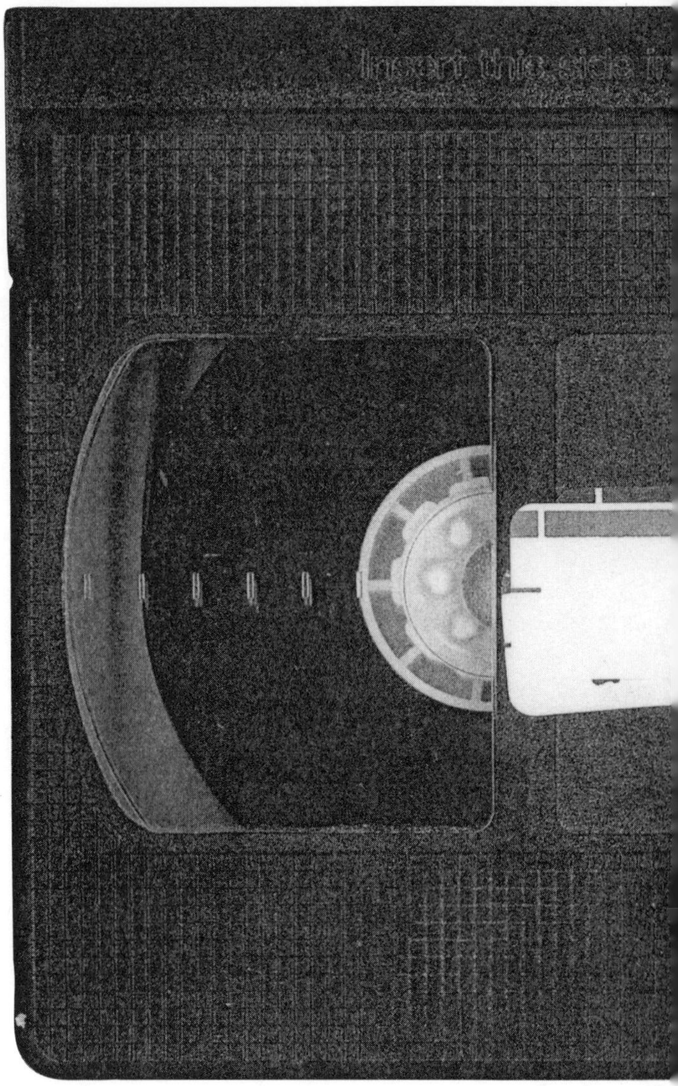
Insert this side in

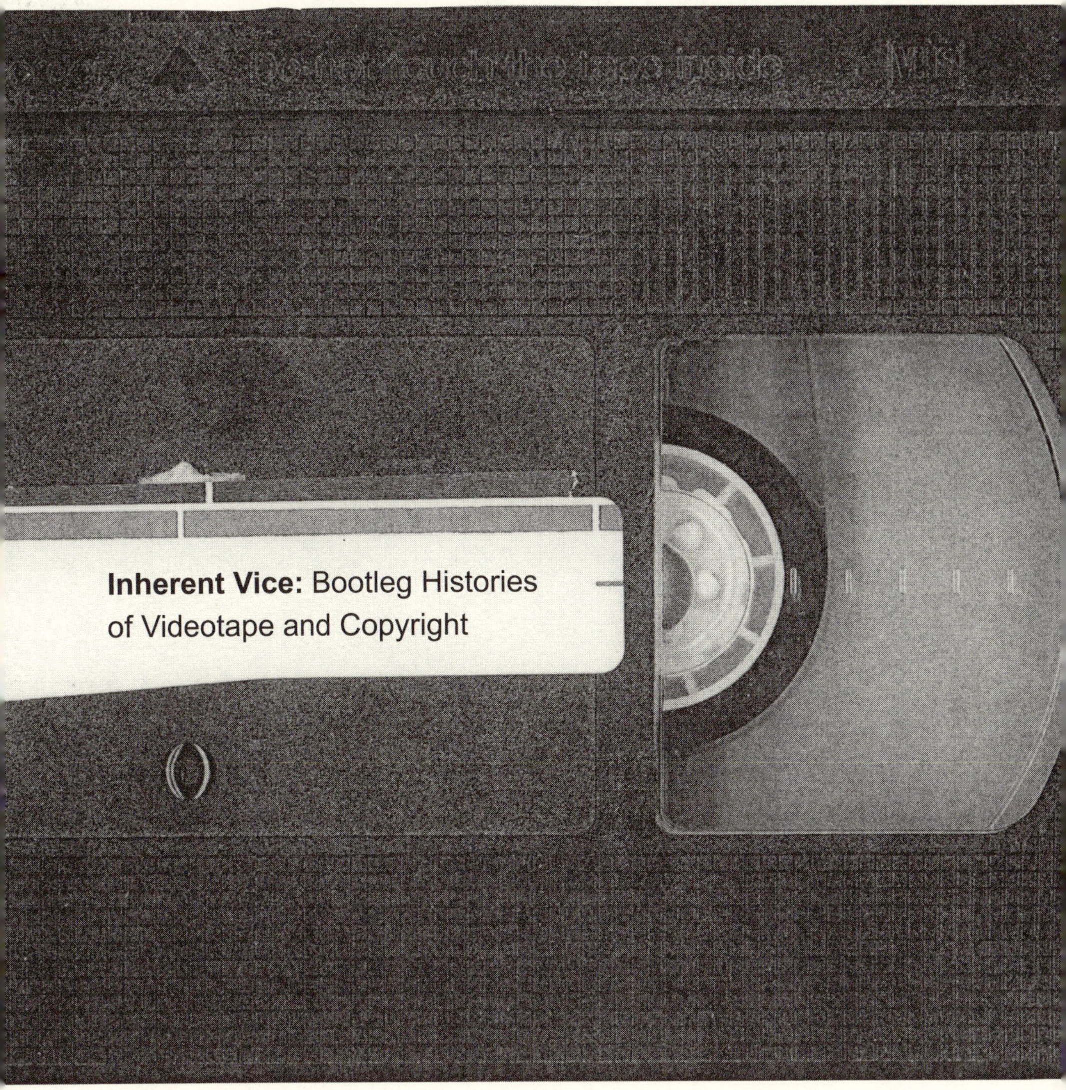

Inherent Vice: Bootleg Histories of Videotape and Copyright

Lucas Hilderbrand

Duke University Press | Durham and London | 2009

Printed in the United States of America
on acid-free paper ∞
Designed by Amy Ruth Buchanan
Typeset in Whitman by Achorn International
Library of Congress Cataloging-in-Publication data
and republication acknowledgments appear on the
last printed pages of this book.

For Catty

Contents

List of Illustrations

Preface

The format wars and legal battles that marked home video's early history have seemingly been rewound and replayed repeatedly in the age of peer-to-peer file-sharing networks, online video streaming, and HD DVD format competition. This book seeks to rethink videotape's recent histories from the vantage point of a cultural moment when DVD (and increasingly downloaded and streaming video) has eclipsed videotape as the primary home video format and when both the entertainment industry and the government have sought to clamp down on "piracy." Any device that has been widely adopted and altered audience uses is necessarily of its own moment and might eventually evoke nostalgia once it becomes (theoretically or actually) obsolete. In fact, the appearance of home video in the mid-1970s might be said to be culturally linked to the purported nostalgia craze of the time by making old movies and syndicated shows recordable for reviewing.[1]

In this book I situate videotape and VCRs culturally—through popular rhetoric, market shifts, legal regulations, and love stories. The book, in turn, can be situated in dialogue with cinema and television studies, histories of new media, critical legal studies, and copyleft advocacy. A substantial body of literature has analyzed the theories and uses of video, yet such work has not captured all the cultural meanings, experiences, or prevalent uses of videotape. One survey of the academic literature on video claimed a lack of critical consensus on video specificity except that it has no specificity.[2] A wave of foundational scholarship about video, which extended from British television and cultural studies and American postmodern theory, appeared in the late 1980s and early 1990s.[3] Other work oriented toward history or the social sciences reflects varied disciplinary approaches to video. On the sociological and ethnographic end of communications approaches, researchers have clocked subjects' uses of VCRs and related technologies, focusing less on what is watched than on how and for how long. This behaviorist approach emphasized individuals' actions and motivations.[4] Industry-oriented communications and political economy work has examined statistics of VCR adoption by consumers and corporate strategies of exploring and exploiting the home video market.[5] Such market research offers a macro view that again abstracts content in favor of hard numbers for units sold and commercial exploitation. When video's aesthetic potential has been explored, it has been as a "problem" for cinema studies or in the separate milieu of video art; although video art reflected upon the technology and ideology of television generally, it ultimately offers limited resemblance to more pervasive entertainment uses of videotape.[6] In analyzing video as a haptic medium, cinema scholar Laura Marks looks to a site of aesthetic analysis close to my own heart: video grain and decay.[7] (More on that in the introduction and chapter 4.) Such cinema studies and communications approaches rarely investigate the history of video technology in dialogue with both aesthetic and legal issues, the strategy of the present book.

Comparative academic histories of "old" and "new" media have been prone to juxtaposing vinyl LPs and CDs or celluloid and streaming digital video while erasing "middle-aged" or residual magnetic tapes and cassettes from the evolutions of formats and practices.[8] Analog videotape was once a new technology, and before too long, DVDs and MPEGs will seem old as well. By treating magnetic tape technologies as merely transitional and inferior to what came before and after, such work presents a distorted and incomplete account that ignores the material and experiential attributes of these recording and playback technologies—and the new modes and expectations of access that they introduced.[9]

Old, middle-aged, and new technologies co-exist, rather than offering a radical break. Historians' attention to new technologies often infers that once a device is commercially available, it is adopted and immediately displaces prior technologies, and new media studies often dwell on the newness of the present or the promise of the future. But technological predictions often miss the mark, as devices are often imagined to become ubiquitous years or even decades before they even become commercially available. And just because a technology has been invented and marketed does not mean it is adopted or instantly becomes part of everyday life. Technological obsolescence doesn't quite work so efficiently, either: analog technologies remain useful and in use. Planned obsolescence, a marketing racket developed through short-lived pop music singles and annual automotive model updates, has extended to frequent "innovations" in computers and cell phones. Hardware manufacturers, looking to develop a new market, and the studios, eager to sell rereleases of familiar content, have pushed the idea of analog technologies' obsolescence. Just as availability does not mean adoption, and market penetration takes time, so does obsolescence. VHS and VCRs linger on as "residual" technologies, patched into TVs to play back old tapes or lingering on in the pre-landfill limbo of basements and garages.[10] As one scholar put it, "The venerable VHS cassette has been around since 1976, a geological tenure in electronic media terms."[11] Thus I agree with arguments against seeing new media as revolutionary; rather, new media reveal continuities, collaborations, and periods of coexistence as technologies change. New technologies do not necessarily kill media when they upgrade the devices.[12] What's new about new media is specific technologies, interfaces, and uses, but these technologies often rework preexisting practices, concepts, and content.

Media archaeology looks for the new in the old, the stories in the past, and the tangents among the facts. Although I haven't followed this as a methodology exactly, as someone who is often more interested in asides and footnotes than in a book's thesis, I can only hope that I have done just this, by looking to the legal feuds and lurid associations in home video's past.[13] My book is unabashedly nostalgic, just as I suspect that the affective uses of videotape have often been.[14] At times, this will mean articulating the obvious, drawing the reader's attention to aesthetics, uses, and materialities of videotapes that were almost instantly taken for granted, that may need to be rethought, or that may only be noticed for the first time now. This will entail mixing subjective and scholarly tones, anecdotal and archival evidence, though the boundaries are not so discrete: some of the anecdotes come from archives. This study is not an ethnography of bootleggers but rather a series of histories, reflections, and analyses of the ways that videos have created, changed, and circulated texts. I have attempted to integrate policy with media historiography, reception studies, material culture, and cinema aesthetics. Thus, I hope that this book not only gives videotape a worthy send-off but also transcends the plastic tape and cassette casings to suggest how thinking about analog video is generative for understanding other times and technologies.

The concept of cultural memory describes less-than-systematic ways in which personal experience, popular culture, and historical narratives intersect. Experiences of home video are largely entangled with memories of media. So many of our personal and social memories are of cultural

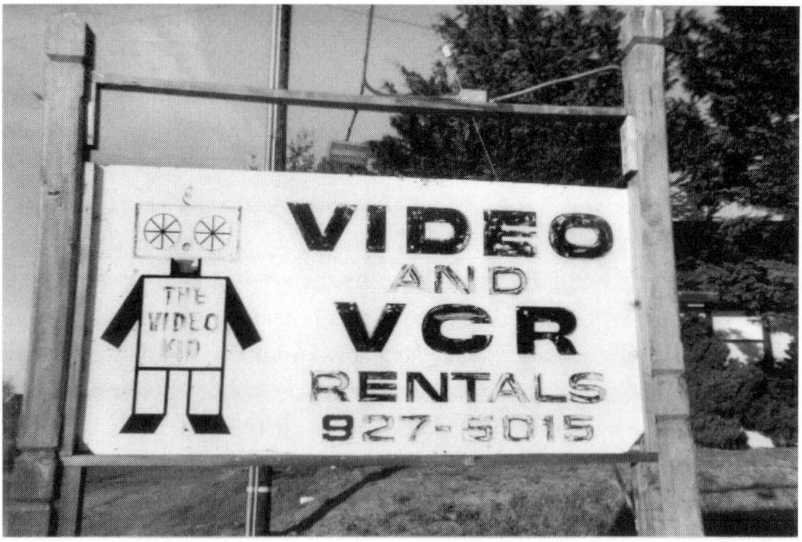

1. The weathered sign in front of an independent video store in Cambria, California, continues to advertise VCR rentals. The robot's belly says, "The Video Kid." Photo by author, October 2006.

productions, whether epiphany-inducing masterpieces or familiar sitcoms. The private tactics and affects of videotape bootlegging in effect help to produce and sustain cultural memories; videotape allows users to save or seek out the media texts that have shaped them and that would otherwise be forgotten in "objective" histories.[15] Writing about both video and cultural memory, Marita Sturken formulates the intersections of the two: she acknowledges the materiality of video and theorizes cultural memory as entangled with history in the way the past is recalled and reexperienced. Videotapes are "technologies of memory" that "embody and generate memory."[16]

If you will indulge me, I would like to share my own memories of videotape since my readings of historical documents and legal codes are inevitably subjective. Videotape has been formative throughout my life. When I was a kid, videotape became my means of accessing the world beyond my small Midwestern town. I loved to browse the video boxes at the public library, the video store, and the video sections at the gas station or grocery store, and to take home as many as I had time and money to watch. In the early 1980s, before my family finally bought our own VCR, we would rent the deck along with the videotapes. We'd regularly lug home a heavy, top-loading VCR in its protective blue nylon foam carrying case. This made the convenience and experience of home video affordable even before the cost of the decks dropped to consumer-friendly rates. Despite being a respectable Baptist family, we had a propensity for renting lowbrow comedies with significant amounts of nudity. "Cover your eyes" was a common refrain my parents would use as we watched *Vacation*, *Revenge of the Nerds*, or *Porky's*. (Of course, I peeked between my fingers, perhaps instilling a connection between video and sexual discovery; rewinding, pausing, and slow motion later became favorite tools during puberty.) Not long after my family did finally get a VCR of its own, I began to hoard it by keeping it in my room, patched into the minuscule television I had saved a year's worth of allowances to buy. When I went east to college, my first major purchase was a VCR of my own, which became a symbol of my adult independence.

Much of my higher education about film, television, and video art—and most of what was interesting—I learned from bootlegs. I first saw *Superstar: The Karen Carpenter Story*, the tape that inspired this project, in an undergraduate film course called Oppositional Cinemas. In addition to examples of Third Cinema and Paper Tiger TV media deconstructions, we also watched the graduate student adjunct's own homemade VCR-to-VCR abridgement of a Lifetime TV miniseries, which reduced four hours of melodrama to a more manageable hour-long text with softened video colors and jump-cut transitions. During and after college, I became a professional bootlegger when, as a film critic, I often received second-generation preview tapes; and as a publicist, duplicating tapes for other critics was part of my job. The more compelling or obscure the work, the more likely I was to keep a copy for myself. In grad school, I saw many more tapes of dubious provenance, including video art, perverse practices, old industrial documentaries, early television, Hollywood films taped off-air, foreign films undistributed in the United States, and recordings of "authoritative" or otherwise unavailable archival prints. Such screenings were typically prefaced by apologies for the tape quality or half-proud explanations of the recordings' pilfered origins.

I have researched and written this book while VHS teetered on the brink of obsolescence, and this project has largely been an attempt to keep the memory of VHS alive. During the temporal vortex known as grad school, DVD effectively pushed VHS out of the market, and video stores across the country began liquidating outmoded inventories of still-functional cassettes. Curiously enough, when I later moved to Los Angeles, I discovered a heartening preponderance of independent video stores that maintained actual videotapes—and not just small sections at the back, but racks and racks of them, up front and banged up from handling. VHS lived on in the home of the entertainment industry that had once opposed it, and this vitality renewed my conviction about the format as I began revising this manuscript. But when I tried to replace the VCR that conked out at my (illegal) sublet, I discovered, to my practical frustration and academic dismay, that new stand-alone VCRs had already become almost impossible to buy. As I hope this account indicates, for me, at least, access, aesthetics, and affect are intertwined.

The introduction defines some of the concepts that have informed my project and highlights the basic issues at play throughout the book, such as video's interventions into the ways audiences use and experience the media and the intersections of copyright regulations and video practices. Chapter 1 expands the discussion of videotape to suggest a complex conception of analog magnetic video's format specificity. I situate video technology historically, in relation to prior analog audio and more recent digital video media, examine changes in its uses and discourses effected by the market, and finally suggest the aesthetics of analog video by examining bootlegs and amateur pornography. Chapter 2 offers critical legal histories of copyright, fair use, and legal restrictions in the era of digital media. In tandem with the historical intentions and legislations of copyright law, I analyze two major Supreme Court decisions that have sought to think through and, to some extent, expand the fair-use doctrine and its relationship to home video recording. *Sony v. Universal* (1984) set a major judicial precedent that has been much debated and much relied upon in subsequent discussions of fair use and personal media consumption. This decision also served as the defense in the later wave of lawsuits against peer-to-peer file-sharing services, as well as the primary allusion in press and critical legal commentary on these cases. This suggests that the Betamax case not only set a legal precedent but also that VCRs established practices that have informed institutional and private paradigms for domestic media that have continued into the digital era. The chapter concludes with an analysis of the Supreme Court opinions in *MGM v. Grokster* (2005), which considered the relevance of the analog ruling for digital file sharing and reconsidered the continued authority of the prior ruling more generally.

The first two chapters work to establish the more institutional—one might say more coherent, though hopefully still surprising—histories of videotape and copyright. Following these foundational chapters, a trio of case studies, while chronological in sequence and contextualized within their specific accounts, deviates from the standard histories of analog video.

These case studies examine practices that reflect myriad ways videotape has enabled access through alternative preservation and distribution and are intentionally distinct in scale, ambition, and milieu—although all of them derive from personal initiative to use videotape to preserve and circulate politically, aesthetically, or socially significant media works. The studies range from a long-term, systematic, institutionalized historical project to record news, to idiosyncratic person-to-person tape dupes and trades that have informally maintained a public life for an underground film, to a loosely structured feminist network for exchanging work.

Chapter 3, the first case study, focuses on the Vanderbilt Television News Archive. This archive was the first project of its kind: a broadcast taping project begun in 1968 to record and collect the nightly network news for political, historical, and scholarly analysis. Following meetings and correspondence with the Vanderbilt archive, CBS sued the archive for copyright infringement. Vanderbilt countered that the archive project was acting in the interest of the First Amendment (which suggests the freedoms of speech and the press) and the Fairness Doctrine (the FCC policy that attempted to balance political perspectives in broadcasting) by providing public access to information. The lawsuit extended over the course of three years; although numerous motions were filed, it never reached a trial. The litigation was eventually resolved in Congress, rather than in court, through the comprehensive revision of the copyright code in 1976, which included a special copyright exemption for libraries and archives to record the news, mandated the creation of the American Television and Radio Archive at the Library of Congress, and offered the first statutory fair-use exemption. Not only did video recording introduce a new relationship to television news, giving it a controversial new status as an object of study during a period of cultural conflicts, but this new relationship also raised critical issues of politics, preservation, and the rights of access.

Moving from innovations in video preservation and debates over the legal status of recordings, I next consider more experiential concepts of aesthetics and affect. The second case study, chapter 4, turns to the bootleg history of Todd Haynes's *Superstar: The Karen Carpenter Story* (1987). This text, which dramatizes a pop-culture history of the Nixon era, was originally conceived as an allegorical text for the Reagan era, one that traced the beginnings of a conservative shift in American political and popular culture and the ambivalent appeal of the seemingly wholesome and reactionary sibling singing duo the Carpenters. The film was withdrawn from official distribution after Haynes received cease-and-desist letters threatening copyright litigation over the film's unauthorized inclusion of the Carpenters' music. But *Superstar* had clearly struck a chord with audiences and has continued to circulate via bootleg videotapes, semi-secret screenings, and eventually DVD-RS and downloadable MPEGS. Thus *Superstar* was a film phenomenon of the home video age, as the common consumer technology aided in duplicating and circulating the text for a wide viewing public that, in an earlier era, would have known of the work only through rumor. The chapter recounts and clarifies this cult film's screening and legal history and then examines the underground tapes as unique texts that encode their own histories of multiple-generation dubbing. Through these tapes, format-specific aesthetics become more pronounced as analog interference and lost resolution cloud the image and distort the soundtrack. Because the film has historically circulated through direct, interpersonal copying and loaning, the cassettes themselves become mementos of specific people or time periods in their owners' lives. Thus *Superstar* bootlegs suggest both aesthetic and affective relationships rarely attributed to videotapes.

The final case study, chapter 5, presents the Joanie 4 Jackie (formerly Big Miss Moviola) video chainletter project as a model for bootleg self-distribution in a turn that moves the discussion away from productive copyright infringement toward willful open-source sharing. This project, initiated by the performance and video artist Miranda July, established an alternative, person-to-person video distribution network for women and girl media makers. Influenced by riot grrrl, zine, and punk principles (though predated by early video collectives and exchanges), the project works like this: female media makers send in a tape of their work, and it is compiled onto a mix videotape (a "chainletter") that is then returned to the makers and available to anyone who wants to buy a copy. The project is specifically analog in its uses of videotape reproduction and the U.S. Postal Service's distribution infrastructure. I examine this project as providing a space for female artists located in western and midwestern towns to express their experiences in American regions rarely portrayed in mainstream or alternative media. The tapes often present autobiographical or essayistic accounts of female experiences, which suggest a form of community building based on shared intimacies that dates back to prior waves of feminist organizing. Begun in the mid-1990s and continuing into the first decade of the new century, the Joanie 4 Jackie project offers an analog video distribution model that predates widespread online file sharing and digital-era public-domain endeavors such as Creative Commons. The participants forgo copyright protection and royalties to express themselves, communicate, and foster a nationwide feminist media network.

Appearing in chronological order, these bootleg studies offer examples of productive video uses in the 1970s, 1980s, and 1990s, respectively, although all of the described practices continue. The different intentions and practices suggest a range of uses of video, and each study attempts to contextualize practices within American culture—political, artistic, and social. Additionally, these studies indicate cultural shifts in relation to copyright law, from attempts to work with and through the law, to resisting it, to inventing participatory alternatives to it. Although each case study presents exceptions to everyday videotape practices rather than exemplifying them, they do indicate the increasing disconnections between copyright law and the ways users interact with media (and mediated communities).

Between chapters, I interject quick, illustrative interludes called "video clips" that focus on specific sites and debates for videotape bootlegging and exchange. In effect, these represent some of the illicit practices that elude sustained studies but must not be overlooked. I have been fortunate to live in the two U.S. media capitals—Los Angeles and New York—while working on this project; certainly this facilitated much of my research. But it was also important to me to look beyond these cities or even nearby Orange County and New Jersey (though these suburbs are present in the clips) to some of the other locations where bootleg taping and access have been so important, such as Nashville and Oklahoma City. *Inherent Vice* examines the ways that practices, regulations, places, and experiences of videotape technology have raised new means and concerns for media participation, preservation, and circulation.

This book is primarily historical in orientation, but in the epilogue, I turn to one of the most popular developments in video sharing of the twenty-first century: YouTube. Although there is much specifically new and wonderful about YouTube, I suggest that the most prominent discourses surrounding it—the democratization of media access and the threat of piracy—recall the decades-old ideologies and panics that have long defined video. YouTube not only revives these familiar tropes, but also facilitates reviewing the video past.

Acknowledgments

One of this book's topics is the formation of connections and communities through videotape. Certainly, the book wouldn't have happened but for the kindness of many friends and some strangers.

I'll begin, as academics so often do, by thanking my dissertation committee. I wanted an advisor whose work I admired and with whom I felt kinship; with Anna McCarthy, I shared inspirations, anxieties, pedagogical strategies, and scholarly methods, as well as gossip, videos, music, and friendship. Howard Besser inspired my interest in the critical issues that copyright law raises for media access and preservation with the offhand remark that sometimes what's ethical and what's legal don't align. (The implication was that archivists face difficult choices in preserving media.) Marita Sturken's research stimulated my thinking well before I met her, and her feedback was always incisive and instructive. During my defense Lawrence Lessig's and Siva Vaidhyanathan's comments were unexpectedly generous, and their questions were generative. Thanks are due to the many other faculty, visitors, staff, and students who helped shape my time at New York University.

To my great fortune, a postdoctoral fellowship in Critical Studies at the University of Southern California's School of Cinematic Arts gave me research support in beginning the process of writing this book. The USC faculty and staff, especially Anne Friedberg, Miranda Banks, Michael Renov, and Bill Whittington were very supportive. Having Los Angeles as my new home also certainly softened the blow of having to leave New York; I suspect I have Tara McPherson to thank for this.

I write these acknowledgments now as a faculty member in Film and Media Studies at the University of California, Irvine—a position I know how fortunate I am to have. Not only a top-notch research institution in a sunny location, UCI also boasts the best colleagues imaginable; I actually look forward to faculty meetings. Everyone has been wonderful, with a few folks who deserve special mention. My fellow media peep Victoria Johnson has been supportive of my work and social life from the start and has generously shared insights into how the UC system works. Kristen Hatch and Catherine Benamou both navigated as UCI newbies alongside me with a great spirit of camaraderie; Kristen, in particular, has become a close friend and has even occasionally taken me in as a refugee from behind the Orange Curtain. True to her name, Bliss Lim makes me happy every time I see her; and Lauren Steimer has been a dove. Beyond my home department, Julia Bryan-Wilson has become a friend and frequent conspirator, and Jennifer Terry has been a fun mentor. I also thank the tireless FMS department staff Vikki Duncan, Peter Chang, Suzanne Wachman, and Kelly Swanholm. And, finally, the students in my graduate seminar "Inventing the Media: Histories of Technology" offered constructive critiques when we workshopped this manuscript in class.

My research was aided and abetted by numerous people, including Caetlin Benson-Allott, Ann Butler at Fales Library, Julia Bryan-Wilson, the *Camera Obscura* collective, Daniel Chamberlain, Andrea Fontenot, Noriko Furunishi, Rosemary Furtak, Tarleton Gillespie, Joshua Greenberg, Jackie Goss and her Joanie 4 Jackie interns at Bard College, Jeremy and Liz Greene, Todd Haynes, Jim Hubbard, Ed Johnson, Lynne Joyrich, Brian Larkin, Ming Yuen S. Ma, Shauna McGarry, K. J. Mohr, Charles Silver of the MoMA Film Study Center, Sirida Srisombadi, Lauren Steimer, Julio Vera, James Wentzy, Patty White, Rob White and *Film Quarterly*'s anonymous readers, Damon Young, the staff of the Margaret Herrick Library for the Academy of Motion Picture Picture Arts and Science, and the interns of the various archives who presumably did the initial clippings and filings that have been invaluable for supplementing my research. For my research on the Vanderbilt Television News Archive, the entire archive staff enthusiastically provided essential access to archival documents and their own memories; Marshall Breeding and his wife Zora were also wonderfully gracious hosts during my time in Nashville. To get the CBS perspective, I had a cordial and frank off-the-record discussion with the executive director of the CBS News archive, Dan DiPierro. For aiding supplemental research, I thank Mike Mashon, Madeline Mats, and the staffs of the Library of Congress Motion Picture, Broadcasting and Recorded Sound Division and the Library of Congress Law Library Reading Room. And thanks, again, to the many respondents to my e-mail queries and postings about diasporic bootlegs, video memories, and *Superstar*.

For images, Austin Kearsley at the UCI Teaching, Learning and Technology Center retrained me to capture video stills, Henry Shipman aided in making some of the VTNA photos in chapter 3 available, and Caroline Burghardt at the Luhring Augustine Gallery provided the image from Pipilotti Rist's *I'm Not the Girl Who Misses Much*.

At Duke University Press, Ken Wissoker has been enthusiastic in acquiring my manuscript, and Courtney Berger has been as conscientious as she is charming in overseeing its publication. Pam Morrison has been a pro as my managing editor, and my copy editor Bill Henry commendably caught many mistakes and indulged my prose. I wanted a beautiful book, and I thank Amy Ruth Buchanan for making a book about an obsolete technology and copyright technicalities so graceful looking. I asked for anonymous readers with expertise in the law and in historiography beyond film studies to test this project with the most rigorous standards possible. I thank my anonymous and not-so-anonymous readers for their generosity, careful readings of the text, and insightful suggestions to improve it.

Thanks to my parents for always supporting me, whatever my interests, and allowing me to be, well, me. My brother Grant set the academic bar high and has always looked out for his little brother. Many friends have offered support and distractions; to name but a few members of my chosen family: Marci Boudreau, Michael Franklin, Bishnu Ghosh, Ali Hoffman, Liza Johnson, Alex Juhasz, Carla Marcantonio, Jeff Martin, Sara Mielke, the MIX festival staff, Candace Moore, Nguyen Tan Hoang, Kimberly O'Quinn, David Pendleton, Ragan Rhyne, Lynne Sachs, Bhaskar Sarkar, Marc Siegel, Lauren Steimer, Michelle Stewart, Juan Suarez, Richard Vos, Tom Waugh, and Agustin Zarzosa. Elena Gorfinkel has been one of my intellectual mentors, and we have shared hours of smut mongering, dancing, and haircuts during our years of friendship. Jose Freire's authoritative pronouncements never fail to amuse or educate, and his kindness has been immeasurable. Joe Wlodarz has read many drafts of many things and shared many a night of cocktails. Dean Otto has kept me true to my sentimental hometown (Minneapolis) and repeatedly shared his house as my vacation home. Finally, I dedicate this book to Allison McCracken, who has been my confidante and cheerleader from the beginning of this project through its completion—and I hope from here forward.

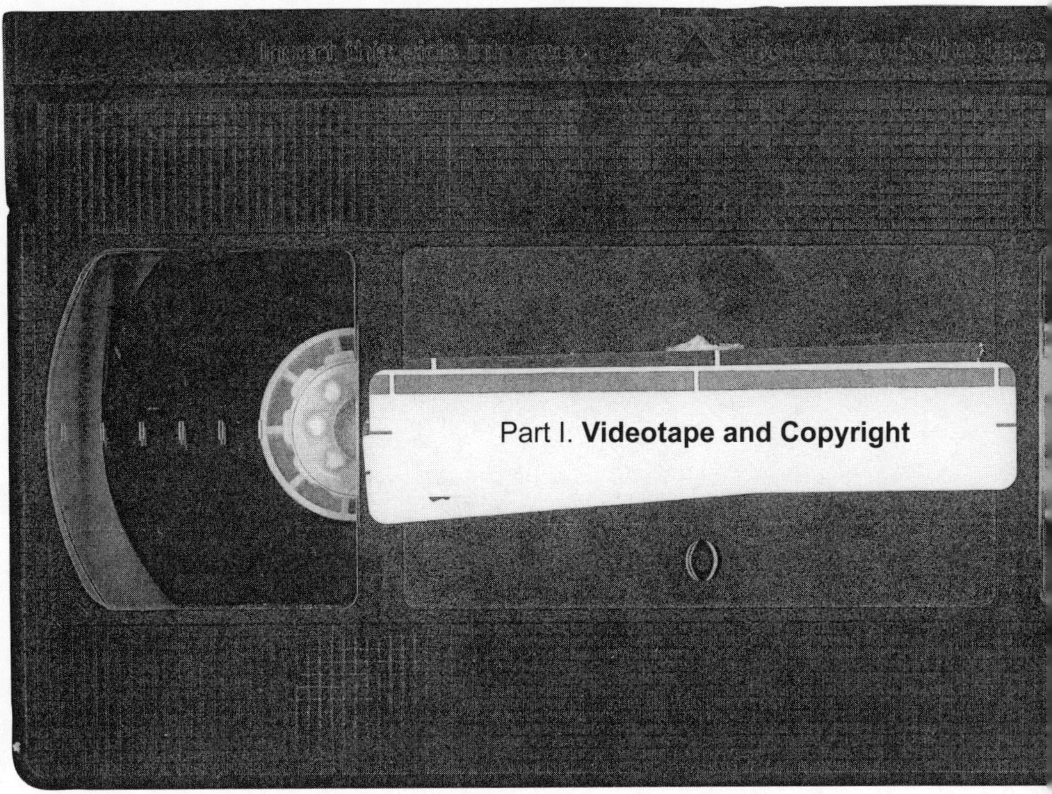
Part I. **Videotape and Copyright**

Introduction: The Aesthetics of Access

On November 14, 2006, *Variety* ran an odd obituary headlined "VHS, 30, Dies of Loneliness." A tacky cartoon of a cassette-shaped tombstone inscribed with "RIP 1976–2006" illustrated the article and reflected its mocking tone. This write-up was curious not only for its lack of urgency—given DVDs' well-established market dominance, this was not breaking news—but also for its distinct lack of reporting: the only quoted source offers the banal assessment "It's pretty much over." The only actual news in the piece was that the studios had decided to cease manufacturing feature films on tape in the near future, though it acknowledged that they had not done so yet and some minor players in the industry would continue to vend the format. Despite the subheading "The Home-Entertainment Format Lived a Fruitful Life," the piece also lacked the reverence or generous historical narrative typically offered in obituaries. Rather, the short, premature, and halfhearted tribute asserted, perhaps all too accurately, "No services are planned."[1]

A month and a half later, with much more fanfare, *Time* magazine named its 2006 Person of the Year: "You." The first pronoun to earn such a distinction and certainly the most indulgent of its readership, "You" was clearly chosen in large part because of the popularity (and, for its creators, profitability) of the Web video streaming and sharing site YouTube (www.youtube.com). *Time*'s cover image featured an illustration of a white iMac modified so that the screen resembled the frame of a YouTube video, with playback controls and time code display. The screen was made of a metallic plastic, so that the reader's likeness was reflected when looking at the cover.[2]

As compelling (and convenient) as the juxtaposition of VHS and YouTube that frames this book might be, let me backtrack just a bit. The *Variety* obituary wasn't the first time someone tried to kill off VHS, though the rhetorical homicide has usually been done with a bit more kindness. VHS's death had already been reported years earlier, with a self-reflexively nostalgic eulogy and another image of a gravestone inscribed with "R.I.P. VHS" in the British entertainment magazine *Empire*. But at least this time the image also included the words "in loving memory," and the article actually paid tribute to "a once great format." *Empire*'s nine-page feature included a surprisingly useful timeline (dating back to 1951) and sidebar features on the format wars, film flops that found sleeper audiences on tape, and capsule reviews of "video nasties" (violent films banned in the United Kingdom in 1984 for fear they would "deprave and corrupt" audiences).[3] My favorite section, however, focused on the most-paused moments in movies—mostly images of gore, nudity, or subliminal messages such as the exploding head in *Scanners*, Sharon Stone uncrossing her legs without panties in *Basic Instinct*, or (news to me) a scene when the clouds spell "sex" in *The Lion King*. This "freeze frame" write-up not only suggested a specific way that viewers used video—and the scenes that inspired such uses—but also acknowledged the aesthetic specificity of such practices. All the images included simulations of video noise streaking horizontally across the frame and the written acknowledgment "It trashed the tape and mostly featured fuzz." In this retrospective celebration of video, the format's limitations not only serve as distinctive markers of the technology but have also become central to its charm. Announcing the death of a technology belatedly acknowledges a kind of vitality. For something to die, it must first have lived.[4]

As a final example, I turn to Radiohead's heart-rending dirge "Videotape," which closes the band's pay-what-you-will download album *In Rainbows* (2007). Rather than a eulogy for technology, however, the song suggests that video mediates the narrator's arrival at the pearly gates and will preserve the life he once lived. The tensions between the analog and the digital are even sonically enacted midway through the song: erratic drum machine beats attack the spare acoustic piano while layers of processed phantom ooohs haunt Thom Yorke's pained vocals. Though the song is not technically an obituary, the connections between videotape and death, between videotape and spinning out of control, and between videotape and better times in the past remain. For any technology to be repeatedly memorialized, it must have significant cultural and personal resonances.

The death of VHS, repeatedly imagined, has been driven by DVDs (digital versatile discs or digital video discs), DVRs (digital video recorders, such as TIVO), and YouTube. With phenomenal speed, VHS has been pushed out of the consumer market and the consumer consciousness, thus demonstrating how quickly a technology that has altered viewing habits and been an everyday presence can become erased from public life. Yet even in their own moment, VCRs were quickly taken for granted. As an industrial history in the mid-1980s commented, "A remarkable change has taken place in our everyday behavior, and yet, like so many things that happen under our noses, it has gone largely unnoticed. Already it is getting hard to remember how strange a device the VCR was when it first appeared, and what a commotion it caused."[5] This book queries the strangeness of analog videotape and stirs up some of the "commotion" once again by revisiting its forgotten beauty and conflicts.

Home video emerged amid debates about its suspect legality and potentially damaging uses, and videotape has begun to disappear amid claims about its technological inferiority and aesthetic shortcomings. Consumer-grade videotape was born and now dies through derogatory definitions and discourses of infringement, danger, degradation, distortion, degeneration, inferiority, and obsolescence. To borrow Radiohead's phrasing, videotape has always been "out of control." With the transition from analog to digital technologies, tape hasn't been the only thing at risk of erasure. Technological locks, licenses, and copyright laws that render illegal some uses of media familiar from the analog age have inhibited the rights of audiences and artists. Fair use, non-infringing uses, first-sale rights, and the public domain have all arguably been rendered obsolete as well by policies that seek to protect the content industry from "piracy." Counter to the prematurely reported demise of VHS and the industry's—and users'—apparent haste to move on to new formats, I position videotape as an endangered format for popular and institutional historiographies and access while also attempting to describe the aesthetics of home video before we forget what it was like to watch VHS.

The coinciding eras of analog magnetic tape and of fair-use copyright exemptions constitute a significant historical period, one marked by actual and potential democratic participation enabled by technology that gave way to largely taken-for-granted privileges and consumptive uses. This project was conceived in recognition that the ethical imperative to preserve and provide access to media content at times runs counter to what the law permits and what technology allows.[6] Thus I point toward productive uses of video recording and the ways they have been defined by, prompted revisions of, and often violated, copyright laws; at the same time, I suggest, such practices exaggerate videotape's formal specificity. I approach these histories through the concept of videotape bootlegging, a set of practices and textual relationships that open up alternative conceptions of access, aesthetics, and affect. Perhaps a sexier way of saying the same thing is that this book is about desire—the desire for access—and about the aesthetics and ethics related to access.

In this book, I have several agendas: to validate analog videotape as a format by offering an aesthetic reading (something that, surprisingly, has not been done in any extended way in cinema or media studies); to offer a history of video technology that problematizes the binaries of old and new media; to emphasize that home video was embroiled in legal struggles to define and determine its uses and that video in turn helped shape the law; to politically suggest the ways that digital copyright laws build on and betray analog copyright; and finally to indicate what we might learn from looking back at copyright history in terms of arguing for users' rights of access in the present and future. Considered in tandem, these formal and legal issues demonstrate how home recording contributed to the legal definitions of fair use, how taping has served as a method of amateur archiving for ephemeral content, and how reproduction and sharing create new meanings and communities. This book presents a study of the very recent past, one that of necessity takes a historical vantage point because both technologies and policies change too quickly to assess the present or to plausibly predict the future.

"Inherent Vice," this book's peculiar title, comes from a phrase librarians use to describe the acidity of chemically processed wood-pulp paper, the manufacturing toxin that supposedly burns through old books, turns the interior pages yellowish brown, and makes them brittle.[7] "Inherent vice," perhaps perversely, cuts to the core of videotape. Home video was introduced as a blank format, essentially as a bootleg technology, for the purpose of recording television without permission. As I argue through the concept of bootlegs' aesthetics of access, the specificity of videotape becomes most apparent through repeated duplication, wear, and technical failure: that is, we recognize videotape as tape through its inherent properties of degeneration.[8] Its inherent vice, then, points to both its intended illicit uses in recording and its format specificity.

Historicizing Home Video

"Video" acts as an umbrella term for *technologies* (broadcast signals, electromagnetic videotape, cathode-ray tubes, streaming digital data, camcorders, editing software, playback decks), *content* (programming and "art"), and *institutions* (networks, cable providers, tape rental outlets, galleries, festivals, file-sharing communities, event videographers). Video as a medium is constituted by all these factors. Broadly sketched, the magnetic tape era extended from World War II until the end of the twentieth century. As a popular format for consumers' use and access, one that has been culturally innovative and politically influential, the videotape can be periodized from the late 1960s into the early years of the twenty-first century. Significantly, when videotape was introduced as a consumer format, it was initially in the form of *blank* cassettes for recording television broadcasts. Additionally, VTRs (videotape recorders)—later more commonly called VCRs—were marketed as video *recorders*, not merely playback-only devices.[9] In contrast to prior vinyl LPs or subsequent CDs and DVDs, magnetic tape allowed people to record their own voices, their own lives, the media, and the world around them to an unprecedented degree. This allowed for a boom both in private tapings and in personal participation in public affairs. Tape also introduced new relationships to network and studio programming, allowing audiences to save and use content at will.

Home video technology was developed and sold to make private recordings, and only years later did prerecorded videos of feature films become widely available. Videotape enabled television audiences to become participatory viewers who interacted with the technology and recorded texts. The extension of magnetic tape's availability to private viewers introduced hopes of media access and use that would threaten the established commercial and political power structures. In small ways, this did occur, although much of the promise proved utopian, like the hype that surrounded the Internet a few decades later. VCR owners rarely purchased prerecorded tapes of movies but instead tended to rent them overnight unless cassettes were priced to own and likely to be watched repeatedly—most frequently this meant workout tapes and kid vids. This marketing pattern was significantly reversed for digital technologies to stave off personal reproduction: CDs and DVDs were introduced as nonrecordable, playback-only consumer technologies, and only belatedly did consumer demand and hardware manufacturers succeed in making them recordable by home users. The delay in making DVD recordable may, in fact, have sustained VHS's life.

"Access" was a buzzword for video in its early activist days, before video became domesticated. For video collectives and artists who used equipment such as the Sony Portapak, "access" referred to new modes of production and the democratization of technology: video introduced means of cultural production that were relatively affordable and easy to use. In addition, the equipment was portable, and the recordings could be played back instantly for impromptu feedback and group discussions. Media access centers started up in major cities and college towns across the country, and with the rise of cable television, public access resources and programming seemed to increase access to television production and cablecasting. As the discourse of such initiatives suggested, it was imagined that video could become a medium for the people and a viable alternative to broadcast networks' programming.[10] And, of course, the utopian promise of media decentralization and democratized production has reappeared with digital video cameras, user-friendly editing software, and video sharing websites.

Video has been both a tool of media access (in terms of production and distribution) and an access medium (in terms of reception). Even without a progressive ideology behind it, timeshifting—the initially marketed practice of recording TV broadcasts for belated playback—was, at base, about access as well: watching whatever whenever, to quote a common Betamax ad. Audience access suggests a partial reorientation of power, even as the content industry has grown increasingly conglomerated. Tom O'Regan has recognized a central contradiction of video access: "*recentralization* of production and distribution in Western markets occurs, paradoxically, alongside such a *decentralization* of control."[11]

Scholars have explored the concept of remote control as representing new modes of viewing in the video age or as employing a rhetorical strategy emphasizing discourses of "control" and "mastery."[12] (It should be noted, however, that government regulations, copyright policies, and manufactured abilities powerfully function more remotely and yet with even more control.)[13] Home video technology was designed to give the audience considerable control over the content, so that it could be replayed, slowed down, fast-forwarded, and reproduced. With videotape, content could be played back on the viewer's own terms and schedules for the first time. This meant not only when to start playback but also the options of pausing to run to the kitchen or rewinding to review favorite moments or scanning past boring bits. Each push of a button on a deck or a remote control involves a willed action on the part of the user. Of course, the concept of television viewers as active participants in making meaning extends at least as far back as the "uses and gratifications" studies of the 1960s, and it has been one of the basic premises of reception and cultural studies.[14] Indeed, the very emphasis on the word "uses" in this methodology demonstrates as much. Yet videotape

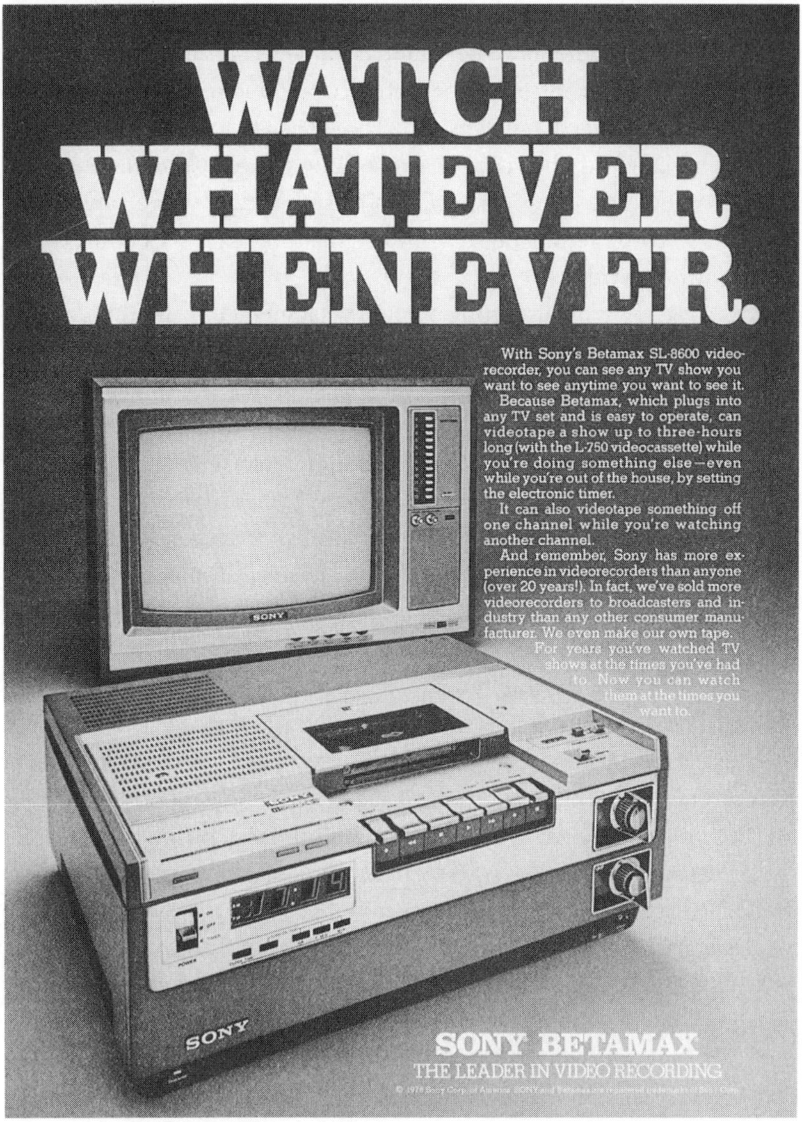

2. The Sony Betamax was marketed as a machine for timeshifting, as exemplified by this prominent print advertising campaign. The slogan "Watch Whatever Whenever" may have been intended to suggest freedom, but it also indicates that content matters less than the technology. The focus here is the machine, not the TV programs to be recorded. Of course, this may also be a corrective: mentioning *Kojak* and *Columbo* in an earlier campaign prompted litigation from Universal Studios. Collection of the author.

changed how audiences become users by introducing new technologies that increased the interactive possibilities for television and introduced expanded practices of controlling, collecting, using, and reproducing texts. In other words, whereas TV audiences had long been conceived of as "active," through home video, they could become "interactive." Certainly there are no more interactive forms of spectatorship than hitting the record button, doing aerobics, or getting off to a porno—the three practices synonymous with early home video.

VCRs suggest a critical starting point in what might be called on-demand culture, wherein audiences want access to entertainment on their own terms: what they want, when they want it. With the rise of video rentals and later TIVO, on-demand programming, YouTube, and streaming content on the networks' websites (not to mention the World Wide Web generally), technology and the market have moved toward an idea (if not an actuality) of infinite and instant access to specific movies or shows whenever the viewer feels the whim. As I suggest in the epilogue, audience attitudes and behavior may suggest a shift toward a sense of access entitlement.

In reality, what viewers actually watch is typically limited by what is available: television programming to be taped or movies released on video. Historically, if viewers forgot to tape a broadcast or its occasional rerun, they just missed out on ever seeing it—unless they found someone else who had taped it. The increasing regularity of the release of new feature films on video, however, introduced an assumption that viewers could just "wait for the video" if they weren't really that anxious to see a particular film or didn't want to pay movie ticket and popcorn prices. On the other hand, spontaneous rentals often proved to be less fun than was hoped. Most VCR owners have wandered around video stores, apathetically browsing for a movie when nothing fits their mood and eventually settling for something other than their first choices. Such everyday experiences may in part deflate overstatements of control and mastery over home video by demonstrating that viewers' choices are often concessionary or impulsive. And different VCR owners will use (or not use) their decks in different ways. Some still primarily use their VCRs for recording broadcasts, while many never did, opting instead for playing rental tapes. And some may have never used their machines themselves at all—for instance, in the cases of grandparents who were given a VCR some decades ago as a holiday gift that really only functioned to entertain restless grandchildren during family visits.

Analog Video and Aesthetics

This project attempts to reclaim analog videotape's format specificity and distinguish it from older analog and newer digital technologies. It undertakes a recuperative mission to recognize that analog generations of consumer electronics profoundly changed the ways audiences became interactive users of technologies and texts and poses an argument that only by looking back to analog formats can we understand the potential innovations and actual limitations of digital ones. Throughout the book, I often use the term "aesthetics" in discussing the specificity of videotape. While I use this term predominantly in reference to formal characteristics of recorded images and sounds, it also suggests a sensory and affective relationship between the audience and (what's on) a given tape and, perhaps in some small way, counters the notions of quality that digital aesthetes use to dismiss analog media. Whereas "analog" has come to more or less mean "not digital," I return to its earlier meaning that indicates mediation and metaphor.

In *Video: The Reflexive Medium*, her recent book on video art aesthetics, Yvonne Spielmann stresses video's status as an electronic medium. Unlike film, in which discrete photographic images are exposed on celluloid and then projected through it, with video, there are no actual or fixed pictures. Analog video sounds and images exist only as electronic signals that are continuously rendered by the television monitor. Even the TV console never reveals a complete image, as the lines of colored pixels alternate—and at a different rate (30 "frames" per second) from film (24 fps). Electronic signals, when stored by magnetic embedding on videotape, are linear and continuous; here they are not images, either, but remain signals that are again to be rendered in real time on the monitor during playback. What is visible within the video screen, then, is never precisely the same or static but always mutable. Videotapes and VCRs, it should be noted, were developed to be used in conjunction with cathode-ray-tube (CRT) monitors. The rise of flat-screen, high-definition LCD and plasma monitors has radically altered television aesthetics (CRT monitors have 480 lines of resolution, whereas HDTVs typically have 720 or 1,080) in ways that exaggerate analog signals' lower resolution.

Electronic video signals, furthermore, are inherently *analog*. Neither indexical nor digitized as binary data, they are representations of the phenomenal world or TV signals reproduced. Whereas analog technologies function through analogy, digital devices operate through abstraction. In digital texts, the numerical reductions to ones and zeros are not representational in a traditional sense, although through software and interfaces, we experience digital texts as representations rather than as series of digits. Video's existence as electronic cannot be denied. But in this book, I focus more on the delivery device with which audiences interact and onto which anxieties and affection have been projected: videotape cassettes. Stored in a tangible format made of plastic strips and a fine glue (this makes it *tape*), the physical storage technology introduces some of its own artifacts and specificity into the signal.[15]

Magnetic tape's inherent functions are recording and erasing, but it is through errors, muck-ups, and decay that users may become most conscious of the tape. Videotape recorders erase tapes before rerecording them, and through human negligence or mechanical failure and quirks, sometimes programs get accidentally taped over or don't get recorded at all. Most home tapers have experienced the frustration of realizing that they have taped over part of a recording that they meant to save, either because the cassette wasn't labeled or cued properly or because the deck was programmed incorrectly. On playback, the viewer may experience jarring accidental jump-cuts between unrelated texts and only then realize that one thing was taped over another. In addition, if commercials are elided or videos are edited using two VCRs rather than higher-end postproduction decks, the transitions between recordings will often produce snowy glitches, squirmy images, or sound distortion as the VCR heads recalibrate.

Videotape presented new modes of televisual temporality, existing both over time (as timeshifting, preservation, or decay) and in time (as duration or manipulated playback speed). Timeshifting was the first publicized use of home video, and it implies that, after being viewed, the recording will be taped over with some other program for a similar purpose. Despite being a storage format with the potential for extended shelf life, video's temporality has often been temporary in practice. When videotape was new, video recordings—whether networks' timeshifted programming, conceptual video art and ephemeral happenings, radical collectives' feedback sessions, even home viewers' timeshifting—were often not intended to last. Even video rentals give prerecorded cassettes a temporary life for individual viewers who took them home as one-night stands. These recordings were not as fleeting as TV tube pictures or electronic pulses, yet they were always implicitly subject to erasure.

Of course, many tapes never were erased or taped over. Though they may now be dusty and damaged, video allowed for a new kind of amateur archiving.[16] As mass media, films and particularly television broadcasts were once simultaneously everywhere and ephemeral. The fact that so much popular entertainment was fleetingly accessible drives the preservative impulse behind recording and keeping collections of tapes. Of course, some have suggested that it's just as well that so much of TV has been lost. In a newspaper feature on "the taping mania" among early home tapers, one journalist posed the skeptical question, "What can you say about a culture dedicated to preserving *My Mother, the Car?*"[17] By no means archivally pristine, home recording nonetheless works to timeshift texts on a semipermanent basis when they become part of a bootleg collection to be saved; if shared, these tapes can serve personal or even cultural-historical interests. Even video rental stores may become de facto repositories for movies that have gone out of print or have never been released on DVD.

If we think of aesthetics as relational, technologies of access, such as videotape, alter the reception of texts by opening up the dynamic between audience and text; audiences can rewatch, fast-forward, pause, or simply turn videos off. In analog video, real time meets reel time. Analog video, because the tape must physically pass the VCR heads to play, exists in "wind" time rather than in nonlinear digital chapters, thus marking temporal distinctions between the experiences of using the two types of technologies. When scanning a videotape in rewind or fast forward—that is, pushing either button while in play mode—the audio cuts out, and the image track often squirms with a few horizontal bars of white noise and slightly skewed picture. Upon returning to play mode, there is often a moment of squiggly distortion when the VCR heads reorient their tracking; heavily used tapes are often stretched out, which aggravates this phenomenon. Yet the viewer will see a continuous moving image as it scans by at an increased gallop. When using DVDs, in contrast, each individual image looks pristine, but the motion is jerky because digital scanning involves skipping entire frames in sequence. After finishing a tape, rewinding often takes several minutes, as the wheels whir and then abruptly stop with a resounding thud that, depending on the VCR, sounds as if it could snap the videotape off the reel. Such aesthetics of playback and fast forwarding call attention to this technology as specifically linear.

By seeing recording errors, the linearity of playback, and especially signs of wear, we begin to see video as videotape. Analog tape emerges as visible and audible through the way the image and soundtrack degenerate through (repeated) reproduction or aging. Each format has a specific aesthetic of failure, and analog videotape has unique modes of decay. Old phonographs

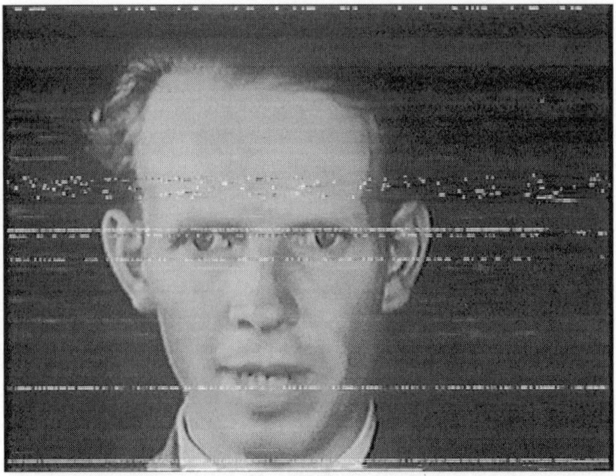

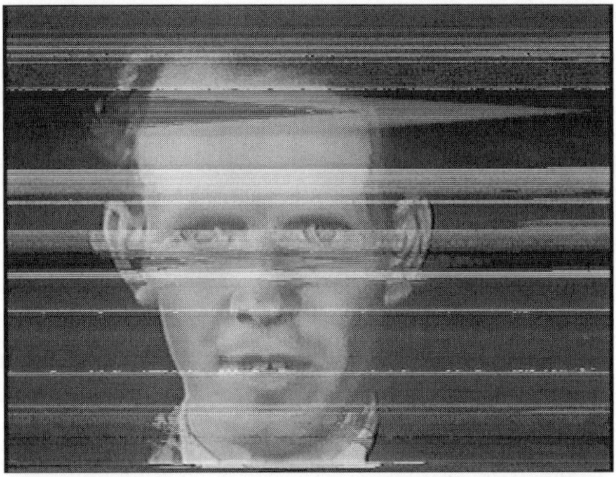

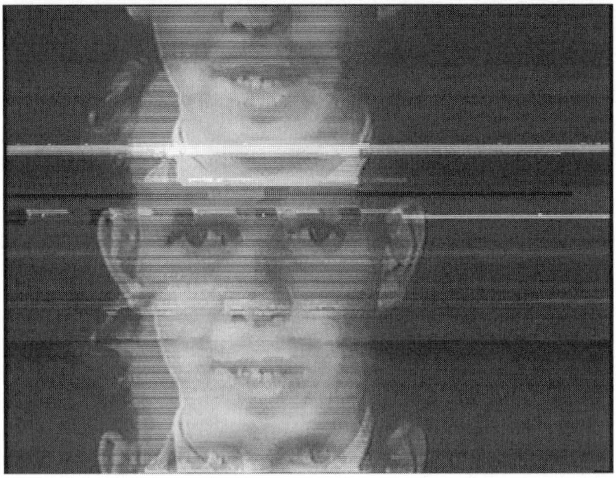

betray crisp crackles, and used celluloid prints bristle with pops, scratches, and splotches; digital media's "corruption" skips, freezes, exhibits blocky interference patterns, or becomes wholly unreadable and inoperable. In contrast, videotape's wear tends toward the softening interference of muffled rainbow flares (called video moiré), skewed images at the top and bottom of the frame (called flagwaving or skew error, caused by stretched or distorted tapes), white specks (called dropout), lines of distortion (called noise bars), exaggerated pixels, jittery framing, and muted sounds. In more extreme cases, tapes damaged by VCRs can cause tracking problems or trigger a default blue screen if the heads cannot detect a video signal. I consider these technical faults to be indexical evidence of use and duration through time. Here the technology becomes a text, and such recordings become historical records of audiences' interactions with the media objects, whether through use (stress from repeated contact between the tape and the VCR heads) or reproduction (analog softening of image and sound). Audiences learned to ignore analog video interference and to filter out the mediations and artifacts, but distortion was always present and perceptible.

Analog media, for which duplication involves degeneration, reflect an aesthetic of access. The altered look and sound of a text through its reduced resolution present both a trade-off for our ability to engage with it and indexical evidence of its circulation and use. We see this in analog photocopies, microfilm, videotapes, and even digital PDFs and streaming videos. And though I hesitate to make reference to the overly cited (though wondrous and inspiring) Walter Benjamin, it strikes me that this is a source of his ambivalence about reproductions of art in the modern age. Artworks lose their physical presence, ritual function, and authenticity when they are reduced to images, yet such images vastly expand the potential audience that may come to learn from and about them. Reproductions exchange aura for access.[18] My dual emphases on videotape's reproductive innovations and decay may seem contradictory, even counterintuitive. But I suggest we cannot experience one without the other.

3a–c. These images were taken from a personal dub of an aged video store copy of *Gizmo!* (Howard Smith, 1977, now out of print), a compilation documentary about odd inventions. Figure 3a shows dropout and noise bars common to old videotapes. Figure 3b shows more severe damage, including flagwaving—the sideways V-shaped skew in the image across and beyond the man's forehead. Figure 3c shows a jittery image that has lost its vertical stability, creating ghostly effects.

The aesthetics of videotape are not merely matters of formalist specificity but also engage broader social and cultural issues of circulation, reception, historiography, and regulation. Two premises of U.S. copyright law have informed this project: first, ideas cannot be copyrighted, only specific expressions or fixed forms can be; and second, the public domain and fair use contribute to the public good by enabling access to, and (re)uses, of texts.[19] The first premise recognizes the formal properties of content, whereas the second suggests that such content, once communicated, enriches society. Our public culture and private lives depend on the mass reproduction and usage of texts. Copyright was developed with the understanding that, in the analog world, copies are necessarily material, and tangibility is a prerequisite for access, use, duration, and copyright protection, as well as for aesthetic experiences. For analog technologies, tangible property and intellectual property coexist; whereas the durable good—a videotape, say—may get worn out, broken, or stolen, the ideas expressed by its content are nondepletable. Ironically, the more the analog device is used, the more productive, valuable, and influential the text or ideas it delivers become.[20]

Copyright and Access

The Hollywood studios were initially wary of home video. If audiences could tape movies and TV shows off the air, studio executives feared that the industry would be devastated by revenue losses. According to this line of reasoning, audiences would stop going to cinemas if they could watch movies for free at home, and advertisers would stop buying airtime for commercials if they thought home viewers would fast-forward through them. As it turned out, of course, neither the theatrical film nor broadcast television industries collapsed, and the studios did gangbusters business because video opened up additional revenue streams and aftermarkets. Home video probably increased film and TV consumption by making it more available. (If any industry was devastated by video, it was the 16 mm educational and industrial film market.) But before the home video market was developed and exploited by the studios, the studios waged litigation against VCRs in the famous *Sony v. Universal* (1976–84) case, and the charge was copyright violation.

Copyright law governs cultural works and creative intellectual property. In the United States, copyright law was enacted early on and was designed in tandem with the U.S. Constitution. It strove to inspire publication (literally, the making public) of books, pamphlets, and newspapers—and later photographs, films, and sound recordings—by protecting authors' or publishers' temporary, near-exclusive rights to profit from such publication. These rights were always conditional—such protection was a reward for sharing insights and arts—and audiences always had vested interests in publication and implied or judicially determined rights to use published materials. At the core of copyright is a contradiction between the public interest and private profit[21]—a conflict that might be called copyright's inherent vice.

Although home video was at first ostensibly a domestic system for private viewing, the regulation and uses of the technology have been linked to principles of the public interest. Copyright protection, fair-use exemptions, and the public domain were all established for the purpose of fostering a rich public culture. The fundamental concept is that each of these copyright categories—whether offering legal and economic incentives for creating original works or providing protections for others to create derivative works—stimulates artistic production and encourages distribution. In broadcasting, one of the major topics for policy and debate has been the extent to which broadcasters must serve public interests and the extent to which the public has rights of access to information that trump networks' and stations' financial interests. As I suggest in the case study on the Vanderbilt Television News Archive in chapter 3, off-air recording realized new forms of access—historical—that raised contentious issues of whether rights owners, politicians, the public, or intermediary institutions have the right to determine public access.

The principle of access is foundational to both copyright and videotape and in effect unites them in spirit and practice. In 1969 the U.S. Supreme Court proclaimed through its ruling on *Red Lion Broadcasting Co. v. FCC* that audiences have the right of access to information.[22] This interpretation of "access" relies on a fundamental belief that the availability of cultural texts, information, and knowledge to a general audience is a public good that serves the public interest. Although Federal Communications Commission regulations have no jurisdiction over copyright and vice versa, the Court's logic in the Red Lion decision indicates an indirect precedent for *Sony v. Universal*. In what became known as "the Betamax case," the Court ruled that "to the extent time-shifting expands public access to freely broadcast television programs, it yields societal benefits," and in effect legalized VCRs.

Perhaps the most famous, ambiguous, and debated of all users' rights under copyright is fair use. Fair use is a general loophole that protects otherwise copyright-infringing duplications of texts for culturally edifying educational, critical, or newsworthy uses. Fair use defined and defended the standard legal uses of home video, and videotape, in turn, provided the medium through which the Supreme Court set its first precedent on fair use. As I will discuss in more depth in chapter 2, the 1976 U.S. copyright code revision introduced the first statutory fair-use exemption. In 1984 the U.S. Supreme Court ruled in a landmark decision on *Sony v. Universal* that VCRs should be allowed in the domestic market because their dominant uses were fair and many potential ones were non-infringing. The eight-year lawsuit not only highlighted the tensions between copyright propriety and audience desires but also served as a major publicity boost for videotape recorders. Much of the early journalistic coverage of home video specifically addressed the lawsuit and the technology's questionable legal status; thus much of the formative public awareness of home video was articulated in relationship to copyright law—an articulation of technology and policy that resurfaced in relation to online file sharing and clouded speculations about the rise of YouTube.

The interdependence of videotape and statutory fair-use exemptions may have started out as a historical coincidence when both appeared in the 1970s, but through the 1984 Court ruling on the Betamax case, they became mutually constitutive as a matter of public policy. As media scholars argued in retrospect of this ruling, "*Sony* did more than legalize home taping and 'time shifting.' It opened up participation in the project of recording the collective memory of this dynamic nation."[23] Fair use also remains critically important to videotape for another reason: individual recordings will not survive long enough, physically or technologically, to ever enter the public domain (when works no longer protected by copyright can be reproduced without permission). A tape's ten-year or twenty-year shelf life before it decays falls far short of the ninety or so years before a work's copyright expires, and preservative reformatting inevitably distorts the text. When the copyright term outlasts the text or the format, fair use may be the only recourse to accessing and using video-originated works.[24] Furthermore, fair use implies that audiences do not merely copy a preexisting work but make *use* of it by interpreting it, building on it, reinventing it. VCRs made television viewers into *users*, and videotapes introduced new *uses* of television.

At first, copyright regulations seemed to favor magnetic recording technology's potential benefits rather than clamping down on potential violations. However, many home recording practices that users have become accustomed to were never explicitly protected by written law; rather, they were deemed legal in the absence of litigation or offered shelter through limited statutory exemptions or judicial rulings. As the technology's dominant uses became domestic, consumptive ones—that is, buying and listening to music or renting and watching movies rather than recording one's own copies—the general perception of magnetic tape shifted away from anxieties about its use as a panoptic means of social control and surveillance (keep in mind that tape technology burst into public consciousness through the Watergate scandal and paranoia thrillers) toward its being a more convenient means of entertaining the self.[25] Despite the music industry's attempts in the early 1980s to claim that home recordings were "killing" the music business or Hollywood's assertions that timeshifting constituted televisual piracy, even everyday recordings of copyrighted material quickly seemed to lack any transgressive edge. Magnetic tape lost its threatening taint, and so citizens perhaps began to take its relatively lax regulation for granted.

Copyright law and litigation have been the most prominent official means of regulating video technology, although increasingly the technology has been designed to go even further in restricting uses and access beyond playback.[26] Restrictive copyright laws, most egregiously the 1998 Digital Millennium Copyright Act (DMCA), have aided and abetted this trend by criminalizing the act of undoing copy-protection hardware or software—even if it is to make otherwise legal or fair uses. These mechanisms are intended to prevent commercial forms of piracy but have seemingly forgotten about important fair and non-infringing uses of reproduction. Together, the law and encryption of digital formats have worked to override many of the fair uses and much of the potential functionality of video; thus, for the time being at least, users can still do more (legally, anyway) with videotape than with digital video, even though the newer formats can offer superior resolution and should allow easier copying and manipulation.

Fair use, I am arguing, is an analog copyright exemption. Fair use is a policy of conditions, ambiguity, and reasonable guesses. Only a judge can say for sure that a particular instance can be defended as fair use, and even then the Supreme Court has final say. Defined by a set of guidelines and few judicial precedents, fair use in the real world rarely operates in a binary way: yes, this is clearly fair use, or no, this is clearly not. Rather, fair use is inexact, approximate, and fluid. In other words, it's analog. The DMCA and especially extralegal technologies to prevent duplication (such as Content Scramble System encoding on DVDs or the absence of a record button on players) instead operate as binary laws: either it's legal or it's not; either it's functionally possible or it's not. These are distinctly digital ways of regulating users' activities and attempts to copy and share media. As a communications and copyright scholar has suggested, "Fair use is . . . antithetical to the design of technologically enforced rules."[27] Technological copy guards (often called DRM, or digital rights management) may prevent even the option of fairly cutting, copying, and pasting, and the DMCA makes it illegal to undo these technologies, regardless of the reason for doing so. Of course, DRM is often ineffectual because anything that can be encrypted can be hacked—and often is, though the law isn't quite so easy to bypass. Therefore, although it may seem that DVD has replaced videotape and the DMCA has to some extent overwritten fair use, videotape and fair use offer lessons in progressive media policy and remain essential tools of media access, even in the era of their apparent obsolescence or irrelevance.

Digital Dilemmas

Access and aesthetics have changed in the transition from analog to digital media and technologies. Even though the predominant analog home video format, VHS, has certain formal limitations, its contribution to the lives of cinephiles and casual viewers alike must not be discounted just because consumers have enthusiastically abandoned it for DVD, TIVO, and streaming video. Some digital formats have made innovations to make media more portable and to make duplication much quicker, and the standardization of letterboxing and higher resolution make DVDs preferable for film buffs. But there have also been trade-offs, losses, and glitches with the turn toward digital home video. Despite the hype, HDTVs are no more "realistic" than old-school tube televisions; instead they are often set to be supernaturally bright and colorful in a way that is transfixing rather than authentic. And, of course, digital technologies are nowhere near as perfect as they are purported to be. Despite innovations in terms of resolution, interfaces, duplication, and distribution, digital media are not necessarily improvements on earlier analog media but rather may be more restrictive of use, duplication, and distribution.[28]

Digital networks have enabled the acceleration of access by reducing texts to data. Technological development does not follow a linear evolution, nor, despite celebrations of "new" media, should we think of current technologies as the final, teleological stage of research and development. The hype of digital resolution as "perfect" and preferable to analog lingers on, despite the failure of "virtual reality" to materialize in the early 1990s and more than a decade of blocky, jerky, and stalled streaming images.[29] Furthermore, as technologies have developed, they have typically become more complex and more dependent on devices and decoding to access texts or information. Contrary to the myth of increased immediacy, newer technologies typically mediate more than old ones, and they introduce new challenges for contemporary access and future preservation. The more advanced the technology, the more likely there will be multiple levels of mediation—hardware, delivery device, software, operating system, encryption, et cetera—and the more likely that one or more of these will break down, become obsolete, or be incompatible. Future media historians will likely have more trouble accessing electronic and digital content than indexical and analog materials simply because it will be harder to find the right device, reconstruct the proper version of software, or decode encryption. Probably the biggest myth promoted in the celebration of digital media is the technology's infallibility; the more dependent on technology and software a file or format is, the less likely it will be to have longevity.[30] Digitization is not preservation. Although plastic digital discs may not disintegrate in the way magnetic tape eventually does, once a file is corrupted or a DVD is scratched, there is almost nothing to be done to restore it. In addition, digital technologies typically become technologically obsolete in less time than it would take a tape to deteriorate. In 2006, librarians and copyright experts assessed that "all digital materials are inherently unstable."[31] In video history so far, analog formats have outlasted digital ones, regardless of physical durability.

Content and hardware companies have introduced anticopy technologies, engineered incompatibility between platforms, and accelerated obsolescence—all of which work to inhibit how audiences access and use digital media. When technology fails to prevent copying, licensing agreements and the Digital Millennium Copyright Act legally determine what users can or cannot do. DVDs have not introduced more control over the content when FBI warnings and sluggishly paced animated menus cannot be skipped or discs are difficult to cue to specific moments in the middle of chapters. The menus and chapters dictate how the user interacts with the disc, and pity anyone who loses a DVD player's remote control, since the complete range of command keys is rarely replicated on the deck itself. The VHS user arguably has much more agency in videotape playback, and the tape stays on the spot where the user leaves it, which facilitates not only strategic viewing but also educational classroom or conference clips. Analog media, while slower, degenerative, and bound to tangible storage formats, is comparatively more flexible in terms of what users can do. Engineers, rights owners, and users of digital media have all learned from analog models for both progressive and repressive developments.

Digital copyright protections and technological encryption are premised on digital media's distinction from analog media; digital data can be replicated without change, whereas analog copies exhibit degeneration. Rights owners fear, therefore, that users will be less likely to pay for media if they can easily make digital clones that are the same as the original for free. Through online networks, digital data can also be exchanged rapidly, anonymously, and without analog technology's prerequisite baggage of tangibility—two more factors that have accelerated content sharing. Just as historians and communications scholars warn against technological determinism (the idea that the device determines how it will be used), so progressive legal scholars also argue against what might be called legal determinism: regulations that would likewise inhibit how technologies are designed and what potential uses can be engineered or rigged.[32]

Bootlegging

Personal recording, within and outside the law, has consistently been practiced and, I argue, exposes analog videotape's formal properties and its fundamental purpose of accessibility. Taping and sharing works can derive from ethical impulses to preserve and provide access to content that may run counter to (and eventually change) the law. While compelling work already exists to advocate for the cultural benefit of appropriation, sampling, and remixing, I suggest that the argument for access should be expanded to include academic and everyday uses of complete works.[33] I advocate certain productive forms of copyright-infringing or legally dubious dubbing while also reflecting on the aesthetics of purloined media.

Bootlegging illuminates the aesthetics of analog videotape because it so often involves multiple generations of reproduction and offers practical models that have challenged, expanded, or provided alternatives to existing intellectual property paradigms. I define bootlegging broadly to include most noncommercial practices of timeshifting, tape dubbing, importing, and sharing of media content that is not reasonably available commercially. Bootlegging functions to fill in the gaps of market failure (when something has not been commercially distributed), archival omissions (when something has not been preserved for historical study), and personal collections (when something has not been accumulated or cannot be afforded). Extending the

Supreme Court's Betamax definition of timeshifting, I consider bootlegging to be fair use of video technologies. In the digital video age, bootlegging also includes excerpting and sharing culturally significant or newsworthy corporate media clips. "Fairness," as a word or ideal, suggests both beauty and justice.[34] Fair-use bootlegging can be a beautiful thing.

Despite the often negative or criminal connotations of the term, I use "bootlegging" to reclaim its productively illicit meanings, its intoxicating pleasures, and its amorous relationships between texts and audiences.[35] In distinction, I define "piracy" as commercial duplication and sale of knockoffs of readily available videos.[36] Pirates steal for profit, not for the egalitarian or productive redistribution of culture and information. Though the terms "piracy" and "bootlegging" are often used interchangeably in industry rhetoric, there is a significant distinction between the two as I use them. Admittedly, gray areas and contradictions in my differentiation remain; bootleg vendors (such as those described in the book's first and second video clips) make money at the same time that they make foreign or obscure tapes available to fans, scholars, and collectors. Yet even in such instances, videotape bootlegging has never really disrupted or threatened the mainstream political and economic power structures. In spite of numerous market misfires and whining about piracy, the technology manufacturers and studios still reap enormous revenues and will surely find new business models to continue doing so.

The Motion Picture Association of America and the Recording Industry Association of America have waged major publicity and legal campaigns against "piracy" in the wake of speculative and actual downturns in the film and music markets as a result of peer-to-peer file sharing and other modes of content reproduction and exchange. Jack Valenti and the MPAA devised rhetoric that suggested that the valuable content industry in the United States would collapse owing to piracy, though there was no actual economic evidence or necessarily even legal grounds for Valenti's claims; rather, he relied on appeals to morality, patriotism, and fear—an all-too-familiar political strategy for the early years of the twenty-first century. The press, the government, and to a lesser extent the public have too often accepted these warnings without sufficiently distinguishing between piracy and productive, if legally ambiguous, non-infringing media reproduction and sharing. Such campaigns reduce the complexity of copyright to a binary of paid uses and piracy. Especially in educational materials aimed at schoolchildren, attempts to train youth to respect the law actually misrepresent it by eliding concepts such as the public domain, fair use, free use, and first sale—the elements of copyright law meant to benefit society.[37] As one of the most insightful digital copyright scholars argues, such lobbies have "succeeded in persuading a lot of people that any behavior that has the same effect as piracy must *be* piracy, and must therefore reflect the same moral turpitude we attach to piracy, even if it is the same behavior that we all called legitimate before."[38] In part, I seek here to shift the discussion away from framing questions of piracy or creativity toward issues of users' rights, access, and preservation, and from a focus on the digital present and future to the recent analog past. To be quite clear, I am advocating for bootlegging rather than piracy.

Geographically, I have focused this book on the impact and uses of videotape recording in the United States, in part because copyright laws, formats, and market factors are territory specific, but also in part because academic work on "piracy" has typically focused on illegal media circulation "over there" in Asia, Africa, and Eastern Europe while ignoring domestic activities.[39] Yet the entertainment and electronics industries have been working overtime stateside: they have restricted access to, and uses of, content through encryption and have successfully lobbied for laws that make circumventing such encryption illegal. Still, I should note that, perhaps even more than in the United States, video has been seen internationally as a threat to intellectual property claims and local governance—and has served a public good. A study of early VCR adoption suggested that the phenomenon was from the start global and largely facilitated by the black market, whether smuggled (in some cases, strapped to camels' backs) to elude laws forbidding foreign media or simply to undercut import taxes. Alternately, migrant workers might bring VCRs back to their home countries, thus introducing the technology in places where it was not yet commercially available.[40] Of course, bootlegs imported from overseas to diasporic populations in the United States demonstrate that such borders and distinctions are porous, as suggested in my first video clip (after this introduction).[41] The materiality of the video image in such bootlegs testifies to the distance between audiences and their homelands and to the illicit network that smuggles videos into circulation: "Video decay is especially significant for emigrants and exiles who treasure old, hard-to-get, or bootlegged tapes from 'back home.' Because they are so hard to find, these videos quickly lose their status as mechanically reproduced media and become rare, unique, and precious objects."[42] Here, there, and in between, the contemporary transition from analog to digital video necessitates a retrospective, qualitative consideration of the specific properties and practices of analog videotape before the format becomes obsolete.

Video taping and sharing can be understood as both public and personal. A scholarly study of concert bootleggers suggests that personal live recordings reclaim popular music as *popular* cultural production. "The larger implications of these bootleggers' accounts is that they help reframe the meaning of popular culture as an ongoing source of cultural production—one that is constantly renewed and revitalized through individual efforts to seek out personal and social relationships. . . . Bootleggers recognize themselves as law-breakers, overly-passionate fans, or self-appointed archivists."[43] Another study asserts, "Bootlegs call into question just what rights the public should have in copyrighted but unavailable material."[44] Yet another proclaims, "An essential element of creativity separates the bootleggers from their piratical cousins."[45] Analog reproduction changes the content recorded, and these variations can be read as personalizing individual recordings. Bootlegging—the private reproduction of copyrighted content for noncommercial personal, scholarly, creative, and community-building uses—is a dynamic practice where policy, preservation, and personal investments intersect.

At times, copyright restrictions erect barriers between what the law allows and our wants as audiences, our needs as scholars, or our intentions as preservationists. When the law acts against the people rather than for them, or when a text that has shaped our culture or our lives becomes inaccessible, what rights of access do we have? And how do we intervene? Often the best option is bootlegging, even though this covert practice may seem morally dubious or even alter the text itself. In response to an earlier incarnation of this project, Lawrence Lessig challenged me to think about copyright policies beyond fair use, the "analog hole" that has so long protected home taping. How else could one reasonably argue for bootlegging? It was a tough question, one for which I didn't have a ready answer. In part, this was a problem of my intended historical frame: I was arguing (and still do) for prior interdependencies of fair use and home video, looking at past legal definitions and working through codes that already exist. Upon reading Lessig's foreword to Kembrew McLeod's *Freedom of Expression*, I realized that he was challenging me to think beyond copyright as we had known it and to advocate for an alternative, future form of copyright.[46] The law is to be questioned, interpreted, and expanded. This is exactly what the Supreme Court justices did in deciding that recording television programs with a VCR could be considered fair use. And it's what they have so far failed to do in the age of digital technologies. I look to video recording practices that have reconceptualized copyright in progressive ways. This book, thus, is an ode to analog tapes and the virtues of their vices.

VIDEO CLIP 1

Diasporic Asian Video Markets in Orange County

Despite what you may have seen on TV in *The OC*, *Laguna Beach*, *The Real Housewives of Orange County*, or even *Arrested Development*, Orange County is one of the most diverse areas of the country and home to numerous diasporic populations. In that Southern California way, many of greater LA's "real" ethnic neighborhoods blend in and out of the generic suburban sprawl. The strip malls may all look alike, but the superficial similarity belies incredibly varied goods, including bootleg videos of foreign content imported from overseas or taped from satellite broadcasts on the West Coast.

In Korean video stores, VHS remains the predominant bootleg format, one that continues to be used extensively for taping television and copying television programs. Dachan Video, located in the Orange Tree Square shopping plaza in Irvine, hosts an impressive collection of VHS tapes of Korean TV serial dramas, arranged by original network (KBS, SBS, MBC) and series. The tapes appear to be consumer grade and taped from local satellite broadcasts of Korean networks; they are probably mass-duped in-house, as the plain white labels have purple tips with the store's name.[1] These labels, in turn, have been computer-printed with the titles of the shows and numerals to indicate each tape's episode or number in the sequence of cassettes. The cassettes are strikingly uniform and only distinguishable by title. Videos here are available for either rent or purchase. The store also features a smattering of classic and children's films on DVD and a larger inventory of legit VHS releases of Hollywood films. Curiously, one nook features only printer cartridges and jugs of replacement ink; no other computer supplies or other kinds of computer merchandise are sold. With large windows, a glass door, and white shelves, the store is brightly lit; nothing seems terribly covert

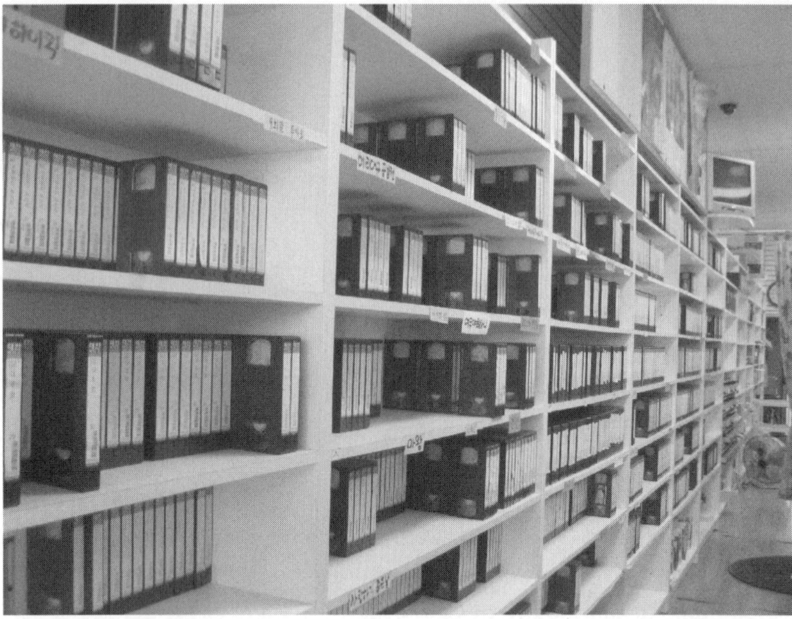

4. The inventory of Korean TV serials at Dachan Video in Irvine, California, December 2007. Photo by author.

about this operation, despite the dubious provenance of the inventory and what appears to be a back room behind a curtain.

Another nearby Korean video store, Irvine Video, is tucked into a corner of the strip mall compound Heritage Plaza amid a stunning range of different cuisines and groceries. The storefront, like the name, is unassuming, and inside the store is more dimly lit. I'm not suggesting it's more sinister; it's just a bit gloomy. The left side of the store appears to be all bootlegs, while the right side at first glance houses the legitimate imports. But the shelves of legitimate tapes, it turns out, slide to reveal a second tier of videos, all of which are dupes. As at Dachan Video, the cassettes themselves are bare, without covers or cases, and are only distinguishable by title; here the computer-printed labels have green tips—the only indication of propriety or distinction from the other store's collection. A poster for KBS America—akin to BBC America for Anglos—both indicates that the store stocks such programs and points to such content's origins. The inventory appears less dominated by TV programs than in the other store, however, as there are numerous films on tape, with a varied selection of Japanese and Chinese cinema in addition to the Korean tapes. As with any other video store, the

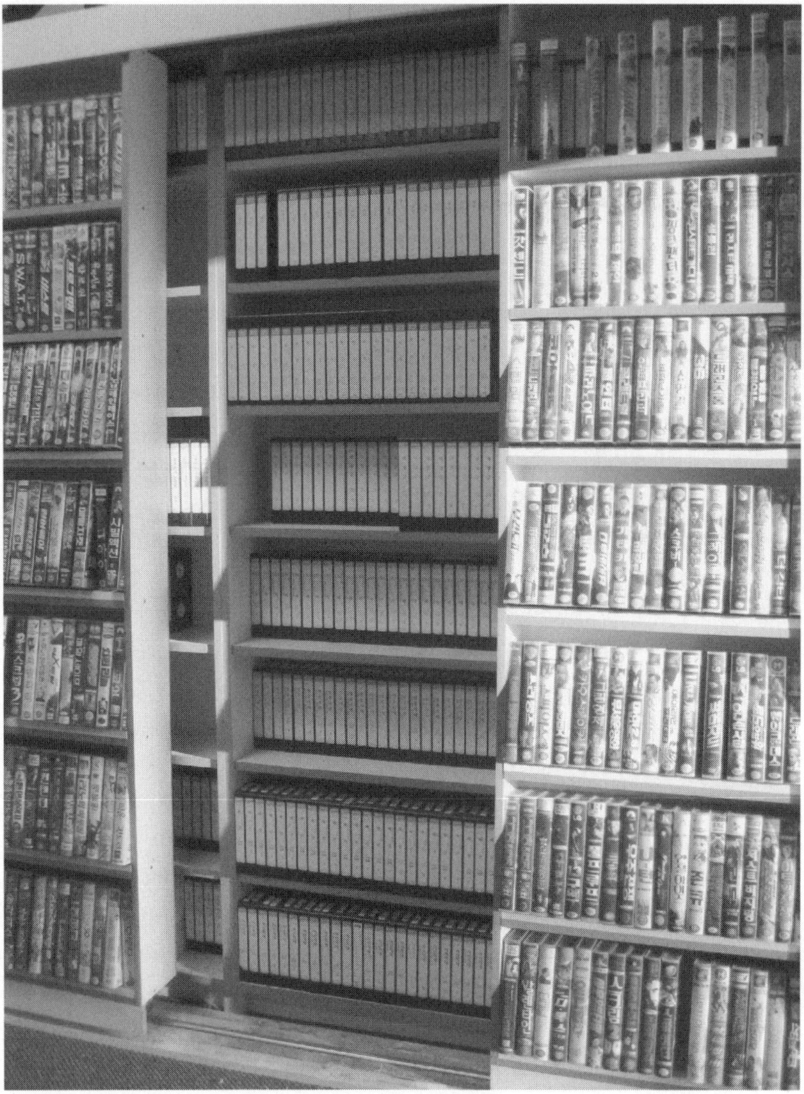

5. Shelves of Korean VHS bootlegs hidden behind shelves of legitimate cassette cases at Irvine Video, December 2007. Photo by author.

selection is distinguished by sections, with all the Hollywood and European releases relegated into a general non-Asian jumble; the selection of Western films is seemingly random, rather than a tight collection of only transnational blockbusters. The only English-language signage is the store's name, unless you count the random display for jars of dental powder. Despite DVD cases here and there, the inventory is predominantly still VHS.

Whereas VHS remains prominent in the Korean stores, it appears to be on the way out at a Japanese market and almost entirely removed from the inventories of Vietnamese shops. High Quality Video, inside the open-air Japanese mall Mitsuwa Marketplace in Costa Mesa, has an inventory of predominantly bootlegged DVD-RS, though a few sections of VHS tapes appear to be on closeout at the end of racks or near checkout. Many of these tapes are in their original consumer-grade blank-tape slipcases and are rubber-banded together as sets; others, for feature films, have color-copied covers made from DVDs (the DVD logo appears in the corner), thus indicating their pirate status. The inventory seems to comprise primarily feature films, mostly Japanese with some Korean and Chinese selections; there isn't any prominent selection of Hollywood films, though when I visited I saw what appeared to be legitimate import box sets of the TV series 24.

At the Asian Garden Mall in Westminster, several stores sell Vietnamese CDs and DVDs. Strikingly, there's a fluidity between the CDs and DVDs, as about half the DVDs are either for karaoke or of live musical performances. All the stores I visited in the mall had prominent monitors playing such contemporary Vietnamese pop performances, which seemed to be staged for TV. The inventories in these stores, unlike Dachan, Irvine, or High Quality Video, look more like professionally produced releases. All the DVDs at these stores have color printed labels and come in sealed plastic wrap. The covers, however, have a distinctly shoddy design aesthetic, and the logos on their backs indicate that they were produced locally in Westminster or in nearby Anaheim, Garden Grove, or Pomona. Most bear some kind of copyright notice, and some warn the consumer, "rental prohibited"—as if that restriction had any actual legal basis. Although these DVDs look less like bootlegs, their legality remains difficult to determine; the various distributors might have paid for distribution rights in the United States, but the copies' cheapness suggest otherwise.

All these video stores operate as businesses, but they also operate to keep their customers in touch with the contemporary entertainment of their (or their ancestors') homelands. Similar stores exist in Thai Town in Los Angeles, the Chinese neighborhood of San Gabriel, and the Filipino

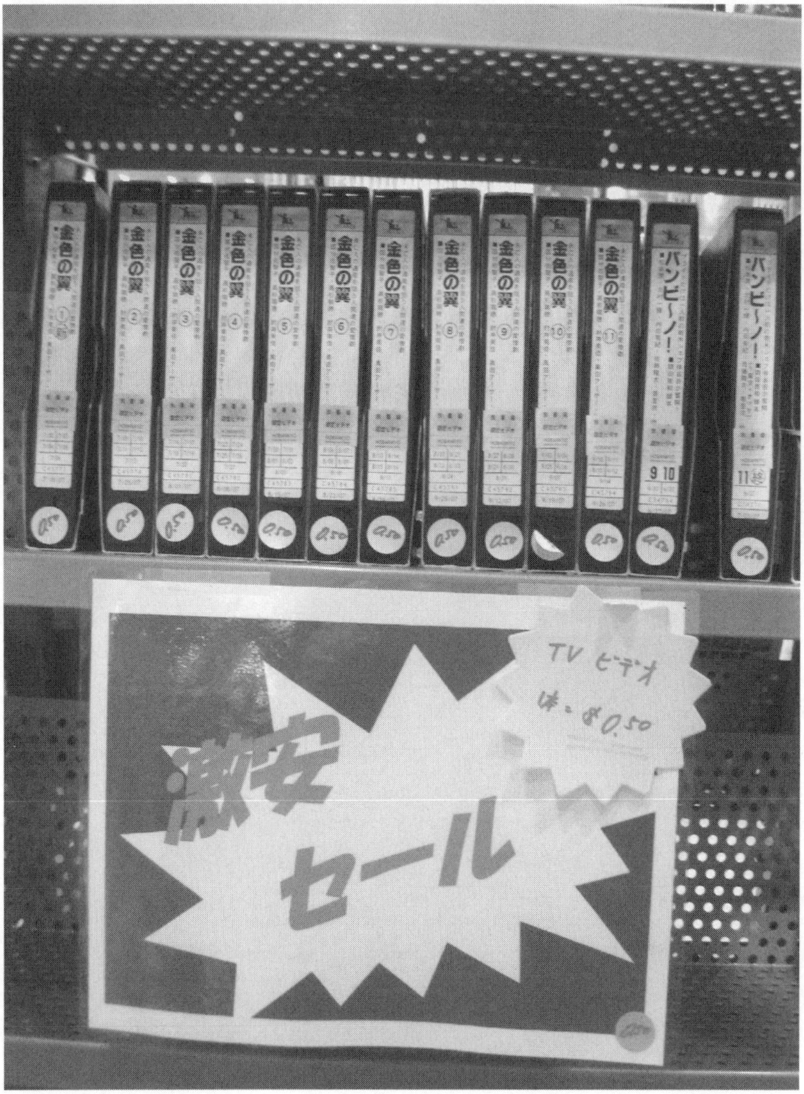

6. VHS tapes of Japanese TV on clearance at High Quality Video in Costa Mesa, California, December 2007. The sign says, “Extra cheap sale! TV videos for $.50 each.” Photo by author.

community in West Covina.[2] According to a friend, a year before our tour of these shops, VHS still predominated at most such stores. These places usually stock current popular TV shows and movies; things that don't sell, my friend informed me, tended to get taped over so that the cassette could be reused for something else—one distinctive quality of videotape that makes it somewhat preferable to disc formats. Diasporic bootlegs are not unique to Southern California but are common in immigrant communities throughout cities along the Pacific Rim and across the country. Although bootlegs exist in a kind of legal limbo—they are generally illegal, since copyright laws are internationally reciprocal—they nonetheless provide a service to diasporic communities and maintain a global market for non-Hollywood media.

1. Be Kind, Rewind: The Histories and Erotics of Home Video

In a VCR user's guide from 1981, the author imagined a scenario of video dubbing that bordered on the stilted dialogue and implausible situations of pornography:

> In order to copy a tape yourself, your options are to buy, borrow or appropriate a second VCR. . . . Who knows what romantic possibilities may be uncovered as you search for a second VCR. In the old days, borrowing sugar afforded a convenient excuse to meet that lovely lady or handsome man next door. Now, modern technology has provided us with a much sweeter line, "Do you mind if I bring over my Betamax and make a dub tonight?"[1]

Although it's perhaps unlikely that someone would respond, "Come on in," to such a flat-footed seduction, videotape seems to have inspired its share of innuendo. It is, after all, a reproductive technology. In another account, this time as the video rental boom was reaching its fever pitch, video negotiated more pervasive hookups without the need for pickup lines; the *New York Times* quoted a video store owner as saying, "Closing time is like closing time at a bar. People get desperate, and they'll go home with anything."[2]

Not only did such blatantly sexualized references pique interest in home video when it was a new and alluring technology, but such curious associations have recurred and lingered even in death.[3] More than twenty years later, an academic "autopsy" of the VCR queerly anthropomorphized the technology by eroticizing it:

> With us but a short while, you demonstrated that the sexual architecture of film was malleable, and although gendered, always incorrectly so, in excess of the binaries we wished to believe human bodies confined them-

selves to. . . . You showed the world what sex with the movies really felt like; you initiated us into the deep satisfaction of holding a tape in one's hand, sticking it in the slot, and making it play.[4]

These speculative, journalistic, and retrospective accounts suggest that VCRs were once objects of passion for some users. Or, as the longtime exploitationeer and adult film entrepreneur David Friedman succinctly asserted, the home video market was "founded by pirates and pornographers."[5]

Videotape has always been a deviant technology, one connotative of vice, at odds with the entertainment industry, a technology in which users can witness the literal degeneration of recordings. This chapter begins and ends with hot-and-bothered discourses of videotape, which have perhaps perverted more quotidian experiences. In between, I examine the technological genealogy of which video is part and the ways that the video market shaped adoption, uses, and meanings for home video. Although I engage video's technological history at some length, I emphasize the materiality and aesthetics of videotape, which tend to fall out of industrial histories of the technology. In addition, the film studios attempted to reform consumer behavior toward renting and purchasing content, but such marketing never entirely killed off home taping and allowed a marginal collector culture to emerge. Meanwhile, mainstream consumptive uses coincided with the rise of amateur and celebrity porn. The erotics and everyday experiences of videotape cannot be divorced from the technical and business institutions that have made home video possible and have wielded considerable power over its uses. But just the same, these official histories offer little insight into the aesthetics and affect of the technology. Thus in this chapter I solicit strange bedfellows in an attempt to offer a multidimensional history of analog home video. This chapter climaxes, so to speak, by reading the lusty associations that bootleg videotapes have provoked and the ways in which they suggest an analog video aesthetic. In analog media, aesthetics and access often exist in an oppositional relationship. But what I call the aesthetics of access in the introduction can also be an eros of access, as some audiences have fallen in love with analog imperfections. This is nowhere more evident than in the published celebrations of bootlegs that romanticize analog video.

Formats and Components: A Technological Genealogy

Audiences may be most aware of technologies when they are new—marketed as performing new functions and requiring new skills to use them—or when they have become old, displaced by new models or different devices that draw attention to what has been lacking all along. Similarly, technologies become most exciting when their uses are illegal—or at least contested. Once adopted and allowed, technologies seem pretty mundane. Thus, looking back at initial advertisements and commentary helps historians understand what was perceived as innovative or unfamiliar about a technology, while retrospective accounts suggest what was once peculiar may have become passé. Once the newness has worn off, users belatedly become hyperaware of ingrained technologies through their breakdowns and failures. Thus my research on video has led me to these liminal moments: its prehistory, its broadcast era, its adoption by artists and community groups, its marketing by rental outlets and studios, and its circulation on the fringes of polite society. Not all of these appear prominently here, but all have informed the versions of history I present.

Videotape generally—and home video in particular—has not been granted the status of a medium. In part, this may be because videotape is a dependent technology: it requires a recording and playback deck, and a VCR has little use value unless it is patched into a television monitor (tuned to channel 3 or 4) on which the recording can be watched.[6] It also requires content, whether homemade, taped off-air from broadcasts, or rented from a video store. Whether seen as a technology for expanding viewership of broadcast television or as the afterthought of feature films' releases, home video has not been conceived as something independent and therefore worthy of attention. Put another way, videotape is a storage device, a category of functional technology to which users don't usually ascribe the status of a medium. Yet, I suggest, videotape has been something more than just a dependent storage device; it has transformed relationships between users and screens and, through its limitations and artifacts, has introduced its own aesthetic qualities as well. That it has been eulogized and eroticized further suggests its cultural importance as a medium. Perhaps a more accurate term than medium is *format*: the specific version of a technology, one that reformats everything it records.

"Video," broadly conceived, will continue to exist; videotape and videocassettes, however, may not. As the analog-to-digital technology transition is well under way—or even a done deal, in the minds of many—it seems essential to retrospectively examine and reclaim analog videotape as a distinguishable and now disappearing format. At the end of the VHS era, we can now approach it as a historically significant format. Videotape was arguably the key component of the first wave of technologies that changed how viewers used their television sets and expanded their viewing options. Before the VCR, the television monitor was a receiver for network and local broadcasts. With the VCR, and arguably building on it, viewers' options expanded to include timeshifted recordings ("timeshifting" means taping television broadcasts for later viewing), original cable programming, rented movies, home movies, video games, and later video on demand and shared online video clips. As one media historian points out, the VCR, HBO, and video games all debuted in 1975, and by 1978 they were visibly cross-marketed.[7] The VCR led the pack as the most widely and quickly adopted way of transforming television, though increasingly such technologies and services are not so much individual media as *components* of a multidevice home entertainment system.

It may be illuminating to offer some statistics up front to reveal how and where video went home. VCRs were once the most quickly adopted new consumer entertainment technology, and yet, though they were on the market as early as fall 1975, in 1982 just more than 5 percent of U.S. television households had acquired VCRs. The increased availability of prerecorded videos containing feature films drove the VCR boom of the mid-1980s. The adoption rate eventually grew to nearly 10 percent in 1983, surpassed 25 percent in 1985, surpassed 50 percent in 1987, and eventually surpassed 75 percent in 1992.[8] During that time, prices for machines steadily declined, while the number of video rental stores grew. DVDs debuted in 1997 and essentially hit similar adoption rates in half the time; I would speculate that such numbers indicate a cultural move toward accelerated adoption of consumer electronics of all stripes as much or more than that DVDs satisfied an actual market need.

Although home video is often thought of as an East Asian, North American, and Western European phenomenon, its cultural impact has been significant worldwide, especially in territories with strict media regulations or regions with little infrastructure for local media production. And, perhaps counter to ethnocentric expectations, the Middle East had one of the most accelerated adoption rates for VCRs. For instance, Kuwait saw 85 percent penetration in TV homes by 1983, compared to less than 10 percent adoption in the United States by this time.[9] Although the videocassette technology is essentially the same worldwide, tapes and players have different regional codings, making them incompatible. (Note that this marks video formats as significantly different from audio ones; an audiocassette or disc plays the same in every country.) The rationale for such distinctions may be related to different television standards in different countries, which would in turn necessitate different input signals, but one of the goals of such incompatibilities is to impede global exchange or transnational piracy.[10] Thus analog video (like scrambled cable signals) regulated uses of technology through encryption regardless of legal rights well before digital rights management.

In historicizing and arguing for the specificity of videotape as a format, I turn now to its constituent parts—its components. I start where video started: with audio. Video expanded out of audio technologies scientifically, commercially, and functionally. The use of magnetic tape, standardized plastic cassettes, and even the types of buttons appeared first for audio. Although this historical review may not exactly be *sexy*, it is at times romantic: music and mix tapes were important and affective common content for tapes. From audio, I turn to video, introducing how it shifted from a broadcast to a home entertainment technology and the very literal way plastic cassettes shaped the ways consumers used video. I then attempt to capture a bit of the lived-in quality of home video by turning attention to the boxy contraptions and entertainment center furniture. I suggest that the videotape's taken-for-grantedness may be because it has in turn been adopted as just another component of how users interact with television on a daily basis, one that has blended in even when it clashes with its surroundings.

Audiotape and Cassettes

In recording and in broadcasting, audio technology has typically preceded audiovisual technology; therefore any history of videotape must remember the relationships between audio and video. In fact, in many ways, video is more closely related to audio technologies and practices than to celluloid, despite direct connection in terms of marketing and content.[11] Because moving-image content transitions between the two platforms so fluidly, this fact bears repeating. As a film historian who stresses the connections between film and video writes, "The two technologies evolved separately, not successively. . . . Video is not cinema; it only looks like cinema. Its technology is essentially the technology of sound transmission, recording, and reproduction."[12] (Not insignificantly, a seminal aesthetic reading of video positions sound before image.)[13]

Audiotape preceded videotape both in the laboratory and in the home; video's development in the lab and its adoption in the home have been informed by sound recording and playback practices. Academic studies of magnetic tape recording have emphasized its impact on production, aesthetics, and distribution within music studies and on technology and political economy in media studies. These cultural histories and theories of audio reproduction demonstrate how common recording practices have been established through misuses (or unintended or unimagined uses) of technology.[14] As early as the nineteenth century, audio recordings reoriented their users' perceptions by initiating a separation of the senses—isolating sound from vision or touch—and listening to recordings became a learned aesthetic practice, what Jonathan Sterne terms "audile technique."[15] Over the decades, trends in performing and methods of listening—creation and reception—also shifted and developed in relation and response to developing recording technologies.

Magnetic tape technology was a post–World War II phenomenon in the United States and Japan, where it was originally developed for broadcasting and business uses and only later became convenient and affordable enough for widespread domestic uses. Thus its development might be considered central to postwar industrial economies and symptomatic of a rise in consumer cultures. The industrial development and market exploitation histories of magnetic tape have been described in depth elsewhere, so I will offer an abbreviated account here. Magnetic audiotape was first manufactured in 1934 in Germany; within four years, tape and the Magnetophon deck were the standard format for recording Reich-Rundfunk-Gesellschaft radio programming. At the end of World War II, U.S. Army electronics specialist John T. Mullin discovered the German Magnetophons and sent two to the army base at Fort Monmouth, New Jersey, and two to his home in San Francisco. Thus the technology was pillaged from the Nazis and imported to the United States as the spoils of war.[16] In 1946 Mullin gave a public demonstration of the technology to the Institute of Radio Engineers. Ampex, which had been making aircraft motors, switched gears to producing professional sound products, thereby capitalizing on a new postwar market. In 1947 Mullin demonstrated the technology to Bing Crosby, who left NBC for the Mutual network so that he could prerecord radio shows without having to interrupt his golfing hobby. Although "liveness" was prized by broadcasters for its immediacy, quality, and authenticity—as well as a method to ensure local stations' dependence on centralized national networks—resistance to prerecording eventually succumbed to tape's advantages and became standard practice in radio and later in television.[17]

Magnetic tape technology was developed to be invisible, so that prerecorded programs were formally indistinguishable from live ones for audiences (though the programs' contents may have been less timely or topical). Transparency and fidelity were considered among the technology's highest virtues for broadcasting and recording professionals. Consumer recording models followed from high-end technologies, typically miniaturized for both reduced cost and user convenience at the expense of fidelity. Memorex even marketed consumer-grade videotape on the basis of its verisimilitude with the famous early 1980s ad campaign "Is it real or is it Memorex?"

Magnetic audio recording technologies were available for office and home uses by the late 1940s, but until the late 1960s they were only adopted by niche users for dictation, hobby recording, party games, and high-fi music reproduction.[18] General users, it seemed, didn't have the need or desire to make their own recordings. And, as the audio historian David Morton has asserted, users were often put off by hearing their own voices played back.[19] Morton also suggests that television, which would eventually drive video recording, initially inhibited home sound recording. "In the early 1950s, television sales skyrocketed and many consumers had to choose between these two fascinating toys. Most chose television" over audio recorders.[20] Finally, in the mid-to-late 1960s, the introduction of 8-track cartridges and compact cassette tapes for recording music—and eventually as a format for buying prerecorded music—boosted consumer adoption.

Audiotape technologies revolutionized recording both for producers and consumers. For producers, magnetic tape could be erased and reused for multiple recordings, unlike prior audio formats that were physically inscribed, scratched, or pressed. Magnetic tape allowed consumers to create their own original audio recordings or to copy music from LPs or the radio. Audiotape was introduced as a recording format, rather than as a playback format, which distinguished tape from both its grooved-disc ancestors and digital disc descendents.

Magnetic tape not only changed the potential uses and productions of sounds but also introduced new audio aesthetics. Tape introduced new sounds through layering, mixing, reverb, and echo effects. As one music scholar writes, "The aesthetic criterion shifted from the sound of the actual performance to the sound of the recording."[21] Since the 1960s sound engineers and musicians have experimented with tape technology by creating sounds derived from the format itself.[22] Tape technology introduced new timbres and allowed for inventive new sonic experiences and musical fusions, which called for new ways of listening and understanding synthetic sounds. For instance, playing a tape at the wrong speed makes voices sound hyper and falsetto when played too fast or lethargic and bass when slowed down, while tapes played backward in songs by Radiohead or Missy Elliott can produce a brain-scrambling sensation. The introduction of digital technologies retrospectively called attention to analog tape's distinctive sounds and limitations.

Widespread consumer usage of magnetic tape technology was made feasible by format standardization and convenient cassette packaging. For both audio and video, cassette cartridges protected the tape and made loading it user-friendly for nonprofessionals without technical training. As a cheaply producible consumer material that took off more or less concurrently with the boom in home entertainment technologies, plastic enabled recording science to become mass media, and plastic contributes to the ways users interact with videotapes as aesthetic experiences and as tangible objects.[23] Various cartridge designs were developed, though this process was fairly slow. Modeled on film cartridges, the Fidelipac (1959) was a single-spool system used for playing short radio spots such as station identification slugs or commercials; although convenient for these uses, the tapes did not have a rewind mechanism and were tricky to fast-forward, preventing popular adoption. The small plastic audiocassette that became the popular standard was developed by Philips in 1962 (some sources say 1964) and was introduced commercially in the following year; importantly, rather than maintaining exclusivity, Philips broadly licensed the design to other manufacturers in order for the format to achieve widespread adoption across competing companies. In the United States, Norelco, the company famous for its electric shavers, produced the plastic cassettes, and they were initially known here as "Norelco cases." Originally the sound quality was suitable for speech recordings but not well suited to music; during the following decade, changes were made to the metallic compounds in the tape's magnetism and in playback heads' sensitivity. At the same time, Ray Dolby, working for Ampex, developed a studio recording method to compensate for inherent tape hiss, involving recording high frequencies at increased levels to drown out the tape's noise and then equalizing the levels on playback. Such recording strategies responded to the breakthrough in cassette portability. Tape players/recorders were initially stand-alone devices but would be integrated into hi-fi stereo systems by the mid 1970s after Dolby's methods made magnetic tape suitable for music recording.[24]

Although Philips cassettes had been manufactured since the mid-1960s, the 8-track (1964) became the first mass-market cartridge format for prerecorded music. Commercial albums could now be played on the go in cars or in hand-held portable players. But the 8-track's single-reel perpetual loop was a glitchy technology, and music purists balked at the fact that record companies would often shuffle song sequences or even cut songs in half to maximize tape time. The 8-track was relegated to thrift store bins by the early 1980s, though it did attain cult status with some collectors. The 8-track's famous failure perhaps predisposed it to kitsch recuperation more than the comparably functional, workaday audiocassette tape format. As has perhaps already been forgotten, 8-tracks were initially popular for home-recording LP records for playback in car stereos or other portable audio players, and there was even a truck-stop black market for pirate 8-tracks.[25]

By 1982, cassette tapes edged 8-tracks out of the market in part because of new portable devices such as the Walkman and "ghetto blasters," and record companies ceased issuing prerecorded 8-tracks almost as soon as the format was eclipsed. The Philips cassette not only accelerated the portability of music and the demise of the 8-track but also boosted the practice of home taping and music bootlegging. The music recording industry campaigned against this audio taping technology in the early 1980s with its campaign "Home taping is killing music" and the piratical logo of a cassette silhouette meant to resemble a skull and crossbones. (During the hubbub over online file sharing, this logo and slogan resurfaced as an ironic T-shirt icon and as part of the BitTorrent site Pirate Bay's logo.) Yet music label and independent studies demonstrated that the more music audiences taped and shared, the more likely they were to purchase more music: "These findings imply that, although related, taping may best be seen as independent ways of expressing a more general, underlying commitment to music."[26]

When home taping technology became widely available to consumers, new possibilities also opened up for compilation audio recordings, as did new affective relationships to music and popular culture that were mediated by tape technologies. Personal mix tapes combine favorite tracks recorded from the radio or albums to reflect particular tastes, sensibilities, or messages (for instance, if the mix tape was made for someone, particularly an object of desire). These mixes may or may not reflect a specific or chronological moment in music history; they may, rather, be historically random but emotionally specific to a moment in a taper's life. (Such emotive uses of analog tape reappear in associations with bootleg videos at the end of this chapter and again in chapter 4.) Thurston Moore, of the band Sonic Youth, published a book about mix tapes that compiled track lists of favorite mixes alongside homemade artwork, images of audiocassettes with handwritten labels, and brief musings on making and listening to musical mixes.[27] The book appeared as iPods and similar MP3 players introduced a new wave of portable music technologies and playlists, suggesting both the cassette precedent for contemporary listening practices and the uniquely analog emotional and laborious commitments (sequencing, cuing, and recording happen in real time) entailed in making mixes. Through cassette tapes, new modes of musical access mixed with new modes of affective investment.

The convenient recording function and portability of magnetic tape cassettes has not only fostered private compilations but also enabled public productions and subaltern bootleg distribution. As cultural anthropologists have observed, cassette tapes (audio and video) have not only fostered the small-scale circulation of works within a community but also had major impacts on international cultural flows, especially in India, Nigeria, Egypt, and Somalia.[28] In many cases the flow of texts constitutes transnational piracy, although "legal or illegal, licensed or unlicensed, the real effect every time a piece of music is copied privately is to promote the circulation of music."[29] And, of course, it's not just non-Western and diasporic audiences who bootleg and pirate music and movies. Dubbing tapes, burning CDs and DVDs, and downloading files have become an all-American pastime that cuts across numerous demographics, from the most privileged, who have advanced technology and could probably afford to pay for their media, to the marginalized people who make their living through the black market. In all these cases, culture is produced and reproduced by private citizens operating outside the domain of major music labels and Hollywood studios. Although less pervasive, videotape mixes, letters, and diasporic bootleg practices (such as those described in my first "video clip" and in chapter 5) have followed from audio compilations.

Videotape and Videocassettes

Home video was a long-germinating project, developed by several competing companies and formats over the course of more than three decades. Engineers expanded on the basic science of audiotape, and they were already at work on video early in audiotape's public life. Videotape stores approximately two hundred times as much information as audiotape, making its mass production and miniaturization a difficult proposition.[30] In its technical development, engineers strove to improve videotape's fidelity by developing magnetic tape that was invisible, inaudible, and imperceptible as tape during playback. Inherent tape hiss or dynamic-range limitations were counteracted as much as possible, and recording capacity was continually expanded so that feature-length films or football games would not have to be split between more than one reel or cassette. (Similarly, videotape's initial popularity in Japan has been credited to the ability to show instant replays of sumo wrestling.)[31] Although typically conceived and used as a transparent, often-temporary access format rather than as a formal medium, analog videotape has specific properties that are distinguishable from live broadcast television or newer digital media, just as different tape stocks reveal varying resolutions and longevities. Furthermore, watching and listening are learned behaviors; the technology, rather than being self-evident, required some degree of education. Content industry trade journals such as *Variety* regularly printed home video glossary features well into the 1980s, indicating that even professionals in the biz needed to be taught about the new technology, its features, and its terminology.[32] For home viewers, instruction manuals may have offered a pedagogical function (though I suspect that many home users never consulted the booklet and thus never learned how to program their VCRs), and even the viewing experience reflects adaptation and new consumption patterns.

Like its audio ancestor, videotape was developed initially for broadcasting and production and was only belatedly made more practical—that is, more affordable, portable, and user-friendly—for consumers. In 1951 both RCA and Ampex began developing videotape; five years later, Ampex presented the first successful model, Quadruplex, which was two inches wide with reels fourteen inches in diameter and recorded images in black and white. The demand for videotape recorders was unexpected. The networks, the earliest adopters of videotape, used the technology for short-term timeshifting. Programs broadcast live on the East Coast would be recorded and played back for broadcast during prime time in the Pacific time zone, which extended the national networks' reach to wider western audiences.[33] Whereas broadcast networks relied on the technology to maintain schedule continuity across time zones (and nationalize control of programming) in a way that simulated liveness, later home tapers randomized when programs would be watched.[34] Early industrial tape was prohibitively expensive, bulky to store, and scarce, so networks reused durable tapes for multiple recordings rather than for archival uses.[35] By the end of the 1950s, the Japanese consumer electronics firms Sony, Matsushita Electric Corporation (parent of JVC and now part of Panasonic), and Toshiba were all competing to develop the first domestic videotape recorders. Perhaps the primary difference between Ampex's and

Sony's early research and development was their intended markets: whereas Ampex was specifically developing machines for commercial broadcasting, Sony was already concerned with the home electronics market.[36]

By the time home video was new, the concept was not. As early as 1955 readers were introduced to the idea of home video and off-air recording, as demonstrated by an article that predicted that reel-to-reel home video tape (HVT, as it was then acronymized) would be the next big thing in home entertainment and available as early as 1966. The article's subheading promised, "A new invention will now permit you to see your favorite program whether you're home or not."[37] Sony actually marketed an early reel-to-reel home video system in 1965 with a splashy two-page advertisement in *Life* that presented the new technology as being explicitly for timeshifting a decade before Sony marketed the Betamax for the same purpose. The ad copy also suggested that consumers could make any use of TV recordings they decided: "You can electronically record anything you see or hear, and play it back instantly. You can record and keep anything you see on your TV set. You can erase the tape immediately and reuse it, or keep it indefinitely."[38] In the early 1970s, more feature articles in prominent magazines such as *TV Guide*, *Life*, and the *New York Times Magazine* continued to educate readers about home video, preparing the market and building expectations years before such devices became common.[39] If anything, home video didn't come quickly enough for some; as one reporter commented in 1972, "That heralded video-cassette era has run into delays."[40] Even technologies that proved to be market failures, such as CBS's EVR (Electronic Video Recorder) and Philips's videodiscs, received considerable reporting. Between 1956 and 1996, more than one hundred video recording and playback formats were developed, many of which were actually marketed; these efforts created a flood of incompatible and quickly obsolete technologies that discouraged consumer adoption (and that now pose major problems for preservation).[41] The year 1984 might be seen as the pivotal moment for home video: during that year, the Supreme Court decided off-air taping was legal, prices for VCRs dropped below $300 and machine sales correspondingly surged, and both *Time* and *Newsweek* reported a "video revolution" on their covers.[42] New-media enthusiasts, please note that "revolutionary" media rhetoric did not begin with the Internet.

When home video caught on, it was initially a novelty for users to decide their own TV schedules and to rent favorite movies. Yet though the phenomenon may have seemed new, the underlying magnetic tape technology and

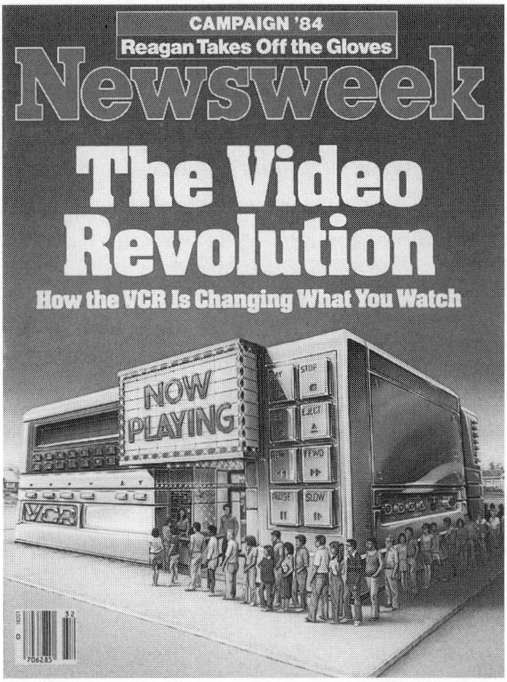

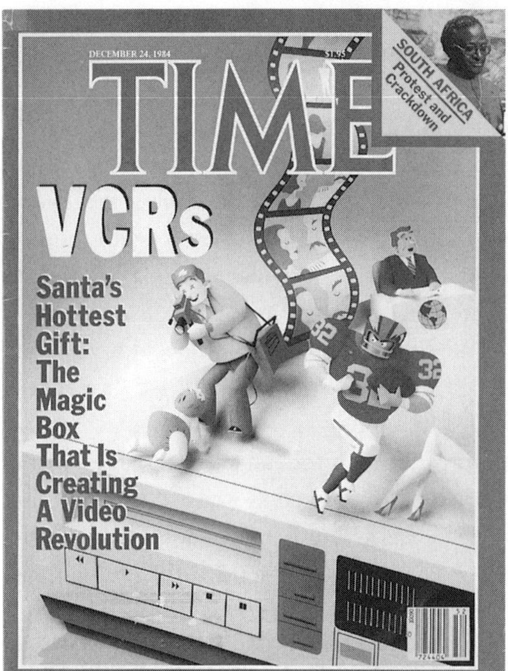

7a–b. In 1984 both *Newsweek* and *Time* proclaimed a "video revolution" on their front covers. Curiously, both magazines depicted the revolution with cartoon images of massive VCRs that dwarf their human users. Collection of the author.

its basic operations would already have been familiar from audio devices.[43] In fact, an early promotional video for Sony's Betamax reassured technophobic potential consumers that anyone who could use a color TV and a tape recorder could operate the Betamax system.[44] Many, if not most, VCR consumers would already have used audiotape recorders, so that the standard menu of buttons—record, play, stop, fast forward, rewind, pause—did not introduce new functions. Some early consumer decks even featured an "audio dub" button with the other primary commands; this function allowed users to add their own soundtracks to video recordings that overwrote the original sound inputs.[45] Even the peculiar necessity of having to push "record" and "play" simultaneously to initiate recording (typical on VHS machines but not on Betas) carried over from audiocassette recorders to many video decks. The VCR's most pervasive functional innovation over audio recorders was the introduction of a clock mechanism that could be set in advance for automated off-air taping.[46] And it was programming clock timers that proved the most famously baffling operation for home video users.

Various companies vied to develop nonbroadcast video technologies for the lucrative mass markets of business and home uses. With sister Japanese (research and development) and American (distribution) corporations, Sony had an early lead, as it proved to be the first to market various videotape formats in the United States that emphasized compact, portable technology—a business strategy that extended from various video recorders to the audio Walkman. Sony introduced 1/2-inch tape with helical scan, a diagonal rather than horizontal encoding pattern that maximized the recording capacity of the tape, in 1965. The company debuted the first mobile reel-to-reel video camera technology, the Portapak, in 1968. In 1969 Sony introduced the 3/4-inch tape cassette, which became a popular professional and industrial format but failed to catch on for domestic uses because of its cost. Finally, in fall 1975, Sony unveiled the Betamax home videotape recorder, the first "successful" home video system to emerge among a crowded field of failed 1970s competitors. This first unit was rather hulking, as the console combined both a cathode-ray tube monitor and tape deck side-by-side; the original suggested retail price was oversized as well at $1,300. Within six months, however, Sony began marketing Betamax decks without the integrated televisions and slashed hundreds off the price tag.[47] In 1976 JVC, Matsushita, and RCA introduced VHS, which would soon overtake Betamax as the preferred format. (Blank JVC tapes still boast "The Inventor of VHS" on their slipcases.) Like Betamax, VHS was introduced as a blank tape format intended to create home recordings from broadcast television signals.

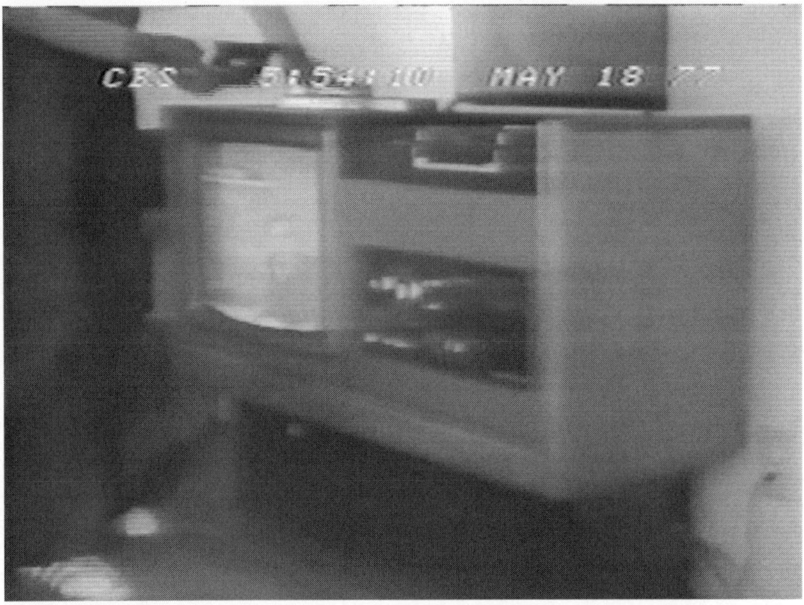

8. The earliest Sony Betamax, model LV 1901, combined a monitor and a recording deck in the same bulky console. Image from the *CBS Evening News* report on the Betamax lawsuit, May 18, 1977.

I return to the "format war" that ensued between Betamax and VHS later in this chapter.

Both models used similar half-inch magnetic tape as their underlying technology, though the encoding and cassette size made the Betamax and VHS formats incompatible. Magnetic tape is made of a thin plastic base, an intermediary level of adhesive, and a layer of oxide particles that can be magnetized to encode video signals or demagnetized to erase them.[48] The video information takes up most of the height of the tape, with diagonal streaks of information; the audio information is encoded along the top of the tape, and tracking control information appears along the bottom. Damage to the tape's edges therefore causes problems in image stability or sound quality. In most VCRs, tapes can be recorded or played back at three speeds: standard play (SP), long play (LP, with double running time but reduced resolution), or extended play (EP, with triple running time but lowest resolution). EP recordings tend to demonstrate grainy colors marked by white staticky specks; similar problems appear with diagonal distress in tapes that have been repeatedly used for everyday timeshifting, so that the magnetic particles seem to be fatigued and less flexible or responsive to recoding.

Because tape is pulled outside the cassette to loop past the recording and playback heads, it may occasionally get caught or tangled by a VCR, though, in my experience, videotapes get snagged around heads and spindles far less frequently than comparatively thin audiotapes.

VHS cassette casings are made of hard, textured black plastic and feature two windows to reveal the reels of tape, along with wee gauge marks. (By contrast, Betamax cassettes only had one window and a larger space for the adhesive label.) This feature allows users to see if the tape is rewound or not, and fluorescent "Be Kind, Rewind" stickers affixed to rental cassettes trained users to double-check by looking. The plastic casing is typically molded so that there are inset, smooth areas for adhesive labels on tapes' tops and spines. A small button on the front right side releases the lever that opens the front flap so that the tape can be accessed by the VCR's pulleys and spindles; this is called U-loading (or M-loading) because of the shape of the tape's path from and back into the cassette.

Cassette cartridges have been essential to making videotape technology a widespread and user-friendly technology, while protective cardboard sleeves or plastic snap cases protect cassettes and keep the interior tape clean for playback. Decorative packaging and labeling also make meaning for tapes by marketing and marking them. A cassette's packaging addresses its user and identifies its content; for example, a puffy case indicates a kid vid, a big box boasts overpriced porn, or a photocopied cover communicates its bootleg status.[49] Both blank and sell-through prerecorded tapes typically come in lightweight cardboard slipcases; children's tapes, in contrast, often come in protective oversized "clamshell" packaging made of stiff cardboard covered with vinyl and with bubbled plastic inset trays for the cassettes. In an e-mail, a friend of mine praised how kids' movies "came in these oversized, brightly colored candy-like plastic boxes that made the most satisfying *smack* when you opened and closed them." Video store tapes have typically been rented out in protective plastic snap cases. These cases are usually clear or black, with molded interior spindles that fit the cassette reels snugly and require the user to insert the tape in a specific direction in order for the case to snap closed without awkward buckling.[50]

Not only have VHS cartridge formats and protective cases very literally shaped the technology, but modifications in VCR decks themselves have responded to changing trends in consumer electronics. During their first decade or so, VCRs were typically heavy, boxy contraptions made of sturdy metal with simulated wood paneling accents. As a friend once recalled, his family's first VCR was "about the size of a microwave." The counters were dials that counted tape length rather than minutes and seconds, the control push buttons were lined up and uniform, like stand-alone audiotape recorders, and the cassettes were inserted or ejected by way of pop-up armatures. All these functions appeared on the tops of the machines, and the earliest remote controls were plug-in devices tethered to decks like headphones. In the 1980s, and increasingly in the 1990s, home entertainment systems became multi-deck and multi-functional. During this time, VCRs became lighter-weight black metal cases with black plastic faces, red or green LCD timer-clock displays, and front-loading trapdoors. Functionality moved from the tops of the decks to their fronts, reflecting both the increased stackability of consumer electronic components and increased dependence on remote controls, which necessitated seeing the front displays from across a room and having remote sensors frontally located. In their late period, VCRs returned to silver as the predominant color as part of a digital era aesthetic, and their shells and interior parts were noticeably lighter weight. (And as the technology has become lighter, it also seems to get more fragile and disposable.)

The more accessory components patched into the TV console, the more it grew to dominate the spaces it inhabited—and the more essential it became to have carts or shelves to accommodate all the electronic toys. In contrast to the early designs for carved-wood radio and television consoles that attempted to naturalize electronic technology and to turn it into "furniture" that matched woodwork and other interior décor, home media components moved away from blending in to becoming their own focal point.[51] This is evident not only in the transition from simulated wood paneling to black plastic boxes on the devices themselves but also in the increasingly synthetic-looking veneer and particle board entertainment centers that house various home electronics devices, such as monitors, VCRs, video game systems, stereos, speakers, and tapes and discs. But before all these products came home, someone had to develop and market them.

On the Market: Consumer Adoption and Changes in the Video Industry

Home video had great promise, but its early history indicates that no one quite knew what to make of it. Sony and other electronics manufacturers hoped that the VCR would be the biggest thing in television since color TV. The Hollywood studios feared the same. After decades of research and development, false starts, and failed launches, home video became viable in the 1970s and boomed in the 1980s. The financial stakes drove incredible competition to determine the dominant format and to define consumer behavior. Like so many other technologies, videotape's mass adoption deviated from its inventors' planned uses, and its popularity perhaps had less to do with the technology itself than the market. Any number of machines might have worked to do more or less the same thing: record television or play movies. As I review at length in the introduction and the next chapter, the Hollywood studios disputed such practices. The history of home video is marked by a series of conflicts between incompatible technologies, between dirty movies and "legitimate" entertainment, between taping and purchasing, and between video stores and the studios. But this history is not just one of binaries; rather, true to its analog nature, such conflicts bleed into one another. Without the rise of prerecorded content, format compatibility would not have been so essential; pornography opened up the market for studio content; users continued taping TV even while renting and purchasing movies; and video stores became a major market for the studios. All these factors contributed to a general teleology that shifted uses of video from recording to consuming—though certainly taping continues. And now again, VCR stalwarts are probably primarily using their decks for timeshifting, whereas they may opt for DVD to watch released content.

The Format Wars

During its first decade, home video was the battleground of a "format war" between Betamax and VHS. This struggle over market dominance ultimately standardized the technology—an outcome that entrenched VHS's lasting prominence as a home video format despite repeated attempts to displace it with other devices. As with audio, cassettes contribute to videotapes' functionality and their tangibility as objects that can be collected, stored, and exchanged. "Format" has been a prominent term and distinction in videotape discourses and practices. Thus the conception of "format" rather than "medium" has perhaps defined how we conceive of videotape and subsequent home entertainment technologies. The so-called war was waged through both VCRs and cassettes, since they were mutually dependent and developed and manufactured in tandem. Consumers' initial choice and investment were obviously in the type of deck, which would in turn determine which kind of cassettes they would buy. But since both Betamax and VHS machines' features and the 1/2-inch magnetic tape were so similar, it was as cassettes that the two formats were made incompatible by manufacturers and most readily distinguishable by consumers. Of course, consumers sometimes didn't recognize the difference, as when my mom brought home blank Beta tapes to go with our first VHS deck. But the recognition that more movies were available for rent on VHS cassettes drove sales of VHS decks. If VCRs had remained primarily a recording technology, incompatibility between formats would have made relatively little difference, and Betamax might have survived longer on the market. In contrast, the continued multiplicity of rival incompatible video game platforms seems like a market anomaly.

Electronics manufacturers were well aware of the commercial advantages of cooperating on a standardized format, and this was originally the plan for home video. According to an early study of videocassettes, "Early in 1970, Sony announced that eight Japanese and European companies agreed to cooperate to establish one standard for videocassettes."[52] However, this obviously did not come to be—at least not in Sony's favor. According to a different business history of the home video format war, Sony felt that it had compromised enormous profits by waiting for other companies to join forces on the 3/4-inch videocassette and recorder, which provided the models for both Betamax and VHS designs.[53] Although it met with other companies to suggest licensing and manufacturing deals, Sony wanted to capitalize on its innovator status by being the first to bring the technology to market. So the company began tooling up its own factories before other companies had joined forces or had a chance to participate in the first wave of manufacturing. Thus, with the Betamax, Sony pursued its own model at the risk of alienating potential business partners and licensees and then expected that its competitors would agree to its specifications. A few companies, such as Toshiba, did manufacture Beta format VCRs (see the Toshiba ad reproduced on page 92), though far fewer than probably would have if Sony had seemed more congenial.

Working together, JVC, Matsushita, and RCA developed VHS as an incompatible competitor to Betamax.[54] In contrast to Betamax, JVC executives argued that videocassettes should have longer recording times (a minimum of two hours, compared to the original Betamax's one hour, to fit feature films on a single cassette), should be less expensive, and should be interchangeable among different brands—like Philips's model with the audiocassette. JVC pursued extensive licensing agreements with other manufacturers, enabling a wider range of brand names and models for VHS VCRs on the market; sheer volume in producing VCR decks enabled the rise of VHS as a viable challenger to Betamax despite its belated start. The conflict came down to a challenge between Sony's exclusive format and everyone else's shared format. VHS decks began outselling Betamax as early as 1978 and by the mid-1980s had become the universal standard, although Betamax's annual sales continued to grow (albeit at a much slower rate than VHS) through 1984.[55]

Histories of the format wars regularly suggest that the Sony Betamax was the better technology in terms of its recording fidelity but that it lost to VHS because it was too late in introducing features such as longer playing time. Beta tapes' initial one-hour capacity reflected that the device was imagined for taping TV programs but not for releasing feature films.[56] The Betamax's smaller cassette size inhibited simply packing more videotape stock onto its reels for longer recording times, and the company angered some of its early consumers by making its subsequent two-hour tapes and decks incompatible with its single-hour versions. However, each format introduced innovations that were quickly matched by the other: Sony introduced wireless remote controls; LP (Long Play) and EP (Extended Play) machines; scanning, slow-motion, and freeze-frame playback modes; high-fidelity sound; and the camcorder. The companies behind VHS introduced portable VCRs and stereo recording.[57] Although Sony continually matched and even surpassed VHS's competitive features, lower-end VHS decks were typically more affordable than Betamax machines, and once the video rental business took off in the early to mid-1980s, a wider variety of prerecorded Hollywood movies—and purportedly hard-core pornography—was available in the VHS format. (An advertisement for the International Home Video Club from 1978 indicates that adult films were available on Beta as well as VHS.)[58] Although Betamax was already losing traction in the video market by the time rental stores became common, rentals more than home taping required format standardization; in other words, if a home user was interested only in timeshifting, the format wouldn't matter as much, since all the tapes he or she used would have been recorded at home. It was with rentals and other prerecorded cassettes that compatibility mattered more for accessing content.

Whereas Sony marketed Betamax primarily for the purpose of timeshifting, VHS did not promote this use as aggressively despite having the same foundational function; this may, in part, suggest why none of the VHS manufacturers were subject to litigation alongside Sony. Rather, as one scholar suggests (though I remain skeptical), VHS was developed as a format for releasing movies in alliance with the studios, and the technology may actually have been designed so that VHS-to-VHS dubs introduced significant resolution loss to discourage piracy.[59]

Public perceptions that VHS was the more pervasive format produced a snowball effect, as consumers were more likely to buy expensive equipment if they thought it would be a good long-term investment: in other words, faced with the choice of two incompatible formats, consumers buy the one they think will become the common standard.[60] Although VHS clearly outperformed all prior home video technologies, even its adoption was relatively slow and deliberate. I suspect that the VCR boom of the 1980s was related not only to the drop in prices for machines and the abundance of movies available for rent but also to a pervasive sense that format stabilization had at last taken hold. Once the VHS deck had become the dominant—nearly exclusive—technology, there was relatively little risk for consumers in buying a machine. Once home viewers invested in a deck and learned how to use it—and after video store owners had invested in their inventories—there was little incentive for either to update formats. Despite continued competition from later competitors, VHS was entrenched as the dominant format for two decades until DVD finally rivaled it.

In contrast, after it lost the home video format battle to VHS, the Betamax—typically called by its nickname "Beta"—has become a major historical reference in conflicts between incompatible formats, such as between DVDs and DivX in the mid-1990s, and again between HD-DVDs and Blu-ray DVDs in the present decade.[61] The term has also functioned variously as a punch line and jeering allusion in discussions of industrial failures.[62] By the mid-1990s, the Betamax was already the subject of profiles on "technostalgia" and was listed among history's "famous flops."[63] Popular history suggested that Sony had stopped making Betamax and switched to VHS in 1988. Thus Sony's announcement that it would cease manufacturing Betamax decks in 2002 made news precisely because reporters—and presumably the public—were surprised and amused that Beta decks had continued to be produced for the prior decade and a half.[64] These references to Beta in business strategies, legal precedent, and cultural memory have far outlived its centrality in practice. The Supreme Court ruling in the landmark "Betamax case" has also provided one of the primary legal arguments and popular-press spins in lawsuits against online peer-to-peer file-sharing networks, such as Napster and Grokster, which I discuss at length in the next chapter. This legal precedent is just about the only positive connotation the term "Betamax" connotes.

In 2008 Sony was finally victorious over Toshiba in the high-definition DVD format war. Like VHS, Sony's successful Blu-ray was the later entry on the market. Unlike the protracted Betamax-VHS competition, however, the HD competition was negotiated through corporate agreements between Sony or Toshiba and film studios, computer manufacturers, and major retailers such as Wal-Mart and Best Buy, rather than decided by consumers themselves. Blu-ray had not, in fact, been outselling Toshiba's HD DVD format when it won.[65] By this time, the content industry had already directed the home video market away from recordable and rental cassettes toward prerecorded sell-through discs.

The Prerecorded Video Market

Like various technologies of audio recording, film projection, and telecommunications, when the VCR was first introduced, the attraction was the marvel of the machine itself. As if by magic (at least according to some early marketing), home video could tape television broadcasts and play them back whenever and as often as users wanted. But home video's sustained viability required a steady stream of content, something to make the device useful and continually entertaining: in other words, movies on tape. Such content conundrums and convergences have reappeared across the histories of entertainment technologies. After the hype of a new device subsides, consumers typically demand content (preferably familiar, reformatted content) to sustain their interest or to justify late adoption. Yet even such consumptive shifts can be seen as a boon to public culture. Off-air recordings and releases of prerecorded cassettes both significantly expanded audiences' access to feature films and television programming. Because the VCR could fix and store recordings for belated or repeated viewing, the content of broadcasting and cinematic exhibitions was now accessible and repeatable; as such, videotape changed the very ontology of film and television. Home video not only introduced a residual market for popular feature films but opened up public lives for films that may have underperformed theatrically but found a broader audience as a rental or might belatedly be rediscovered. Videotapes of classic, independent, documentary, and foreign films that simply didn't screen in theaters in small cities and towns were more likely to be stocked in local video stores, which allowed nonurban audiences to access them.

Broad shifts within the video market suggest almost decade-by-decade patterns. In the 1970s, home video was generally defined by recording; in the 1980s, by renting; and in the 1990s, by sell-through purchases. Of course, such uses and consumption patterns overlapped and coexisted, but these reflect the most publicized uses of VHS for each period—and how the content industry responded to, and attempted to increasingly control, the market. Tellingly, in 1987 a headline in the *New York Daily News* asked: "Are You Renting? Are You Buying? Taping, Maybe?" The article indicates shifts in what people were doing with their VCRs, curiosity about the prevalence of those uses, and a pervasive assumption that taping had given way to other forms of consumption despite statistics indicating it was still the most common practice.[66] Although home video was introduced as a timeshifting technology, the industry, once skeptical and litigious of it, eventually found ways to profit from home video. Even if actual home taping continued, the releases of movies on tape, which began in the late 1970s but boomed in the 1980s, and the rise of video stores shifted the most visible uses away from recording toward renting and purchasing prerecorded content.

As Joshua Greenberg has observed, video rental stores played a significant role in changing the market and the meaning of video by differentiating content from technology. Video stores vended *movies* and often strove to evoke theatrical moviegoing through prominent displays of posters and cardboard stands, marquee-style blinking lights, and even candy racks next to the checkout. Frequently the shrink-wrapped video boxes on shelves, which customers could handle and read while browsing, were empty, and the actual cassettes were kept behind the counter. This strategy—primarily intended to prevent shoplifting—reinforced the alienation of content from cassettes. In video stores, emphasis was on the movies rather than their delivery device.[67] Before a mass market for sell-through videotapes of movies or the proliferation of electronics and entertainment superstores such as Best Buy and Circuit City, electronics venders sold the decks but did not typically rent or sell major quantities of prerecorded tapes. Video stores, by contrast, offered entertainment options but did not usually sell hardware beyond blank tapes and head cleaners. The availability and convenience of prerecorded movies on tape drove the most publicized uses of home video away from recording toward renting, and consumers had to go to different types of stores to buy a deck and to rent movies. Greenberg suggests that by the mid-1980s there was a paradigm shift from thinking of (blank) tapes as subsidiaries to VCRs to marketing the machines as merely functional vehicles to play the innumerable movies available for rent, which were now the primary attraction.[68]

However, before video releases of popular feature films became the norm, in the earliest days of video there were only two prominent programming options: television programs that users had taped themselves and prerecorded porn flicks. As a report in 1977 indicates, pornography was the predominant content available for prerecorded cassettes, though reports conflict about its continued market dominance by 1979: one report on top sellers suggests that only the high-profile porno-chic features *Deep Throat* and *The Devil in Miss Jones* ranked among the top fifteen sellers, whereas one merchant was

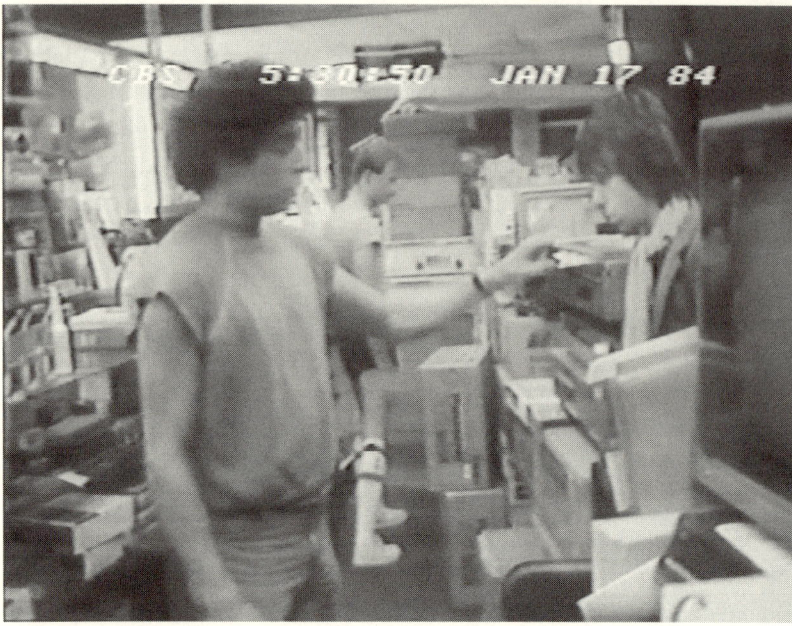

9. The *CBS Evening News* report on the Supreme Court decision in *Sony v. Universal* in 1984 included footage shot inside a store where customers were browsing VCRs. Compared to chain superstores to come, such as Best Buy and Circuit City, this electronics store is crowded and cluttered with various devices and hardware—but not with movies on tape.

quoted as saying, "We're selling 50 times as many porno tapes as any of the other prerecorded material."[69] The adult industry sold 950,000 tapes in 1979, and 1,300,000 the following year.[70] Yet by 1980 the increasing availability of Hollywood titles diminished the market share of porn, and by the mid-1980s new obscenity laws prompted legal action against video stores in Ohio, Alabama, Arizona, and Florida, while family-friendly chains initiated corporate policies to cease renting porn.[71]

Early on, home taping was seen as a threat, and the studios were reluctant to release movies on cassette. (Although concern about piracy was an oft-stated reason for the studios' reluctance to enter the video market, a 1980 labor dispute with the Screen Actors Guild about residual payments to performers if films were released on tape further discouraged and delayed massive releases. A similar situation played out as the Writers Guild went on strike in fall 2007 for royalties to DVD and online video releases of TV shows.) In the late 1970s, Fox was the industry leader in exploring the burgeoning home video market by licensing the rights to films such as *The Sound of Music* and *M*A*S*H*. Fox quickly decided to cut out the middleman by buying him out (the company acquired Magnetic Video as a subsidiary in 1979), and other studios tentatively began forming home entertainment divisions as well. When the number of available prerecorded video titles crossed the 40,000 mark (actually, 40,111) in 1985, the number made news. This figure was reported as a surge over the 14,998 titles available in 1979, although in retrospect, it's probably the 1979 figure that is more surprising.[72] The quality and easy access to Hollywood movies on tape made home taping less imperative. But almost all these films were priced far beyond what most movie audiences could afford to buy. The solution for lowering the cost of seeing movies on video became overnight rentals.

Between the end of the 1970s and the mid-1980s, independent entrepreneurs developed the video rental business. They relied on legitimately released prerecorded cassettes, but video stores essentially determined the market more than the studios—much to the studios' chagrin. The video rental business exploded through a wide range of entrepreneurial experiments, which included Fotomat's drive-through service (1979), video kiosks in movie theater lobbies (1982), private viewing rooms inside video stores (1984), and rental outlets at 7-Elevens (1986), and, perhaps most tenuously, U-Haul moving equipment rental centers (1984). The Video Club of America established a mail-order video club in the late 1970s, as did Time-Life (which already had a book club); Columbia House (already a record and tape club) began its video division in 1981. Businesses specialized in providing technology such as Rent-a-Beta decks (1982), VHS machines for rental (also 1982), and movie vending machines.[73] Greenberg has also observed that various record, electronics, and camera shops ventured into selling and renting prerecorded movies on tape as a way to diversify inventory and boost profits while working the format into existing business models.[74] Many of these experiments were short-lived or phased out as the technology and dedicated video stores became mainstream, though grocery stores belatedly became one of the most common sites for (sometimes subcontracted) video sections. This industrial history suggests that the video market was primarily developed by businesspeople independent—and often geographically far removed—from Hollywood. Various press profiles indicate that surviving the video rental market was not as easy as the hype or the hopes of speculators.[75]

Video stores were able to rent cassettes because of the first-sale doctrine of copyright law—a provision that allows owners of tangible copies of media works to use, rent, resell, or dispose of the object as they see fit without paying additional royalties to the rights owner. The first-sale provision protects libraries, used-book and music stores, and video rental shops. The industry was no fan of what it viewed as a legal loophole. An early *Variety* report may have reflected the studio's attitude when it grudgingly admitted the legality of the practice with the turn of phrase "unauthorized (though legal) renting."[76] In 1983, fed up with not getting a bigger piece of the rental pie, the studios unsuccessfully lobbied for repeal (or at least revision) of the first-sale law.[77] Although they presumably preferred video rentals to home taping, the studios initially viewed the rental market as "an unqualified disaster."[78] The studios and video companies releasing films on tape generally priced them high and tried various attempts to extract royalties on rentals. As early as 1980, the studies considered implementing "rent-sell" or tiered pricing strategies to maximize their revenues from the rental market—though with mixed results.[79] For rental stores, the biggest advantage of profit-sharing agreements with studios was the ability to stock massive quantities of the most popular new releases without having to buy each copy at the inflated debut rate. With franchising and new releases guaranteed to be in stock, Blockbuster and Hollywood Video eventually drove innumerable mom-and-pop video stores out of business. With national chains refusing to stock pornographic or even X, NC-17, or unrated videos, stocking pornography for rent became a survival strategy for many independent and local chains. Urban shops catering to cinephiles and retailers in rural towns have remarkably maintained their independence, but alternative video stores have long been an endangered species in the suburbs.[80]

Of course, despite the increased access to tapes with prerecorded content, people continued to use VCRs for home recording. However, in terms of the technology's public profile, once the Betamax case was resolved, the debate over private taping almost ceased, and marketing for video stores and weekly new releases became far more prevalent. Rentals became the dominant purpose for home video in public discourse if not in actual practice. A Nielsen study in 1984 found that off-air taping remained the primary use for VCRs but that recent consumers were more likely than early adopters to rent videos, perhaps offering an early indication of a shift in uses for home video as the market penetration expanded.[81] (Also according to Nielsen data, in 1984 the top six taped programs were daytime soap operas.)[82] Continued concerns over home taping and piracy were confirmed by the studios' adoption of anticopying encoding on tapes and efforts to block new reproductive machines from the U.S. market. Macrovision anticopy technology was used in nearly half of all prerecorded tapes by 1987.[83] Yet dual-cassette VCRs reinforced recording as the primary purpose for decks; these were contested by the MPAA as early as 1985 and kept out of the U.S. market until at least 1989.[84]

For consumers, early acquisitions of videotapes not only reflected the market but also suggested a kind of logic; aside from a handful of blockbuster or classic films, the popular material available for purchase was predominantly something that viewers would probably want to watch either privately (pornography) or repeatedly (workout routines). On the other hand, the self-consciousness many users would have felt about exercising in public aerobics classes may have paralleled the embarrassment many would have felt in adult theaters; thus body shame may have been central to home video's early success.[85] A perennial chart topper and inspiration for numerous sequels, Jane Fonda's *Workout* (1982) worked up a sweat as the best-selling video for about a year and a half.

The Hollywood studios eventually began experimenting with lowering prices on the most popular titles for general audiences to purchase. When Paramount released *Raiders of the Lost Ark* (1981) as a priced-to-own title in December 1983, the preorders alone topped *Workout*'s total sales. The studio's sudden and massive success with *Raiders* was widely reported in the trade press—and in mainstream press suggestions for holiday gifts—and indicates a decisive moment in the industry's accelerating development of the home video market. Paramount quickly reduced the price point on its most popular movies and quickly saw several more of its titles (including *Star Trek II: The Wrath of Khan*, *An Officer and a Gentleman*, and *Flashdance*) become instant top sellers. Eventually children's titles, especially Disney's animated features, became the most popular titles—both because they were popular and also, as in one of the original reasons for purchasing videos, children often watched them repeatedly. One statistic suggests that adult and children's videos each constituted 20 percent of the video rental market by 1990.[86] Despite the popularity of music videos on MTV and their tendency for repeated viewing, only *The Making of Michael Jackson's "Thriller"* achieved blockbuster sell-through status. (On a tangential note, I vividly remember being thrilled at seeing a performance by Michael Jackson in rewind-scan mode so that he moonwalked, impossibly, forward.) In the early 1990s, the press began reporting that the rental market was stagnating, but the sell-through market continued to grow.[87] The studios, of course, preferred having millions of individual consumers purchase tapes rather than thousands of video stores doing so. By the time DVD hit the market in 1997, the trend toward purchasing had been established, and the new technology provided an opportunity to exploit it.

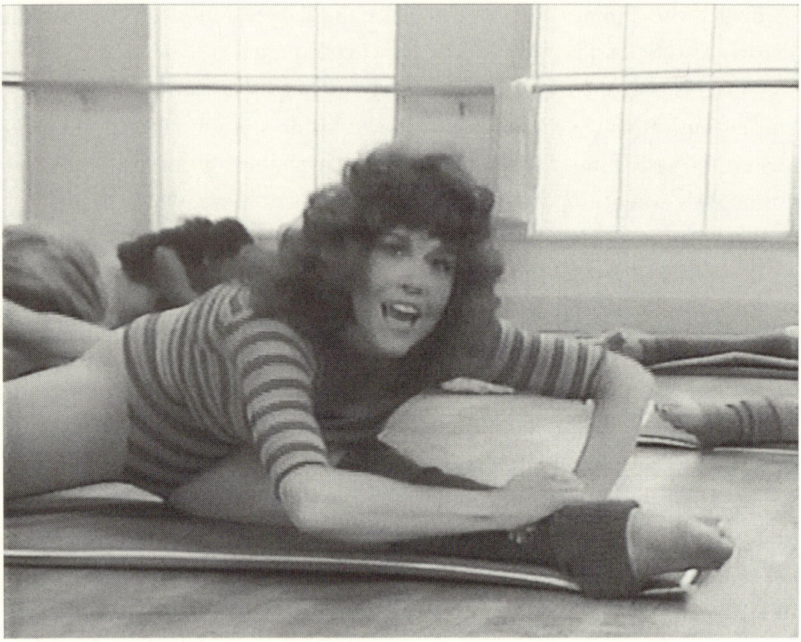

10. Jane Fonda's *Workout* (1982) was one of the first sell-through blockbusters. Workout videos not only created new and interactive uses for television but also often frustrated spectatorial relations to the screen, as many aerobic positions can be so strenuous or awkward that keeping an eye on the monitor is difficult (if not physically impossible).

Yet DVD history demonstrates a reversal and acceleration of VHS's market patterns; DVD was introduced primarily as a purchased format, with Netflix, Blockbuster, and other companies growing a rental market only after significant adoption of the technology had already taken place. Finally, of course, DVD burning and copying technologies and DVRs became widely available as the final major stages of use before, and coinciding with, the introduction of the next-generation high-definition video disc formats. Simultaneously in the present decade, digital video recorders (DVRs), such as TiVo and the various cable company knockoffs, have revived timeshifting as a temporary practice. DVRs, at base, are hard drives, and early TiVos, which did not feature DVD-burning capacities, emphasized short-term recording rather than collecting or long-term storage because the drive typically required regular deletions to make room for more recordings. By recording programs that TiVo "thinks" its user would like, it accelerates deletion and essentially urges its owner to get hooked on new shows. In addition to the initial investment in the TIVO hard drive, users must also pay a monthly subscription fee, making it significantly more costly than VCRs. What DVRs are good for, then, is helping viewers watch more new television rather than stockpiling favorite shows and to continue paying for the privilege. For those desiring long-term access, DVRs function as a short-term programming repository until the DVD box set release.

I offer this account of video's industrial history to suggest the ways that recording eventually became less central to videotape's format identity. Home video's uses and discourses were dynamic during its first three decades, establishing market patterns and consumer expectations before digital video formats. With the institutionalization of home video as a delivery device, mainstream users may have watched fewer and fewer aging tapes or grainy dubs. On the other hand, studio control of the market created the need for a bootleg circuit for those works that were not or could not be legitimately distributed. Such underground tapes are marked by their lower reproduction values and labeling, formal distinctions that, for some, create new and alluringly naughty meanings. Even the standardization of professional video pornography may have prompted a new boom of indecent recording by couples and curious celebrity hounds. I turn now to these off-color sites to explore video's vices.

The Vice Squad

Throughout this book, I propose that bootlegging is exemplary of videotape: it foregrounds the technology as a recording format, it exposes the formal degeneration of the signal, it stresses the importance of access, and it raises issues of intellectual property rights. Bootlegging is also, significantly, an *amateur* practice—both in its common connotation as nonprofessional (unpaid) and in its original meaning as *amorous*. Imported from French, the term "amateur" literally refers to the lover, not the unskilled—and I thus argue that bootleggers (and lovers of bootlegs who may not do the duping themselves) have personal convictions about, and affectionate connections to, their recordings.[88] Bootlegs implicitly reveal audiences as users of videotape technology. Bootlegs' status as illicit, amateur copies indicates that they were made and that their source copies were probably actively sought. And analog videotapes, through intergenerational distortion of the image and sound tracks, materially record and reveal this process of creation and history of circulation. Bootlegs, in particular, demonstrate this aesthetic of access because they are typically multiple generations removed from a source or master tape. They suggest wonderfully lurid relationships.

Audiences who find digital recordings to be impersonal may deem analog media "romantic." This, however, is nothing new. In the nineteenth century, romanticism arose in part as a response to industrialization; tradition, community, and subjectivity were newly valorized as ways to resist technology's seeming ruptures, commodification, and reason.[89] By 1936 romanticism became an audible sensibility, as a music critic differentiated between people seeking fidelity in recordings and those seeking passion: "The Realists stood out strongly for as accurate a reproduction as possible of the actual sounds recorded, but the Romantics held that a certain sacrifice of accuracy was permissible, nay even desirable, if it induced a quality more pleasing to the ear."[90] Some "romantic" technicians and artists have even used analog distortion for its unique affectations. As sound scholars have argued, in considering technological reproduction, we must rethink issues of fidelity and authenticity to move away from conceptions of an original performance that precedes recording. Rather, fidelity and authenticity are a ruse, an ideology to promote newer and more expensive formats. Infidelity is the marker of the analog amateur. Bootleggers are promiscuous and polyamorous.

Have Tape, Will Copy

Bootlegs have been central to fan and film collector culture since the introduction of home video. Although it would be impossible to prove definitively, I suspect that videotape changed the very nature of media fandom and collecting. Through home video there could be a shift in collecting practices from seeking out various forms of *objects related to* the production or promotion of a film to collecting *the film itself*. Of course, there was a small Super 8 and 16 mm collector's culture that was already doing this, a specialist cult that I would correlate to the early home-taping videophiles. Through the mass marketing of prerecorded tapes and "collector's edition" DVDs, there was a mainstreaming of movie collecting culture—one that increasingly had less to do with specialized knowledge or unique objects but that instead contributed to a cultural popularization of geekdom. Yet even as DVD has grown the market for priced-to-own movies and collector culture, many of the most intensely interesting, perverted, or loved texts exist only outside legitimate distribution. The true collector collects those objects that have to be found (and copied) rather than simply purchased at Best Buy.

In his history of videotape as a mediating technology, Greenberg described early fan conventions where Betamax owners would swap tapes or "daisy chain" their Betamax decks in orgies of dubbing.[91] More recently, bootleg videos have circulated through semi-institutionalized networks of tapers, collectors, traders, and vendors—sites where hard- and soft-core pornography mingles with cult, horror, and fantasy cinema. Whether operating on an equal-trade or commercial basis, interpersonal connections, mail-order catalog services (advertised in fanzines), and cult film conventions provided the primary circulatory routes for bootleg tapes before the Internet. (One such convention is described in my second video clip, following this chapter.) With personal websites, discussion boards, e-commerce, and auction sites, the Internet has facilitated advertising and access to rare video dupes, available for trade or sale, and permits hyperlinks between commercial sites and between blogs and vendors. Such sites have the potential to act as personals or social networking sites, making matches, facilitating community exchange, or, perhaps more often, awkward social gestures that go unanswered, as when I've e-mailed queries about bootlegs. Even in cases of commercial exchange, such bootleg operations are typically the work of individuals rather than teams or companies—especially in the cases of eBay and other direct sales. But e-commerce has not entirely rendered the tangible and personal obsolete. Many preexisting bootleggers developed websites to facilitate their continued mail-order endeavors and reduce catalog printing costs, although printed fanzine ads still drive traffic to websites, and convention booths continue to promote wares that are simultaneously available online. Thus analog practices continue and commingle with digital video burns and downloads, though DVD-Rs have largely displaced VHS in consumer demand. Vendors with large inventories tend to focus on imported schlock or cult texts that were never released on video, thus prioritizing the unavailable while avoiding risky sales of pirated commercial releases. In some cases, FAQ (frequently asked questions) sections on the websites insist that they are not breaking copyright laws by distributing films without U.S. distributors; more accurately, they are just unlikely to be sued.[92]

Not surprisingly, studies of video collecting have been attentive to the materiality of tapes, issues of access, and affective relationships between collectors and their videos. This research asserts videos' specific interventions into viewers' lives. (Still, in many cases, such essays are squirreled away—one might even say repressed—in the back of general anthologies on spectatorship or television, suggesting a still-uneasy position in between film and television studies.) Charles Tashiro's first-person essay on video collecting has been the seminal academic essay for this small body of work; the author suggests that our collections reflect our subjective idiosyncrasies as well as the tastes with which we feel obliged to identify.[93] More revealingly, however, in Kim Bjarkman's study of television tapers and collectors, their off-air recordings are labors of love, which take extensive time and tape commitments to shows that fall short of topping the Nielsen ratings. These tapers share recordings on a not-for-profit basis and exchange only commercially inaccessible content, maintaining a strict distinction between bootlegging and piracy (as suggested in the introduction). When commercial-free box sets are officially released, the demand for dubs of collectors' home recordings may drop significantly, but the text and the viewing experience are altered. If, for instance, an off-air recording includes commercials and interstitial local news promos that would be elided in commercially released DVDs of television series, it can not only reproduce a fairly exact simulation of historical flow but also document the economic and political context for the program. Off-air recordings also include the original musical cues, which are often replaced in commercial video releases because of expired or overpriced licensing agreements. The research subjects—and Bjarkman herself—act as curators of what has historically been an ephemeral medium: television.[94] As material documents of cultural memory, bootlegging functions hegemonically—participating within consumer capitalism and reproducing official texts while in some small way opposing it.

Perhaps the most sustained coverage of the phenomenon of video bootlegging has appeared in the fan magazine *Film Threat*'s ongoing feature "The Bootleg Files." This column has reviewed an impressive range of the most famously circulated and sought-after bootlegs—works that may have become offensive or humiliating over time or that have become key texts yet have not found sustained commercial distribution. The works profiled include film classics (of sorts), campy and embarrassing television events, historically significant documents, and cult films, such as *The Eternal Jew* (1940), *Song of the South* (1946), the Zapruder film of John F. Kennedy's assassination (1963), "The Homosexuals" (a famous 1967 *CBS Reports* special), *Linda Lovelace for President* (1975), *The Star Wars Holiday Special* (1978), *Superstar: The Karen Carpenter Story* (1987), and even Georges Méliès's *A Trip to the Moon* (1902, listed as historically the first bootlegged film). These profiles offer summaries of each work, as well as speculative reasons for each film or show's suppression, chances of legitimate commercial release, and the prevalence of bootlegs.[95]

For cult film audiences who often relish low production values and schlocky scripts as part of the films' appeal, the addition of bootleg video aesthetics—whether from sketchy distributors or personal copying—may well enrich the text and add to the experience. As an art-horror film scholar has remarked of bootleg aesthetics, "The illegality is emphasized in the tape's very mode of viewer address. . . . The very rawness of the image becomes both a signifier of the tape's outlaw status and a guarantor of its authenticity. You know this is the stuff you weren't meant to see simply because the image quality is so bad."[96] A global policy study observed such degeneration as a market strategy: "To prevent others from pirating his pirated tapes, he made a point of retaping them to the edge of fuzziness before rental."[97] Tape reveals its reproduction and can be used to police its uses. Both of these accounts of distortion—one incidental, the other intended—point to ways video aesthetics mark the text as forbidden. The idea of the forbidden here, of course, cuts both ways—as temptation and as warning. The white noise, the jittery image, the unnatural colors, the grain, the momentary loss of signal that triggers the blank blue TV screen or the flash of tracking: these are the marks of damaged dupes. Such effects can be frustrating, or they can intensify one's attention.

On other occasions when critics have pondered their rendezvous with videotape bootlegging, the topic has inspired purple prose and deviant pleasures. My favorite is a delirious revelry in which the writer plays fast and loose with his associations, drawing analogies between the worn-out aesthetics of duplication and the intensely carnal pleasures of sex, drugs, and rock 'n' roll:

> The harshest reds had been strained to a porn-zine labial pink, the blues and blacks dulled to a bad-meat gray. And the whole look of the frame changed; softened slightly with each generation—the images wavering in some liquid video purgatory—until the whole thing resembled some sort of a vertiginous underwater snuff film. . . . Bootleg culture parallels drug culture, both in its word-of-mouth distribution system and in the kick of possessing, or simply being near, the forbidden object.[98]

This critic connects the fleshiness of the tapes to the viewer's affective response—one in which emotional reaction is as embodied as it is intellectual. His mixed metaphors and florid language vividly convey the sensual, illicit, and formal pleasures produced through reproduction. Although not writing of bootlegs specifically, Laura Marks has also theorized video's haptic aesthetics in relation to its low resolution and electronic manipulability:

> Part of the eroticism of this medium is its incompleteness, the inability to ever see it all, because it's so grainy, its chiaroscuro so harsh, its figures mere suggestion. . . . But haptic images have a particular erotic quality, one involving giving up visual control. The viewer is called on to fill in the gaps in the image, engage with traces the image leaves.[99]

In effect, Marks suggests a submissive sexuality in watching grainy video. Video leaves the viewer wanting more.

What is described in each of these effusive bursts has remained marginal as a theory of aesthetic specificity for analog video. Yet the ways that they evoke the technical properties of videotape suggest that, just maybe, these ways of seeing video actually speak to its aesthetic better than any other. That there's something sensual about these passages also seems to reveal some of the formative ways in which video came to be defined. Inherent vice, indeed.

Videotape's Last Great Fling

Repeatedly in the history of reproductive technologies, pornography has been one of the earliest and most commercially successful forms of content. Although it has become accepted as a truism that pornography was the most prominent content available for prerecorded cassettes in the late 1970s, it was also already recognized as something home users with access to a camera could make themselves. In the "home video" epilogue to a 1977 book on the ways in which art practices defined video as a medium, analog aesthetics are eroticized with a description that prefigures Marks's remarks quoted earlier:

> Video pornography is first-rate. The fuzziness makes it hard to see, and your natural impulse to stare is heightened by the difficulty of figuring out exactly what is going on up there. The effect is like a striptease: Now you see it, now you don't. And your imagination will inflame you more than a realistic picture could.[100]

Whereas pornography has been credited with advancing the market penetration (as they say) of VHS in the late 1970s and early 1980s, beginning in the mid-1980s, the phenomenon of amateur porn exhibited a pervasive new and kinky video aesthetic.[101] In a way, pornography flipped the mainstream home video market's trajectory over, innovating the prerecorded content market and later returning attention to recording through amateur porn and celebrity sex piracy.

In the most literal realization of its etymology, *amateur* porn has circulated as a popular category of amorous analog video. Amateur pornography began as a kind of virtual swinging: tapes were swapped among the makers in a kind of bootleg network. Such exchanges demonstrated a potential market, one that was soon exploited and institutionalized by porn video distributors, making the practice a hybrid of personal expression and professional marketing.[102] Part of the appeal—and, arguably, progressive representational politics—of amateur pornography is that it shows people with average bodies (i.e., breasts without implants, cocks shorter than ten inches) engaging in real sex for pleasure, maybe even love, rather than for money. (Of course, gonzo pornography pretty quickly moved the genre beyond amorous sex acts into pure exploitation.) The makers' less-than-ideal physiques and the realities of at times awkward or mundane sexual performance were complemented by the recording's subpar production values—low light, grainy image, hand-held camera jiggle, overlong takes, indifferent framing, ambient buzz and mechanical noise, and often inaudible conversation. The genre's failure at simulating Hollywood's—or even studio porn's—fantastic realism or invisible construction both made it seem more intimate and called attention to the familiar specificities of video technology itself. These dual attributes have been read as asserting a kind of authenticity that is typically missing from professional porn. In addition, both the aesthetics of amateur pornography and its bootleg circulation make its participants seem somehow more plausibly sexually available to the viewers.

If by the mid-1980s rentals and sell-through shifted the discourses of video from a recording format to a playback format, in the late 1980s and throughout the 1990s the camcorder reestablished the public visibility of video as a recording technology. As the video equivalent of Super 8 home movies, camcorders (a portmanteau of camera and videotape recorder) reasserted the "home" in "home video" and became synonymous with the phrase. Home video as a term has come to connote family values, since weddings, birthday parties, births, vacations, and school plays or sports events may have been the most prominent subjects for original home video recordings.[103] Of course, camcorders have also facilitated more radical uses, such as grassroots alternative video production and activist documentation. Miniaturized 8 mm analog and even digital video camcorders have typically continued to use cassette tapes as storage formats, maintaining experiential continuities for the user as the technologies changed. Most home videos, short of capturing the kinds of slapstick accidents broadcast on *America's Funniest Home Videos* each week, held little interest beyond the friends and family of the subjects documented. As for tapes that strangers were actually curious to see, well, sex tapes pretty much top the list.

Camcorders, like bygone Polaroids, have allowed couples to make private documents of intimate sex acts without the worry of clerks at a film-processing lab ogling the images. The practice of recording private sex acts emerged not long after camcorders entered the consumer market. Of course, there's no way to track such uses, or how often recorded sex acts were watched or rewatched by the people who made them. However, some of these tapes were not only watched but also shared. The phenomenon of self-taped sex acts attracted significant public attention with the controversy surrounding Rob Lowe's private caucus with an underage woman at the 1988 Democratic National Convention (and a second sex recording featuring Lowe participating in a *ménage à trois* with another man and a woman shot in Paris) and with the release of *sex, lies, and videotape* (Steven Soderbergh, 1989), in which the protagonist (played by James Spader) masturbates to taped interviews with women recalling their sexual histories. Various celebrities have since been "caught on tape," from Tanya Harding to R. Kelly to Paris Hilton.

Perhaps the most reproduced and most studied illicit recording of the VHS era was the Pamela Anderson and Tommy Lee sex tape. Images were published in *Penthouse* and footage was posted online by Club Love at an early stage of streaming video. An official if unauthorized home video version, *Pam and Tommy Lee: Hardcore and Uncensored*, scored as the best-selling adult title of all time, remains available as a legitimate DVD from the porn giant Vivid Entertainment. Different cuts of the tape, with varying contents, running times, and titles, soon began circulating; for instance, the bootleg I acquired, labeled *Down and Dirty with Pam and Tommy Lee*, does not contain *Hardcore and Uncensored*'s intertitles or some of the scenes about which I've read. One scholarly reading of the tape focuses on the genre codes of amateur porn and of performance at play in the tape, suggesting that the mundane content (some of which does not appear in my tape) authenticates the document. This article goes on to suggest that in its production context the tape was a home movie, but its publication changed its mode of address into pornography for the viewers.[104] In another textual analysis, the author remarks on the tape's affirmation of love, sex, and marriage. "The overall effect of the entire tape is—counterintuitively—not a highlighting of the sensational parts, but a placing of explicit newlywed sex in the context of love, affection, enthusiasm, mutual playfulness, and exploration . . . exactly what is left out of pornography."[105] Although I adore this

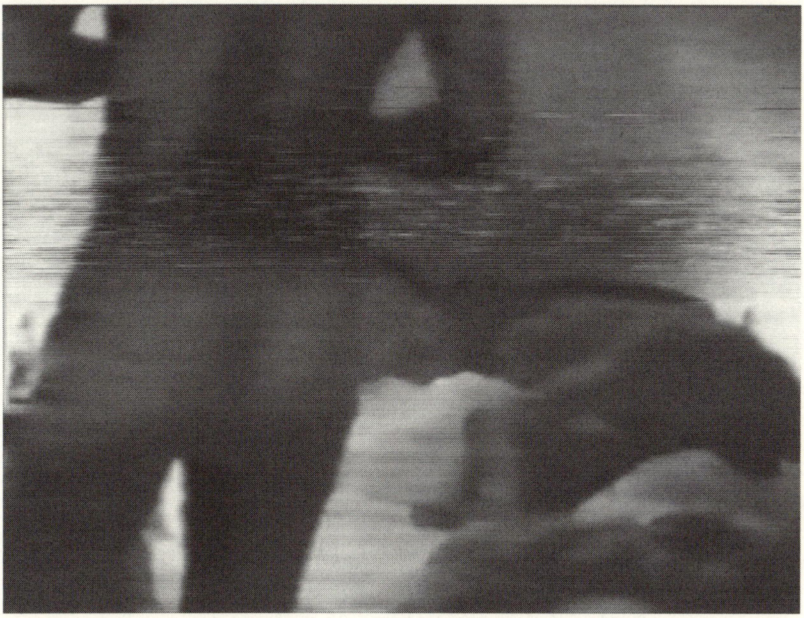

11. Rob Lowe approaches the bed to join in a *ménage à trois* in his second sex tape, which Al Goldstein showed on his Manhattan cable access show *Midnight Blue* and released as part of a highlights DVD. This image shows the low quality of camcorder footage, made even dimmer by generations of reproduction and age.

reading and redemption of the tape—and of Anderson and Lee—I suspect that the editing down of their vacation video to get to the titillating parts and (one might presume) the fast-forwarding of viewers, again, to get to the titillating parts may in effect elide such a message of blissful monogamy and hot marriage.

In part, the nonprofessionalism of the camerawork emphasizes the recording's nonprofessional, nonpublic status; the image is shaky at best, while water droplets on the lens and sun glares further blur it. These home video aesthetics only intensify the authenticity of the document for voyeuristic viewers, visually marking the text as private. The camera functioned as a sex toy for the couple, and their tape—if they ever intended to watch it—was for their eyes only (though at one point Anderson brags about Lee's cock to their imagined future children, as if *they* will watch the home video). All the shots are point-of-view shots, which places the viewer in a position of identification; for straight male viewers, this may entail the pleasure of having impressive penile endowment and the vicarious thrill of seeing oneself fuck and get sucked off by Anderson. These professional performers

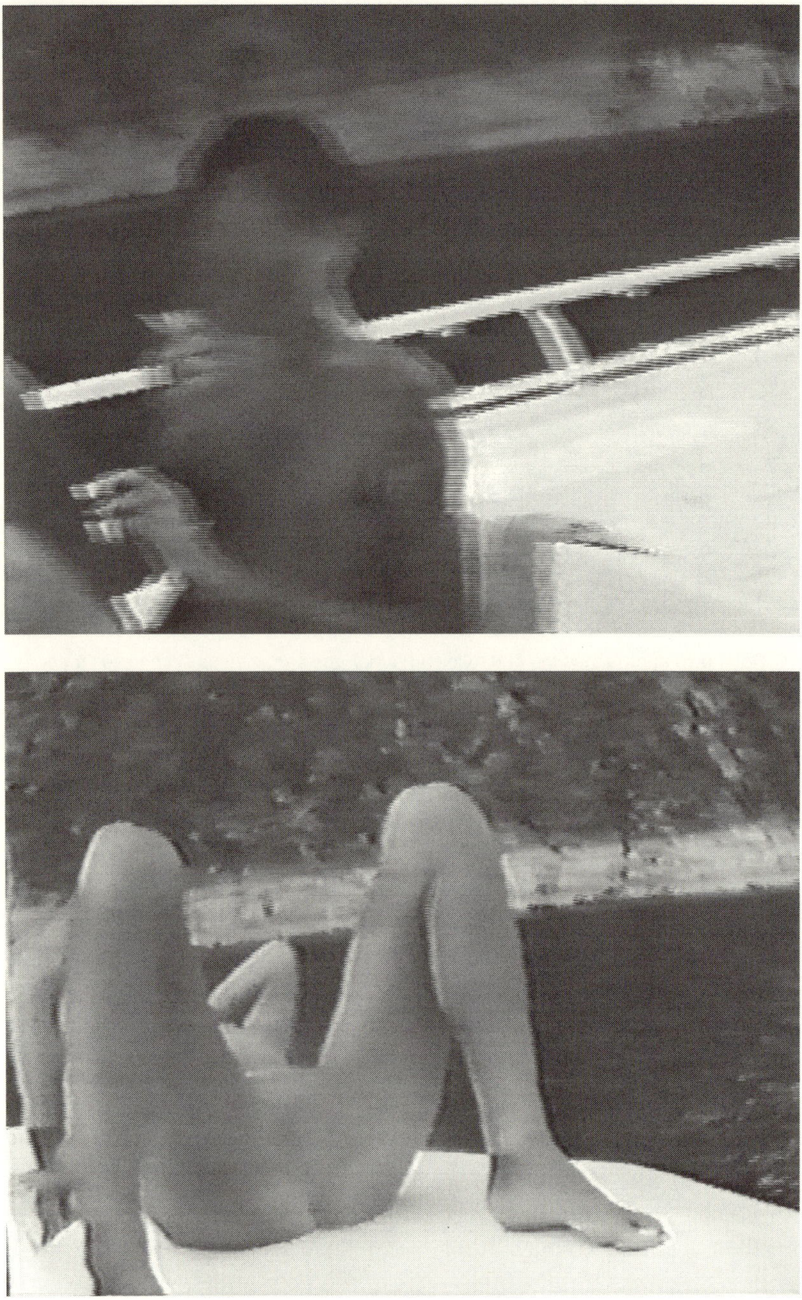

12a–b. The awkward framing of hand-held amateur pornography, combined with water on the camcorder lens and generations of bootlegging, has rendered Tommy Lee's face and Pamela Anderson's pussy into suggestive blurs.

were performing exclusively for themselves—an inversion of the codes of popular amateur video pornography, though the Anderson-Lee tape certainly shares some generic elements with this genre. Anderson and Lee's home taping was a personal recording of a private affair—an amateur video in both senses of the word.

Yet, accentuating the tape's amateur production (and perhaps foreshadowing the dissolution of the couple's romance), all the sex tape images that were reproduced for prurient consumption were marked by further decay. Video has a resolution of 72 dpi (dots per inch), in comparison to print's standard minimum of 300 dpi, up to 2,540 dpi for glossy publications; this means that even frame enlargements published in *Penthouse* would have looked crummy at best. Alternatively, viewers who watched a streaming version in 1997 would have seen a small, jagged digital (and probably frequently frozen and "buffering") image, and viewers of pirated cassettes would have seen the result of multiple-generation VHS copies reduced in image and sound quality. And the more pirated tapes circulated, the more likely free peer-to-peer bootlegs began to appear as well. Degradations would have filtered the images and sounds of all these reproductions, thereby making the couple's healthy copulation seem a bit more sleazy and illicit to viewers, which arguably contributes to the thrill. By accentuating the viewer's voyeuristic desire while titillating it, the aesthetics of access visible in Pamela Anderson and Tommy Lee tapes and other bootlegs suggest the way video mediates desires.

Writing on a different analog medium (underground homoerotic graphics) that circulated through seedy bookshops as photo or postcard reproductions, Thomas Waugh has suggested that analog degeneration not only alters the text but suggests audience participation: "The pre-Stonewall viewer automatically participated in the underground through his thrill at the dim and blurred little anonymous bootleg image, adding his fingerprints to those who had preceded him on the circuit even where he did not copy it himself, and thereby contributing to its collective authorship."[106] Videotape amateurs and bootleggers' sticky fingerprints are, in a sense, all over video pornography and cult films. Such evidence is not merely putrid interference; it signifies the inherent vices of analog video—and personalizes it as well. At a certain point, the distortion can become beautiful or arousing or even (as I suggest in chapter 4) emotionally moving.

Videotape is a technology of duplication, one introduced for recording. Playback, of necessity, could only come secondarily. It was always also commercial. As much as I may romanticize the technology and its liberation of moving images and sexual mores, I cannot deny this fact. This love was always for sale. Major international corporations developed and marketed numerous iterations of the technology; Hollywood studios struggled to profit from it; entrepreneurs rented it out; pornographers exploited many a money shot. Even the impulse toward bootlegging is to some extent a response to the market: we tape what we can't get otherwise. Videotape introduced and expanded audiences' access to, and uses of, media. As I have suggested here, some video practices have carried over from learned audio ones, and many practices were affected by the prerecorded video market. I also suggest that such analog formats have in turn established patterns for digital ones. But the importance of videotape is not reducible to a technological teleology or capitalist critique; in this chapter, I've tried to reflect the overlapping and conflicting factors that have contributed to video's cultural complexity.

I believe that videotape changes not just what we can watch but also how we do so. Would it be too much to say that we see differently when we see something recorded on video? Sony, JVC, the studios, and the video stores may have trained us as consumers, but certain modes of viewing continue to exceed these lessons. We experience videotape meaningfully, materially, and erotically. And when home users hit the record button, they also experience videotape participatively and embed their marks in the process. Perhaps these attributes primarily distinguish analog from digital formats, as the transition from analog to digital implies dematerialization and loss-free reproduction. At least in theory. In practice, digital formats compress and malfunction too.

As if learning from the "mistakes" of permissive analog video and its loose regulations, the premise of endless, rapid, perfect digital cloning prompted restrictive new attempts to regulate media through copyright codes, licensing schemes, and technological encryption. These analog and digital policies and judicial interpretations that crack down on video vices are the subject of chapter 2.

Chiller Theatre Toy, Model, and Film Expo

The semi-annual Chiller Theatre Toy, Model, and Film Expo is the largest event of its kind in the New York metropolitan area.[1] The event appeals to a wide range of fans of cult and marginal cinema, from horror and sci-fi to East Asian action and anime to pornography. Because home video has largely killed the midnight-movie subculture and the Internet has largely rendered fan exchanges virtual or even anonymous, the convention provides a potential site for personal interaction. The convention is a social event; attendees go with groups of friends or as families, and part of the convention's appeal is the promise of momentary conversation with has-been cult celebrities who sign autographs for a fee. The Chiller's thousands of attendees include the expected geeks and costumed characters (though *Rocky Horror*–inspired costumes are as numerous as *Star Wars* and *Star Trek* ones), as well as goths, metal heads, and postpunk hipsters. But the convention is surprisingly middlebrow, and most attendees look like average suburban families.

Counter to any utopian notions of fan communities, the event is primarily about commerce. Participation is expensive, between the entry fee, overpriced hotel food, and the overwhelming mass of commodities vying for impulse purchases—not to mention transportation and lodging costs. The convention hotel gets almost bursting with vendors' displays of bootlegged or imported videotapes and DVDs, toys, posters, T-shirts, and vintage cult film and girlie magazines. Precious little space is reserved for noneconomic activities, such as talking or people watching, to offer respite from the crowds or exhaustion of immersive shopping. Most of the merchandise could be found online or through mail-order catalogs, but the convention provides the satisfaction of handling and comparing the goods, discovering unexpected items, and interpersonal exchange.

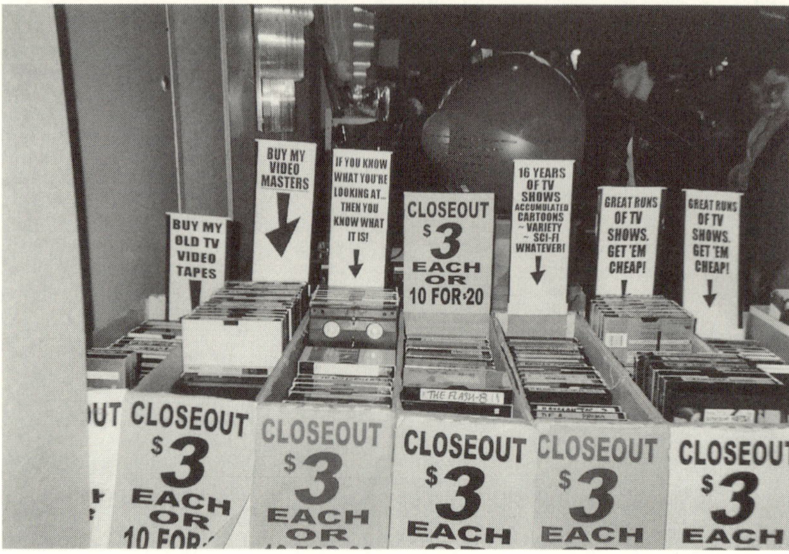

13. VHS bootlegs on closeout at the Chiller convention, October 2004. Photo by author.

When I attended in spring and fall 2004, DVD had already become the predominant in-demand format, and vendors' stocks of VHS tapes were being phased out. One vendor who was transitioning from VHS to DVD had numerous boxes of VHS tapes with handwritten labels identifying television series, seasons, and episode numbers that were being offered as part of a "closeout" sale for three dollars each or ten for twenty bucks. Various laser-printed signs hailed passersby to "buy my old TV tapes" and, alarmingly for preservationists, "buy my video masters." The tapes were relegated to the edge of his display, with additional boxes of tapes stashed under the table for customers to rummage through. This vendor's stock represented a time capsule of video collecting in the late 1970s and 1980s, with entire seasons of television programs and specials systematically taped off-air—programs that have more recently been released as box sets on DVD, thus rendering the old VHS tapes less valuable, though they clearly evoke more personal labor and collector care.

The dealers who had remained faithful to VHS tended to have music-oriented inventories. One vendor, who was wary of talking to an academic and forbade me to take pictures, had a large collection of concert video bootlegs that ran the gamut of popular musicians. Another specialized in Scopitones (short film predecessors to music videos), feature films starring musicians, and vintage pornographic shorts. Some of his inventory was bought out from other vendors, while some appeared to be reproduced by him. He has been installed in the same corner during both my visits to Chiller, and he has also been a regular presence in New York's East Village and Williamsburg, catering to hipsters out at night and on the weekends. These tables boasted some of the most unique content, work that couldn't be readily imported or that had not yet been digitized for proliferation on DVD-R.

In general, the inventory at various tables showed significant redundancy, though often in different versions, so that the same features were available at different tables as legitimate import editions, as pirated DVD-RS with grainy photocopied covers, or as videotaped dupes with Avery labels on their spines. Whereas displays featuring tie-in products such as T-shirts and toys cater to a more specialized clientele, on the video tables there was more likely to be something for everyone. The primary purpose of attending, it seemed, was shopping—and, in shopping, discovering an unexpected rare video.

2. The Fairest of Them All? Home Video, Copyright, and Fair Use

The transition from VHS to DVD has not been instantaneous, nor has it been comprehensive. These competing formats have coexisted awkwardly and will continue to do so as long as there are tapes and VCRs that remain functional—and as long as some of the texts recorded on tape remain inaccessible on disc. The tension between analog and digital extends beyond videos: books, newspapers, and paper documents continue to be printed and used in the age of the Internet. Digital technologies have introduced new and faster methods of access to information, as well as higher-resolution reproductions of moving-image works. Yet through encryption devices, menus, predefined fields, DVD chapters, and website deactivation, digital technologies may also limit how we use, or if we can even access, texts. Thus many users prefer analog formats for some uses, and archivists have recognized that tangible copies long outlast electronic files.

The transition from analog to digital media regulations has also been marked by trade-offs, incompatibilities, delays, and gaps rather than a clean break. When technology and uses change, the question arises whether the old rules apply. Obviously copyright law continues to govern digital media, so the old rules still apply in the legal sense, but it is debatable whether they are adequate. The Digital Millennium Copyright Act (DMCA) of 1998 attempted to bring the U.S. copyright code up to speed with the technological developments of the information age. Rather than comprehensively revising the law, however, the act was incorporated into the analog-model copyright code, wedged within and alongside preexisting statutes, so that the law functions as a hybrid creation. These digital bits of legal code entangle the previously existing analog rules in a network of specifications, subsections, and cross-references that resemble a mess of wires and circuits.

Such complexity has resulted in a copyright code filled with disconnections between permissive uses of analog media and the comparatively restrictive uses of digital data. (One troubling remedy to this contradiction has been legislation to close the "analog hole.") These distinctions have prompted considerable controversy owing to the sense that contemporary copyright law clamps down on the ways audiences can legally access and use media and the ways some uses have been criminalized.

Here I delve into the relevant histories of copyright legislation and judicial interpretation since 1976 to examine the regulatory continuities and interdependencies between analog and digital media. I approach the era from the mid-1970s to the late 1990s—the coinciding period of statutory fair use and the explosion of home video—as being permissive of users' rights and access compared to the present. Whereas in the previous chapter I examined the history of videotape, here I focus on legislative and judicial policies that have established fair use and employed it as a guide to define home video practices. Most VCR users have probably only rarely (if ever) thought about copyright, quickly adopting the habit of fast-forwarding through the FBI warnings that became ubiquitous on prerecorded tapes. (Later DVDs are often programmed to make such antipiracy warnings unskippable, though that's no assurance that viewers actually read them or pay them much mind.) Although it should perhaps go without saying, copyright matters, and the issue should concern anyone interested in film and media because it has long been the primary legal means of regulating texts. Home videotaping was very nearly outlawed by the courts, a turn of events that would have had major consequences for audience (and academic) access to films and television programs.

The considerable liberty for users in the early, anonymous, and unregulated days of home video, the Internet, and even YouTube has repeatedly given way to more constrained, corporatized, and consumptive uses. VCRs, camcorders, computers, and other popular electronic devices were initially celebrated for democratizing the media; they expanded the ways audiences could create and access texts by making the technologies of production and reproduction widely available. New media's potential often raises libertarian claims and utopian rhetoric. But uses of such technologies are often eventually reined in by laws, policies, market forces, technological design, and software—a combination of government and business regulations that Lawrence Lessig has succinctly but effectively termed "code." As Lessig argues, in the digital media age, the content, the distribution, and the hardware are typically all owned or controlled by corporations with vested interests in regulating them. Technology often governs actual practices beyond what the law advises.[1] Thus convergence is not merely a matter of synergy and content reformatting; it also describes the current trend in regulations in which law, commerce, and technology converge as code. Not all forms of regulation are regressive, of course; some protect personal privacy or the public interest. But copyright law, in particular, has increasingly served the interests of big media at the expense of audiences and, to a certain extent, creators. The one major victory for audiences and access amid this trend during the past few decades has been the defense of off-air video recording (that is, taping broadcasts) as fair use. This history is instructive for both future-fixated enthusiasts of digital media and depressed DMCA detractors to remember.

This chapter introduces some readers to the fundamental concepts and relevant history of copyright—as well as faces the considerable challenge of convincing more than a few skeptics that the law is not only important but also *interesting*. At the same time, I also attempt to say something relevant to readers already well versed in intellectual property issues and participating in what has been called the "copyleft" movement. After a brief primer on copyright, I focus on the intentions, histories, and analyses of two specific copyright statutes (fair use and the DMCA) and two Supreme Court decisions (*Sony v. Universal*, a.k.a. the Betamax case, and *MGM v. Grokster*) that have set precedents in the wake of these legislated copyright codes. The first half of the chapter focuses on the establishment of fair use within analog media; the second half focuses on digital copyright codes—and the ways they have revised and reestablished analog interpretations. The Betamax case played a vital role in clarifying and ensuring audiences' rights as media users—rights that have been eroded with the transition to digital technologies and regulations. In the Grokster case, the second-generation peer-to-peer (P2P) file-sharing service (Napster was the most famous first-generation P2P), which was technically similar to the better-known Kazaa, was shut down by the Supreme Court for contributing to rampant unauthorized music sharing. The legal legacies of both Betamax and Grokster have long outlived their practical lives, existing as residual court precedents in the age of their obsolescence.

A reductive version of this chapter's history would suggest that the good old days of analog media were progressive and that digital media codes are reactionary. I have observed that when people learn about the extent of the DMCA's restrictions, they respond with shock and outrage, which tends to turn either to pessimism or to willful disregard for the law. Neither outcome seems to me productive. Rather, I suggest that in a legal system in which judicial rulings are typically based on precedent, analog history continues to matter and bear influence. By recognizing the ways in which the Betamax case demonstrates that the law can be *interpreted* rather than merely followed or applied, we may just have a precedent for thinking about how copyright can still protect the rights of audiences. Although some legal scholars might contend that the Court's ruling on Betamax invented the law rather than followed it, I think that the decision realigned fair use with copyright's constitutional principles.[2] I also suggest that it's significant that the 1984 Betamax decision was the initial, foundational court interpretation of the 1976 fair-use statute. If the Supreme Court's seminal precedent on fair use expanded its domain, why shouldn't subsequent rulings follow this lead?

Fair Use and the U.S. Copyright Code

Copyright governs textual reproduction and distribution; the law was established in the interest of promoting new cultural works by offering their creators and producers temporary market monopolies over their creations. Copyright works through a bargain: artists and publishers are granted protection to commercially exploit their works in exchange for making them publicly accessible. This means that copyright is intended to serve the interests of the audience as much as it rewards publishers, distributors, writers, filmmakers, musicians, and artists. Thus tensions arise between the public interest (exemplified by public domain and fair use) and private property (copyright protection more generally), though the private property rights are granted to benefit the public by giving an incentive for the creation and publication of new cultural works.[3] L. Ray Patterson and Stanley W. Lindberg argue that users' interests in copyright law are as important as those of authors and entrepreneurs, yet because users' rights of access are implicit, they are often forgotten.[4] More recently, Jessica Litman has revisited the concept of personal use as a right—one that was always vague and that recently seems to be getting squeezed: "Even the most rapacious copyright owners have always agreed that some uses are lawful even though they are neither exempted or privileged in the copyright statute nor recognized as legal by any judicial decision."[5] In addition, Litman points to a useful definition of the inherently vague concept: " 'Personal use,' in the broad sense, means consumption or adaptation of intellectual properties by individual users for their own purposes, including uncompensated sharing of those works with others."[6]

Copyright law in the United States is unique, as it was one of the foundational premises of American democracy; provisions for the promotion of "useful" arts were written into the Constitution. Article I, Section 8 states: "The Congress shall have the power . . . To promote the Progress of Science and the useful Arts, by securing for limited Times to Authors and Inventors the exclusive Right to their respective Writings and Discoveries." The constitutional purpose of copyright has been stressed by public-domain and fair-use advocates, though in practice the copyright code has operated more like a property law. The first congressional copyright act is telling in at least two ways: the way in which it defines the new nation and the way it inverts the original conceptions of authors' rights. For an upstart nation founded on the principles of the freedoms of speech, the press, and religion, copyright was an important issue to set from the earliest stages of legislation—both in terms of ideologically promoting authors' rights to expression and in the necessity of the state to prevent monopolies. The copyright act was structured in a dually self-serving way so that *only* U.S. citizens or residents could copyright works domestically and receive financial return, but it encouraged the import, piracy, and cheap distribution of foreign texts and ideas. As a developing nation, the United States considered foreign works public domain for the benefit of its citizens and creators; today, of course, the government and corporations do not encourage similar strategies of other developing nations. Instead they institute trade sanctions.[7]

Whereas in Europe authors maintain their creative rights and contract out their distribution rights, in the United States copyrights are foundationally about publication rights as a matter of statute. The European model for copyright privileges what are called authors' "moral rights," the inalienable rights of the artist or author to say if and how a work can be reproduced. Moral rights do not exist as part of the U.S. copyright code. So European creators have more control over public uses of their own works, but in the United States (in theory, at least) the power is balanced so that the public has more freedom to use and build from others' creations. Over the past thirty years, the United States has revised its copyright code to conform to international copyright standards, and the DMCA was part of a move toward standardizing laws to facilitate reciprocity in enforcing and restricting copyright between nations.[8] Yet the foundational philosophies of European and U.S. copyrights are incommensurable; this has made for complicated and contradictory policies in an age of transnational corporations and global circulation.

In the United States, authors must frequently surrender their copyrights to distributors or publishers in exchange for publication. For example, a director who sold a film to Miramax at the Sundance Film Festival in the 1990s no longer controls the release, marketing, or profits from that film; the Weinstein brothers, who brokered the deal and handled the film's initial release, don't have a say anymore either. Disney, which owns Miramax, does. Or, another example, to get their work published, most authors sign over their copyright to whoever publishes the article or book—unless the author is famous or adamant enough to retain his or her rights. This may save the author the headache of negotiating every reprint or course reader deal, but it also ensures the publisher a cut of any residual profits. Among the benefits of more accessible reproductive technologies and of the Internet as a distribution system is that self-publication and self-governance become more feasible, thus opening up the potential to bypass corporate publishing. Copyright has also been redefined in the artists' and authors' interests with the rise of Creative Commons licenses, through which creators define their own terms of protection and grant users more rights than under traditional copyright law.[9]

And though I've encountered many people who tend to think of policy as dull and artless, copyright actually insists on aesthetics and recognizes the importance of tangibility or interfaces: the law does *not* protect *ideas*, only *expressions* in *fixed forms*. This distinction, of course, has become more difficult to maintain in the so-called information age. In a way, this premise reveals the analog logic of copyright law; it is the expression, the analogue, that is protected, not the idea itself. This also allows multiple books about a given topic—the ways that sex in Hollywood movies has been censored under the Production Code and the later ratings system, let's say—to convey the same basic information, but as long as the writing style and rhetoric differ, none of these books can be considered to infringe each other. The fixed-form criterion also presumes the necessity of formats to communicate, as delivery devices (books, records, celluloid, videos) have historically shaped the work. These issues of access and aesthetics, often overlooked, are as inherent to copyright as they are to videotape.

Copyright history, like video history, includes many attempts to capture the market that never quite made it: all the bills and amendments that didn't quite pass, the judicial rulings that might have gone the other way or that were ultimately overturned. These might be seen as akin to all the technologies that were developed but never made it to market or ultimately failed to be adopted by consumers. Although I don't go in to every particular for what might have been, I make this point to suggest that the law need not have turned out the way it did, just as technologies have often been adapted for unforeseen uses. The law is often arbitrary and complex and almost always politically compromised. It is full of clauses to serve special interests and oddities specific to their historical moments; it is intended to be impartial and (as much as possible) impervious to change. But like video (and many other things), the law becomes most self-evident when it fails or becomes outmoded. All of this suggests that analog history still matters, not only to give a more coherent sense of the past but also to help understand how we got where we are today.

Fair Use

Fair use has emerged as one of the most contested and celebrated concepts in U.S. copyright law. It is an exception, a contradiction, and yet the core of copyright. Fair-use exceptions are unique to the United States and extend the foundational purpose of copyright protection: to promote cultural progress by permitting reproductive uses of still-protected works for societal and intellectual innovation.[10] The fair-use provision states that use or reproduction of copyrighted material for "criticism, comment, news reporting, teaching . . . , scholarship, or research, is not an infringement of copyright." Although fair use is applied on a case-by-case basis by judges in the event of litigation, it is generally safe to assume that you, as a researcher, could make a personal copy of this chapter at a library, that I could quote from a *New York Times* article about the developing video market in the previous chapter, and that the reporter could describe scenes from a popular video release, because these are all (probably) fair uses. Fair use pertains only to excerpts and reproductions of works that are protected by copyright; if the original work has not been copyrighted or its protection has expired, it is in the public domain, and fair use need not apply. And, as is too rarely articulated, fair use indicates not only reproduction but also *use*, suggesting that copying can be productive as well as consumptive.

In 1976 Congress revised the U.S. copyright code to include a provision for fair use as Section 107, thus permitting private reproduction of excerpts from protected works for critical, educational, and scholarly purposes. Fair use had long existed as a concept in case law (dating back to 1841 and 1869)[11]—wherein lawyers would argue or judges would allow occasional common-sense exceptions to copyright regulations—but fair use had never been statutory law (that is, legislated, written law). The existing copyright code, dating from 1909, was clearly out of sync with recently developed technologies, such as radios, televisions, photocopiers, audiotape, and the emergent videotape. A copyright bill establishing fair use as statutory law was first presented in Congress in 1964, but the copyright revision was not passed until 1976. The fair-use provision remained unchanged during those twelve years of legislative defeat and revision, which suggests that fair use was one of the long-standing and agreed-on purposes of the revision.[12] The 1976 copyright code revision was the most extensive in U.S. history, following more than a decade of study, Senate hearings, deliberation, and defeated bills—all of which strove to modernize the law to adequately correspond to international standards, contemporary commerce, and consumer needs. Writing the fair-use provision into law was an attempt to balance interests in favor of the public good while creating more strict copyright controls in favor of rights holders. The revised law has been explicitly identified as a "compromise" that "attempt[ed] to redress past wrongs, to shift the balance of copyright protection from publishers and producers to individual authors, and to codify the rights of both authors and users to materials communicated by all media, including new technologies."[13]

The fair-use provision was written to be flexible and abstract, following principles previously offered in judicial rulings. Four factors determine whether these uses can be deemed fair:

—the purpose and character of the use,
—the nature of the copyrighted work,
—the proportion of the excerpt used in relation to the entire work,
—the market impact of the use.[14]

These four criteria were designed to be considered in tandem, making fair use not so much a law as a set of guidelines. They are "nonexclusive"—meaning that other factors could be considered when relevant—and not all factors are weighed evenly in each court decision. Such legal ambiguity has prompted criticism of the provision as weak or overreaching, depending on how it is applied. For instance, in 2004 a judge and a legal scholar suggested that these guidelines are "misleading" and confusing; counter to their apparent meanings, the "purpose" of the use can be commercial, entire works can be reproduced, and the market impact from derogatory critical use (such as a bad review) is not distinguished from a use that merely supplants demand (such as a condensation or alternative version). These commentators even go so far as to say that the second factor, the "nature" of the work, is "empty" because of its ambiguity.[15] Fair use was and remains at the court's discretion to decide on a case-by-case basis.

Fair use is by definition exceptional, and its exceptionality makes it particularly difficult to establish general judicial precedents or guarantees of users' rights. Despite these qualifications and conundrums, critical and scholarly uses of a work are more likely to be considered defensible than commercial condensations, and generally the smaller the portion reproduced, the more likely the derivative use will be considered fair. The economic interests of the copyright owner have tended to carry the most weight of the four factors, and some legal experts consider fair use to be a policy that applies only to reproductions of entire works in cases of market failure (meaning that a work is not readily available for purchase at a reasonable price). The "market failure" interpretation suggests that works that can be reasonably purchased or licensed cannot be reproduced without permission or payment; in this scenario, out-of-print or undistributed works may be copied more freely. This interpretation suggests that fair use, as *free* use, should be permissible only when no reasonably accessible or affordable copy can be purchased or licensed.[16] This version of fair use, like mine in the introduction, conceives of the defense as a question of access.[17]

Commenting on the 1976 copyright law's inclusion of the fair-use section, the copyright office attorney Harriet L. Oler emphasized that fair use is not a user's *right* but merely a potential *defense* that only the courts have the authority to allow:

> It is not an exemption from the owner's exclusive rights, but a defense to an infringement action. The distinction is subtle, but important. It means that a use of a copyrighted work which would otherwise constitute a literal copyright infringement may be adjudged a fair or free one, and that user may successfully defend such a use in a copyright infringement action.[18]

Oler quotes the House of Representatives report on the 1976 copyright revision bill, which states, "Section 107 is intended to restate the present judicial doctrine of fair use, not to change, narrow or enlarge it in any way."[19] More recently, Lessig succinctly assessed that "fair use in America simply means the right to hire a lawyer to defend your right to create."[20]

Fair use was designed to protect educational, news reporting, and political commentary uses, but it was not designed as a *creative* exception. Despite copyright law's founding mission to "promote the useful arts," there is not necessarily protection for *artistic* repurposing—only creative reworkings that offer some type of critical examination of a preexisting work. Fair use has become an increasingly weak defense in an age when copyright holders are more likely to litigate. Both rights owners and appropriation artists are often reluctant to pursue expensive litigation or take the chance that Supreme Court decisions would set unfavorable precedents; consequently there are relatively few judicial precedents, as most infringement lawsuits settle out of court. Many artists and educators hope that fair-use provisions will protect any and all appropriations of copyrighted content, but there are no guarantees.

Beyond Fair Use

As I suggested in the introduction, this book reminds readers of the complexity of copyright and users' rights. Copyright doesn't work the way the content industry would have audiences believe: that either audiences pay for access or they're pirates. And fair use is not the only mechanism within copyright law to facilitate users' rights. Thanks to the public domain and the first-sale provisions, some uses are noninfringing or "free" (as in freedom, not as in cheap) rather than fair uses. A work enters the public domain when its copyright protections expire. Once the rights expire, anyone can copy and distribute copies of the text, rework it in its original medium, or adapt it into another medium. Most works are most profitable when they're new, so authors or publishers reap sufficient rewards under this system to make creativity and distribution worthwhile. When the U.S. copyright code began, the term for protection lasted fourteen years with the potential for renewal. Congress has repeatedly extended that term limit, thanks to lobbying from publishers, studios, writers, and artists. Today copyright protection lasts for the life of the author plus seventy years or, in the case of works of hire, ninety years. Although classic literature and a few films have "fallen" into the public domain, works created in our lifetime will probably never be available for public-domain uses while we're alive. The first-sale rule basically allows the owner of a video (or book or CD) to do anything to or with that physical copy—watching it, defacing it, loaning it, throwing it away, or reselling it—short of copying it. This policy allows public libraries, used bookstores, and video rental outlets to exist. One of the central tenets of copyright is the distinction that the consumer may own the tangible delivery device (the videocassette) but not the copyrighted content (the movie or recorded TV program). To reiterate: copying a public-domain work is noninfringing because the original work is no longer protected; using a tangible copy of a video is noninfringing because it does not involve copying. Fair use protects users' rights to make copies of copyrighted works.

With digital media there are few noninfringing or free uses because almost every use of a Word document, a music file, an e-mail, or a website involves creating a copy. Thus, as Lessig has argued, fair use has been rhetorically overextended in the digital media age to defend not only fair uses but also uses that were previously noninfringing or free in the analog environment.[21] According to Lessig, fair use has been overburdened with covering whole additional categories of uses that are beyond the provision's intended scope. Elsewhere, Litman asserted that fair use was not designed to determine the legality of personal uses and is therefore mostly ill equipped to do so.[22] As I argue in this chapter, the Betamax case demonstrates that fair use can be more flexible than is conventionally thought.

Furthermore, the DMCA locks out user access and fair uses of much digital media. In a brief supporting Grokster that was filed before the Supreme Court, media scholars indicated both the importance of fair use and its limitations in educational and scholarly uses of media:

> teaching and research often require the unauthorized copying, distribution, re-fashioning, and performance of copyrighted works without permission from the copyright holder, and thus have cleared a space within the strictures of copyright law to allow for such publicly beneficial uses. The foundation of that space is "fair use," which, though an affirmative defense to the accusation of infringement, has granted educators a certain measure of comfort that they would not be sued by copyright holders for infringement. However, the penumbra of perceived "users' rights" that emanate from Sec. 107 of the Copyright Act has proven inadequate to protect many important acts central to teaching and research.[23]

But, as in the Betamax case, fair use may be the best measure we have to protect personal and productive copying.

Copyright and Preservation

Preservation was not the intended function for videotape—or for many other reproductive technologies, for that matter. Nor was preservation why copyright was invented. But it has become one of their benefits, and one of the ways in which both can enable access. Significantly, U.S. copyrights are administered under the domain of the Library of Congress, further fusing the intentions of promoting creative progress with the national repository of knowledge. Such preservation promises future access. The connection is also a logistical one: formerly, copies of works had to be submitted for copyright, thereby providing the source for the Library of Congress's acquisitions. As film historians are well aware, many of the extant early films are available only because of deposited paper prints of each frame (films were originally protected only by copyrighting each frame as a separate photographic image); these have been rephotographed, frame by frame, to reconstruct these early motion pictures. As can be seen repeatedly in the histories of technology, innovative media are often believed to be immortal when they are introduced. Long-term preservation and distribution are often neither feasible nor prominent concerns during new media's early phases. Requiring copyright deposits indirectly ensured that at least one copy of whatever was copyrighted would be maintained for posterity; unfortunately, it's often the new and fleeting technologies that do not yet qualify for copyright protection.

Copyright was further linked to preservation through Section 108 exceptions to reproductive restrictions for libraries and archives and through the mandate for the American Television and Radio Archives, both of which were passed as part of the 1976 copyright code, as I discuss further in the next chapter. In both its location within the copyright code and its legislative history, Section 108 seems to be the younger sibling of fair use, Section 107. Section 108 pertains specifically to libraries and archives and offers specific types of copyright exemption in the interest of preservation and access. Yet the 1976 copyright act was not otherwise especially oriented toward preservation: although damaged books could be reproduced and broadcast media would now be collected, under the general code, published works were no longer required to be registered to be protected in accordance with the Berne Convention rules, and thus the Library of Congress no longer automatically receives deposits of all protected publications.[24] This shift relieved authors and publishers of bureaucratic labor, but it has also created potential gaps in the library's collection and confusion among users about unregistered works' copyright status. By removing registration and deposit requirements, the law created new problems in determining who owns a work, if it is protected, and whether free or fair uses apply; in addition, the law created a preservation gap that may necessitate private citizens to intervene in collecting, copying, and preserving cultural texts.[25] Videotape technology introduced one new format for such amateur archiving interventions, and fair use and Section 108 have served to help protect at least some of these practices.

The Betamax Decision

By the time the new copyright code was passed, the first mass-market domestic videotape recorder, Sony's Betamax, had been introduced in the U.S. market (in September 1975), and VHS soon followed (in 1976). These technological innovations had been in development about as long as the fair-use bill. In 1976, just as the copyright act was finally revised, the Hollywood studios Universal and Disney teamed up to initiate a lawsuit against Sony, manufacturer of the Betamax machine. The studios argued that the Betamax was a copyright-infringing device that allowed and encouraged viewers to record the studios' television shows and that the Japanese company was liable for contributory infringement. In 1979 a district court judge ruled that consumer taping was fair use; two years later, a circuit court overturned the decision on appeal, and the case was subsequently taken to the Supreme Court.[26] In 1984 the Supreme Court ultimately ruled that videocassette recorders should be allowed because of their potential for productive noninfringing and fair uses. This decision was the Court's first precedent-setting decision relying on fair use since the exemption had been codified. Thus fair use not only protected VCRs, but VCRs helped to define fair use.

Although I approach this legal history as an advocate of personal videotape recording and of fair use generally, as I read the Supreme Court's decision in the Betamax case, the judges integrated these two issues somewhat arbitrarily and haphazardly. As a law that merely legislated judicial reasoning, fair use was created and, in the Betamax case, broadly interpreted by the courts. As a strict application of the fair-use guidelines as legislated, the dissent may actually be the more persuasive opinion. This alarming conclusion initially bothered me: what if the Betamax decision, so progressive in protecting audiences' rights, was legally wrong? Should I just pretend not to have noticed, rather than undermine my own argument by addressing the matter? Ultimately I realized that this revelation presented an opportunity to advocate for similar judicial interpretations in the future. The Court's majority saw fit to expand the definition of fair use to include personal consumptive uses as a way to broaden the potential audiences for television programming in order to serve a broader public interest.

The Betamax case both sought to define what audiences were doing with their machines and whether such uses could be defended as fair uses. The litigation was premised on the logic that recording television broadcasts off-air was a violation of the studio's copyrights and detrimental to the rerun and still-speculative home video markets for its programs. According to a reporter for CBS *Evening News*, Sony compared timeshifting to taping radio programs off-air, whereas Universal compared the practice to stealing a car.[27] (The content industry would make similar theft comparisons during its campaign against peer-to-peer file sharing.) The studios also feared that home taping might diminish the networks' commercial revenues if advertisers felt they weren't reaching live prime-time audiences or feared home audiences were fast-forwarding through their spots. Not insignificantly, Universal's parent company, MCA, had financial interest in the success of the DiscoVision video system, a speculative competitor of Sony's Betamax. One of the earliest Betamax advertisements suggested that, with the device, audiences could watch two Universal-produced programs (*Kojak* and *Columbo*) that were broadcast simultaneously on competing networks by watching one and taping the other. Sony apparently believed the campaign would please Universal by expanding its audiences; Universal, however, was not pleased.[28] Universal enlisted Disney as a co-plaintiff, purportedly because of Disney's reputation for vigorous intellectual property protection practices; together they pursued litigation against Sony for manufacturing the Betamax, a handful of Betamax retailers, and an individual Betamax user. The studios pursued an injunction against the manufacture of subsequent machines and damages for contributory copyright infringement. The Betamax suit was filed before VHS had any significant presence on the market, and separate litigation was never pursued to challenge manufacturers of VHS machines.

In spite of the Betamax lawsuit and apparent resistance to releasing movies on tape, the studios were not necessarily opposed to home video before it became a reality. Nor have executives denied their shortsighted business models in retrospect. MCA president and Universal executive Lew Wasserman was quoted in a 1970 book on emerging video technologies: "It's not the hardware that is important. It is the entertainment and who owns it. We have two thousand features available for cassettes. If only ten percent is suitable for cassettes—what a library!"[29] These comments indicate a tension between technology and content and between who will profit from the developing market—a clear staking-out of commercial territory six years before Wasserman's company started litigation against Sony. But this comment also indicates that Wasserman saw the potential for residual profits through the home video market—and he hoped to exploit it. A decade and a half later, other studio executives reflected on how the studios, by their reticence to enter the home video market, had lost out on an early market share to home tapers and independent rental stores. In 1984, Steve Roberts, president of Twentieth Century Telecommunications, told *Newsweek*: "A whole black market had grown up to satisfy consumer demand we were ignoring. . . . So we decided to get into the bootlegger's business and make some profits ourselves." In the same article, Twentieth Century Fox president Alan Hirschfield admitted, "The film companies through the years have failed to have much foresight about the future. . . . We didn't do [it] with TV. We failed with cable, and we allowed others to seize the distribution of home video."[30]

The litigation did not halt the manufacture of machines, nor did it drastically change marketing that educated potential customers in uses that the studios contested. A special advertising section titled "The Wonderful World of Home Video" in the October 30, 1978, issue of *Time* featured an illustration with the caption "Build Your Own Movie Library!" and a Toshiba ad for its Beta-format VCR urging home tapers to avoid commercials ("Get rid of Mr. Whipple, ring around the collar and the pain caused by aspirin commercials") with its remote-control pauser, a tethered device that looks like a cross between a disposable cigarette lighter and the response button that contestants clutch on *Jeopardy*. The ad only works, of course, if the reader watches enough TV to recognize the ad campaigns without mentioning the products (Charmin toilet tissue in the case of spokescharacter Mr. Whipple and Wisk laundry detergent for the plight of ring around the collar) and might therefore be annoyed by them. The fine print at the bottom of the page, however, offers a disclaimer that essentially undermines everything that appears above: "CAUTION: The unauthorized recording of copyrighted material, television programs, films, video tapes and other materials, may infringe the rights of copyright owners and be contrary to law and by the sale of this equipment, we do not represent that such material can be recorded." Yet that's exactly what the ad copy does represent.[31] This advertising section appeared well after the Betamax case had been filed and after Sony had pulled its initial ad campaign suggesting that viewers tape shows while watching something else—purportedly the marketing strategy that initiated Universal's rancor. (Another version of the campaign's history suggests that Sony pulled the plug because it couldn't manufacture machines quickly enough to meet demand. Yet Sony Corporation of America president Harvey L. Schein told *TV Guide* that the lawsuit "gave credibility to our advertising campaign. . . . The movie companies were recognizing that Betamax could do what we said it can do.")[32] By 1978, rather than mention specific programs, Sony ads urged customers to indifferently "watch whatever whenever." (See figure 2 on page 9 for a reproduction of this ad.)

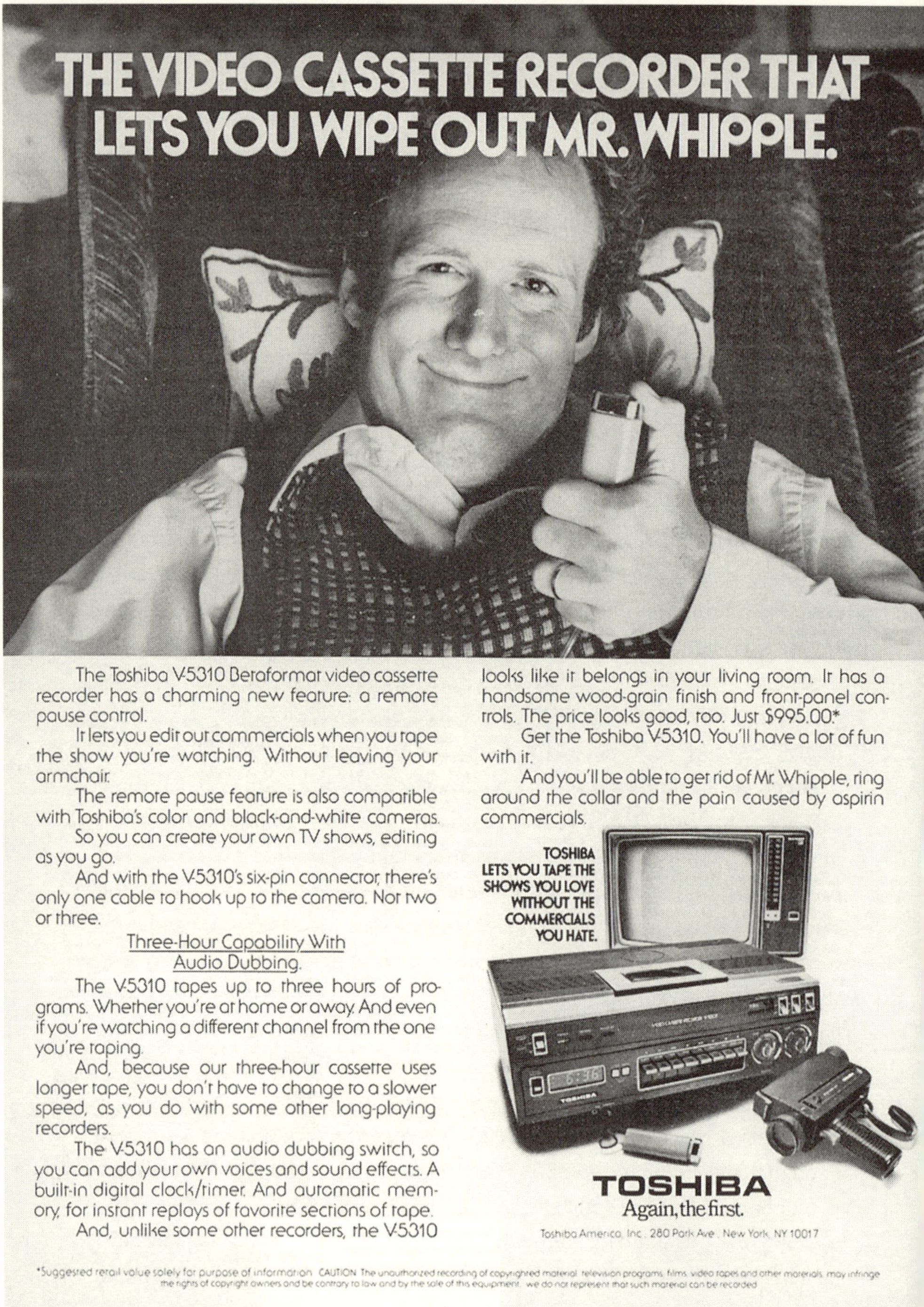
THE VIDEO CASSETTE RECORDER THAT LETS YOU WIPE OUT MR. WHIPPLE.
The Toshiba V-5310 Betaformat video cassette recorder has a charming new feature: a remote pause control.
It lets you edit out commercials when you tape the show you're watching. Without leaving your armchair.
The remote pause feature is also compatible with Toshiba's color and black-and-white cameras.
So you can create your own TV shows, editing as you go.
And with the V-5310's six-pin connector, there's only one cable to hook up to the camera. Not two or three.
Three-Hour Capability With Audio Dubbing.
The V-5310 tapes up to three hours of programs. Whether you're at home or away. And even if you're watching a different channel from the one you're taping.
And, because our three-hour cassette uses longer tape, you don't have to change to a slower speed, as you do with some other long-playing recorders.
The V-5310 has an audio dubbing switch, so you can add your own voices and sound effects. A built-in digital clock/timer. And automatic memory, for instant replays of favorite sections of tape.
And, unlike some other recorders, the V-5310 looks like it belongs in your living room. It has a handsome wood-grain finish and front-panel controls. The price looks good, too. Just $995.00*
Get the Toshiba V-5310. You'll have a lot of fun with it.
And you'll be able to get rid of Mr. Whipple, ring around the collar and the pain caused by aspirin commercials.
TOSHIBA LETS YOU TAPE THE SHOWS YOU LOVE WITHOUT THE COMMERCIALS YOU HATE.
TOSHIBA
Again, the first.
Toshiba America, Inc., 280 Park Ave., New York, NY 10017
*Suggested retail value solely for purpose of information. CAUTION: The unauthorized recording of copyrighted material, television programs, films, video tapes and other materials, may infringe the rights of copyright owners and be contrary to law and by the sale of this equipment, we do not represent that such material can be recorded.

To determine the legalities of the technology, the Supreme Court attempted to define the format specificity of the Betamax machine. By inventing the technology's legal definitions, the Court—like users, hardware manufacturers, marketers, journalists, video store entrepreneurs, and eventually studio executives—contributed to the creation of the meanings and discourses surrounding the device, thus suggesting that the role of VCRs in culture was not self-evident or predetermined but developed. Both the majority and dissenting opinions in *Sony v. Universal* enumerate the primary elements of the videotape recorder (VTR) as a tuner that receives broadcast signals, a recording head that encodes signals onto tape, and an adapter that decodes the video signal for output to a monitor. (However, only Blackmun's dissent observes that Sony also manufactured playback-only Betamax decks without tuners and that the studios made no objection to these machines.)[33] Both opinions also single out pause and fast-forward commands as central to the device's appeal and functionality, especially as they relate to methods of omitting advertisements during recording or zipping through them during playback. Both opinions refrain from comparing Betamax and VHS models, thus at once narrowing the scope of the decision to the specific allegations against Sony and potentially refusing to take positions on videorecorders more broadly. By 1983, when the case was argued before the Supreme Court, VHS had already outpaced Betamax on the consumer market.

The Ruling

The Court's ruling in *Sony v. Universal* was described by Dan Rather on *CBS Evening News* as "high court, high tech, high stakes."[34] In a narrow decision, the Court ruled for Sony. This final Betamax ruling relied on three premises: first, that home video recorders must be allowed because of their potential for noninfringing uses; second, that the dominant uses of the machines were for timeshifting, which the Supreme Court considered fair use; and third, that Sony could not be held liable for its customers' misuses of the machines. The judges were clearly aware that some home tapers did, in fact, elide or fast-forward through commercials when timeshifting and that some video collectors built home libraries of tapes. But for the Court, the legitimate and potentially beneficial uses of the technology outweighed

14. Although published while the Sony-Universal lawsuit was working its way through the courts, this 1978 advertisement for Toshiba's Betamax-format VCR explicitly markets the device for eliminating commercials while recording TV broadcasts. The fine print, however, suggests that recording television might not be legal. Collection of the author.

such violations. The fair-use component of the ruling was originally its more controversial element and received more attention as a precedent-setting opinion. However, the finding that a technology's potential productive uses override illicit uses has been the focus of debates decades later in lawsuits relating to peer-to-peer file-sharing networks.

The first decision on *Sony v. Universal* came from a California district court in 1979. In this, the first of three *Sony v. Universal* rulings, the decisive factor was an expansive definition of fair use to include private taping for entertainment purposes. In this ruling, Judge Warren John Ferguson's definition was premised on the fact that consumers received broadcasts freely and that access was the fundamental project of fair use—interpretations that resurface in the Supreme Court's majority opinion.[35] Ronald Bettig, in his analysis of this initial ruling, extrapolated that "access is . . . one of the underlying tenets of copyright law as evidenced by the fair use doctrine."[36] In 1981 a Court of Appeals overturned the district court on the premise that timeshifting was not a "productive" use and therefore not a fair use and suggested that a majority of infringing uses overrode potential noninfringing ones.[37] In addition, the Court of Appeals argued, "the statute does not list . . . 'increased access' as [a] purpose within the general scope of fair use."[38] At the core of these divergent rulings was a different standard for determining fair use. The first equated private, noncommercial use with fair use; the second determined that such instances also had to be *productive*, that is, to produce knowledge or a derivative work for the public's benefit. The fair-use principle thus produced debates between private and public uses, entertainment and edification. And it hinged on the issue of access.

The logic of the Supreme Court's majority ruling suggests that access in and of itself was sufficiently productive to constitute fair use in this case. A memorandum indicates that Justice Stevens's thinking was founded in part on the principles of access to information and the public interest—concepts that have been central to broadcast regulation and, as we will see in case of the Vanderbilt Television News Archive, media preservation. Justice John Paul Stevens wrote, "Time shifting makes television programming available to viewers who would otherwise miss it."[39] The Supreme Court's majority Betamax decision offered a generous interpretation of fair use that conflated nonprofit private use with fair use in line with the district court's initial ruling and put the onus on the plaintiffs to demonstrate their economic injury (which they could not). On the first page of its majority decision, the Supreme Court held that "any individual may reproduce a copyrighted work for a 'fair use'; the copyright owner does not possess the exclusive right to such a use."[40] In the footnotes to the opinion, Justice Stevens writes, "The statutory language does not identify any dichotomy between productive and nonproductive time-shifting."[41] The interpretation of timeshifting as fair use seems to ignore that fair use typically indicates transformative use of a portion of a copyrighted work; in an off-air recording there is no change to the content of the original broadcast, except perhaps when viewers omit or fast-forward through commercials and thus use the recordings in a way that alters the experience of the source material. Such practices of avoiding commercials were, of course, one of the primary concerns that motivated the lawsuit in the first place; studios and networks feared the economic structure of television would collapse if advertisers withdrew sponsorship in response to viewers' newfound ability to bypass commercials when timeshifting. Thus the case presents a curious application of the fair-use exemption, one that set the precedent for much subsequent confusion on the part of users, artists, and rights holders. Research into the history of the ruling has revealed that fair use was not even the basis of the decision in the initial draft of Justice Stevens's opinion—at the time anticipated to be a dissent rather than a majority—when he reasoned that "private copying did not infringe," which would not necessitate a fair-use defense.[42]

The Supreme Court opinions on *Sony v. Universal* demonstrate the gaps and tensions between politics and strict interpretation of the law. Considered in comparison to the dissent's strict statutory analysis, the majority opinion clearly expanded the domain of fair use to mean private, consumptive use. The dissenting opinion, authored by Justice Harry Blackmun, actually demonstrates closer analysis and consideration of judicial precedent and legislative history. The distinctions between fair use and free or noninfringing uses are significant to copyright generally, and they also clarify the contradictions of the Supreme Court's ruling in the Betamax case. The majority opinion distinguished between fair uses and noninfringing uses of off-air recording; the justices decided that timeshifting was fair use and that recording public affairs or permitted programming was noninfringing. But this distinction conflates free use with fair use, rather than free use with noninfringing use. The justices interpreted that recording complete programs off-air that were broadcast over public airwaves and received freely (and free of charge) was fair use; defined through application of the first-sale doctrine, this is closer to free use.[43] In some cases, timeshifting could certainly be fair use, though it would seem that not all timeshifting would qualify. Timeshifting falls somewhere between the two: it uses texts that are given to audiences to consume, but it also involves reproduction of copyrighted works. From the published histories of the case that draw on drafted opinions and memorandums circulated among the justices, it seems that fair use was employed as a compromise to protect off-air taping rather than applied in a straightforward way. Yet because fair use is really just a codified placeholder for judicial interpretations and granted exceptions, the Supreme Court was in the position to redefine the concept to include consumptive free uses. This may be a case where the end justified the means, but the contradictory logic has also resulted in a cloudy legal and rhetorical model for subsequent fair-use defenses.[44] Despite the decision's infamy, the case has remained prominent in fair-use analysis and advocacy.

The dissent raised multiple issues, including distinctions between timeshifting and "library building" uses of recording (the latter posing a greater copyright infringement), the fact that entire programs were typically recorded (in perceived violation of the "amount and substantiality" criteria of fair use), the potential future economic impact and competition that saved home recordings posed to rebroadcasts or rereleases of the same content (just because users don't sell their tapes doesn't make them noncommercial if they would otherwise purchase official releases), and the distinction between nonproductive personal consumptive use and productive fair use (which creates knowledge through scholarly, critical, and educational reproduction of excerpts). In the dissent, Justice Blackmun argues:

> When a user reproduces an entire work and uses it for its original purpose, with no added benefit to the public, there is then no need whatsoever to provide the ordinary user with a fair use subsidy at the author's expense. . . . It may be tempting, as, in my view, the Court today is tempted, to stretch the doctrine of fair use so as to permit unfettered use of this new technology in order to increase access to television programming. But such an extension risks eroding the very basis of copyright law, by depriving authors of control over their works and consequently of their incentive to create.[45]

The dissenting justices' two major objections to the majority opinion were the questionable interpretation of fair use and the practices of consumers who used their VCRs to build personal libraries of recordings. Both issues are central to my political position. This dissenting opinion maintains the division made by the court of appeals between "productive" fair use and "nonproductive" timeshifting, though it acknowledges some of the gray areas in making such determinations. Generally, however, I suspect that television scholars, who may have the largest claim for fair-use recordings, would also be among the academics most likely to reject hierarchies between their "productive" viewership and general television audiences' "consumptive" kind, given the emphasis within the discipline on audience practices and fan cultures. I consider collection building and personal recording to be potentially productive uses—and therefore fair uses. Personal library building of commercially unavailable content has been productive in personal enrichment that manifests in indirect ways and maintains user access to work that has gone out of print or never been made available through commercial mass releases. Through reproduction and exchange of videocassettes, these personal collections and recordings keep media works in the public sphere for viewing, study, and creative reuse. The accumulation and circulation of videotapes have not just functioned as a potential subversion of copyright owners' economic propriety but also contribute significantly to the production, distribution, and preservation of information, history, culture, and media.

Blackmun's dissent examines the four factors of statutory fair use and finds that timeshifting for private entertainment falls short of all four criteria; the majority opinion, despite its reliance on fair use, does not follow the statutory instructions this closely. Additionally, Blackmun argues, "neither the [fair-use] statute nor its legislative history suggests any intent to create a general exemption for a single copy made for personal or private use. Indeed, it appears that Congress considered and rejected the very possibility of a special private use exemption."[46]

In their study of the 1976 copyright act, Patterson and Lindberg stress the too-rarely observed distinction between personal and fair uses:

> *An individual's use of a copyrighted work for his or her own private use is a personal use, not subject to fair-use restraints. Such use includes use by copying, provided that the copy is neither for public distribution or sale to others nor a functional substitute for a copyrighted work currently available on the market at a reasonable price.*
>
> One key point here is that personal use is not subject to length restrictions, but is limited to a single copy not intended for distribution. The user who goes beyond these limits must resort to fair-use criteria to determine the appropriateness of the use.[47]

These legal scholars also point out that, as written, the fair-use doctrine does not distinguish between "competitors and consumers," which has misleadingly insinuated that personal uses are akin to commercial ones.[48] The Betamax majority opinion's blurring of personal and fair uses may be key to its murky grounding in law and failure to provide a strong precedent for subsequent decisions. By the time of the *Napster* and *Grokster* decisions, however, the No Electronic Theft Act, later part of the Digital Millennium Copyright Act, would criminalize digital copying whether or not it was commercial or private.

The question may also arise, if home taping was fair use, why did those pesky FBI warnings at the beginning of prerecorded movies continue? The Court was deciding on off-air television taping, not on tape-to-tape dubbing. Timeshifting was fair use in large part because television programming was in many ways ephemeral and could not reasonably be accessed later. Even shows in syndication had unpredictable schedules. Besides, timeshifting was supposed to be temporary. Duplicating a rental tape for long-term home viewing was not timeshifting. In addition, prerecorded movies were more or less readily accessible at video stores for rental, and although many VCR owners may have balked at the price for tapes, the fact that some individuals did buy cassettes at $70 or more a pop indicated that movies *could* be purchased at a (relatively) "reasonable" price. If a movie is out of print and thus unavailable, a stronger case might be made that dubbing a personal copy is fair use.

Implications of the Decision

Sony v. Universal epitomizes the notion of a "landmark" Supreme Court ruling. As legal historians have noted, "*Betamax* is the cornerstone of all subsequent fair use jurisprudence."[49] Indeed, the Betamax case has been analyzed in depth and incalculably referenced.[50] Despite the Supreme Court ruling's influence and employment as a judicial precedent, it was by no means a clear-cut case. A California district court favored Sony; the federal appeals court favored the studios. At the Supreme Court, the decision was five to four for Sony, a close verdict that legal historians have revealed nearly went the other way (three to six). The drawn-out narrative and sudden reversals in the Betamax case might seem exasperating, even implausible, if they were the stuff of fiction. Yet, as in one of my favorite lines of movie dialogue, "Life doesn't imitate art. It imitates bad television."[51] The Supreme Court's reevaluation of the Betamax precedent in the age of Internet file sharing was similarly divided: three justices suggested reconsideration, three maintained support for the precedent, and three appeared neutral. Thus judicial positions on the case were and remain nearly evenly divided.

Although this decision has been used as a touchstone in arguing against various copyright revisions and infringement lawsuits, the Supreme Court justices were careful to state that the decision was an interpretation of the law as written up to that time and that Congress had the discretion—and perhaps the obligation—to legislate new copyright rules specific to the new video recording technology.[52] Copyright historians contend that every new technology introduces a period of market change and anxiety for content owners, but that any preemptive regulation will erode users' rights. Rather than controlling the technology and criminalizing the uses that new technology allows, new business strategies need to be developed to create a balance of profits and public interests. The responsive and proactive methods of regulating copyright for technological innovations are among the underlying debates in the Supreme Court's opposing opinions. The majority opinion of the Court stated:

> From its beginning, the law of copyright has developed in response to significant changes in technology. . . . The judiciary's reluctance to expand the protections afforded by the copyright [code] without explicit legislative guidance is a recurring theme. . . . Sound policy, as well as history, supports our consistent deference to Congress when major technological innovations alter the market for copyrighted materials. Congress has the constitutional authority and the institutional ability to accommodate fully the varied permutations of competing interests that are inevitably implicated by such new technology.[53]

Justice Blackmun's dissent, however, suggests that such judicial positions pass the buck:

> The Court's decision today provides little incentive for congressional action. . . . The Court has tended to evade the hard issues when they arise in the area of copyright law. I see no reason for the Court to be particularly pleased with this tradition or to continue it. Indeed, it is fairly clear from the legislative history of the 1976 Act that Congress meant to change the old pattern and enact a statute that would cover new technologies, as well as old.[54]

The Betamax decisions necessarily examined the law as it had been written. But despite the 1976 law's relatively recent vintage, home video was not a reality or a major concern for legislators when they proposed, revised, and

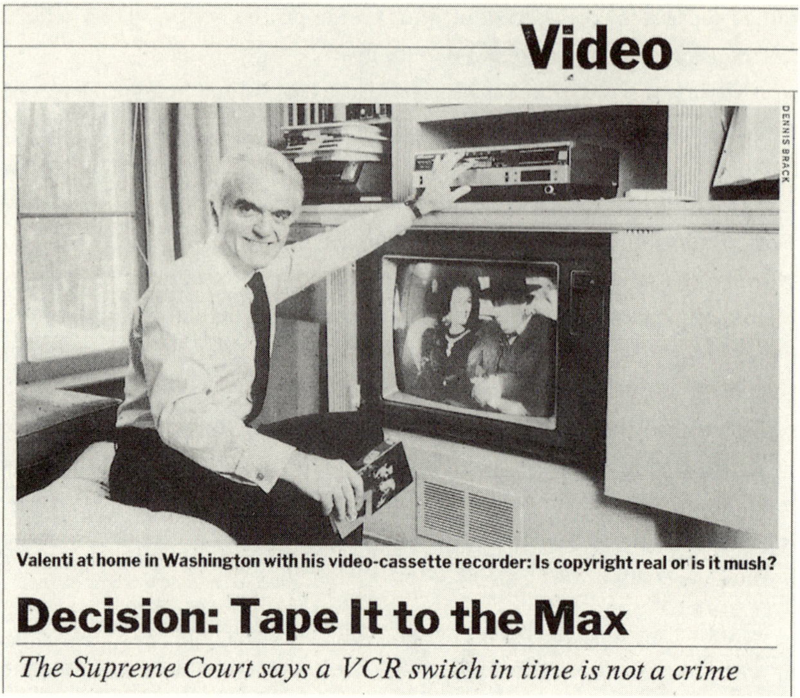
Video

DENNIS BRACK

Valenti at home in Washington with his video-cassette recorder: Is copyright real or is it mush?

Decision: Tape It to the Max

The Supreme Court says a VCR switch in time is not a crime

15. When *Time* reported the Supreme Court's decision on *Sony v. Universal*, the magazine showed a bit of sass by illustrating the article with a picture of the Motion Picture Association of America president and piracy paranoiac Jack Valenti smiling in front of his own VCR. Of course, the tape in his hand is a prerecorded film classic, not a home recording from television. *Time*, January 30, 1984, page 67. Collection of the author.

finally enacted the copyright code. Similarly, the rise of peer-to-peer file-sharing networks and practices just after the DMCA's passage indicates how quickly a future-looking copyright code can become outmoded.

The Supreme Court's majority opinion in the Betamax case advocated legislative statutes rather than judicial precedents for defining the boundaries of copyright law for new technologies. Despite continued lobbying from Hollywood, Congress did not pass any legislative revisions to criminalize timeshifting; the legislature's inaction has been attributed to the fact that the Court decision came down during an election year, and no congressperson up for reelection was likely to take a stand against a popular consumer device.[55] Meanwhile the VCR's potential for productive uses largely gave way to consumptive uses through industry exploitation of the home video market. In an indirect way, the Hollywood studios won the battle against such productive uses by providing commercial alternatives to them.

Whereas Congress has never successfully legislated legal qualifications or restrictions for timeshifting or video-specific fair use, it has attempted to regulate digital media technologies, much to the chagrin of fair-use and access advocates. From a certain perspective, one might say that Congress learned all the wrong lessons from *Sony v. Universal*. Or perhaps the content industries' lobbyists have just proved more persuasive than considerations of the public interest.

With increasing conglomeration and global power, the content industries have become more powerful influences than ever before—both on official policy in Congress and in the marketplace through synergistic agreements with technology manufacturers. Significantly, these technology manufacturers and content producers are no longer necessarily distinct entities. For instance, Sony, formerly only a consumer electronics firm, has been in the entertainment business for decades now, following its acquisition of CBS Records (in 1987) and Columbia Pictures (in 1989). Getting into content was part of a controversial business strategy to recover from the Betamax debacle, as well as a move toward having a proprietary catalog of content to drive adoption of Sony's technologies.[56] Before the rollout of its second-generation DVD format, Blu-ray, the corporation also acquired MGM to expand its catalog of film titles available for exclusive release on its format.

The histories of consumer technologies reveal that speculations about the devices that will be invented, marketed, and adopted frequently prove premature by years (even decades) or off the mark entirely. If scientists and media moguls cannot reliably predict which inventions will catch on—or how they will be used—certainly legislators cannot, either. Copyright has historically been a responsive system of law for the sound reason that any attempt to craft a "future-proof" policy will probably introduce unnecessary restrictions that impede users' rights of access and miscalculate future issues. Yet in the rush to protect proprietary interests when computer networking and digital reproduction were beginning to catch on, Congress has turned toward predictive copyright legislation.

Digital Copyright

For most of its history, copyright has been a responsive regulatory system, so that media such as photographs, film, and phonorecords became protected only after their adoption and widespread use. In the digital media age, not only has Congress overextended copyright protections and the Courts so far allowed this turn, but also technologies themselves have been designed to prevent many potentially legal methods of reproduction. As Lessig argues, vertical integration is increasingly allowing corporations to control various levels of "code"—the technology, the distribution, and the content. And "code," as a form of regulation, takes both technical and legal forms. The law has turned from being considered and reactive to being predictive, while technologies now preempt usage beyond what the law restricts and without any certain recourse for appeal.

The past few decades have witnessed shifting strategies, and the DMCA was not without precedent. Yochai Benkler observes that current corporate and governmental strategies date back to the 1970s, not merely as recently as the "new media" 1990s when synergy and the content industry's influence on copyright law accelerated.[57] In the early 1970s, protection was extended to magnetic tape audio recordings, protecting still nascent prerecorded mass-consumer formats such as 8-tracks and cassette tapes. Later, the passage of the 1992 Audio Home Recording Act (AHRA) added a chapter titled "Digital Audio Recording Devices and Media" to the copyright code and set a precedent by not protecting intellectual property per se but *regulating technology* and introducing policies that *criminalize tampering with encryption codes and copyguards* as well as importing devices that bypass encoding. This revision challenges the international circulation of content, even if a recording that is commercially available in one country is not available elsewhere. As Litman points out, the 1992 Audio Home Recording Act revision was introduced because of anxieties that digital audio tape (DAT), already a professional format, had the potential for widespread digital piracy when it was introduced as a consumer format; DATs, however, never took off as a mass-media format, and the legislation stuck around longer than the format it was legislating.[58] Although the AHRA introduced a dangerous precedent for inhibiting reproduction and access of digital technologies, its progressive policies for analog media are too often overlooked. The AHRA introduced a copyright exemption to protect home taping with analog technologies for noncommercial personal use. Thus the AHRA distinguishes analog from digital technologies and maintains that analog bootlegging serves the public interest by protecting private access.

After this gradual shift in policies between the 1970s and early 1990s, policies took a decisive turn between 1995 and 1998, marked by the Federal Antidilution Act of 1995 for trademarks, the FCC's extensive new Telecommunications Act of 1996, and the No Electronic Theft Act of 1997.[59] The No Electronic Theft Act (NET) criminalized noncommercial personal copying for the first time and was absorbed into the DMCA in the following year; this law essentially equated noncommercial private duplication with piracy.[60] In 1998 the DMCA extended the principles of the 1992 and 1997 revisions to apply to digital media and devices generally and mandated the inclusion of copy prevention technologies in analog ones. In addition, the 1998 "Sonny Bono" Copyright Term Extension Act (CTEA) extended the duration of all copyrights by twenty years—even retroactively.

The DMCA was the result of a task force set up by President Clinton, which published a white paper in 1995; the legislation was passed in 1998. These dates are important because, as the report of the Committee on Intellectual Property Rights and the Emerging Information Infrastructure (a National Research Council task force that evaluated the DMCA) observes, the 1995 report was researched in the earliest stages of mainstream use of the World Wide Web and was necessarily based on speculation.[61] I would add that 1998, the year the DMCA was passed, marked the height of the dot.com boom, when the market suggested the Internet's specifically commercial potential and delirious profits were being made all around. The law came out of the Clinton-Gore policies of privatization and neoliberalism, which attempted to build Internet infrastructures and foster new cultural works by making the Web "safe" for corporate investment and content.[62] The DMCA was clearly fast-tracked to protect a quickly developing market, but compared to the dozen or so years of debate that went into the 1976 copyright act, the DMCA seems like the overzealous product of political haste. Policies with the goal of starting up the Internet should have taken the form of short-term funding initiatives or regulatory guidelines rather than a permanent addition to copyright law; with the goal of establishing Internet commerce by and large achieved, the law is overdue for reevaluation—a reconsideration that the Supreme Court has yet to undertake.

Further making a mess of things, the DMCA legislation seems intended to respond to computer-based uses but applies broadly to all digital (and some analog) media and technologies. The rationale for differential regulations of analog and digital media derives from distinctions between the two. In the analog world, access requires tangibility and ownership. For analog media, such as books printed on paper, publication is quite literally a process of making a work public, and the work enters the public record (if not the public domain) in object form. Copyright protects against pirate reproductions but does not monitor access to, or uses of, a book.[63] The purchased copy is the *physical* property of the consumer even as it is the *intellectual* property of its creator, publisher, or distributor, and the copyright holder has no jurisdiction to control how owners use their private goods.

Aesthetically, analog media are typically considered more indexical than digital ones, although the term also suggests interpretation—think of its etymological cousin "analogy." But owing to this interpretation and expression, analog copies reveal resolution loss from generation to generation.

Although I have argued that for users the practices, experiences, and expectations of digital technologies often mimic prior analog ones, I must concede that at the level of duplication and distribution digital technologies are in many ways new and different and that they may not be effectively regulated by analog copyright law. Digital formats may not require tangibility, scarcity, or even expression. The distinction between ideas and expression is potentially lost when content is merely information without physical form. In addition, the very foundational concepts of copying and theft are turned on their heads. Let me explain.

Technically, all digital works are reducible to information—a string of zeros and ones. Digitization (processing analog forms into binary code) and networking collapses ideas and expressions: in the digital world, all expression is reduced to data. Digital content may not have tangible forms or creative expression, and the very concepts of copying or publication become complicated. Computer technology renders accessing and reading a work indistinguishable from copying—a digital copy must be made to open a file, download a web page, or send an e-mail attachment. As data, information can be cloned without generational loss between copies, although there may be compression errors. As data, binary code can also be sent virtually to innumerable, anonymous other network users. Actually, the information and ideas that are expressed in all "intellectual property" are nonrivalrous in terms of access—though the profitability of such intellectual property may fall with saturation. Anyone with a television set and a clear signal can watch a show on broadcast television without depriving others of the same privilege; anyone can sing a song in the shower without preventing others from singing the song at a karaoke bar; anyone can quote a statistic from a magazine article at a dinner party without limiting an economist from analyzing the same figure. In a strange way, even though digital technologies may seem to undermine copyright, there are striking parallels between the nonscarcity of ideas and data. Analog tape, as I have emphasized, reveals a bootleg aesthetic of degeneration between copies, and master tapes can age or break down. As tangible delivery formats, cassettes also maintain an inherent scarcity and require at least a modicum of human contact. Unlike shoplifting, neither downloading nor off-air taping involves stealing an actual scarce object. The copies created do not take away from their owners, though they might diminish the market in the sense that audiences might be less likely to pay for texts of which they've already made free copies.

Congress applied the most restrictive and conservative type of protection to all digital devices, regardless of their differences. One of the problems with the DMCA is that it does not distinguish between kinds of digital media or technologies. Playing or recording a DVD is quite different from most computer applications, even though they are all "digital." Consequently the DMCA introduces a contradiction, as observed by a copyright critic:

> Copyright was designed to regulate only copying. It was not supposed to regulate one's right to read or share. But now that the distinctions among accessing, using, and copying have collapsed, copyright policy makers have found themselves faced with what seems to be a difficult choice: either relinquish some control over copying or expand copyright to regulate access and use, despite the chilling effect this might have on creativity, community, and democracy.[64]

The DMCA demonstrates that Congress has chosen the latter. A National Research Council report states that "control of reproduction is the mechanism, not the goal," of copyright law.[65] As *The Digital Dilemma* states, "When access requires reproduction, as it does for works in the digital form, the right to control reproduction is the right to control access."[66] Yet once a technology is obsolete—or a single erroneous one or zero corrupts an entire file—a digital work is nearly impossible to restore, thus introducing potential crises for preservation and future access.

The DMCA has been much critiqued, with the implicit hope of revising or overturning the law in the near future. Fair use and sharing (popularized as "creative commons") have become the focus of a boom in media and policy activism against the DMCA and the CTEA.[67] Through both practice and theory, hackers, librarians, archivists, lawyers, artists, students, and scholars have attempted to demonstrate alternative copyright models, to build public awareness of impending crises of access, and to sway restrictive legislation and judicial rulings. In particular, fair use is seen as endangered by anticopying technologies. After all, if you can't copy something in the first place, you can't very well make a fair use of it. And it's the anticopy technologies, not fair use, that are specifically protected under the DMCA. The law states succinctly and sweepingly, "No person shall circumvent a technological measure that effectively controls access to a work protected under this title."[68] The fair-use code remained unchanged, and no adaptations or "additional provisions" were made to allow for fair digital use.[69]

The DMCA effectively forbids users to make fair uses of media if technology has to be circumvented—for instance, if a scholar wants to copy a frame from a DVD for publication, the fact that encryption must be cracked makes what would be permissible and easy to do with videotape illegal for digital formats. Likewise, it is illegal to deprogram or reverse-engineer any encryption system in digital media devices, so that consumers cannot legally break through firewalls to copy DVDs or remove a region-encoding chip to play a European DVD in a North American DVD deck. For media scholars and cinephiles, this poses a crisis for access to cultural imports or bootlegged copies of unavailable works. The pervasive availability of multiregion playback decks and of online postings with instructions for hacking DVD region encoding has rendered this law difficult to enforce, but it remains troubling. In response to the anticircumvention component of the DMCA, we might ask, as one copyright scholar does, "If pirating is already illegal, why do we need this law? Congress decided it was easier to regulate machines than people."[70]

Encryption offers a short-term fix to provide market protection that has detrimental long-term implications for preservation when content cannot be retrieved later. Encryption predates digital media, though it is both more debilitating for nontechie users and more restrictive legally. For videotapes, Macrovision, the most common antipiracy technology, works by means of an encoded signal that jams the video image if the playback VCR is patched into a second VCR. Through scrambling, Macrovision introduced its own bootleg aesthetics, which makes the image pulse from light to dark while leaving the soundtrack unimpeded; the result is still watchable (in the sense that the viewer can still more or less see the action) if annoying. This method also indicates bias that the image track is more important than the sound track. In contrast, scrambled cable channels really did screw up the image into purple and black squiggles that were truly indecipherable, though the sound remained likewise unaltered; I vividly recall hearing the flirty come-ons and moans behind the teasing streaks when channel surfing past the Playboy channel during late-night babysitting gigs. Macrovision continues to block analog output from a DVD player to a VCR, but for digital output, Content Scrambling System (CSS) is an equivalent, common form of digital rights management (DRM). CSS does not merely make a signal difficult to decipher; it disables usage completely unless the disc and the player have authorized encoding to unlock the information. Even these temporary protections are partial, as anything that can be encrypted can also be hacked by covert code experts.[71]

DRM also supports the market strategy of accelerated technological obsolescence by functionally discouraging users from reformatting texts when they upgrade from one technology to another. Consumers are supposed to repurchase the same content again and again as new formats appear—just as happened to music lovers who bought redundant CDs of albums in their vinyl and cassette collections, or is currently occurring with movie fans who purchase HD-DVDs to replace the DVDs that replaced their off-air recordings from HBO. Industry officials reportedly do not expect DRM to prevent piracy but rather to circumscribe individuals' uses and discourage their attempts to make unauthorized uses.[72] The contradiction is blatant: encryption technology punishes everyday customers, not pirates. And in the process, it inhibits legal uses and activities that were formerly enabled by analog technologies.

If the DMCA policies seem overreaching, the penalties are even worse. The punishments for digital copyright crimes—essentially property theft—are way out of whack with material property theft crimes. As Lessig points out, if each illegal download is punishable by up to $150,000, someone who downloads a ten-track album could be liable on ten counts for up to $1,500,000. Someone else who shoplifts the same album in physical form from a record store will only face a maximum $1,000 penalty.[73] This wild discrepancy between penalties assumes future potential actions—making downloads accessible for mass access to others—rather than proven past ones. In its infamous lawsuits against music downloaders, the Recording Industry Association of America (RIAA) has sought the maximum damages and then subsequently settled for each defendant's life savings. These policies and penalties demonstrate how far the law has strayed from the public interest and private uses as outlined in the Constitution and defined in the Supreme Court's Betamax decision.

In all fairness, Congress was clearly aware that the DMCA might go too far in its restrictions and instituted Section 1201, a legislated checks-and-balances mechanism. Section 1201 directs the Librarian of Congress, in consultation with the Register of Copyrights, to evaluate whether protections for encryption technology counter fair use and free speech and to introduce specific temporary exemptions to the copyright act every three years. Although designed as a safety valve, Section 1201 has been criticized for actually eroding fair use, bypassing judicial intervention, and moving policy decisions from the legislature to civil servants.[74] In November 2006 the copyright office introduced its first ever exemption to the DMCA for hacking DVDs, as authorized by the code's Section 1201. The DVD exemption provides a three-year permit for film and media professors to create clips from DVDs for use in classroom instruction.[75] Although this marked a major victory against restricted legal and technological locks for a specific class of users and uses, it stops well short of protecting all potential academic and educational uses, much less the innumerable other noninfringing uses of DVD content.

Despite narrow, temporary exemptions allowed via Section 1201, the DMCA challenges preservation of digital media content after the technology becomes obsolete if specialists cannot hack the code or casing to save and reformat a work on another platform. Digital controls have the potential to lock up content, effectively censoring future historiography. This crisis for preservation has prompted inquiries into creating digital-specific amendments to the Section 108 exemptions for libraries and archives. In spring 2006, the Section 108 Study Group suggested that digital media and technologies are "inherently unstable" and thus necessitate preemptive copying and digital rights management circumvention in order to be reformatted and preserved.[76]

When media are in transition, copyright becomes a weapon of the coup. This often happens in moments of upheaval, when producers and owners attempt to maintain their prior control and claim new market rewards for old media content. Just as analog technologies established many of the marketing and consumption patterns for subsequent digital ones, so too digital regulation revises prior codes rather than wholly inventing them—but there are fundamental incompatibilities between the two, which the law maintains as contradictions rather than attempting to patch up and adapt like an RF modulator (the black box that converts digital signals into analog ones, thus allowing DVD players to be hooked up to older TVs).

By governing the hardware as well as the software—and in asserting preemptive rather than reactive policies—copyright law has imposed increasingly restrictive rules for technology, access, and use. The DMCA was not a single, epistemic shift in copyright law, but it was one of the most extensive revisions since 1976 and is symptomatic of policy protecting corporate manufacturers' and content producers' property claims rather than the potential public good of promoting more liberated practices. A risk arises that if encryption technologies and licensing agreements control access and ownership in addition to reproduction, then there may not be any tangible content left to be collected or preserved. An exception granted to libraries and archives allowing them to make access or preservation copies of their materials offers a small remedy, but it still leaves the public record in the hands of the few, and popular cultural memory may be vulnerable to erasure.

Peer-to-Peer Lawsuits

Despite the extensive DMCA legislation and the considerable debate it has generated, analog media policy and interpretation have remained central to responses to online peer-to-peer file-sharing networks, such as Napster, Grokster, Kazaa, Limewire, and BitTorrent. The Betamax decision not only set a major precedent for analog technology and the interpretation of fair use but has also continued to provide the standard rhetoric for debates on how digital media can (and should) be regulated. Among the pundits, legal scholars, friends of the court, legal defense teams, and judges who have taken positions on the various litigation against P2PS, the Supreme Court ruling in the Betamax case has been the standard legal precedent. Yet in the digital era, the analog fair-use precedent was no longer deemed viable; rather, the question came down to corporate liability and noninfringing potential.

The music industry has suggested a direct, inverse relationship between music downloaded and record sales; this logic suggests that if someone downloads a song, he will not pay for it, but presumes that he *would have* paid for it if he hadn't downloaded it. The first part of such a claim—that users won't pay for songs they already possess—is probably true more often than not. The second part, however, remains dubious, as downloading has become a way to preview unknown artists or rehear old favorites in fits of nostalgia, instances wherein users probably would not have bought a complete CD. The alleged loss of revenue distinguishes the argument against P2PS from the prior case against VCR timeshifting (though there was the threat of indirect revenue loss due to reduced TV advertising). Television broadcasts are given to the public for "free" rather than "stolen." (Again, this conflates free use with fair use. Never mind broadcast networks' commercial revenues or that such a rationale does not easily apply to cable or satellite services.) The economic argument against VCRS was more preemptive than actual; the record companies, in contrast, were facing a changing market and a downturn in sales. Of course, there's a compelling argument that downloaders were the industry's best customers; those most active in downloading were also the most likely to buy records.[77] In addition, downloading calls for rethinking the music industry's business model; free downloads can effectively promote lucrative live performances and merchandise.

But even more than financial, the primary distinction between analog timeshifting and digital network file sharing is one of scale and infrastructure. Whereas the process of multiple-generation reproduction and redistribution was relatively uncommon among VCR users, it is the foundational structure of digital file-sharing systems. File-sharing networks can be sustained only through the premise and practice of redistribution; these systems work only if, once a file is downloaded from one user, it will be made available to be downloaded by subsequent seekers. The more a file is downloaded, the more prominently it will come back with hits from searches, and the more quickly it can be downloaded as a composite file from multiple sources. With VCRs, access is a matter of reception; with downloads, access is a matter of redistribution. As long as home taping was kept private—neither traceable nor publicly competing on the market—bootleggers were essentially safe from legal action; privacy insulates bootleggers from getting caught. Internet technology, however, enables tracking of licit and illicit copies.

The structure of reproduction and sharing was the key to legal determinations in lawsuits against the P2Ps. Two primary models of P2P networks have emerged: centralized and disseminated. Napster operated a central server that indexed its users and facilitated the flow of content between them; thus it oversaw and to some extent could have regulated the files being exchanged. In the case that shut down Napster's early operating model, the U.S. Court of Appeals for the Ninth Circuit ruled that the major distinction between Napster and Sony's Betamax was in the P2P company's capacity for continued monitoring and prevention of copyright infringement. Whereas Sony had no control over the uses of a VCR once it was sold and taken home, Napster had contact with users and could have blocked infringers and infringing material. Napster, however, chose not to do so. Grokster, in contrast, operated on a decentralized and significantly less controllable model: software was dispersed so that individual users could search each other's computers directly via a network without a central server. (Like the more famous Kazaa, Grokster operated through a FastTrack protocol.) Grokster thus had far less control over its users, although it was seen, like Napster, to operate primarily in the interest of facilitating mass copyright infringement—and, lest it be forgotten, it was a business with income from user-targeted advertising.

In the lawsuits against Sony, Napster, and Grokster, the litigation focused on questions of a technology creator's liability for its users' practices.[78] These cases were not (for all practical purposes) directed at users themselves but aimed at the companies that enabled users, yet by targeting and disabling portals, the lawsuits potentially disabled user-end practices. In both the Napster and Grokster cases, the defendants' downfalls in part came from their ability to intervene and protect against copyright infringement. One legal scholar observed that "while not all of [the] briefs asserted the lawfulness of Napster's particular operation of peer-to-peer file sharing technology, all concurred that peer-to-peer file sharing technology offers a valuable means of communication whose dissemination should not be jeopardized by copyright infringement."[79]

Also at stake was the *Sony v. Universal* ruling's assertion that a technology with the capacity for substantial noninfringing uses must be permitted; this factor was the P2PS' best chance for protection. While recognizing the potential for noninfringing uses of P2P networks, the Supreme Court ruled that this was a misapplication of precedent on the question of liability: Sony was not liable because its only contact with users was at the point of sale without further inducement to violate copyright laws, and the dominant practice (timeshifting) was decided to be fair use; in contrast, Grokster was in recurring contact with its users and induced them toward blatant copyright infringement. (The Court did acknowledge, however, that P2P networks have given "users the opportunity to download the briefs in this very case" as an example of a productive nonprofit use.)[80] The opinion concludes by upholding the prior Betamax opinion while simultaneously ruling against the P2P network. The relevance of the prior opinion's assertion that the Betamax "need merely be capable of substantial noninfringing uses" to be permitted on the marketplace was clearly the point of contest and interpretation in decisions on Grokster and even between the Supreme Court justices. In a surprise but short-lived victory, an appeals court favored Grokster over the music labels; thus, for a moment, it seemed that a peer-to-peer would be protected—shielded in part because of the Betamax precedent. However, that decision was unanimously overturned by the Supreme Court; yet six of the justices signed one of two "concurring" opinions that debated the relevance of the Betamax ruling in the wake of Grokster and similar technologies and software.[81]

The Court's literalist opinions for Grokster resemble the Betamax dissent rather than the more progressive majority. In a concurring opinion, Justice Ruth Bader Ginsburg dismisses the argument that Grokster has demonstrated such capacity. "Here, there has been no finding of any fair use and little beyond anecdotal evidence of noninfringing uses."[82] In his concurring opinion, Justice Stephen Breyer challenges this position by listing examples of shared public-domain films, research, authorized music files, photos, and open-source software and asserts that the ratio of noninfringing Grokster downloads (10 percent) slightly exceeds the ratio of authorized uses of VCRs (9 percent) asserted in the Betamax case.[83] Breyer's opinion would thus seem to validate Grokster's position by suggesting parallels between the two cases. Instead his opinion builds to commend the Betamax decision's foresight and soundness while concurring with the ruling against Grokster.[84] Breyer suggests that the Betamax ruling protects technological development by limiting liability for manufacturers and developers, though only for what might be called "neutral" reproductive technologies: "*Sony*'s rule shelters VCRs, typewriters, tape recorders, photocopiers, computers, cassette players, compact disc burners, digital video recorders, MP3 players, Internet search engines, and peer-to-peer software. But *Sony*'s rule does not shelter descramblers, even if one could *theoretically* use a descrambler in a noninfringing way."[85] Breyer argues that legal precedent protects P2P networks, like other reproductive technologies—at least in the abstract. Breyer opposes decryption technologies, however—presumably in deference to the DMCA, which is never explicitly referenced. But Breyer never explains the legal logic or basis of this distinction; nor does the opinion clearly articulate the relationship between Grokster and "a descrambler" that would distinguish it from "sheltered" P2P software.

Neither the *Opinion of the Court* nor the appended concurring opinions explicitly reference the DMCA as informing or effectively altering considerations of fair use or contributory infringement. Considering the distinctions the DMCA makes between digital and analog media—and the ire that the DMCA has provoked among public-domain and fair-use advocates—the absence of any sustained inquiry into Grokster's essentially digital processes is surprising. The Supreme Court does not question the analog-digital distinction nor, apparently, consider it relevant in this case. Despite much activism against the DMCA, it appears to have had little bearing on the Grokster ruling. Or, perhaps more likely, the Court was reluctant to set a DMCA-specific precedent here. (And, Lessig has pointed out, the ruling was also in some ways pointless because the availability of Grokster's open code made the programming and know-how readily available for copycat networks to be constructed and even improved to replace the specific network disabled by the decision.)[86]

Rather, the Court used the Grokster decision as a means—even an opportunity—to reassess its own Betamax ruling rather than to test the DMCA. The justices contrasted *Grokster* with *Sony*, ultimately affirming the prior decision's continued authority. Thus the court's decision on online file-sharing systems seems to mimic the contradiction of the DMCA's claims not to alter the preexisting fair-use provision. This testifies that both Congress and the courts recognize the value of fair use in the analog world—and shows their inability to reimagine how to maintain it in the digital one.

Although digital copyright policies may be interpreted as consistent with previous congressional practices of revising copyright law to protect business interests in emerging technologies, these regulations of the mid- to late 1990s have instituted comparatively extreme restrictions on consumer access and uses. If anything, the acceleration of market adoption and technological obsolescence in the digital media era should inspire *reduced* copyright terms rather than longer ones for copyright to serve public interests in access. Yet even though policies may have become more oppressive in terms of users' legal entitlements, a countertrend among users themselves has pushed back through demonstrated practices of sharing texts and, at times, willfully transgressing the law.[87]

Transitioning

Videotape and fair use have been useful tools to expand what was thought legally permissible. Timeshifting shifted from a questionable exception to the copyright rule to a standard practice in the public interest. Digital technologies, regulations, and rulings thus far have counteracted permissive analog policies. I do not intend to suggest that the DMCA has effectively prevented many of the productive uses of digital media. Users continue to download songs and videos and to hack and burn DVDs. At times, such practices are conducted in full recognition that such actions are illegal; users may be motivated either by beliefs that the content industries make too much money anyway or by presumptions that the chances of getting caught, targeted, and sued are extremely low. In other cases, users may not realize that they are committing crimes by doing things that would be comparable to fair uses of analog media.

As Litman has suggested, people don't abide by laws they don't respect—or understand.[88] The DMCA, by everyday evidence, seems to be such a law. It's remarkably easy to hack some forms of DRM, for instance, by downloading Mac the Ripper to unlock DVDs for duplication on a computer. Some people have advocated for private copying as a form of civil disobedience to counter a copyright code that excessively rewards copyright holders of the most commercially successful works.[89] Whereas it might seem that, by justifying bootleg videotape practices, I toe this line as well, I am actually advocating learning from and sustaining (legal) fair-use practices more than I am endorsing (illegal) civil disobedience. Copyright gray areas and fretting about potential litigation do much to inhibit preservation, redistribution, and scholarship, so that many more productive uses would be made of media if users felt less at risk of taking a legal hit. Flouting a practice's illegality, conversely, may work against its adoption as a common practice or its acceptance as a practice that should be legalized. Both strategies must be employed, even overlap, though I suspect it is more efficacious to speak in terms of fair use than civil disobedience.

The examples of bootlegging analyzed in the case studies that follow raise issues of preservation, access, audience participation, creative endeavor, perception, affect, identity, and community. Collectively these case studies argue that fair uses of analog videotape recording have functioned to document our history, to distribute rare works, and to personalize texts; such innovative uses and aesthetics are currently threatened by digital media technologies and regulations.

Part II. **Case Studies**

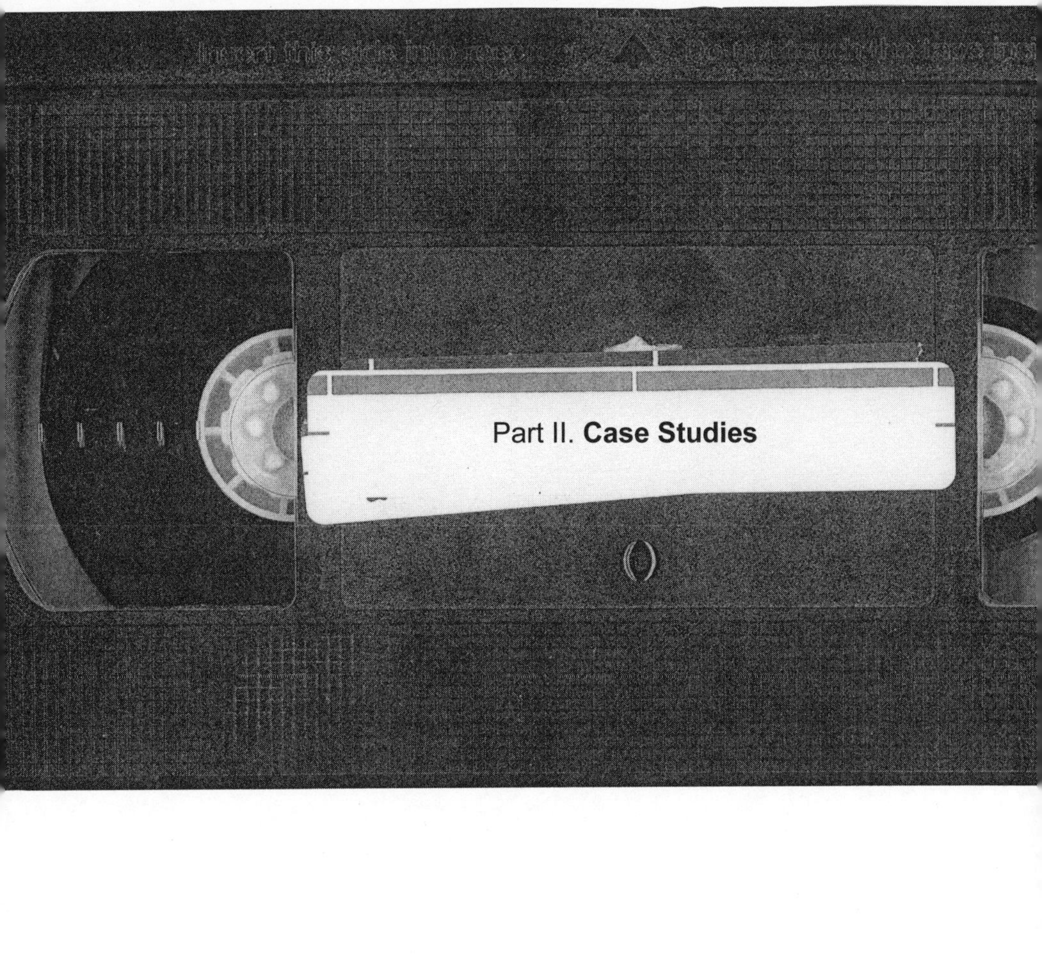

3. The Revolution Was Recorded: Vanderbilt Television News Archive, Copyright in Conflict, and the Making of TV History

Imagine a historical blackout. Not ancient history, but recent history. Maybe you want to examine Cold War political discourses. Maybe you want a tape of what happened in the world the year you were born. Or maybe you seek television coverage of the radical uprisings around the world in early 1968, such as the Prague Spring, the Columbia University student sit-ins, or the May protests in France. You might think that it would be easy enough to track down a copy of network television news reports on these topics, which were broadcast by major corporations to millions of homes across the United States. But you would be wrong. No comprehensive collection exists for complete network news programs that were broadcast before late 1968. And none of the extant fragments of news coverage before that date that are housed in network archives are readily accessible to the public.

One of the lesser-known revolutions of 1968 has had one of the longest legacies. In August, an independent project in Nashville began recording the three major U.S. television networks' nightly news broadcasts from the local affiliates. Begun as a private citizen's intervention to record a period of cultural and political conflicts, this endeavor soon became institutionalized as the Vanderbilt Television News Archive (VTNA), which continues to record, collect, index, and make available national news broadcasts. The programs are recorded as aired, complete with commercials and promos, rather than collected or licensed directly from the networks. Researchers who use the VTNA can view news programs on-site in Nashville or can request to have copies of selected programs, segments, or even commercials compiled and mailed to them. The archive offers an exemplary model for institutional, systematic video recording to provide access to media history—a model that incurred litigation from CBS and helped reshape U.S. copyright law.[1]

CBS sued the archive for copyright infringement in 1973, alleging that the archive reedited and leased its broadcasts to users. The archive's primary defense was to argue its role in serving the public good: that by providing users access to information, it was performing a service protected by the First Amendment. Secondarily, it claimed that the copyright law, dating back to 1909 and long in the works for revision, did not protect live broadcasts such as TV news programs. The suit dragged on for three years, as the stakes were considered monumental and the law was ambiguous at best. Meanwhile Congress, inspired by the VTNA's efforts and public debates over news bias, eventually developed a two-pronged approach to protecting TV news preservation, both of which were ultimately amended to the new copyright act: a new exemption for libraries and archives to record broadcast news programs off-air and the creation of a new national American Television and Radio Archive. ("Off-air" taping is the term for recording broadcasts during live transmission, not to be confused with recordings of programs that are no longer on the air.) These two provisions eventually passed along with the new comprehensive copyright act in 1976, and the legal battle between the Vanderbilt archive and the network was thus settled. Copyright became the means of both challenging and ultimately ensuring public access to television records. The VTNA has become a major historical resource, not only for finding out "the way it was," to modify the CBS news anchor Walter Cronkite's nightly farewell, but also the way it was told.

Whereas the previous two chapters laid the groundwork for discussing the specificity of videotape and the ways that copyright has defined its permissible uses, this chapter presents the first of three historical case studies where these issues intersect. Here I examine the practices, discourses, and institutionalization of network news study and preservation, as well as how these issues were challenged and mandated specifically in relationship to copyright law. Following introductions to the founding of the VTNA and the political attention to network news, I offer parallel legal histories: first, the congressional processes of amending the U.S. copyright code and creating a national collection of television programming, and second, the copyright litigation brought by CBS against the VTNA. Spurred by these two events, debates about the politics of network news broadcasts and strategies to access such programming pervaded in many sites of power and cultural negotiation, such as archives, networks, Congress, the Library of Congress, lawyers' offices, courtrooms, the press, and the White House.

Establishing the Vanderbilt Television News Archive

The VTNA was central to a multifaceted rise of analytical and archival impulses in making television—and television news in particular—an object of study between the late 1960s and mid-1970s. The so-called crisis of democracy of the late 1960s in turn sparked recognition of a crisis of access: access to ephemeral coverage of the "television war" overseas and shifting social mores domestically. Within the VTNA's first few years, politicians and press commentators claimed a liberal bias in the news media, Congress held hearings to investigate television news editing practices, published studies attempted to systematically analyze the political slant of the news, surveys attempted to assess the influence of the news on public opinion, CBS sued the VTNA for copyright infringement, and Congress intervened not only to protect the archive but also to mandate the creation of a national TV repository.[2] Simultaneously, media studies emerged as an academic field of study, and by the mid- to late 1970s, various TV archives opened to establish television collections and give access to programs now deemed to have historical significance. Videotape enabled such punditry, research, and preservation, but the developing technologies outpaced copyright regulations and thus raised issues not only of politics but also of policy.

Paul Simpson founded the VTNA after he toured the three network news departments in March 1968. He did not originally have an archive in mind; he had visited the networks to see how the news programs were produced in order to understand if and how a liberal bias infiltrated reporting. A conservative insurance salesman, he thought that the New York–based news producers were out of sync with much of the rest of the United States—they probably were—and that such national news coverage reflected the liberal urban attitudes endemic to the coastal metropolis.[3] During his visit, he learned that video recordings of complete broadcasts were kept for only two weeks before the tapes were erased and reused, meaning that in most cases the programs were lost.[4] For Simpson, this was a devastating democratic and historical loss. How could media analysts and historians—not to mention interested citizens—understand or participate in American politics if they couldn't look back at what had happened and how it was reported? As Simpson would often argue, he believed that television news should be available to researchers just as old newspapers are available on microfilm at libraries. (Though, like microfilm, early video recordings of news broadcasts exhibit the aesthetics of access; they suffer from murky black-and-white

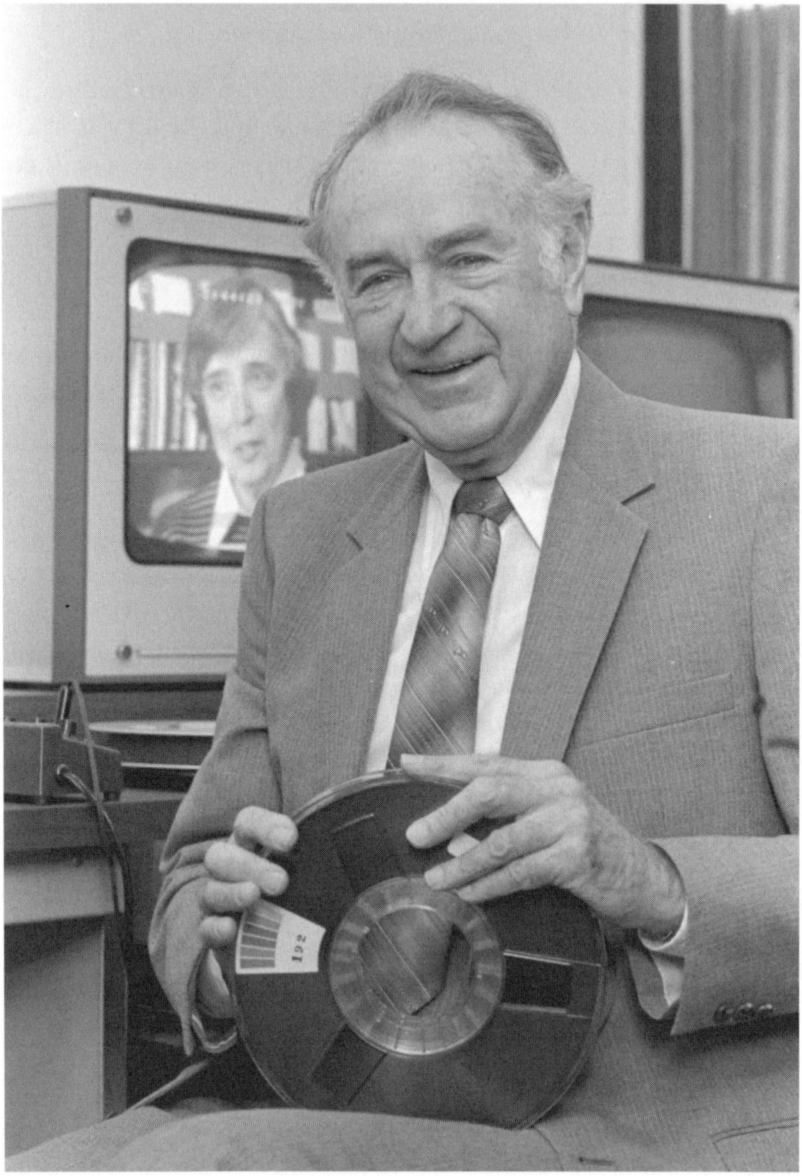

16. Paul Simpson, founder of the Vanderbilt Television News Archive. Photo courtesy of Vanderbilt University Special Collections and University Archives.

reproduction that mucks up the original's resolution and may prematurely make the text seem dated.)[5]

Simpson began planning a TV news–taping project to remedy the three networks' failure to save and provide access to their broadcasts. Before the VTNA, the only systematic off-air television news recording project was being conducted by the Department of Defense, which had been monitoring coverage of military efforts in Vietnam and sending compilation recordings to officials abroad since 1965.[6] Although CBS News maintained its own archive of transcripts and film elements from its documentaries and new reports, these were not readily accessible to researchers unaffiliated with the network. Nor did they maintain complete copies of what was actually broadcast, so that footage of Walter Cronkite reading news reports or introducing prefilmed segments was lost. News skeptics were especially concerned that transcripts of the news, such as those kept by CBS, would not communicate nonverbal forms of bias, such as intonations, expressions, or innuendoes.[7]

Simpson's news recording project in Nashville was originally intended to be a test of feasibility, and he hoped that the Library of Congress would quickly take on its own broadcast recording operations for national access and safekeeping. In March 1969, Simpson met with senators Howard Baker (Republican) and Albert Gore (Democrat) and representatives William Brock (R) and Richard Fulton (D), all from Tennessee, who in turn wrote a joint letter to Librarian of Congress L. Quincy Mumford advocating a study for a public news collection project. The study was approved, and library staff visited the VTNA in June. Mumford also wrote to the network presidents to discuss collaboratively establishing a news archive. ABC demonstrated interest, NBC showed slight interest without follow-up, and CBS did not respond.[8] Although the Library of Congress staff agreed that a TV news archive was a desirable endeavor, the project was not considered feasible, as it would require far more monetary, equipment, space, and staff resources than were available. The networks were clearly resistant to making deposits of video copies of their news programming or to loaning tapes for the library to duplicate. Thus the library would have to record programs off-air the way Simpson's project had been doing, but Library of Congress studies also determined that a considerably more costly video system would be required for producing archival-quality recordings.[9] And so by default Vanderbilt University, the temporary test site, became the long-term home for the nation's television news recording and archiving project.

Simpson's pilot operation had to explore and invent off-air taping and video preservation procedures as the project developed. The archive began as an amateur collection—a stockpiling of news broadcasts initiated by a politically passionate man. Simpson collaborated with Ampex, a major videotape developer and manufacturer, to establish the project with the best and most suitable technology available. He met with a local vendor and flew to Ampex offices to work out the technical logistics. Ampex recommended one-inch, black-and-white reel-to-reel equipment, which the project adopted. The technology was still largely experimental, and the endeavor was hugely expensive without institutional endowment. During its history, the archive has used three recording formats. From 1968 to 1979, it used 1-inch, type-A black-and-white Ampex magnetic videotape with a 1/2-inch reel-to-reel EIAJ backup recording system (which produced significantly fuzzier tapes). Access copies could be made on 3/4-inch U-matic, although it was not yet the primary recording format. In May 1979, the VTNA adopted 3/4-inch cassette color video as its master format, and VHS was introduced as the backup format. In May 2003, the VTNA migrated to the digital MPEG 2 format for its master nightly recordings, as well as for a recent digital preservation project.

Significantly, tapes of the VTNA's early recordings *look* dated, both in terms of the plain news desk sets and minimal onscreen graphics and in terms of the video texture. The aesthetics of broadcast television, mixed with analog tape recordings in black-and-white or faded color, age these programs in a way that gives them nostalgic charm and credence as historical documents. Since the early 1970s, the VTNA's nightly recordings have been encoded with information about the network, date, and time at the top of the frame; this facilitates indexing and filling user requests and acts as precise carbon dating for later scholars. But it also marks the Vanderbilt archive as the source when footage has been repurposed in documentaries, such as *Far from Poland* (Jill Godmilow, 1984) and *Roger & Me* (Michael Moore, 1989). A guidebook for news archives suggested such stamping, along with reusing degraded VHS tapes, among strategies to discourage users from making unauthorized copies: "Burn in a time code and transfer the image to VHS tape. . . . As poor a quality VHS copy as is possible should be sent. The quality of VHS tape usually is too poor for use in productions."[10] As I suggest with bootleg aesthetics in the next chapter and with the network logo watermarks that resurface on YouTube in the epilogue, video reproductions document such artifacts and source information along with the texts and, in effect, record their histories of circulation. Analog reproduction, rather than replicating or compressing information bit by bit, effectively layers the news documents.

The VTNA has undertaken two comprehensive reformatting preservation projects, the first analog and the second digital. The first was a long-term effort to transfer the original 1-inch open-reel tapes to 3/4-inch cassettes, which took more than a decade from 1979 to the early 1990s. By comparison, digitizing the collection from 1968 to the present decade took less than two years; the archive's back collection of recordings is now stored on servers and burned to backup DVD-RS. News recordings are also shipped in bulk on hard drives for the collection of the Library of Congress. Another, short-term preservation project for recordings from 1974 to 1975 demonstrates that seemingly everything about the VTNA has some tie to U.S. policy in the 1970s: "Videotape is a petroleum-based product and, unfortunately, some manufacturers were skimping on the brew during the oil embargo during the 1970s; consequently, the tapes of the 1974 and 1975 newscasts were falling apart."[11]

When I first met with Vanderbilt University's library technology officer Marshall Breeding to discuss the archive's preservation project, he stated that MPEG-2 DVD was not an ideal format for preservation copies of most moving-image works but that they were suitable for the archive's purposes because the source material—taped off-air on magnetic video—did not have pristine images or sound in the first place. This may indicate a departure from the archive's foundational belief that seeing and hearing the broadcasts were necessary to understanding the subtleties of expression, intonation, and innuendo that biased news reporting, although it is consistent with broader cultural denial of analog formats' distinct looks and feels—as well as how television news is frequently used as an information source without consideration of aesthetic form. For the digital preservation project, the informational content has been prioritized over fidelity to analog broadcast and tape aesthetics. When I visited the archive for research, the staff said that the current digital recordings look better than prior analog ones, and that even the reformatted preserved copies look superior to the originals because of the time-based corrections—though even the digital versions are not perfect, since the source tapes were already marked by some decay. The archive staff also pointed out that the "entire" image is now visible on the computer screens, whereas cathode-ray-tube monitors crop the image. (Of course, the original broadcasts were viewed on cathode-ray tubes, meaning that the whole image was visible before and the decropped images now show excess information.) During this period of digital reformatting and digital off-air recording for master video sources, VHS initially remained the access format, seemingly to prevent extensive user-end digital duplication; as of this writing, users can currently request news compilations on tape or DVD. Although the archive is capable of streaming digital files to users at subscription universities, all the networks except CNN have indicated that they would consider such distribution copyright infringing.

Making the VTNA Collection Useful

Back in 1971, the news recording project at Vanderbilt made a major organizational leap forward when James Pilkington came on board as its administrator. (He served as the VTNA's administrator until the late 1980s.) With Pilkington and an expanding staff, the operations of the VTNA became more systematic and could be broken down into three primary activities: recording, indexing, and compiling user-requested tapes. These remain the basic functions of the archive, with the addition of periodic preservation and reformatting efforts. From Pilkington's perspective, abstracting and indexing the recordings were essential to the long-term usability of the collection. Indexes and abstracts facilitated finding specific news reports, for both the staff and users. Print abstracts began periodic publication in January 1971, and the format was revised as the monthly *Television News Index and Abstracts* in January 1972. These publications were distributed free of charge to a mailing list of networks, libraries, and interested parties; in 1994 print publication ceased, and these resources have since been launched to the Internet.

Using the indexes and abstracts, researchers can identify and request specific news segments that they want to see from among the thousands of recordings in the VTNA collection. The archive then compiles tapes of specific user-requested segments from different broadcasts and different networks. The staff does not select the segments for compilations themselves but instead insists that users make their own choices; this insulates the archive from any charges of misrepresenting network news coverage. Further facilitating uses of the collection, the archive ships these compiled tapes directly to users for research at their convenience rather than demanding on-site viewing in Nashville. (These compilation tapes are sent on loan, like library books, and must be returned; users are not supposed to make and keep personal dubs of these research compilations, though surely in some cases they do.) The most requested portions of the collection are recent events and Vietnam War–era recordings, which suggests that the early period's politics remain central to the archive's vitality. Massive special col-

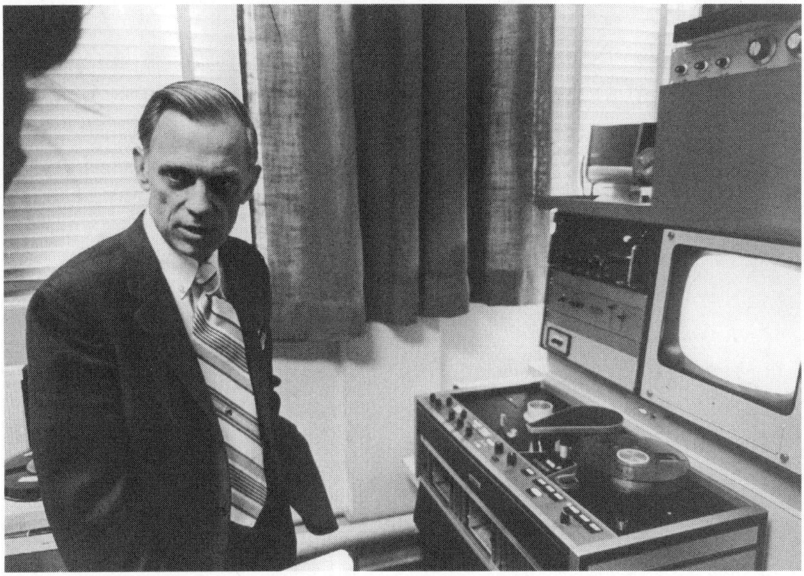

17. James Pilkington, VTNA administrator. Photo courtesy of Vanderbilt University Special Collections and University Archives.

lections, such as the Watergate hearings, are underused, however, because owing to limited resources they have never been comprehensively indexed and abstracted.[12]

Simpson conceived his archive to be accessible to users of all political stripes, and its systematic process of recording all nightly news broadcasts without staff interference or intentional omissions has imposed a structure that does not manipulate the news programs. The enterprise could be read as an embodiment of Cold War political and corporate liberalism—a nonpartisan recognition of the benefits of social welfare and civil rights.[13] In spite of the political context in which it was created and the uses that have been made of the collection, the VTNA's recordings are just recordings. Making meaning or writing histories or finding political biases requires that researchers make selections and interpret them independently of the technologies. Building on my claim about the relationship between audiences and videotape, these recordings necessitate that television viewers become television *users*. And although the VTNA may be operationally neutral, it is not without ideology—the ideology that information and historical documentation should serve the public interest by being accessible. This is the same ideology that served as the basis for U.S. copyright laws and the exemption to copyright for off-air videotaping.

Today the VTNA's collection includes the following materials:

ABC *World News Tonight*, August 5, 1968–present
CBS *Evening News*, August 5, 1968–present
NBC *Nightly News*, August 5, 1968–present
ABC *Nightline*, September 12, 1988–present
CNN *WorldView*, October 2, 1995–November 3, 2000
CNN *Wolf Blitzer Reports*, February 1, 2001–December 31, 2001
CNN *NewsNight*, November 5, 2001–October 28, 2005
Anderson Cooper 360, November 1, 2005–present
Fox News reports, February 15, 2004–present
Coverage of Democratic and Republican National Conventions, elections, State of the Union addresses, Watergate hearings, American hostages in Iran, Persian Gulf War, September 11 attacks and aftermath, and the Iraq war, as well as selected news specials dating back to 1968.

Suggesting the project's attention to public affairs, Simpson chose to begin taping on August 5, 1968, with the nightly news reports and coverage of the Republican National Convention. His initial plan was to record the news programs and major presidential campaign events through the end of the election. The news was Simpson's passion. The VTNA was his legacy.

The Politics of the News

The Vanderbilt Television News Archive was formed at one of the most culturally and politically tumultuous periods in American history. And perhaps more than at any time since, network news appeared to take a central role in public life. A purported liberal media bias became one of the hot topics and political platforms of the Nixon era. Within a year of Richard Nixon's and Vice President Spiro T. Agnew's election, the Republicans in power began a long and vitriolic campaign of lambasting the media for what they considered unfavorable reporting. At times these attacks would take the form of public addresses and, at others, private harassment or congressional investigations. Network television news was *the* national news source during the Vietnam War period; television not only "brought the war home" but also became a battleground of its own as war coverage brought television news under scrutiny. CBS and other prominent news organizations, such as the *New York Times* and the *Washington Post*, were the targets of recurring

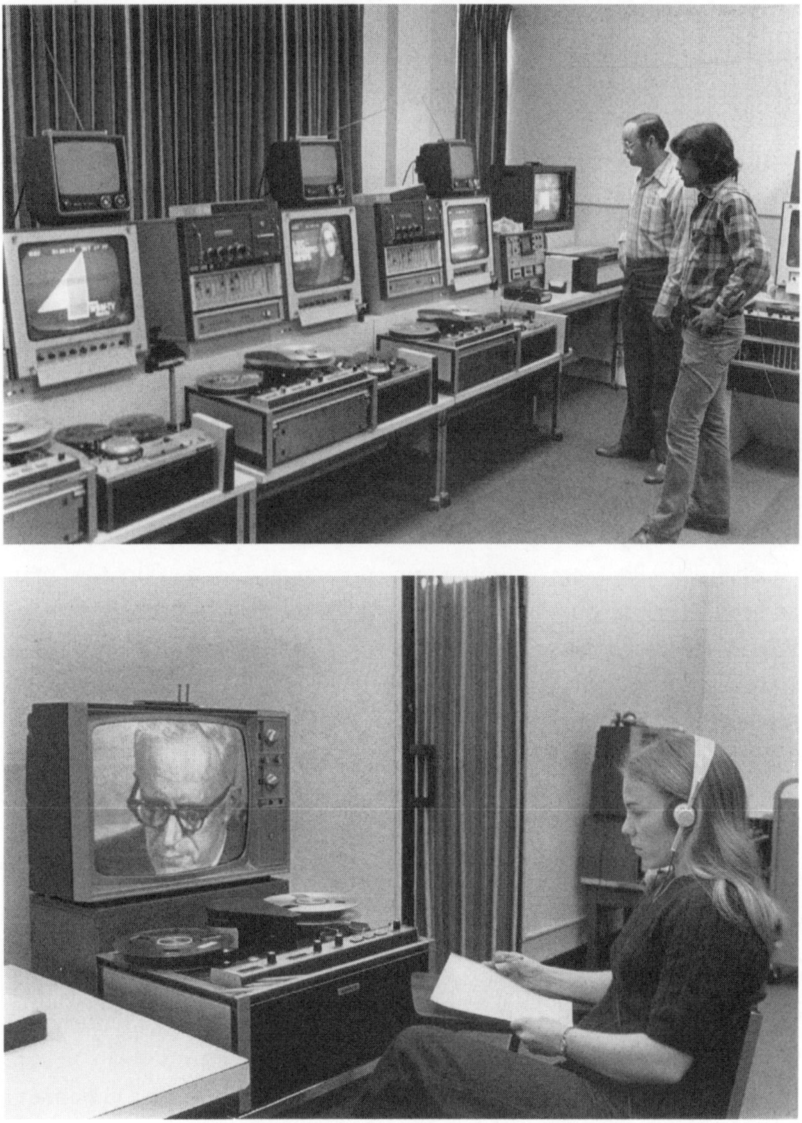

18a–b. Video recording and study stations at the VTNA in the early days. Photos courtesy of Vanderbilt University Special Collections and University Archives.

scrutiny from analysts, political groups, and the government for their allegedly distorted reporting. Audiences lauded CBS News anchor Walter Cronkite as "the most trusted man in America," yet some politicians distrusted his potential influence.

Numerous political and academic studies in the 1970s attempted to evaluate the impact of the media on society, and some surveys suggested correlations between television consumption and political dissent. Numerous profiles of news practices and political influence were conducted during this period. On broadcast news production, the former CBS News president Fred Friendly published *Due to Circumstances beyond Our Control* in 1967, and Robert MacNeil published *The People Machine: The Influence of Television on American Politics* in 1968; both books were influential on Simpson. Subsequent independent critiques of the news included William J. Small's *To Kill a Messenger: Television News and the Real World* (1970), D. L. Shaw's and M. E. McCombs's *The Emergence of American Political Issues: The Agenda-Setting Function of the Press* (1971), Edith Efron's prominent *The News Twisters* (1971) and the more vitriolic follow-up *How CBS Tried to Kill a Book* (1972), and Edward Jay Epstein's *News from Nowhere: Television and the News* (1973), which focused on the influence of corporate organizational structure on NBC news in 1968 and 1969.[14] Some of these books referenced or relied on the VTNA as a resource.

During this time CBS was the most watched, most revered, and presumed to be the most influential network news outlet. Conservatives also suggested that its news division was the most liberal and thus the most irresponsible. Three controversial moments—all of which were broadcast by CBS—have become the standard references as the most significant broadcast moments in the debates about media bias during the Nixon era: a speech by Spiro Agnew in the fall of 1969, the CBS Reports documentary *The Selling of the Pentagon* (1971), and the two-part report on Watergate in 1972 by *CBS Evening News*. *The Selling of the Pentagon* was a searing indictment of the Pentagon's taxpayer-funded public relations exhibitions and pro-military propaganda. Written and directed by Peter Davis, who would later make *Hearts and Minds* (1974), the film was so explosive that it prompted harsh and skeptical newspaper editorials, rebroadcasts, and even a congressional investigation to determine if it had manipulated a military spokesman's interview through improper editing. It also won raves and a slew of awards. With the two-part story on the Watergate break-in and investigation, CBS News picked up on the *Washington Post*'s early reporting on Watergate at a time when few other print or broadcast journalists would;

the network's attention helped validate the story by making what had been local news into a national scandal. Airing on Friday, October 27, 1972—eleven days before the presidential election—the first part was fourteen minutes long, consuming an unprecedented two-thirds of the program. Under pressure from Nixon's special counsel and media watchdog Charles Colson and CBS's chairman William S. Paley, the news division delayed the second part by a day and cut it from fourteen to eight minutes.[15] Despite these Watergate reports, Nixon and Agnew easily won reelection.

The VTNA first came to public and political attention for its recordings of coverage of the 1968 Democratic National Convention. The convention, held in Chicago, was famously the site of riots and police violence against protesters. Later the VTNA's tape stock source, Ampex, asked the archive to produce a compilation tape of news coverage of the events for the 1968 International Police Convention in Hawaii. (The connection between Ampex and the IPC is unclear.) Simpson and technician Ron Moulton obliged, eager to test their equipment and tapes to produce their first compilation. (Compilations for general researchers would not become common until a few years later, with the introduction and widespread adoption of the 3/4-inch video formats and eventually VHS.) They chose to use footage only from NBC, which had the highest ratings and most extensive coverage during the convention. While assembling the tape, they realized that the network had shown footage of "the same heavy man in a plaid shirt and a beard being arrested and put in the paddy wagon three times."[16] The footage was shot from three different angles, aired unedited and unpreviewed. Because of a strike by local telephone company employees, television reporters were not able to send live feeds to the networks. Instead film had to be shot and processed, causing a significant time delay and a rush to broadcast footage as quickly as possible. Of the resulting repetitions of coverage, Simpson surmised, "This technique gave a mistaken impression of the nature of the violence during the convention."[17] This, it seemed to him, was evidence of news distortion—produced and later discovered by circumstance. An early report on the off-air taping project that appeared in the industry journal *Broadcasting* a month before the 1968 election pointed to the endeavor's complex political implications. The article presciently stated: "The question posed by this preservation and eventual retrieval of network news is whether it will benefit future historians or prove a noisome index of alleged bias in the way networks report the news. Both aspects have surfaced in an investigation of the recording project."[18]

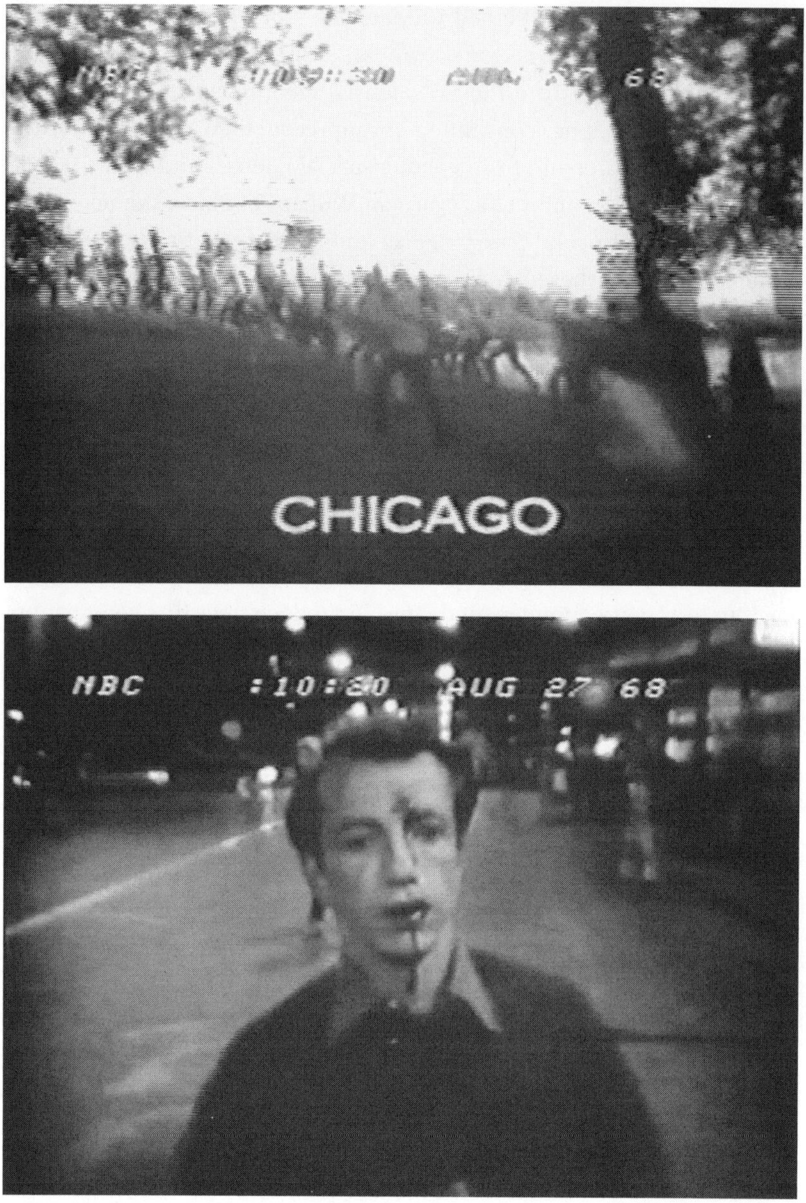

19a–d. NBC coverage of the protests and violence during the 1968 Democratic National Convention. *The Huntley-Brinkley Report*, August 27 and 28, 1968.

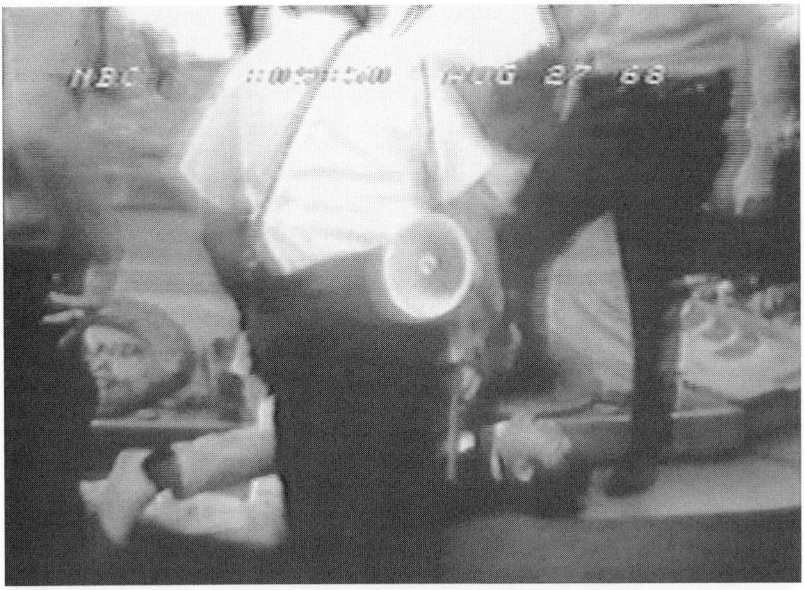
NBC
AUG 27 68

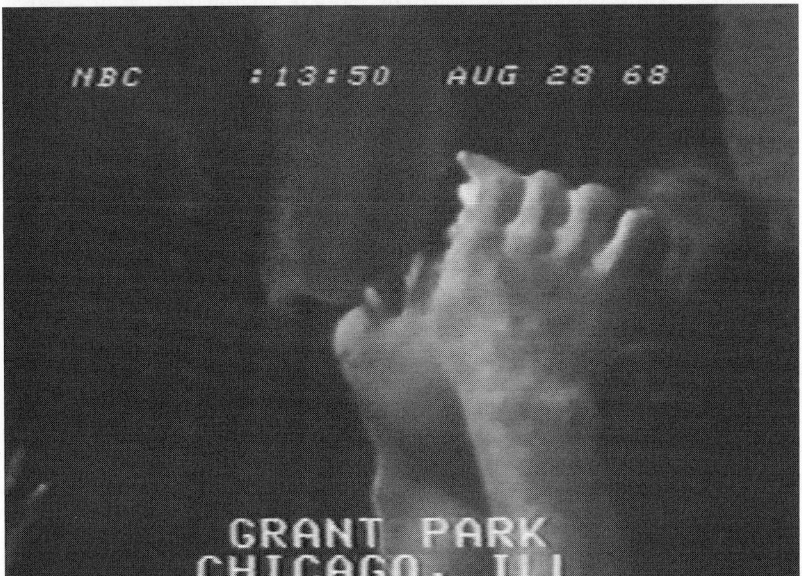
NBC :13:50 AUG 28 68
GRANT PARK
CHICAGO, ILL.

At the request of Senator Baker's assistant, Simpson presented the convention compilation tape at the Executive Office Building adjoining the White House in October 1969. Congressmen Baker, Brock, and Fulton (with whom Simpson had met in the spring to propose the Library of Congress collection), three Nixon administration executive staff members, and a few others attended the screening. But the playback was also patched into a closed-circuit system accessible to offices throughout the building and was apparently viewed by staff members who did not want to be seen at the semipublic screening. Later, the White House speechwriter and adviser Patrick Buchanan, who had watched the presentation on closed circuit, requested that Simpson return to Washington so that Buchanan could review the tape. They viewed the whole tape together, and Buchanan incorporated a reference to the taped convention coverage in a speech that he wrote for Agnew.

On November 13, 1969, Agnew addressed a regional Republican meeting in Des Moines to decry the state of American journalism. This speech indirectly made Simpson's compilation of network reporting into national news. All three networks broadcasted the speech, which also made the next day's front pages of the *New York Times* and the *Washington Post*, both of which also reprinted the speech in full. This was unusual attention for statements by a vice president and marked an important moment in Agnew's rise to prominence as a popular public figure and orator. His speech is consistently referenced as a pivotal moment in histories of network news and profiles of Agnew and marked, as Jules Witcover called it, "the birth of Agnewism."[19] The critique also echoed one of Simpson's primary convictions—that the national news media are concentrated in the liberal enclaves of New York City and Washington, D.C., which do not represent the values of the rest of the country. The Vanderbilt news-taping project, initiated to allow for news analysis, had done its job.[20] And it helped stoke public debates about liberal bias and the Fairness Doctrine (a Federal Communications Commission policy mandating equitable access to radio and television airtime for opposing political viewpoints).

Republicans continued to use the archive's collection to substantiate subsequent bias complaints. In spring 1971, the Republican National Convention called the VTNA to arrange a screening of compiled coverage of the Laos incursion; Senator Bob Dole (R-Kansas), the convention chairman, followed up on the request with a letter. Pilkington and Simpson compiled the CBS and NBC reports aired between February and early March 1971 for a screening at the Senate Office Building. The Republicans announced the event, "sponsored" by Senator Clifford Hansen (R-Wyoming), to both congressional bodies and the media. The Senate screening received prominent coverage in the trade magazine *Variety*, with an all-caps front-page headline, "GOP MARKS TV NEWS LAOS-Y," and a top center story, "Senators Screen Tapes, Scream." Such trade reporting certainly caught CBS and the other networks' eyes. The story's lead states, "An unprecedented screening of news tapes last week led to a new barrage of GOP criticism of network television news coverage—and also underlined a little-noticed program by Vanderbilt University to preserve the evening news shows of ABC, CBS and NBC."[21] The report quotes Senators Hansen, Dole, and Brock attacking the news media's bias and was linked to a separate story on Senator Baker's proposed legislation calling for a national TV news archive (discussed later in this chapter).[22]

The White House had begun monitoring the news even before its congressional colleagues had begun calling on the VTNA as a resource. The Watergate investigation and subsequently released memos revealed the extent to which the Nixon administration had monitored and attempted to intimidate the networks news divisions, especially in the case of CBS. In summer 1969, Nixon's staff produced a four-hundred-page summary of television coverage.[23] If the media portrayed the Vietnam War as a losing battle or the United States as a country in crisis, they feared, such news reports might undermine their power. So the news became the site of anxiety as viewers tuned in for the facts while politicians attempted to manipulate them or cry foul.

It appears that Republicans and the Nixon staff successfully minimized critical coverage on occasion, and it seems plausible that such pressure tactics also generated some network self-censoring tendencies on a more quotidian basis. Such political monkeying with the media was nothing new, of course; it just reached an apex. Nixon had used television to his advantage early in his career through his famous "Checkers speech" during his run for vice president in 1952 and later sabotaged himself when he spoke out against the press by commenting that reporters wouldn't have "Nixon to kick around anymore" after losing the California gubernatorial race in 1962. By the time he became president, Nixon didn't watch television news, and he did not typically intervene personally. Rather, he delegated his staff to write summary reports each day, to bully the networks in private, and to make his complaints public in addresses.[24]

There were multiple subsequently published memos between Nixon's special counsel Colson and the White House chief of staff H. R. Haldeman

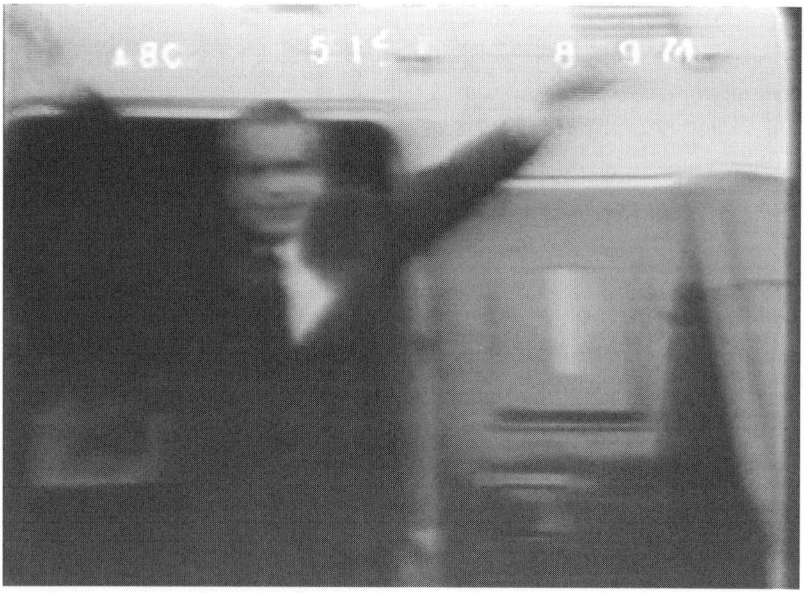

20. VTNA loaner tapes begin with a video promo featuring highlights of news history as recorded by the archive, such as President Reagan with Mikhail Gorbachev, the Tiananmen Square showdown, the fall of the Berlin Wall, and the Oklahoma City bombing. But the first clip in the video timeline, appropriately, is this fuzzy footage of President Nixon.

commenting on the news and their effective intimidation of the networks in 1970 and 1971, for example, "I've had a feeling, watching the news, that CBS is trying hard to do better. I believe that this is because of . . . pressures" and "I don't know what's next, but at the rate they are going they might even start having Cronkite praise the Vice President. I'll bet this is really paining these guys."[25] In a February 1971 memo, Colson boasted, "I have developed a good personal relationship with Paley which has been very helpful to us on a number of occasions."[26] In the following month, Colson met with network and news executives and later composed a memo which stated, "CBS have improved considerably over the past couple of months since my visit with them."[27] For nearly three years after their first private in-person meeting, Colson reportedly called Paley or CBS president Frank Stanton about once a month—more than he called executives from the other networks—to complain about bias.[28]

While the Nixon staff was keeping a watchful eye on network broadcasts, they likewise kept tabs on the start-up news archive in Nashville. Despite prior screenings on Capitol Hill, members of the Nixon staff "discovered" a potential ally down south. In May 1972, Colson sent a memo to White House communications director Ken Clawson suggesting that the administration publicize the VTNA.[29] In this memo, Colson argued that the public's interest (as well as Nixon's) would be served by greater public awareness and use of the VTNA, suggesting a cocksure belief that history would vindicate the president. By innuendo more than intent, the VTNA was often associated with the Nixon administration and conservative members of Congress during this period. These were the archive's most prominent early users, and they were its most powerful political allies.[30] But such connections to the Right have at times led to misperceptions of the archive's equal-access mission.

Of course, not all network news inquiries during this time set out to characterize the networks as lefties, nor were all of the VTNA's users conservative. For instance, during its early years, the archive filled orders for such varied clients and researchers as the documentary and TV historian Erik Barnouw, the *National Enquirer*, the *Columbus Dispatch*, Elizabeth Dole, Phyllis Schlafly, the leftist documentarian Emile de Antonio, the U.S. Army, NBC, the New York State Special Commission on Attica, the Alternative Educational Foundation, the Senate Watergate Committee, Universal Studios, Warner Brothers, Common Cause, the Twentieth Century Fund, and the National Organization for Women.[31] The VTNA was a major resource for private and public interests—left, right, and center—during the rise of attention to television as politically influential and worthy of historical study.

Legislating TV News Preservation

The VTNA not only stimulated political interest in a publicly accessible repository for network news programs but also demonstrated that one was feasible. But questions remained: who would continue the endeavor, and was it even legal? While the executive branch of the government had pursued public and private campaigns against unfavorable news reporting, the legislative branch conducted its own inquiries and potential remedies. Although various hearings were conducted during this period to examine bias allegations under the rubric of the FCC's Fairness Doctrine, ultimately more efficacious measures would be conducted as part of the ongoing copyright revision. The VTNA inspired two initially discrete bills that became components of the comprehensive copyright act, which eventually passed in 1976: a mandate for a national broadcast programming repository and an exemption from infringement liability for libraries and archives to record broadcast content. Thus nearly a decade before fair use (Section 107 of the copyright act) would provide the basis of the Supreme Court's ruling that off-air recordings for private use must be permitted, off-air videotaping directly shaped legislation of the exemptions for libraries and archives (Section 108). Although distinct from Section 107, Section 108 can be seen as the logical, institutional extension of fair use. Like allegations of bias from the White House and the archive itself, this legislation has also been seen as a response to the cultural upheavals and partisan politics of the time.

Senator Baker began introducing statements calling for the formation of a national TV news archive into the Senate after learning of Simpson's off-air recording project in his home state. Baker has generally been credited as the driving force behind legislating a mandate for the Library of Congress to create a television news collection. In December 1969, Baker made a statement on the Senate floor to suggest that the library should make videotape dupes (at the library's expense) of the networks' master tapes of news broadcasts. Baker framed his statements with references to Agnew's pivotal speech on journalistic bias the prior month.[32] Baker's intention—like Paul Simpson's—was for the Library of Congress to take over from Vanderbilt.

The following spring, Baker introduced his first bill in the Senate (S 3720) calling on the library to create a national news broadcast repository.[33] This and subsequent bills mandated the Library of Congress to

> (1) obtain, preserve, and index videotapes or films of—
> (A) nationally televised evening news programs; and
> (B) such other nationally televised programs as the Librarian of Congress determines to be of substantial public interest, including, but not limited to, public affairs programs and other programs dealing with current events;
> (2) produce subject matter tapes or films which shall present a collection of programs or portions of programs obtained under clause (1) of this section, in the order in which such programs or portions were broadcast, dealing with a particular subject during a given period of time, without any alteration or change in such programs or portions of programs; and
> (3) make available for purposes of study or research copies of videotapes of films obtained or produced under this section.

Baker's bill also included specific budgetary allocations for initial investment and annual operations. Demonstrating industry agreement with the proposal, the Radio/Television News Directors Association passed a resolution in September 1970 in support of legislation creating a broadcast news archive at the Library of Congress.[34]

The bill didn't go anywhere, however, so Baker reintroduced similar legislation to the Senate on March 10, 1971 (as S 1169) and again on September 27, 1973 (as S 2497).[35] Baker's bills essentially called for the Library of Congress to replicate the VTNA services, including recording news broadcasts off-air and making user-requested compilation tapes. His statements on the Senate floor to explain these bills regularly made reference to the existing practices at Vanderbilt and contextualized the need for such an archive because of the politics of the era. For example, in his 1971 pitch, he argued, "Because America and the world are in such ferment at the present time, it is essential that future generations be given a reasonably accurate picture of what was going on in the 1960's and 1970's. Such a picture would be impossible without reference to television news coverage."[36] With this second attempt, he also reiterated references to the Agnew charges of bias and more recent complaints made by Nixon about coverage of the Laos operation. A note written by a Library of Congress staff member and attached to a copy of the bill in the library's files suggests enthusiasm for the proposal but skepticism about the tactic: "Unfortunately, they get right into partisan politics, so the whole thing may go out the window."[37]

Although the bill calling for a national news archive—and the VTNA staff's recollection of it—retrospectively seems to be totally identified with Baker, he was not alone in introducing such legislation.[38] There were as many attempts at legislation on the matter in the House as there were in the Senate. In fact, the same day that Baker introduced his first bill, April 15, 1970, Fulton, a fellow Tennessean, introduced a twin proposal (HR 17010) in the House of Representatives.[39] Later, Representative Spark Matsunaga (D-Hawaii) proposed his own bills, which appear to be unrelated to Baker's efforts or the VTNA, first in January 1971 (as HR 35) and again in January 1973 (as HR 2853).[40] Matsunaga's bills also called for a national news repository at the Library of Congress but did not specify services to be provided to users. Although his participation seems to have been minimized in subsequent accounts of the American Television and Radio Archive's creation, Matsunaga's bills may actually more closely resemble the ultimate mandate.[41]

All the bills that had been introduced through 1973 focused on creating an archive at the Library of Congress as a way to relieve Vanderbilt of its taping duties and to make the project a public one. But as none of the measures had managed to pass, and as CBS had initiated copyright infringement litigation against Vanderbilt University, Baker tried a contingency maneuver. While maintaining that a national collection should be created, on August 15, 1974, he introduced separate legislation specifically written to exempt the Vanderbilt project from liability, which he amended to the overall copyright revision bill (Amendment 1803). Baker had consulted with Barbara Ringer, the register of copyrights, and he determined that such an amendment was the best emergency indemnity for the archive.[42] Given that this proposal now came after the Watergate scandal had burst open, he also shifted his political rhetoric from quoting Nixon and Agnew to referencing investigations of them: "Who, for example, could imagine studying the events of the Watergate period without being able to study the network news reports produced during that period[?]"[43] This was one of many instances when the VTNA's taping practices would be linked to post-Watergate demands for access to information, this time by the highest-ranking Republican on the Senate's Watergate investigation committee.

Baker's bill was integrated by a unanimous Senate vote as an amendment to the overall copyright bill as part of the Section 108 exemptions for libraries and archives. The Senate passed the full copyright revision bill the same day, but it was not passed in time for the House to act on it during the same congressional session. A similar bill was reintroduced in January 1975, though it was not brought to the floor until early 1976. In 1974, Ringer had begun advocating that the prior Baker and Matsunaga bills for the Library of Congress to initiate its own TV collection should also be integrated into the copyright revision bill, although the mandate was not scripted into the copyright act until the House did so during revisions in 1976. Nonetheless both methods to preserve news preservation—the Vanderbilt exception and the mandate for the Library of Congress—became part of the new copyright code.[44] Throughout this legislative history, the VTNA was the mobilizing force and model behind congressional action mandating what would become a national repository for TV and radio programming—both news and entertainment. The CBS litigation against Vanderbilt made the issues all the more urgent and prompted a general provision for libraries and archives to tape news and public affairs programming off-air.

Passing the amended copyright act, however, was not so easy. As a whole, the act rewrote the copyright law, had been in negotiation for more than a decade, and had both vague and complex exemptions (such as fair use and the various exemptions for libraries and archives). These exemptions were among many potential points of contestation. After the Senate passed the bill, the House conducted extensive hearings on copyright during 1975.

Among the witnesses were CBS vice president and general counsel Robert Evans, VTNA founder Simpson, and Register of Copyrights Ringer. Evans testified to CBS's opposition to the provision protecting the right of libraries and archives to tape televised news programs off-air, arguing that the measure would "discriminate unfairly against owners of 'audiovisual news programs' by making their rights inferior to the rights of the owners of other copyrighted works." Arguing for privatization, he continued, "Moreover, the problem addressed by these unusual provisions is not one that requires Congressional action because it is being resolved by private initiative."[45] Of course, the private initiative Evans advocated was the network's, not Simpson's or the VTNA's. CBS's extensive internal archiving practices and its licensing agreements with public institutions (discussed in the next section) demonstrated greater interest on its part than the other networks to preserve the news and, laudably, to make it accessible for study. I interpret such attempts as not only tactics to challenge Vanderbilt's practices but also to strengthen CBS's reputation and resource as *the* broadcast news of public record. These agreements functioned to validate its image of quality television and claims of public interest journalism. But CBS clearly wanted to dictate the terms on which its "public" records were consulted and used.

In the fall, Ringer gave the hearings' closing testimony and attempted to summarize the proceedings and controversies, giving special attention to copyright Sections 107 and 108—the sections devoted to fair use and to exceptions for libraries and archives, which she saw as intertwined.[46] In discussing the history of the VTNA and the Baker bills, Ringer commented that the archive founder and staff "may have gone a little further than they should have," though she later stated personal support for the project in spirit.[47] "The public issues underlying the case, and the Baker amendments to section 108, are important, difficult, fascinating, and in some ways, dangerous," Ringer stated.[48] She argued against Baker's off-air taping exception by offering an alternative formulation, similar to CBS's—that is, swapping out the exception for the separate proposals for a national broadcasting archive. Ringer did, however, suggest a "grandfather clause" for Vanderbilt to continue operations.[49]

The Senate unanimously passed the copyright revision bill in February 1976. In the House, consideration of the bill was initially postponed owing to disagreement.[50] In April, Representative Ed Pattison (D-New York), "acting on behalf of CBS," proposed amending Baker's Section 108 clause by qualifying access of tapes in news archives as being for "private study and scholarly research." The network's pressure for rewording the provision was reportedly connected to CBS's long-standing annoyance with politicians' attacks on the media. In May an apparent compromise was reached, which modified the language of the Section 108 exemption to restrict access of news tapes to "lending" only (rather than permanent sale or gift) and to state that borrowers may not copy tapes on loan. The modification was passed by a unanimous vote.[51] The House passed a slightly revised copyright bill in late September. To negotiate the differences between the Senate and House versions of the act, a conference committee was organized and issued a report. The Senate conceded to most of the House's revisions, including the changes in Sections 107 and 108. The report was approved and passed by both congressional bodies, and President Ford signed the United States Copyright Act of 1976 into law on October 19.[52]

Seven years after Senator Baker first broached the subject of TV archives on the Senate floor, and numerous bills, debates, and hearings later, the enacted Section 108(f)(3) succinctly states: "Nothing in this section . . . shall be construed to limit the reproduction and distribution by lending of a limited number of copies and excerpts by a library or archives of an audiovisual news program." The VTNA, the inspiration for the exemption, remains its primary beneficiary. The American Television and Radio Archives, under the guidance of the Librarian of Congress, was likewise legislated as part of the 1976 copyright revision as Appendix I, Section 113, though it was slower to start and more restrictive in its collection and access policies. When the Library of Congress did cultivate a television collection, its source for network news was the VTNA. The Vanderbilt archive continues to supply copies of all its nightly news recordings to the library.[53]

CBS Contests the VTNA

By recording and collecting news programs without permission, the VTNA both violated and validated the networks. On the one hand, the archive made ephemeral corporate news subject to retrospective scrutiny; on the other, it asserted the long-term significance of television news. In CBS's litigation against Vanderbilt, the network claimed copyright protection and objected to the "editing" of their programs—a term that recalls the congressional investigation of the network's *The Selling of the Pentagon*—onto compilation tapes for researchers that were then loaned. Politicians and scholars often singled out the "Tiffany" network for criticism, but CBS was intent on protecting its reputation and integrity. Its cultural prominence and its role in these debates also suggest why access to CBS News broadcasts remains essential for historians and media scholars, thus prompting a clash of interests between the corporation's prestige and profits and the public record. Despite speculation that bad publicity from bias attacks and political harassment may have motivated the lawsuit, no available documentation indicates that the legal action was retaliatory.

The conflicts between the network and the archive have generally been framed as a struggle that pits private property against the public interest. In defending the news-recording project, Simpson and the Vanderbilt lawyers not only relied on the technicalities of copyright law but also frequently invoked the FCC mandates of fairness and public-interest broadcasting, as well as First Amendment rights. Broadcasters were granted public airwaves, they argued, and in return they were required to act in the public interest. In the Supreme Court's influential *Red Lion Co. v. FCC* decision (1969), the Fairness Doctrine was redefined in expanded terms of audience access: "It is the right of the viewers and listeners, not the right of the broadcasters, which is paramount. . . . It is the right of the public to receive suitable access to social, political, esthetic, moral, and other ideas and experiences which is crucial here."[54] This broadcasting policy, however, was separate from copyright law and had little or no direct bearing on it, except as a parallel matter of principle.

The VTNA attempted to extend the Fairness Doctrine's access principle from broadcasts to broadcast *recordings*. The off-air news-taping project was not technically a *public* project, nor was the videotape or recording equipment derived from a scarce, government-regulated public resource (broadcast spectrum). Technically, the mandates of public interest and fairness pertained to initial broadcasts; none of these policies were designed for retrospective access, which had not been possible up to that point. The question raised by the archive was whether the networks were as accountable to future historians as they were to their original home audiences. The networks and the news departments had certainly had their fill of references to the Fairness Doctrine; the policy was the basis of repeated criticisms, studies, and investigations during this time. When the Fairness Doctrine was no longer considered politically useful by Republicans in the 1980s, it was eliminated.[55]

Among the debates that raged in the pages of litigation briefs were attempts to wrestle with and define the medium and material specificity of television broadcasts to argue whether copyright could apply. CBS surely deserved some kind of protection to prevent its programs from being resold or rebroadcast, but whether the network's claims to copyright protection were valid remained debatable. The transmissions of CBS News were clearly expressive but had no tangible form; broadcast live, they did not exist before the VTNA's recordings but were recorded simultaneously. Live television broadcasts were not yet protected under the existing copyright law. Until this time there had been little need to protect live broadcasts, as off-air videotaping technology was still rare. As Vanderbilt's lawyers argued, the archive was not copying CBS's recordings but making its own from free, public broadcasts. Furthermore, such recordings functioned to promote public access to information—not in the news moment but as history. Recording changed the temporality of the news. The lawsuit occurred before the passage of the 1976 copyright act and was ultimately undone by it, as the key issues involved were specifically addressed in the act's revision of the copyright code. The new copyright code not only introduced fair use and exemptions for libraries and archives, as discussed in the previous section, but also legislated the first protections for live broadcasts and other nontangible electronic media.

The network and the archive had extensive interactions—cautious, then collegial, then increasingly hostile—for more than five years before the lawsuit began. Simpson was in contact with the networks' news divisions before even embarking on his recording project. He and James Pilkington remained in cordial communication with CBS News president Richard Salant and consulted with CBS News archivist Samuel Suratt regularly.[56] CBS's vice president and legal counsel Robert Evans, however, had long seemed more leery of the VTNA's potential legal and economic threat to the network. In April 1972, Evans sent the archive his first written warnings. In a succinct letter to Pilkington thanking him for sending a sample issue of the archive's new *Television News Abstracts and Index*, Evans asserted that the VTNA's activities were "a clear infringement of our common law copyright[s]." Evans then suggested a free licensing agreement "in an effort to avoid litigation."[57] This proposal would have granted permission for the VTNA to continue recording the news for archival accumulation and on-site use, but it would have forbade reproduction, excerpting, abstracting, indexing, or off-site circulation. In effect, such a license would have undone much of the archive's mission and function. In the fall, Simpson and Pilkington met with a CBS representative in New York. The network's position was that the indexes were costing the network huge revenue loss.[58] This appears to have been the end of discussion between the archive and the network until July 1973.

Midway through 1973, CBS's Nashville-based legal representative, Val Sanford, sent a letter to Alexander Heard, chancellor of Vanderbilt University. "Since this activity first came to the attention of CBS, it has recognized that while the Vanderbilt program may provide a useful public service, it also involves both an appropriation of valuable property rights of CBS and a dangerous precedent for further appropriations by others." The letter also stated that the VTNA had refused CBS's licensing offer and informed the chancellor that episodes of *The CBS Evening News with Walter Cronkite* were registered for copyright. Sanford closed with an ultimatum: "Unless Vanderbilt accepts such a license or will agree to cease the taping off-the-air of the broadcasts of CBS, we have been authorized to take appropriate action to enforce CBS' rights."[59]

Beginning with CBS's early communications to the VTNA and continuing into the lawsuit, the network urged establishing a licensing agreement between the network and the archive. Such a license would effectively recognize CBS's intellectual property rights and dictate the terms under which the archive and its users could record, excerpt, compile, duplicate, and circulate the network's news programming. VTNA repeatedly refused such arrangements because the practices and uses of the material would be determined by the network rather than by the archive or its researchers. CBS did succeed in establishing network-determined arrangements for donated collections and off-air recording elsewhere, however. Although these were publicized as serving the public interest and increasing general access to its news materials, such agreements were also clearly undertaken to undermine Vanderbilt's claims that its operations were providing a civil service that was not otherwise being performed. But the arrangements CBS made—with the National Archives and Records Service (NARS, now the National Archives and Records Administration) and with various school systems—set strict limits on circulation and reproduction of collections or the longevity of retained recordings. Both of these models undermined access and preservation of the news by forbidding excerpting, compiling, and off-site usage or by requiring erasure of recordings after thirty days.[60] Such licensing agreements then, as well as in the increasingly prevalent digital subscription business models today, allow for short-term access during the paid-for period but may not allow for long-term access to documents.

Despite CBS's efforts to establish television news collections through public archives, Vanderbilt maintained that its operations were essential to democratize user access to the tapes and to maintain the availability of the other networks' news programs. Despite being a private university, Vanderbilt refused to cloister tapes in the ivory tower and adamantly supported the broadest feasible scenario for public access. Additionally, videotape technology was not yet common in libraries, rendering the loan policy of the NARS ineffective. The licensing agreements that CBS urged and activated during the early to mid-1970s may have encouraged more institutions to adopt video technologies and to use television news, but these agreements were largely designed to counteract the VTNA's access policies and to bolster the network's public image during the lawsuit.

For approximately six months during 1973, lawyers representing CBS and Vanderbilt exchanged letters that stated and restated their respective positions. CBS claimed proprietary rights in its broadcasts and did not want the VTNA or any of its users to copy, condense, or circulate them. Vanderbilt asserted that the archive was providing a public service and that the CBS broadcasts were not covered by copyright in any case. The earliest broadcasts that the VTNA had recorded were not in fact registered for copyright; during the tense period leading up to litigation, CBS began registering programs as unpublished "motion pictures other than photoplays not reproduced for sale" and then, in the midst of the suit, switched to registering new episodes as published works. The copyright law at the time was of little guidance, for it was unclear how the live news broadcasts could be protected by copyright. But it was perhaps even less probable that a blanket exemption could be granted to the VTNA's extensive recording project if a judge determined that the news programs could be protected. In the flow of letters before litigation, both sides staked out positions, proclaimed rights, and tested rhetorical strategies—some of which were developed, some of which were dropped, in the subsequent lawsuit.

In a letter to Sanford following an in-person meeting, Vanderbilt legal counsel Jeff Carr presented a four-point defense of VTNA's practices: first, the broadcasts must be videotaped to be accurately documented; second, the material must be abstracted in published indexes for public access; third, the material must be duplicated onto access tapes to prevent wear on master tapes; and fourth, users must be able to select specific segments for viewing as they would for print research in a library.[61] In a later exchange, Sanford presented a three-part argument for CBS's position: first, the archive could not monitor or control inappropriate uses of the loaned tapes; second, reproducing and distributing such tapes might, under copyright law, be tantamount to publishing and therefore infringe the network's rights; and third, these services competed with current and speculative educational and other ancillary markets for CBS News programs.[62] Further letter exchanges and a meeting between Carr and Sanford confirmed irreconcilable points of disagreement.[63] Finally, the epistolary battle ended and the lawsuit begin.

Litigation

On December 21, 1973, CBS filed suit against Vanderbilt University, the custodian of the archive, in the U.S. District Court in Nashville, requesting an injunction against taping, surrender of previously recorded tapes to the network, and reimbursement of legal fees.[64] The official court complaint emphasized the originality and expense of CBS News productions, their registration under copyright, and the network's objections to VTNA practices; the complaint also stressed that Vanderbilt was charging a fee for its service and "consistently treated the Plaintiff's property as its own, which it considers itself free to use as it will."[65] The claim that the VTNA treated the news programs as "its own" derived from an agreement that users were required to sign when borrowing tapes. The agreement forbade further duplication or broadcast of loaned materials and was designed both as a goodwill gesture toward the networks and as a way of absolving the archive of liability for users' infringements.

In the motions, briefs, and other documents filed by both CBS and Vanderbilt during the course of the lawsuit, the two sides repeatedly addressed complex and circular issues of the ontology of broadcast television, the jurisdiction of copyright, the public interest, rights of access, and the preservation of news media. Thus the matters at stake were not merely a corporation's financial interests but the broader relationship of copyright to the public good and the current law's apparent incapacity to continue regulating pervasive television technologies and practices. The lawsuit was portrayed in the press as a landmark case with the potential for appeals all the way to the Supreme Court, which indicated that the case was viewed by both its participants and its public commentators as being of vital importance.[66]

Vanderbilt filed two motions to dismiss the case in March 1974, along with supporting briefs. The first brief began by clarifying the archive's history and practices, but the argument did not respond directly to CBS's original complaint. Rather, it offered an alternative argument that the public interest superseded CBS's proprietary claims, thus making a First Amendment argument extending the principles of free speech and free press to the right to receive access to information and ideas. In addition, the brief offered a critique that copyright was being regulated by default through technology rather than by copyrighting of the texts themselves, decades before the Digital Millennium Copyright Act:

> National television newscasts constitute a distinct marketplace of ideas which is monopolized by the television networks. This monopoly is

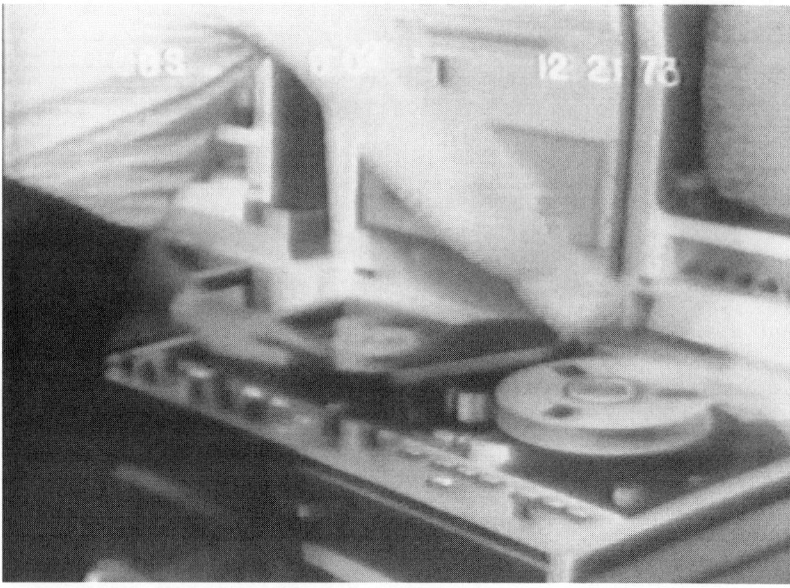

21. The first off-air recorded footage that appears during the VTNA promo at the beginning of its loaner tapes comes from the local CBS affiliate's coverage of the network's lawsuit against the archive. The footage's significance is probably lost on most borrowers, but its inclusion on all tapes suggests the lawsuit's continued importance to the archive's identity. WTVF News, December 21, 1973.

> enhanced by the fact that the television networks, unlike the printed media, can control later access to news they present by reason of the technology of television. *CBS now seeks further to extend its monopoly by a claim of copyright, thereby gaining the power to control access to its newscasts by law, as well as by reason of technology.* This cannot do, because this power would deny the public the right "to receive suitable access" to the news.[67]

Along the same rationale, the motion argued that the speech was not just CBS's but also (even predominantly) the speech of public officials, for which access could not be restricted.[68] The brief also challenged the monopoly granted to CBS by its copyright protection. "Plaintiff appears to believe that a copyright gives it power to control any use of copyrighted material." A concept of use versus infringement was developed: "It is fundamental that 'use' is not the same as 'infringement,' that use short of infringement is to be encouraged."[69] As I argued in the introduction, the concept of "use" is central to both fair use and to the way videotape technology changed audience's relationships to television.

Vanderbilt's brief supporting its second motion to dismiss alleged that the copyright registrations for broadcasts of the *CBS Evening News with Walter Cronkite* were invalid and that CBS's use of the category of "motion pictures other than photoplays not reproduced for sale" was a manipulation of the law for protection yet served as a loophole that absolved the network of depositing archival recordings in the Library of Congress. It was clear that copyright code legislation had not kept current with technological innovation, but the copyright office had already been registering videotape deposits as motion pictures since 1961. According to the copyright office, videotapes were considered "merely a technological improvement on motion pictures" and "a cassette is not different from a tape or disc. The mere fact that it is enclosed in a box does not make it different under copyright law."[70] A 1970 Senate report also suggested that "the physical form in which the motion picture is fixed—film, tape, discs, and so forth—is irrelevant, and the same is true whether the images reproduced in the physical object can be made out with the naked eye or require optical, electronic, or other special equipment to be perceived."[71] Thus copyright law up to that time denied format specificity.

A potential pitfall in this case was that CBS was not even copyrighting *tapes*. It was attempting to copyright live "programs," and Vanderbilt's second motion emphasized the very intangibility of television broadcasting. Vanderbilt contended that live television broadcasts were ineligible for copyright because Congress had never amended the law for its protection. The point Vanderbilt made here was that copyright pertained to expressions in fixed forms, not to ideas themselves. This was the underlying regulation of analog copyright: protection, like access, demands physical substance. Not only were electronic transmissions neither fixed nor written, but, the brief argues, they were also ephemeral, which renders copyright protection irrelevant.

In June, CBS filed a seventy-seven-page reply brief that claimed that its news programs were properly registered for copyright and that portrayed the VTNA as a pirate operation competing with CBS's own services. The brief reiterated the copyright principle that expressions in fixed forms can be copyrighted but ideas cannot. CBS stressed the authorship and expense entailed in producing its news program, which made it an *expression* of news events rather than mere facts or information. Incidentally, this concept of expression admits to the possibility of bias because it relies on interpreting and packaging the information, not merely conveying it. Additionally, the brief repeatedly argued that the news *programs* were copyrighted, not the *broadcasts.* The brief distinguished between publication, which in copyright indicated making copies publicly accessible, and performance, which indicated ephemeral exhibition without copies. CBS identified its evening news broadcasts as *performances* that were therefore "not reproduced for sale," but claimed that it copyrighted the *programs*, not the broadcasts. These programs were fixed on videotape simultaneously with the live broadcasts but did not exist before broadcast; therefore they were not copyrighted before broadcast.[72]

Vanderbilt challenged the concept that CBS could claim copyright over programs taped simultaneously with live broadcast. Vanderbilt contended that CBS belatedly requested retroactive copyrights for its programs, with deposits and registration taking place a month or so after broadcast. This meant that the programs—if they were even eligible for protection—had not yet been copyrighted when the VTNA taped them.[73] The rebuttal extensively quoted a 1965 hearing before the House of Representatives on copyright revision when representatives from the National Football League sought protection for live broadcasts that were simultaneously recorded on videotape.[74] This method of retroactive copyrighting for recorded broadcasts was precisely what CBS sought for its news programs. But clearly the NFL, which at the time had CBS as its primary network partner, understood that its recordings of live games could not be copyrighted. Congress had not passed any copyright code amendments between the hearings in 1965 and the lawsuit that would recognize or authorize such a procedure.

CBS also focused on its internal archiving practices, suggesting that Vanderbilt's operations competed with the network's own research access policies and its developing markets for residual uses of the news material.[75] It is unclear how or how often access was granted for requests to research, view, or use the material or how much the network charged; Vanderbilt made its services available to any interested user and had standardized, below-cost rates for use. Although the network claimed to offer services comparable to those offered by the VTNA, CBS could not provide access to other networks' programs to allow for comparative analysis. Nonetheless CBS's arguments on the basis of copyright law and unfair competition were strong. Although CBS was not claiming specific monetary damages because of competition from the VTNA, it was in the process of exploiting ancillary educational and audio markets for its news products and was keenly watching the nascent home video technology as a site for future development.[76] CBS also stated that it sought to develop an index for sale to libraries and schools, with which the

VTNA's *Television News Index and Abstracts* would compete. Yet these indexes had different purposes: the VTNA's functioned as a directory for using the tape collection, whereas CBS's would merely be a reference book.

In a subsequent response to Vanderbilt's filings, CBS opposed Vanderbilt's tactic of representing itself as acting in the public interest by suggesting that the (private) university was no more a public institution or representative of "the public" than the network.[77] The network also argued against Vanderbilt's suggestion that CBS had registered its programs as "unpublished" works to avoid deposit and preservation of the programs at the Library of Congress.[78] Indeed, the network surely devoted more resources to maintaining its materials than the library ever could. This document continued to wrestle with an attempt to legally define the ontology of broadcast television. Indicating that its previous brief had been perplexing, CBS attempted to clarify its copyright procedures and protections with a question-and-answer format. The network claimed that it copyrighted the expressed program, which was simultaneously "performed" as a broadcast and "written" on videotape. The claimed copyright neither protected the performance, which was ineligible for protection, nor the physical tape, but the "expression."[79] The distinction remained so precise as to be incomprehensible, and such rhetorical claims to protection further underscore the law's insufficiency at the time to properly address broadcast technologies. Despite the obvious slippage in this reasoning, this (simultaneous recording) was how live broadcasts eventually became eligible for instantaneous copyright protection under the 1976 copyright act revision. L. Ray Patterson and Stanley W. Lindberg, scholars of copyright law, would later call such "electronic" copyright protections a "fiction" that veered from the purpose of the copyright code to protect corporate interests.[80] Of course, such protections were not yet in effect at the time CBS's brief was filed.

A respite from court filings lasted for several months following the frequent exchanges in 1974. During this time, CBS sought to secure its copyright claims and strengthen its argument by changing its registration categorization. Beginning in February 1975, CBS began registering the *CBS Evening News with Walter Cronkite* programs as *published* works and submitted an amended and supplemental complaint to reflect this change in June. In the amended lawsuit, CBS continued to claim copyright on programs broadcast between April 16, 1973, and February 14, 1975, as unpublished works in addition to the published subsequent broadcasts. The network again sought an injunction against future recording, return of existing tapes, and legal expenses.

In the amended complaint, CBS stated that the now-published programs were broadcast with notifications of copyright and that two copies of each program were deposited with the register of copyrights, thus fulfilling two requirements for protection.[81] But the complaint did not explain any technological difference between the programs before and after the classification change that would suggest a qualitative change in production or distribution or would distinguish the programs as unpublished or published.

With another round of motions to argue legal process in late 1975, both parties ultimately requested a court hearing.[82] They had apparently grown tired of filing motions and saw an oral pleading and judicial decision as the only resolution to the dispute. But the case seemed to stall in 1976. At the end of March 1976, the district court issued an order to deny Vanderbilt's requests for dismissal or summary judgment because matters of fact were in dispute and because of the complexity of the case.[83] Thus, it seemed, the case would finally go to trial. However, the court did not rush to act on the prior motions or to hear the case, which had now lasted more than two years. As an overview of the litigation hypothesized, "There was apparent reluctance on the part of the court in Nashville to place the case on the docket," possibly because the 1909 copyright law was insufficient for the case's circumstances.[84] A letter from Sanford to Carr stated, "The criminal docket is likely to monopolize Judge Gray's court this fall," and recognized the copyright revision pending in Congress. Because of the circumstances, Sanford indicated, CBS would put a hold on further filings or proceedings.[85]

Following the passage of the new copyright code with the Section 108 exemption for libraries and archives to tape the news off-air, CBS requested the dismissal of the lawsuit, without prejudice, in early December, and the court officially dissolved the case on December 20, 1976.[86] It was an anticlimactic ending to a lengthy conflict. Despite the limitations of the existing copyright law, CBS would probably have won its lawsuit. The copyright office had been accepting videotapes as functionally equivalent to film for copyright registration and deposit, and the register of copyrights had made public statements that the VTNA's actions violated copyright as Ringer interpreted it. But such a ruling would immediately have been rendered moot by the revised copyright legislation or, potentially, overturned by a higher court. The lawsuit has retained a somewhat legendary status in the archival community, and there remains hearsay about continuing animosity between CBS and the VTNA.

Public Responses and Repositories

The press coverage of the CBS-VTNA conflict suggested that it was a crucial matter of the abuse of power versus the public interest. By far, the majority of the press coverage and public opinion sided with Vanderbilt and expressed outrage that CBS News was apparently trying to suppress its broadcasts from the public record at the same time that it was demanding that Nixon release all his subpoenaed audio recordings. Commentators understood the lawsuit as a conflict of its time, specifically through the lens of the Watergate scandal, which had pointed to the importance of journalistic integrity and full disclosure—not to mention magnetic tape.

In an ironic twist, both the Nixon administration's rise and fall—charted by its attacks on the press and its undoing by it—would validate the need for the VTNA project and draw attention to it.[87] The Watergate investigations revealed Nixon's covert taping practices and that eighteen minutes of his personal surveillance recordings had been erased, thus drawing public attention to the technology and to its political and potentially controversial uses. Wayne Sargent, publisher of the *Nashville Banner*, commented on the lawsuit:

> Naturally, in this day and age, nothing can happen without it having some relationship to Watergate. [*TV Guide*] Columnist Kevin Phillips has already suggested that CBS has no more right to erase its tapes, either in New York or at Vanderbilt, than did the someone who, by mistake or on purpose, caused an 18 minute gap in the President's tapes.[88]

More succinctly, Alexander Cockburn began a *Village Voice* column, "CBS is eager to join President Nixon in the tape wiping business."[89] Thus the news tapes were seen not only as recordings of the news but also as historical evidence, and the press alleged that destroying the tapes or restricting access to them was tantamount to conspiracy. Tape recording and erasure, in this historical moment, seemed to be synonymous with Nixon, who was perhaps the most famous taper in the United States.[90]

The Vanderbilt Television News Archive began as a personal initiative, and as a pilot program its operations may not have been wholly within the law. Yet it quickly became a model institution that spread the television archive fever among networks, universities, museums, and the national government. The VTNA's project began amid developing academic interest in television and preceded a boom in television archives. Simply put, television became institutionalized in the academy and in archives during the 1960s and 1970s. CBS, the VTNA, and copyright all played roles in these trends. CBS and its staff participated in encouraging scholarly attention to television and in claiming television as part of the public's cultural heritage through the development of scholarly analysis, internal archiving, and public museums. The VTNA acted as a resource both for the broadcast news surveillance and political scapegoating of the period and for a working model of archiving and accessing television for subsequent collections.

Whereas television news itself was topical, television more generally became "old" in the 1970s, when it was newly understood as having a past worth preserving. Derek Kompare writes, "The seventies marked the beginning of television's *historicity*, that is, its articulation into discourses of history and memory."[91] The attention to news and its preservation appeared simultaneously with the interest in preserving film and media more generally—arguably reflecting a conservative impulse to preserve film heritage amid cultural shifts or simply an interest, like Paul Simpson's, in documenting the changing world. One history of moving-image media preservation notes, "In the decade spanning 1967 to 1977, moving image preservation gained a national platform for the first time."[92] Extending from the film preservation movement, in the mid- to late 1970s, TV archives became a zeitgeist phenomenon. Erik Barnouw suggested that a popular rise in the mid- to late 1970s of retrospection and archival impulses was an attempt to iron out the kinks of recent social and political conflicts. He posited 1976 as a moment of pervasive historicism; the year marked the national bicentennial, the opening of the Museum of Broadcasting, and the copyright provision for the American Television and Radio Archives.[93] Capitalizing on the "simpler" and "wholesome" values of 1950s family sitcoms, the incessant syndication of "classic" television programs commingled with a pervasive nostalgia culture in the early 1970s that generated a new sense of television's role in cultural memory and prompted interest in studying and archiving its content. Attention to new videocassette formats contributed to this paradigm shift toward television as well: not only *should* television programming be saved, but now it *could* be.[94]

The most publicized sign of television's new credibility was the 1976 opening of the Museum of Broadcasting in New York, which had major ties to the TV industry.[95] The William S. Paley Foundation—the CBS CEO's philanthropic endeavor—commissioned a study from 1967 to 1971 to examine creating a television archive. The concept for this institution clearly predates the VTNA's origins, though the museum did not come into existence until nearly a decade later. In 1975, Paley founded and funded the Museum of Broadcasting, and it opened the following year. Despite its connections to the prior study of archiving, the museum has never had a comprehensive collection, nor has it functioned as an archive. A publicly accessible private institution, it acquires its materials through direct agreements with the networks and producers and attempts to showcase only the "best" or "most representative" sampling of quality television and radio. The collection functions for casual tourist viewing and public symposiums with media makers and personalities; the museum only secondarily serves more in-depth scholarly research, and the collection can be viewed only on-site.[96] This perhaps illustrates the different missions of different types of memory institutions: whereas subject archives aim to *preserve* specific, in-depth collections and cater to specialized historical research, encyclopedic museums aim to *exhibit* representative samples of a wide array of objects or texts and cater to a generally educated audience. Libraries, a third category, aim to *circulate* nonprecious texts to a wide, public audience. The Museum of Broadcasting, true to its name, operates like a museum. The VTNA functions as a hybrid archive-library. (In contrast, the CBS News documentary producer Perry Wolff commented on the network's access policy, "The name of the organization is CBS News. It's not the CBS Public Library.")[97]

Also in 1976, the film archive of the University of California, Los Angeles, expanded its name to include television, and the Peabody Award Archive was established at the University of Georgia.[98] In 1977 the International Federation of Television Archives (FIAT/IFTA) was created by a group of European broadcasters—ARD (Germany), BBC (United Kingdom), INA (France), and RAI (Italy)—and has since become a major international professional organization with annual conferences. In fall 1978, Fay Schreibman opened the short-lived Television News Study Center at George Washington University, which functioned as a satellite viewing center for the VTNA collection and reportedly doubled requests for the archive's materials.[99] It did not house its own collection, although it recorded weekend network news programs and coverage of selected special events, which it sent to the VTNA.[100] While all these organizations have significantly expanded access to televisual history, all face the challenges of ephemerality, technological obsolescence, funding, and limited resources.

Despite its ultimate lack of legal ruling or precedent, I have recorded some of the lawsuit's major arguments at length here to suggest their insights into tensions between obsolete intellectual property law and emerging technology. Such incompatibility, as I suggested in the previous chapter, has returned in the age of digital technologies and the Digital Millennium

Copyright Act. Such a retrospective examination of the lawsuit suggests why access, legal exemptions, and archives were such essential issues in the 1970s, and, I hope, illuminates their continued urgency today.

Conclusion

Before the VTNA, network news was coverage of the moment—nightly transmissions without an imagined future or sustained value. With the advent of video recording, the news could suddenly be fixed, reviewed, preserved, duplicated, recirculated, and studied. This introduced a new relationship to news programs as documents, and it raised the networks' accountability to a public that could now use and reexamine recordings as historical evidence. News programming was a matter of major political and public discourse, and its preservation became a matter of policy and legal intervention.

The establishment of the archive and the lawsuit brought on by the network both emerged during the turn from the 1960s to the 1970s—a period marked by intense political divisions, new forms of democratic participation, theories of ideology, and attention to television's role in enlightening society. Whether the agenda was critical or celebratory, new collections and practices emerged that enabled television to become the subject of public debate, covert surveillance, and academic analysis. Recording and copyright played significant new roles in these modes of television study and historiography through off-air taping technologies. The VTNA's ambitious recording project not only created a major public historical and cultural resource but also motivated the networks to take better care of their own archives and spurred Congress to create a national broadcast collection. Before the 1976 copyright code revision—a glacial process that started several years before the lawsuit—Vanderbilt's actions may have been illegal, but they operated on the principle that the public good superseded the law.

The VTNA's legal battle offered a preview of the conflict that would ensue a few years later in the Betamax case, as the studios' proprietary rights in TV programming clashed with questions of the viewing public's rights of access. Most potential users' first knowledge of the VTNA probably came through press coverage of the CBS lawsuit, perhaps not unlike the publicity boost that home video received from the Betamax lawsuit. As with the Supreme Court's definition of fair use in that case, copyright was expansively interpreted and revised to permit productive uses of videotape as an access format. The legislation of Section 108, with its exception for libraries and archives to record the news off-air, and the copyright code's mandate in

Appendix I for the creation of a national broadcast programming archive demonstrate that Congress used copyright as a means to permit public access and to preserve media. Thus this study, true to the nature of copyright generally, demonstrates the ambivalence of intellectual property law, which simultaneously attempts to provide exclusive rights and productive exemptions. Access was contested and created through copyright.

VIDEO CLIP 3

Experimental Film on Video: A Frameworks Debate

In early February 2006, a Portuguese film instructor posted an inquiry about how to find the Austrian experimental filmmaker Peter Kubelka's work on video to the Frameworks Listserv, an e-mail discussion group about underground film. The poster commented that he had seen Kubelka's work on bootlegs but wanted a better copy for "teaching purposes." The inquiry stoked a long-running debate about whether films should be viewed on video, but this time the argument focused on bootlegs and the ethics of screening work that was transferred to video without the artist's consent. Kubelka has never intended his work to be seen on video, some subscribers replied. The original poster responded half apologetically, "If it wasn't for that bootleg tape, I would surely die without watching his films."

The Listserv discussion pointed to a tension between ethics and access. Here I will quote excerpts from two posters that established the basic arguments on both sides, as well as another respondent who offered both clarification and ambivalence. After explaining that many of these bootlegs come from college campus facilities with telecine devices,[1] David Tetzlaff offered a defense of bootlegs in educational instances:

> I think the people who decry the availability of films on video, and would only have them shown in proper public screenings with legitimate film rentals don't really understand education as a whole. . . . And I would argue that it is exactly this kind of usage . . . that the Fair Use clause means to protect by "educational use." It is, in fact, a great asset to our culture to have a wide selection of film materials readily at hand in a way that they can be used on the spur of the moment in off the cuff inspirational ways, both in teaching and elsewhere. I don't believe this violates any

> artist's intent as the context doesn't say "here you have fully experienced this art in its true and complete form." The use isn't even *about* the work, really, just employing certain elements of it to include in an intellectual stew and stir up the pot.

Fred Camper maintained that an artist's intent for how his or her work should be viewed must be respected. Educational contexts should not exempt such intentions, he responded:

> There are a couple of problems with this. . . . One is that even though this school does continue to rent prints, these study-only copies have been known to inadvertently make it into classroom screenings, which should not be a big surprise, no system being perfect. Another is that unauthorized dupes are sometimes made for personal use by grad students and others, and it wouldn't surprise me if such dupes, even worse than the VHS originals, sometimes make it into classroom screenings when said student gets his or her first teaching job at Podunk State which of course has no rental budget and no working film projectors either. But what galls me the most about this practice is that no attempt is made to exclude from video dubbing the films of those filmmakers who have lost income by never authorizing the transfer of their films to video for aesthetic reasons, because the makers feel their films should simply not be seen on video. . . . It certainly "feels" to me like it should be illegal.

Camper identifies two arguments against screening bootlegs, the first being economic and the second being aesthetic. Whereas the economic argument would hold a stronger case for copyright infringement in the United States, Camper seems more concerned with the issue of artists' "moral rights" to determine if and how their works may be reproduced or exhibited. Although moral rights are central to European copyright and may "feel" as if they "should be illegal," they do not actually exist in the United States. Instead, respecting moral rights here is merely a matter of good manners. Although this distinction may seem crass, in the United States it actually serves the audience and the public interest by protecting all kinds of ingenuity and rights for uses of texts—especially in an era when copyrights beyond the world of underground film are so prominently governed by corporations rather than individual artists.

But back to the e-mail debate. Again arguing for access, Tetzlaff responded:

> Folks, bootlegs are one of the most common ways people outside of major urban centers develop a lasting love for these odd little works of outsider art—somebody initiates them into the world of experimental film by showing them a crappy video they're not supposed to have.

Among the dozens of e-mails from different respondents, the two positions were typically categorized as either Tetzlaff's or Camper's—that is, access versus the artist's intent and film purism. Film studies instructors were among the advocates for access and educational uses of bootlegs. Jonathan Walley indicated a mediation of sorts:

> I think the debate has (at times) conflated two issues. The first is whether or not video is an adequate form for viewing experimental film, whether the videos are legitimate copies or not. The second issue is whether or not making unauthorized video duplicates of film prints is ethical. . . . I can't say I know exactly where I fall on this issue—an unauthorized copy of an experimental film in my personal collection deprives the filmmaker and/or distributor (those folks fighting the good fight, like FMC [Film-Maker's Cooperative] and Canyon [Cinema]) of funds, but on the other hand it enables me as a teacher to expose my students to said film when: (a) I lack the funds to bring the film in as a print, or; (b) I lack the time to arrange the booking and shipping of the print. This isn't to say that the "wrong" of unauthorized copying is balanced by the "right" of spreading the word about avant-garde film by any means necessary, but to point out potentially mitigating factors related to the practice of copying.

Although only tangentially articulated in relation to copyright, the discussion illustrated the different ethical arguments at stake, as well as the trade-offs between aesthetics and access. Significantly, bootleg reproductions and screenings of experimental films were believed to be most prevalent in college classrooms.

An even more voluminous series of e-mails revisited these basic issues in a Frameworks discussion about UbuWeb in June 2008. A web portal for streaming versions of experimental films and video art, UbuWeb (www.ubuweb.com) was founded by poets invested in sharing inspiring media works with or without permission. The site boasts an impressive centralized collection of avant-garde media, but, like YouTube, its videos appear in low resolution. These streaming videos, like second-generation analog dubs, counteract medium-specific film techniques and may undermine experiments with duration when the user can simply fast forward or click ahead.

As a free web-based project, the site facilitates much more access to rare works than bootleg cassettes ever could; the Internet also makes this work available for viewers who live far from the few cities where such work might screen or who are not enrolled in college film courses. Certainly some of this access inspires users to seek out official screenings of film works, whereas for most users, the small and grainy images probably suffice. A few of the listserv respondents praised UbuWeb, more condemned it, and most were conflicted: access was generally praised, while the low-fidelity aesthetics and disregard for artists' rights were bemoaned. Streaming videos reiterate what I've been suggesting analog bootlegs did before: they point to ways that form and regulation are interdependent and that copyright guides how video access gets determined.

Filmmakers, programmers, and scholars are the predominant participants in the Frameworks e-mail forum, but these debates parallel what has long been the fundamental conflict for film archivists: preservation and access. For archivists, this binary exemplifies the issues central to their profession. On the one hand, preservation is essential to ensure the longevity of works so that they can be seen in the best condition possible. On the other, films are meant to be seen, and screenings may inspire interest in saving at-risk works.[2] Preservation can postpone or restrict access to wonderful texts, but exhibition always introduces the risk of damage to the materials. Videotape often serves as the compromise at archives in the form of access copies transferred from film prints or masters to VHS tapes that researchers can use for reference. Copyright, on the other hand, can be used to interfere with both preservation (if rights owners decide a title has little commercial appeal or may embarrass a parent company) and access (if a title has been withheld pending later commercial release).

4. Grainy Days and Mondays: *Superstar* and Bootleg Aesthetics

The Carpenters had "only just begun" when a male narrator dryly delivers the following speculative historical analysis:

> The year is 1970, and suddenly the nation finds itself asking the question, "What if, instead of the riots and assassinations, the protests and the drugs, instead of the angry words and hard-rock sounds, we were to hear something soft and smooth, and see something of wholesomeness and easy-handed faith?" This was the year that put the song onto the charts that made the Carpenters a household word.

The deep, authoritative voice is juxtaposed with flickering pixelated period images shot off the surface of a television monitor: falling bombs, California governor Ronald Reagan, an American flag, a flurry of angry protestors, Richard Nixon with his daughter Tricia, a stock photo of a happy heterosexual couple, and the final triumphant moments of a beauty pageant. Immediately after this montage, the opening piano notes of "(They Long to Be) Close to You" knell on the soundtrack as the film cuts to the inside of a recording studio. The camera pans to show Karen in the booth, and just at the moment when she should begin singing, "Why do birds suddenly appear . . ." she coughs instead.[1]

"Karen, are you all right?" asks her brother Richard.

"I'm sorry, Richard," she replies. "Goddamn, I'm really flubbing it up today, aren't I? I'm sorry, guys. I don't know what's the matter with me."

"Just relax. Take a deep breath," Richard coaches. "Look, we'll just do it until it's right. Just do what I tell you, and it will be great."

Karen responds, "I just want it to be *perfect.*" And in her retake, it is. This sequence appears early in *Superstar: The Karen Carpenter Story* (1987), a

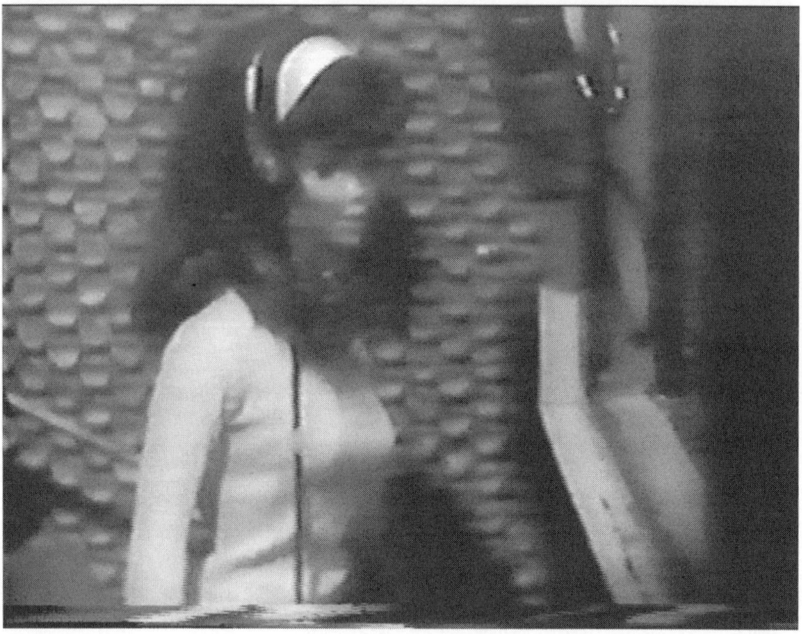

22. Karen in the recording studio in *Superstar*, about to record "(They Long to Be) Close to You."

forty-three-minute 16 mm film that uses dolls to portray sibling supergroup the Carpenters' rise to fame and singer Karen Carpenter's struggle with anorexia. Filmmaker Todd Haynes presents the Carpenters' music and personas as conflicting with their historical context and with their own lives and desires. *Superstar* strips away the surface sheen of media images and exposes the human frailty behind easy (if often melancholy) listening.

A beloved and moving oddity, *Superstar* has been suppressed from legitimate distribution since 1989 as a result of its unauthorized use of the Carpenters' music. And yet it survives through bootleg circulation. This featurette remains perhaps the most famous nonpornographic bootlegged video, and it launched Haynes's career as an acclaimed filmmaker. In 2003, *Superstar* ranked forty-fifth on *Entertainment Weekly*'s list of the top fifty cult films. Fan magazine *Film Threat* commented on the *EW* poll, "Most of the choices were predictable, more than a few were fairly silly, but one stood out since it was the only film which attained cult status strictly because it can only be seen via bootleg video: . . . *Superstar*." Also indicating the film's cult status, it was reviewed in the sixth issue of *Shock Cinema*, a New York-based zine that bills itself as "Your guide to cult movies, arthouse oddities, drive-in swill, and underground obscurities!"[2]

In the previous chapter, I examined practices of video recording and copyright negotiations that fueled television news study, political controversy, and preservation during the Nixon era. Now I turn to a semifictionalized text that presents a snapshot of that time period from the vantage point of the mid-1980s and later became a bootleg phenomenon during the 1990s. Rather than an institutional model of bootlegging that influenced official political action, *Superstar* sharing remains a popular act of civil disobedience. Thus this chapter shifts its primary focus away from technology and copyright per se toward aesthetics and reception.

The Carpenters' distinctive sound has been credited to their extensive use of overdubbing, a multitrack studio recording technique in which different layers of sound are recorded separately but played back simultaneously. This technique, an innovation of magnetic tape recording, offers a multilayered, complex fusion of the discrete tracks on playback. In particular, the overdubbing of Karen Carpenter's vocals gave her voice a resonant timbre and warm tone. As I suggest in this chapter, a different kind of overdubbing—bootlegging—likewise gives unexpected texture and qualities to videotapes of *Superstar*. VHS tapes of *Superstar*, which have proliferated through multiple generations of dubbing, betray the fuzzy images and warbled soundtracks of analog video reproduction—what I have been calling the aesthetics of access.

Appropriated music and images expressively function within the film to reproduce the mass-mediated context of the Carpenters' work and to represent a cultural memory of the 1970s. Videotapes of the film, by extension, inscribe a bootleg aesthetic that exhibits the audience's engagement in a clandestine love affair—watching, sharing, and copying the illicit text so that viewers' reception of *Superstar* is historically, perceptually, and emotionally reshaped. Videotape duplication of the work formally changes the text, so that its thematic concerns—distorted mass media and their relations to subjective and bodily breakdown—become rendered on the surface; significantly, this analog duplication also records the cult audience's participation in reproducing *Superstar*. Bootleggers' participation is not limited to distribution but is also aesthetic and affective. Because the tapes have primarily circulated through personal connections, they also become souvenirs of relationships. This chapter presents the film's production, exhibition, and legal histories before examining uses of appropriated media within the film and bootleg aesthetics inscribed onto videotape reproductions.

Ladies and Gentlemen: The Carpenters!

Haynes's *Superstar* is at once a portrait of a historical period and a critique of popular culture's failure to adequately respond to it. As performers whose image promoted conservative family values, *Superstar* positions the sunny Southern Californian Carpenters as something of an anomaly during a period of social revolt and political crisis (as discussed in chapter 3). They were, however, an extraordinarily popular anomaly who scored twenty Top 40 hits between their debut single "Close to You" in 1970 and anorexic Karen Carpenter's lethal heart attack following an overdose of Ipecac syrup in 1983.[3]

In portraying Karen's life, Haynes presents the cultural context for the group's fame and her body issues. He simulates the Carpenters' domestic and professional dramas with a cast of Barbie-type dolls—and occasionally human body doubles and talking heads. In the process, the filmmaker structures the narrative through the generic modes of star biopics, disease-of-the-week TV movies, health educational films, and feminist documentaries. Haynes imitates and combines familiar film and television genres not to critique these modes but to strategically use them to present allegorical narratives that function as shorthand for expressing the characters' emotional states and for producing audience affect. Haynes's generic tactic in *Superstar* prefigures the themes and stylistic modes that have remained central to his subsequent films, including *Poison*, *Safe*, *Velvet Goldmine*, and *I'm Not There*. Haynes not only combines disparate narrative methodologies but also textures the film by interweaving a variety of media and aesthetic styles.[4] His work in *Superstar* was influenced by the shift in the late 1970s and early 1980s from purely formalist experimental cinema to an avant-garde cinema of narrative experimentation used to explore social issues.[5] As Barbara Kruger summarily raved in her *Artforum* review, "It is perhaps this small film's triumph that it can so economically sketch, with both laughter and chilling actuality, the conflation of patriotism, familial control, and bodily self-revulsion that drove Karen Carpenter and so many like her to strive for perfection and end up simply doing away with themselves."[6] *Superstar*'s allegorical connections between Karen's anorexic wasting and the emaciating effects of AIDS would have been nearly unmissable at the time of the film's release. I suspect the more historically removed we get from the public panics over AIDS in the 1980s, the less the text will be received allegorically, and *Superstar* will increasingly be seen as "just" about eating disorders and media culture.

For readers who have not seen *Superstar* or do not have ready access to see it again, I begin with fairly detailed descriptions of a few early montage sequences to convey the film's complex structure. The film opens with a black-and-white point-of-view shot—"A Dramatization," as it is marked—that shows Karen's mother searching through a house and finding a dead body lying in the closet. The film then quickly changes tone as a male narrator's authoritative voice raises rhetorical questions that promise to be answered to make sense of the horror. Mundane images of suburban California homes drift across the screen as the fancy cursive credits appear and Karen Carpenter's disembodied voice sings the familiar, sad opening verses of "Superstar." After the discovery of Karen's corpse, the song has a surprisingly chilling effect—until it shifts up-tempo for the chorus, when the sad love song inexplicably turns celebratory, drowning out the heartache scripted in the lyrics of youthful love and desperate hopes: "Don't you remember you told me you loved me, baby?"[7] The song's shift in tone presents a dual affect of melancholy and feigned joviality; such emotional tensions and transitions appear throughout the film's shifts in genre and address, alternately conveyed with irony and sincere mourning. If the film can be read as camp, it is only in the way suggested by Richard Dyer: "passion-with-irony."[8]

Although predominantly shot using dolls for actors, *Superstar*'s framings, camera movements, and editing adhere to live-action modes. (The film was shot as live action rather than as stop-motion animation.) Comically, the establishing shot for the family home in Downey, California, is superimposed with the label "A simulation." The domestic and performance scenes are shot in the manner of Douglas Sirk's melodramas (prefiguring Haynes's *Far from Heaven*), with pans showing Karen framed in windows or in the background with relatively few close-ups. When the Carpenters perform "We've Only Just Begun" for a television broadcast, the camera movements and cutting resemble the construction and décor of the period's TV variety show musical numbers. The sequence segues into a standard music montage, with various cuts away to different activities documenting the Carpenters' offstage lives, presented in hokey Super 8 rear projection; the illusion is percussively ruptured, however, by repeated shots of a human hand hitting "a lackadaisically brandished tambourine."[9] The film allows the audience to giggle early on at the dolls' stunt casting and joke moments—such as Karen's cough or shots of human body parts—before becoming progressively more tragic.

Frequently the film operates in dual registers, as in a parodic educational film-within-the-film about anorexia, which is laughably didactic yet conveys substantial information. Although presenting a pathology in factual medical terms, the construction of the sequence mocks the pedantic documentary form, broken up as it is by overly awkward live-action shots of women on the street asking basic questions such as "What is anorexia nervosa?" and "Do they really think they look good like that?" Adding to the comic effect while reconnecting the pseudo-doc to the narrative's plastic world, doll arms substitute for human stand-ins to illustrate the "normal" arm (chubby baby doll arm) and the "anorexic" body (Barbie-type doll body). The following "Top of the World" sequence recasts the meaning of the first line, "Such a feeling's comin' over me," as a reference to anorexic euphoria. This montage begins with a graphic match, cutting from a turning globe to a turning disco ball, and Karen's world-tour diet of salads, iced tea, and Ex-Lax becomes a routine, edited with a rhythmic series of shots of a bathroom scale dial turning to measure Karen's diminishing weight. The sequence ends with the Carpenter family watching a performance together on television. While Richard and the parents cheer the TV act, Karen complains, "I looked really fat." The film posits that her self-perception was increasingly mediated by television broadcasts and music critics' barbs.

Much of the fuss over the film has emphasized the novelty and, with a sentiment of skepticism undone, effectiveness of the doll stars. The doll

23. Karen during a live performance in *Superstar*. Is that a Lite Brite in the background?

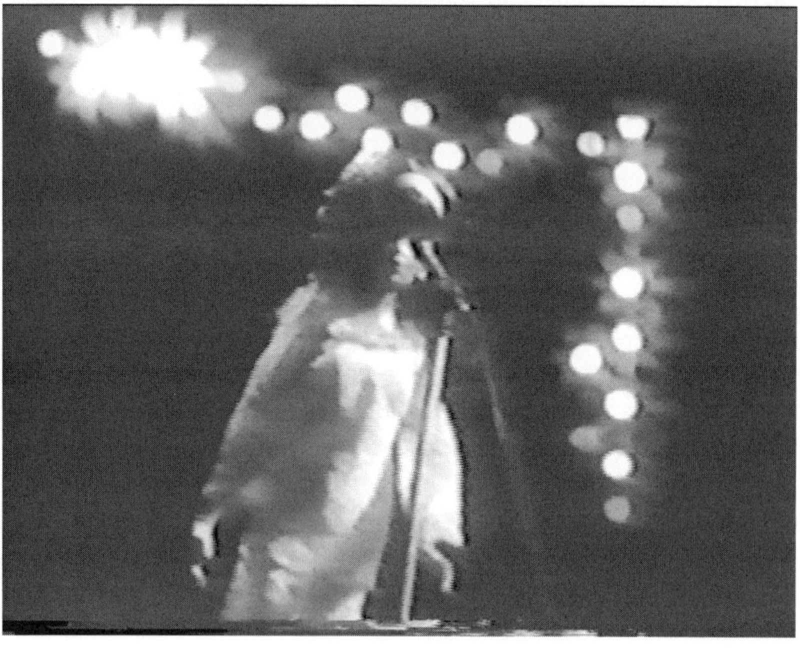

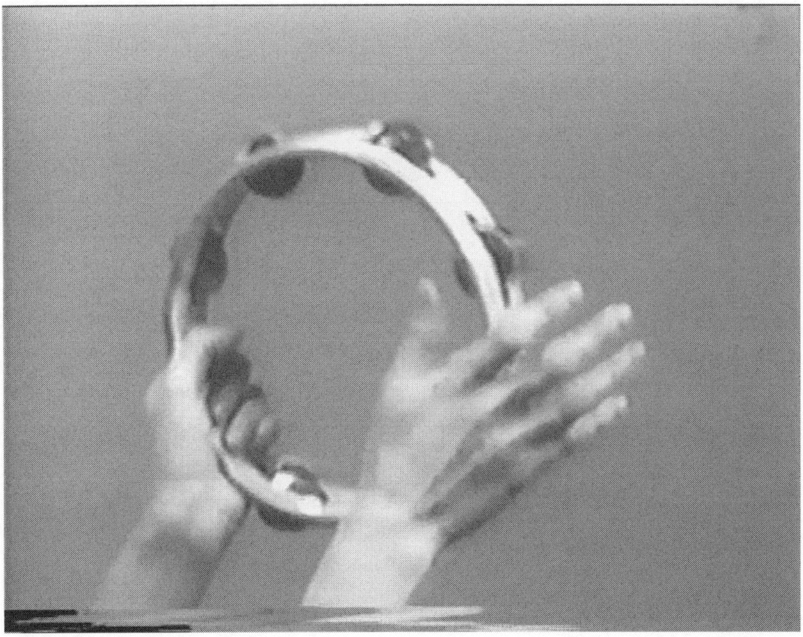

24. *Superstar*: The intrusion of a human body part into the doll world with "a lackadaisically brandished tambourine."

scenes, however, make up only about two-thirds of the screen time, and the "acted" doll scenes with dialogue look stiff in comparison to sequences when the Carpenters' songs provide the primary soundtrack and inspiration for fluid montage sequences. As in melodrama (literally, drama-plus-music), the Carpenters' songs trigger the emotional cues throughout the film, and Karen Carpenter's authentic singing voice imbues the dolls with their much-acclaimed subjectivity. Viewers of *Superstar* may find themselves in the ambivalent position of singing along to songs they might otherwise be embarrassed to enjoy, as Coco Fusco observed in her self-reflexive review of the film:

> I was stunned by the realization that I and everyone else in the room knew every lyric by heart. Those sappy tunes had infected us all, just as much, if not more than, the Grateful Dead. And the extraordinary response to the film, which transformed the 27-year-old Haynes into an avant-garde superstar just weeks after the *Village Voice* proclaimed the death of avant-garde cinema, signals that the film hit an ever-vibrant pop-cultural nerve.[10]

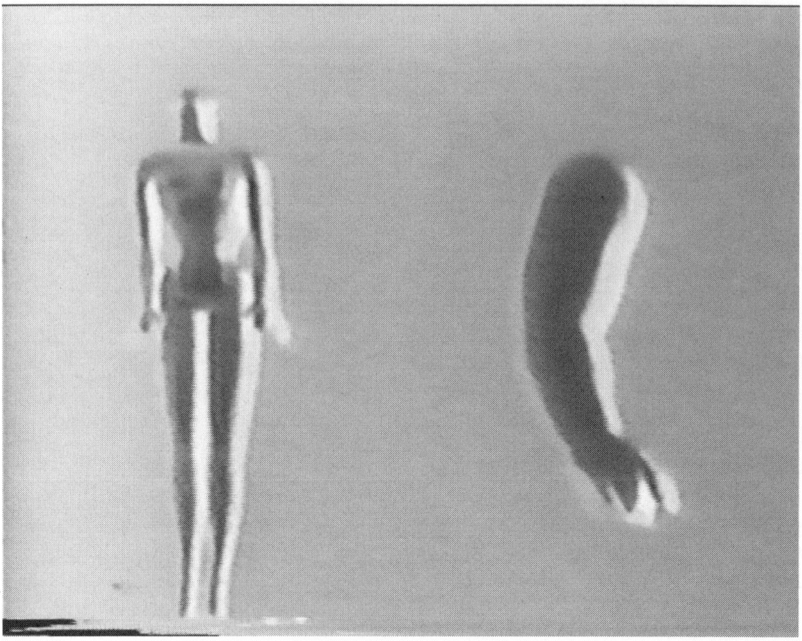

25. *Superstar*: The anorexic body (Barbie-like) and the normal body (baby doll arm).

Without the melancholic sound of Karen Carpenter's sonorous voice and occasionally ironic literalizations of the lyrics, *Superstar* simply wouldn't work. Throughout *Superstar*, musical montages function not only as dress rehearsals for the complicated musical structure of Haynes's later *Velvet Goldmine* (1998) but also, as in *Goldmine*, present the visualizations of music that provide the essential narrative exposition while exploiting the songs' emotive potential.[11] Rather than relying solely on the dolls' emotive capacity, the film's wit and affective ability are attributable to its use of the Carpenters' music, formal and generic play, and, on video, the material degeneration of rerecorded tapes.

For All I Know: A History of *Superstar*

Although writings on Haynes's oeuvre have alluded to the film's status as "an underground classic" and bootleg favorite, they have not attempted to account for its prevalence or the ways in which bootlegging has altered the text. *Superstar*'s reception has been influenced meaningfully by the conditions of its exhibition and circulation, even more so since its withdrawal from licit distribution. Therefore it seems essential to revisit *Superstar*'s history and perhaps correct some of its production and distribution lore before reading the bootleg aesthetic of the film's copies on analog video.[12]

Exhibition History

Superstar debuted at the downtown New York spaces Films Charas and Millennium in July 1987. In August the film screened again as part of Karen Carpenter Night at Pyramid, a gay-friendly postpunk nightclub on Avenue A that was a hot spot for dancing and performance at the time.[13] When *Artforum*'s two-part fortieth-anniversary issues offered a retrospective look at the 1980s art scene, *Superstar* was singled out as one of the two featured milestones for the year. (The other was Andy Warhol's death.)[14] In late 1987 and early 1988, the film continued to screen, on film or as a video installation, at various venues in the city, including the Naked Eye Cinema at ABC No Rio, the New Museum of Contemporary Art, the 55 Mercer Street Gallery, Artists Space, the Collective for Living Cinema, and the new Museum of the Moving Image. Beyond New York City, the film also had a vibrant life across the country, with extensive popular screenings in 1988 and 1989. It screened at the USA Film Festival in Dallas, where it won the National Short Film and Video Competition; the San Francisco International Film Festival, where it won the Golden Gate Grand Prize for Short Narrative; the United States Film Festival (renamed Sundance a few years later); and the Toronto International Film Festival. Concurrently with the film's festival events, it screened at museums, colleges, artist centers, and rep houses as part of special events or midnight runs in Washington; Chicago; Baltimore; Milwaukee; San Francisco; Berkeley; Los Angeles; Pasadena; Seattle; Boston; Cambridge, Massachusetts; Rochester, Ithaca, and Poughkeepsie, New York; and South Norwalk, Connecticut.[15] In addition, the film screened several times at the influential music venue Maxwell's in Hoboken, New Jersey, where the film crossed over from film and gallery audiences to music ones, including members of Sonic Youth, who later covered "Superstar" for the tribute album *If I Were a Carpenter* (1994). Haynes suggests that these screenings "established the film in the alternative music world, where it surely influenced a Carpenters reappraisal."[16]

During the two years after the film's release, *Superstar* was quickly integrated into the curriculum for college courses and was being used at eating disorder clinics as an educational and discussion aid, presumably screening on video. Additionally, tapes were circulating among film industry folks, who would watch *Superstar* over lunch hours or at parties; preview tapes had gone out to the press and curators as well. Haynes also sold approximately sixty VHS copies of the film, complete with homemade covers and transcriptions of the difficult-to-read intertitles within the film, through a bookstore in Los Angeles, and bootlegs were already available in alternative video stores across the country.[17] Thus legitimate and bootleg tapes already began circulating simultaneously with the film's theatrical and gallery screenings.

The public screenings and private viewings recounted here, though short of comprehensive and ultimately impossible to exhaustively document, demonstrate the film's extensive screenings across the country. In addition, the range of venues and presentational modes suggests the varied ways the film was positioned for audiences: as an avant-garde art film, as a party musical, as a fan text, as a video artwork, as a midnight cult flick, as a festival indie, as a museum piece, as a pedagogical tool, as a therapeutic text, and as a collector's item. These multiple identities and modes of address may in part suggest the film's appeal to varied audiences and reflect the film's complexity.

Legal Problems

If the film's gimmick of using dolls for actors helped make it infamous, its ultimate withdrawal from official distribution because of legal trouble has made it legendary. Significantly, Haynes was conscious during production that his film might court unwanted advances—from both the Carpenters and Mattel. Coscreenwriter and coproducer Cynthia Schneider, now a lawyer, was beginning her foray in the legal field during production and was conscientious about avoiding allegations of libel by only portraying biographical details that had previously appeared in print. Late in the film's production, Haynes also attempted to secure the rights to the Carpenters' music by sending letters to the various music publishers. "Top of the World," cowritten by Richard Carpenter, was among Haynes's requested tracks and figured prominently in the film. (All the other songs were written by other composers.) Haynes received an immediate response from Richard Carpenter's representative asking for more information, and Haynes replied with a synopsis and personal statement of intention, stating that the film was sympathetic to Karen Carpenter and explaining that it was a student film that would not be screened for commercial purposes.[18] Two months later, Richard Carpenter's representative replied that Haynes could not make the film, use the songs, or portray any biographical information. By that point, *Superstar* was in late postproduction, and Haynes decided to complete the film anyway. Soon the film began to screen publicly, but for the next couple of years, Haynes did not hear back from Richard Carpenter's representatives—or other music publishers or record company officials. Significantly, Haynes's press release for *Superstar*'s first three screenings acknowledges its outlaw status in the first sentence: "*Superstar* is an unauthorized film . . . using Barbie-sized dolls."[19] The phrase "Barbie-sized dolls" is especially interesting because it seems to anticipate and circumscribe Haynes's first near lawsuit following the film's release.

Barbie • Mattel, the manufacturer and owner of Barbie, her pals, her products, and her trademarked identity, first took notice of the film in 1988. The corporation was already involved in lawsuits against knockoff products and clearly intent on protecting its market share by whatever legal means necessary. The company expressed concern to Haynes about associations between their products and death, fearing that portraying a Barbie doll as anorexic would mar her happy, healthy image. Mattel sent Haynes a series of letters, including one with copies of the patents for Barbie and her various individual body parts; Barbie was not merely a brand but also a precise width of her arm or curvature of her torso. The dolls used in the film were an assortment of Mattel and Mattel-like products (for instance, Dionne Warwick was reportedly embodied by the head of a Michael Jackson figure attached to a female doll body),[20] mostly found at thrift stores and rendered unrecognizable by appearing in period garb with remolded faces.[21] Barbie's name and logo never appear in the film, and the authentic Mattel products are indistinguishable from the knockoffs. As a gesture of good faith, Haynes sent Mattel a letter offering to add a disclaimer or credit in the film—either stating that the dolls in the film were not Mattel products and not to be confused with them or adding a note of gratitude to the company for its (after-the-fact) permission.[22] Mattel never pursued full-fledged legal action or sought damages against the film. (Haynes does not know precisely what influenced Mattel's decision to stop correspondence.) Since the film's release and suppression, however, there seems to have been a flurry of doll media and criticism, and Mattel has threatened works such as Mark Napier's Internet project *The Distorted Barbie* (1997), Tom Forsythe's photo series *Food Chain Barbie* (1999), and the Brazilian short *Barbie Can Also Be Sad* (*Barbie tambien puede estar triste*, Albertina Carri, 2001).[23] In addition, Barbie studies emerged as a hot 1990s subdiscipline of feminist cultural studies and critical pranks with the production of the tape *Twist Barbie: Lynn Spigel Dreams of Plastic Feminism* (Paper Tiger TV, 1994) and the publication of Erica Rand's *Barbie's Queer*

Accessories, M. G. Lord's *Forever Barbie: The Unauthorized Biography of a Real Doll*, and *The Barbie Chronicles*, edited by Yona Zeldis McDonough. Perhaps most famously, the Barbie Liberation Organization was a mid-1990s intervention group that switched voice boxes in talking Barbie and G.I. Joe dolls to break down gender stereotypes; the dolls were returned to stores, where they were purchased by unsuspecting consumers. The group's actions are documented in the tape *BLO Nightly News* (1994).

One issue that plagues the Barbie name is its common usage. Even Haynes, who learned to be careful about describing the dolls, frequently uses the term "Barbie" as shorthand. The term "Barbie" has, in effect, experienced "genericide"—when a trademarked name no longer refers exclusively to a specific brand identity but is used to generically refer to the product itself, so that through common usage "Barbie" has come to mean pretty much any doll of a certain size and style.[24] What is perhaps especially interesting about attempts to control the use and identity of a specific, brand-trademarked doll—beyond its market dominance and cultural significance—is that it contradicts the basic premise of doll play: children (and adults) use dolls to enact imagined, unauthorized stories. At times these fabulations are based on corporate-owned mythologies and brand identities (playing Barbie), but just as often—if not more so—doll play rehearses general scenarios (playing "house" or "school") or reenacts actual personalities and events (playing Karen Carpenter through Barbie).[25] Part of *Superstar*'s transgression is rendering private play in a public forum.

Music Rights • *Superstar*'s legal troubles resumed in October 1989, when Haynes received three cease-and-desist letters: one from Richard Carpenter's music publisher (Almo Music Corp./Hammer and Nails Music, Inc. ASCAP), one from the Carpenters' label (A&M RECORDS), and one from the Karen Carpenter Estate. These letters and subsequent correspondence charged that *Superstar* violated copyright laws through unauthorized use of the Carpenters' music, logo, likenesses, and life story. As celebrities, the Carpenters were public, newsworthy figures, and Haynes's retelling was conscientiously nonlibelous because it could be substantiated through press and printed biographies. Richard Carpenter's objection to uses of the Carpenters' logo and likenesses, which function as authenticating markers within the plastic mise-en-scène, points to a desire to literally preserve the duo's image(s). But it is the Carpenters' music, used without permission or licensing, that remains the most insurmountable obstacle to the film's aboveground circulation.[26]

Using songs in films requires not only licensing the recording and underlying music publishers' rights but also paying synchronization rights. A synchronization license, as the term suggests, applies whenever recorded music is matched with moving images, thereby exploiting the dramatic potential of the music and potentially altering the song's original intended meaning through the juxtaposition. There are few legal recourses for including music without clearing such rights. As I remarked in chapter 2, fair use does not protect *artistic* appropriation but does protect critical or transformative reuse—thereby necessitating a political edge or formal reinvention. Perhaps a case could have been made that *Superstar* uses the Carpenters' songs in critical, even scholarly or culturally and emotionally transformative manners. The glitch in the film's potential fair-use defense lies in the song clips' duration; subsequent decisions on music sampling have suggested that reproducing mere seconds of a song constitutes infringement. Music, whether integrated into derivative songs or applied in films and videos, is perhaps the hardest category of work for claiming fair use, and music rights holders have been among the most aggressive in licensing and litigating. Parody, as a subcategory of fair use, has somewhat more wiggle room, but the songs themselves are not parodied by their usage in the film, and claiming that they are would undermine the film's dramatic effect and perhaps Haynes's artistic intentions.

The press has characterized the motivation behind the injunctions as the result of Richard Carpenter's personal offense at the film, but these assumptions remain unsubstantiated.[27] However, it is clear that the case against the film was never phrased in terms of the artist's or record company's revenue losses. If anything, *Superstar*'s popularity increased sales of the Carpenters' albums and functioned as an incredibly effective promotional vehicle for the by-then-unfashionable duo. Haynes was not asked to pay any damages for copyright infringement; instead the legal correspondence demanded that the film be completely removed from circulation.[28] To date, Haynes does not know if Richard Carpenter has seen the film, although Haynes has made efforts to make the film available for Carpenter's consideration. However, Richard Carpenter did participate in the made-for-television biopic *The Karen Carpenter Story*, which aired in 1989 and with which *Superstar* may have seemed to compete; in the liner notes for the duo's thirty-fifth anniversary double CD collection, he expressed regret about the TV project.[29]

Attempting to negotiate, Haynes requested that the film be allowed to continue screening nontheatrically and noncommercially as an educational tool for schools and clinics, offering to donate all proceeds from rentals to the Karen Carpenter Foundation for Anorexia Research. Haynes's proposal was declined, and the final agreement stipulated that the film could not screen publicly and that Haynes had to do everything he could to stop circulation of videotapes—such as recalling them from video stores. Richard Carpenter did allow for one major concession, seeming to understand a young artist's need to build and promote a career: Haynes was permitted to show the film to critics in relation to his other work. Since 1989, Haynes and his lawyers have made efforts to clear the ban on the film so that it can be released again; clearing the music rights remains the necessary precondition for *Superstar*'s reemergence.

Back in Circulation

For a film that has been removed from distribution and has been historically difficult to access, *Superstar* has had an astonishing, irrepressible afterlife. Although its primary mode of circulation since late 1989 has been through an informal underground network of shared bootleg videotapes, *Superstar* continues to be seen in large-audience (if not always exactly *public*) settings. University classrooms continue to rank among the most prevalent venues for illicit—if educational—screenings. I've heard of a screening in, curiously enough, an Introduction to Video class; the film has also been taught in classes on narrative structure, alternative cinemas, film theory, feminism, American popular culture, documentary theory, and introduction to art. One friend first learned of the film when it showed in the first weeks of his brother's freshman-level intro to film class for production students, apparently screening early in the semester as both an eye-opener for youths who had never seen anything like it and as a model for what low-budget filmmakers could accomplish. Other friends have recalled seeing the film in the early 1990s in informal settings, from a Dallas nightclub to a party in a rented Los Angeles storefront to a cult film club's monthly bar night in Washington to a meeting of the São Paulo Carpenters Fan Club to a television broadcast in Amsterdam. In the mid-1990s, the film is rumored to have screened at film festivals and micro-cinemas in Baltimore, Ann Arbor, and San Francisco and at a major art museum in New York City. Since 2000, museums, micro-cinemas, theaters, and festivals from coast to coast (and to some extent overseas) have also repeatedly made this "surprise," "secret," "early" Haynes "short" available for public consumption—in rare cases on 16 mm, often making a point to publicize that fact. *Superstar* typically screens within the context of the filmmaker's other work or within doll-themed programs and is either shown unannounced or promoted through keywords (in quotation marks in the previous sentence) for in-the-know audiences.

Other public events have explicitly lauded the work's illicit status for the counterculture kids, advertising the film by title and assuredly showing bootlegged videos. In 2002–3 *Superstar* toured as part of the exhibition *Illegal Art: Freedom of Expression in the Corporate Age* to Anthology Film Archives (New York), the Roxie Cinema (San Francisco), and the Prince Music Theater (Philadelphia) and continued traveling, with dates scheduled into 2006. Ironically, the publicity for the *Illegal Art* show ran the disclaimer "used without permission" at the end of its *Superstar* blurb, a note that did not appear in other descriptions for individual works.[30] Free bootleg screenings also launched the grand opening of an alternative-cinema venue in Columbia, Missouri: "We showed it three times over the course of the night, with the theater filling each time with a new group of people. . . . It was like nothing most of the people at the opening had ever seen and I like to think that it started them down a path of transgressive cinema."[31]

The drive to show and share the film must be worth the gamble for venues—a testament to programmers' and audiences' love for it. To my mind, the most telling promotional text for a *Superstar* screening appeared in the calendar listing for a 1998 event at the Blinding Light Cinema in Vancouver, where it screened repeatedly: "Though we swore we'd never show it again . . . due to overwhelming public demand we are pleased to present this long-banned underground classic. . . . The mediocre quality dub which you [will] see here, [is] viewed with a certain charm and respect rarely given to degraded video."[32]

Grainy Days and Mondays: Theorizing Bootleg Aesthetics

As the Vancouver screening advertisement mentions, the bootleg tapes of *Superstar* typically reveal lost resolution from multiple generations of duplication, so that the color looks washed-out and the audio sounds distorted. The typical transfer format—NTSC VHS—ranks among the lowest-fidelity commercial tape stocks, and VHS-to-VHS dubs reveal steep resolution loss from generation to generation. This residue places the *Superstar* bootlegging phenomenon within a specific technological moment: it was possible only after personal VCRs were pervasive, but the generational deterioration specific to analog recording predates digital video reproduction. (Digital copies are also now available on DVD-R or online as streaming or downloadable MPEGS.)

Since the film went underground, the isolated hush-hush and self-consciously transgressive 16 mm screenings offer film purists opportunities to see the work in more pristine condition. I would suggest that the proliferation of degenerate copies of *Superstar* contributes to the allure of an idealized filmic original. The same might be said for home video generally, which prompted a comparative valorization of seeing classic films in restored prints on the big screen. When I saw *Superstar* projected on 16 mm, the auditorium was packed with people who had seen and likely owned copies but probably had never seen the film "in the flesh." As a low-budget film shot over the course of a couple of weekends, even in its original format, *Superstar*'s titles are still nearly illegible, the film generally grainy, and the sound still rough. Seeing the film on film made me nostalgic for my warped dub at home. For me, part of the experience was missing.

At the risk of getting all poststructuralist, video reproduction calls into question the very notion of an "original" film. Yet at the same time as degeneration helps to invent the categories of originality or fidelity in reverse, I suggest that it also creates new, personal, and arguably technologically specific meanings. Analog duplication of the text, rather than destroying the original's aura, creates a new kind of aura that references the indexicality of analog reproduction and sensuously suggests the personal interventions that made the copy possible. Materially, the fall-out of the image and soundtrack mark each successive copy as an illicit object, a forbidden pleasure that has been watched and shared and loved to exhaustion. Furthermore, the de-resolution of the tapes formally reflects the story of Karen's wasting away. The film's theme becomes expressed on the surface, even as it frustrates and interferes with standard spectatorial engagement with the narrative as the visual and audio information become obscured.

Haynes not only appropriated music for his film but also repurposed television footage. Taped from television with a VCR and then played back and reshot in 16 mm from the surface of a monitor, these images appear with the film camera's flicker out of sync with the televisual pixel scanning, so that the images are distressed by black lines rolling vertically across the screen as well as loss from reproduction between formats. Although Haynes says he worked to minimize the deterioration effect during production, a trace of the format mismatch remains and contributes to the film's expressive effect.[33] Of course, film has been shot off television monitors since the TV medium's first transmissions; before the invention of videotape recorders, live television broadcasts were documented—kinescoped is the official term—by filming screens receiving the signal. This was the standard process, which continued in many instances well after the development of magnetic tape and accounts, in part, for the flicker and extreme contrast in extant early TV footage. These images both suggest a nostalgic, decayed quality and foreground their plasticity.

Haynes uses found footage as television transmissions and media-effected memory in *Superstar.* TV monitors appear within the miniature mise-en-scènes throughout the film, and footage is intercut to rupture the diegesis of the doll scenes. Although the references are identifiable in the distressed footage of President Nixon, the American troops in Vietnam and Cambodia, the protests on the domestic front, and moments from *The Poseidon Adventure* (1972), *The Brady Bunch*, and *The Partridge Family*, they do not necessarily refer to specific speeches, moments of war, or episodes of sitcoms but hearken to a general cultural memory of the time. Here Haynes's appropriations function less as recontextualizations or subversions of corporate media than as a historicizing method to present the cultural context for the Carpenters' anachronistically wholesome star personas and music that "led a raucous nation smoothly into the '70s." But this purported smoothness jars with the rough-textured television-to-film (to bootleg video) footage, emphasizing a disjuncture between Karen Carpenter's soothing voice and the controversies documented and remembered.

Media Affects

As a film about simulation, hypocritical images, media reproduction, and self-destruction, the narrative and its aesthetic to a certain extent challenge each other, even as they are conceptually complementary. The film was conceived as a test case of sorts to see whether inanimate dolls can generate spectator sympathy and identification, and of course they can. Barbie cocreator Ruth Handler has even commented that the original doll's "face was deliberately designed to be blank, without a personality, so that the projection of the child's dream could be on Barbie's face."[34] But the identification experiment is neither seamless nor hermetic. As I have already described, the film is made up of abrupt generic shifts and jump-cut ruptures that foreground the text as image and sound, not as a diegetic world.[35] In one of the most rigorous analyses of *Superstar*, the author decodes the signs and queer meanings in the film:

> The cumulative effect of pastiching together contrived dramatic scenarios enacted by plastic dolls, the Carpenters' now dated and hopelessly sentimental music, and found footage from seventies sitcoms serves to expose

the patent artifice (and outrageousness) of these images/texts/structures and the inadequacy of the ideologies they embody.[36]

Although an insightful reading of the film's construction, this analysis does not consider the film's perceptual or emotional resonance. I disagree with the author's appraisal of the Carpenters' music, and therein may lie our different responses and agendas. To my chagrin, I've also heard more than one person suggest that casting Barbie as Karen Carpenter reflects their supposedly shared lack of personality or depth. Made just four years after her death, *Superstar* used the Carpenters' music before a retro cycle had reclaimed it and re-presents Karen Carpenter to audiences too alternative or too cool to have taken her seriously the first time around. Haynes demonstrates enormous affection for Karen Carpenter and admiration for her vocal talent, even though she is represented by a disfigured doll.

The appropriation aesthetic of image loss from duplication that appears within Haynes's film—complemented by a Carpenters soundtrack—presents a historical distance that can be read nostalgically. At the same time, this image loss exerts violence against the images and frames them as representations. As I read the film, the critical analysis of media influence is persistently in tension with the emotional allure of an entertainment utopia. A fondness and respect for Karen Carpenter is essential for a sympathetic engagement with the film. Haynes has recalled his complicated relationship to the entertainment of the period: "The early Seventies had felt like the last moment of pure, popular culture fantasy and fakeness that I shared with my parents, when we were still united in this image of happy American familihood. . . . And The Carpenters' music seemed especially emblematic of that time."[37] What Haynes describes is simultaneously a desire for, and a distrust of, a perfectly constructed pop past.

In the film, Karen begins to demonstrate disillusionment with the media as well. When she has moved to Century City to live on her own, a solitary and starving Karen stares blankly at her giant-screen TV, and the footage becomes staticky. Karen's loss of self-control and subjective breakdown are portrayed through the disarray of television images edited amid documents of Holocaust-emaciated corpses and a doll being spanked. Simultaneously, overlapping samples of Carpenters songs and snippets of dialogue replay on the audio track. Thus Haynes creates his own effect of Carpenters overdubbing on the soundtrack. The effect both materially deconstructs media images and formally expresses Karen's self-perception as mediated by television; the media's direct effects on Karen are made even more explicit

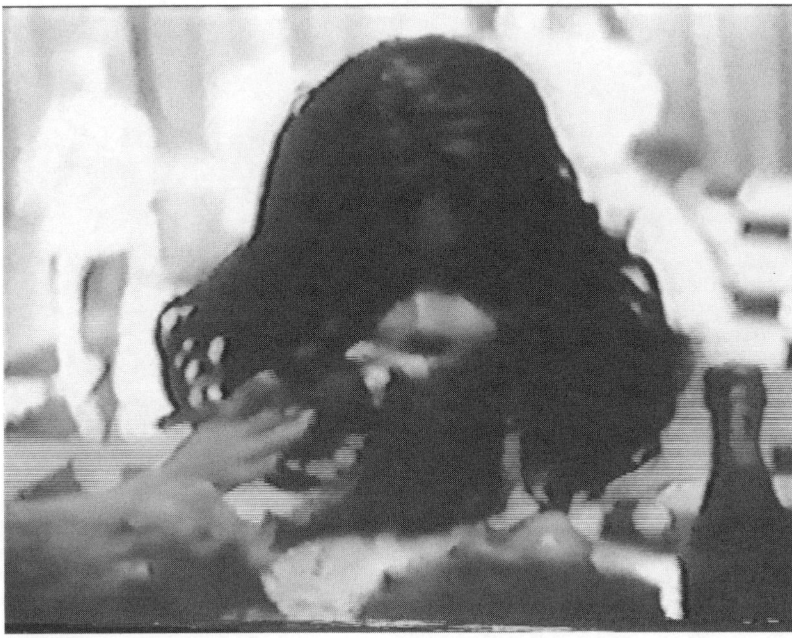

26. *Superstar*: Framed in front of a staticky TV monitor, Karen's subjectivity is influenced by the media.

through close-ups framing Karen in front of imposing televisual transmissions. The distressing of appropriated footage functions expressionistically as a device conveying Karen's psychological state, reflecting the film's themes in its form. Subsequent repeated video reproduction on bootleg videotapes has compounded this effect, so that the image loss with each successive VHS-to-VHS dub aesthetically reflects Karen's subjective and bodily wasting: her disappearing body becomes manifest in the material information loss. Her hollowed-out and remolded face is reflected in the grain of the video pixels.

Bootleg Aesthetics

My research on videotape began in response to a seeming lacuna in relation to the aesthetics of analog video and the ways in which bootlegging can be read as a cinephiliac practice. Relatively little had been written describing the effect of decay and reconfiguration that occurs when video is reshot on film—or when it is then repeatedly recorded from video to video. In chapter 1, I reviewed the existing celebrations that view bootleg aesthetics as formal changes in the work or as evidence of illicit origins. Alongside such

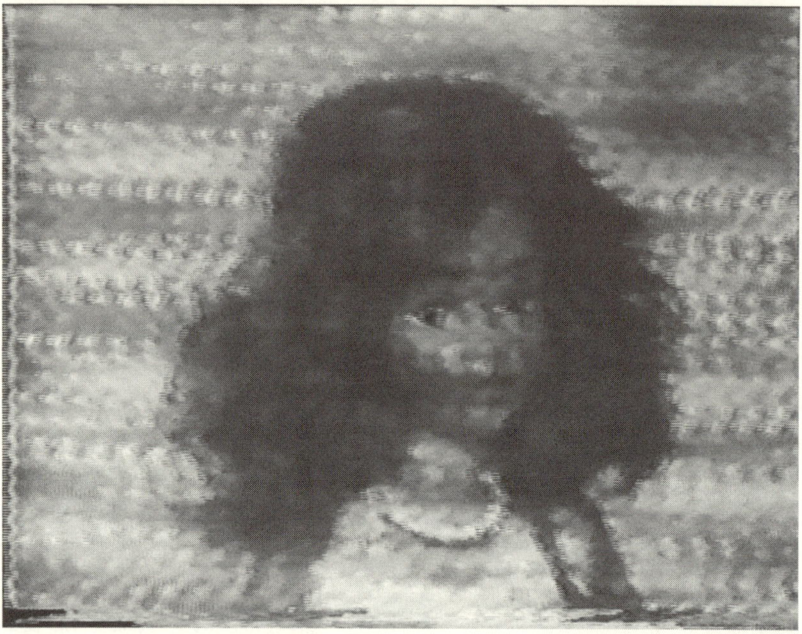

27. *Superstar*: A dissolve from a close-up to static suggests Karen's psychic distress and bodily breakdown.

typically brief accounts, I have looked to, and been influenced by, the theoretical and historical work on audio technologies and listening practices to conceptualize video aesthetics. For instance, writing about audio, Rick Altman has argued that "recorded sound . . . always carries some record of the process, superimposed," and that distortion is inherent to all recordings.[38] Likewise, book historians have suggested that in the analog world, readers leave traces of their reception through physical wear, markings and marginalia, or even cutting and pasting.[39] By extension, I suggest that each videotape transfer can be understood as having a unique effect on the duplication and that each cassette becomes a singular text that contains and compounds its own history. The distress and disappearance of the video signal, which cause tracking problems for far-from-heavenly VHS tapes, call attention to the tapes as copies—analog, personal copies. These blurry bootlegs foreground duplication and remind viewers that they are indulging in a pleasurably transgressive viewing act.

There are appreciable distinctions between *Superstar*'s internal image appropriation and the audience's video bootlegging of the film. The effects of Haynes's nonsynchronous TV-to-film recording differ from cultist video-to-video reproduction: sharp pixelation, scrambled signals, and visible rolling black lines are clearly present in Haynes's appropriation, whereas the video dubbing makes the image less focused and washes out the color intensity. (The putrid colors on these tapes might also be seen as reflecting the ugly palates and cheap productions values of TV shows of the 1970s.) Viewers of the bootlegs engage with the text on a format-specific basis, knowing from the film's first moments (if not from word of mouth even earlier) that they are watching a self-reflexive collage of images that have been further decayed through wear and reproduction. But, to trot out an oft-cited argument by Roland Barthes, video reproduction of the text materially records the audience's (reader's) use and abuse of the text, rendering the "death of the author." Haynes is quite likely the most theoretically influenced and self-conscious contemporary American auteur, but Barthes's paradigm-shattering argument that readers, not authors or critics, produce textual meanings is helpful in articulating the role audiences play in re-creating and redistributing *Superstar* and the differences between the internal and external distressed-image effects. Haynes's unauthorized star study effectively becomes "un-author-ized" through video reproduction. To phrase the issue in Barthes's terms, Haynes's use of found footage *expresses* both Karen's psychological state and Haynes's media critiques, whereas the video-to-video bootlegging *inscribes* histories of the videos' circulation.[40]

Haynes's expressions are not erased by bootleg inscriptions. Rather, the effect is one of mediation as the compound filtering of multiple-generation bootlegs alters the viewing experience. Watching a bootleg presents a constant negotiation of one's own perceptual attention; the viewer must choose to focus on the distortion or attempt to peer *through* it to see Haynes's original intended images and must fill in the muffled pop tunes from memory while listening closely to filter through the garbled dialogue.[41] Of course, seeing and listening more generally are also learned processes of filtering sensory stimulation, and watching a film or video entails actively not seeing: by directing our attention to the screen, by ignoring audience noises, and by relying on the innate perceptual slowness that allows for the persistence of vision.[42] Likewise, there are all kinds of auditory phenomena and sound effects that exist beyond the standard range of human hearing or attention but nonetheless contribute to the soundtrack.

Precisely because analog video interference forces the audience to focus and filter perceptual attention, I suggest that watching distressed tapes of *Superstar* presents a model of spectatorship perhaps more illustrative of the semiotician and psychoanalytic film theorist Christian Metz's formulation

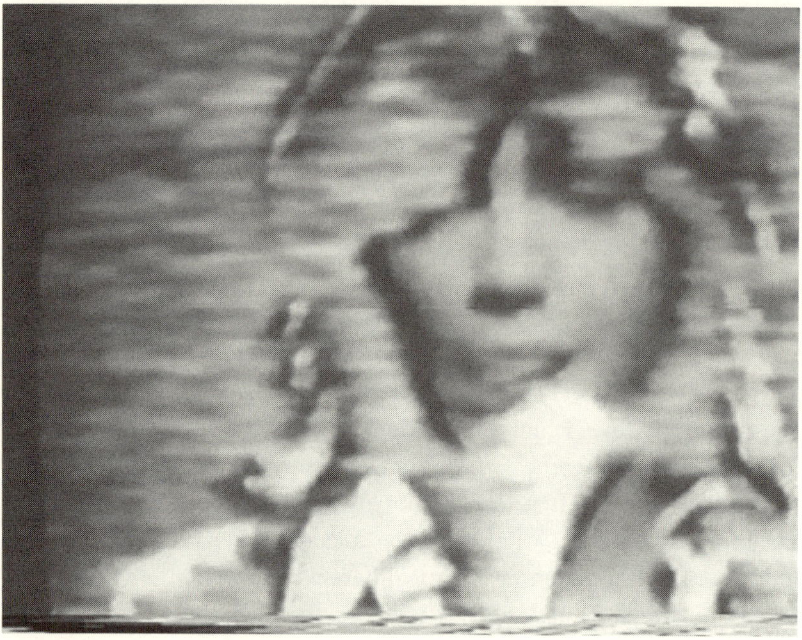

28. Haynes's appropriated image from *The Partridge Family* reveals formal distress.

of cinematic identification than classical Hollywood cinema (although the ideological effects certainly differ). The video viewer becomes more aware of the format through its distortion, and thereby primary identification *is* with the viewer's own gaze, as Metz suggested, while anthropomorphic identification with the dolls must be secondary.[43] Though Metz was attempting to move beyond the phenomenology of classical film theory,[44] the phenomenologist Laura Marks engages Metz's model. Marks acknowledges the erotics of image deterioration, whether owing to age, wear, or artistic intervention. Marks proposes that cinematic identification is grounded in a bodily relationship to the screen and that films and videos that present hard-to-see, deteriorating, or pixelated images offer a haptic, melancholic empathy. But rather than presenting death as horrible, these mortified images offer the viewer new, tangible, intimate, and frequently beautiful relationships to material loss.[45]

Metz and Marks present fundamentally differing approaches to human sensation: Metz divides the senses between those of contact (taste, smell, touch) and those of distance (sight and sound, the senses of spectatorship), whereas Marks desires to close the gap between touch and sight through the concept of haptic vision.[46] Yet, as Marks herself must be aware, no matter what kind of contact we think we feel, we know we are not *touching* the image. When video reproduction alters the tape's surface, it does so in a way that forces us to recognize our own visual and aural concentration. Rather than identification, I suggest that what Marks recognizes is that the spectator's own subjectivity is personal, desiring, sensual.

As I argue in the next section, subjectivity is additionally produced through relationships to the videocassettes themselves. Metz and Marks converge on a cinephiliac point: "The cinema is a body . . . a fetish that can be loved."[47] The intersections of materiality and affect can best be articulated through the concept of the fetish. Fetishism—in religious, Marxist, Freudian, and vernacular conceptions—describes the associative values invested in things that transcend their forms as objects. In the late 1980s and 1990s, cultural scholars and historians turned to fetishism as a new methodology for historical materialism.[48] Bootlegged tapes of *Superstar* function in multiple ways as fetishes: as precious objects, as the products of reproductive labor, as substitutes for absent film prints or commercially produced videos (not to mention Karen Carpenter herself), and as souvenirs of the fans who have made them. Perhaps appropriately for *Superstar*, plastic cassettes of the film, like dolls, are often anthropomorphized and imbued with sentimental meanings. And like Karen Carpenter, VHS has been hugely popular but rarely given its due praise or deemed worthy of aesthetic analysis.

(They Long to Be) Close to *Superstar*: Reception Studies

Superstar's unplanned bootleg circulation presents a democratization of distribution at the same time as it makes access elitist; seeing or obtaining *Superstar*—at least until it became available through eBay or file-sharing networks—depended on insider connections or serendipity. In addition to conceptual connections I have suggested between the anorexic narrative and formal degeneration, the wear and fall-out of tapes present material evidence of fan use, duplication, and dissemination—marking an otherwise impossible-to-retrace and unwritten history of circulation.

Whereas the footage Haynes reshot and inserted works (in part) to locate the story within a specific historical setting, the defocusing and paling effects of video duplication suggest the tapes' geographic and temporal dispersion.[49] The uncontainable and in many ways untraceable exchange of tapes produces a proliferation of meanings, responses, and personal engagements with the text. I like to think of the exponential duping and distribution of bootleg tapes as being akin to scattering Karen Carpenter's ashes—not tossed

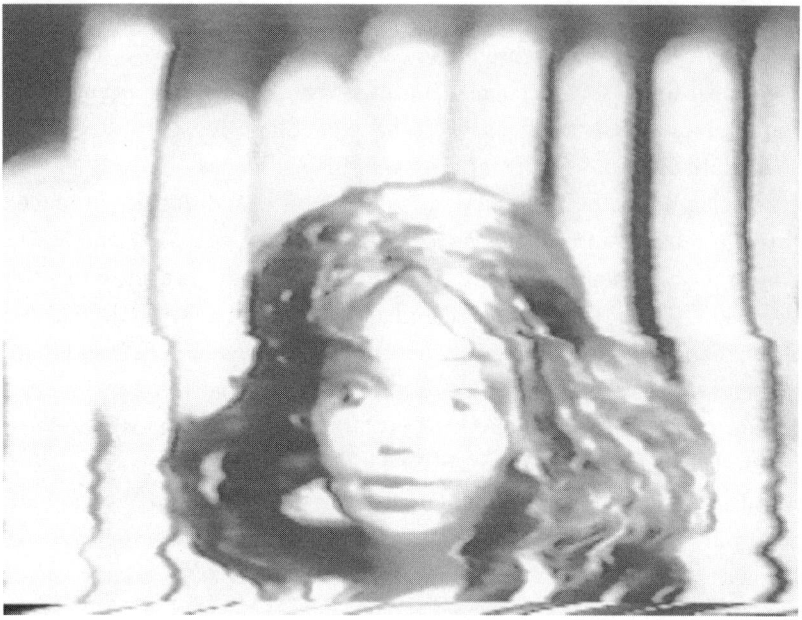

29. Washed out and distorted, Karen's face is disfigured by video reproduction.

to the wind or into the ocean but into the collections of fans and cinephiles. And, of course, there is the alternate perspective that bootleg circulation keeps the film and Karen Carpenter alive.

Surveying

In the case of *Superstar*, bootlegging's resonance for viewers cannot be limited to playback aesthetics. Indeed, the cassettes themselves come to be, to appropriate an academic book title, "an archive of feelings."[50] In initially researching the film's and tapes' ephemeral circulation, I sent out an informal mass e-mail inquiry to friends and colleagues who I assumed had seen it, asking where they had first seen it and if they had acquired their own copies. Later I posted surveys on the experimental film Listerv Frameworks and the gay filmmaker and programmer forum PQProfessionals. Here and in my project more generally, the anecdotal and the colloquial serve to suggest the personal and the everyday relationships and experiences users have with videotape.

To my surprise, I received numerous responses, especially from acquaintances and strangers, that detailed the specifics of their personal experiences. These anecdotes revealed a spectrum of encounters and collection policies, all of which ultimately demonstrated considerable personal attachment to the text. I received stories about illicit means of accessing personal copies, such as secretly duping a tape borrowed from a professor, stealing a tape from a boss, and nearly stealing the tape from a roommate. One person claimed that his source had been taped off-air from Japanese television. Some tracked down copies at specific alternative video stores, swap meets, or fan conventions in Los Angeles, San Francisco, Seattle, Austin, Chicago, Toronto, New Jersey, New York City, and Northampton, Massachusetts. Most friends told all, but a few were adamant that their *Superstar* suppliers "remain nameless." Some attempted to account for the degrees of separation between their copy and the filmmaker—and, by extension, there were frequent speculations about what duplication generation their tapes were (third generation seems to be a popular if unlikely estimate). I was told personal preservation strategies, such as supervising all screenings to avoid having a loaned tape lost and, impressively, remastering a bootleg onto the sturdier Betacam SP format. One bootlegger's source was a Hi8 tape, supposedly duped from a master, which he stole from a visiting professor; but karma came back to haunt him when "a friend borrowed it from me and, despite lots of promises, I never saw it again." A few reported that old bootlegs had worn out from use and loaning and that they had tracked down replacement copies. A couple of people even reported having watched the tape on first dates; the lure of seeing the rare film apparently functions as a viable seduction technique. (This hasn't quite panned out for me, unfortunately.) My dissertation advisor recounted showing a tape when she taught a youth media production class in Chicago; the copy was a black-and-white dub, but nonetheless the kids responded so strongly that *Superstar* became a model for their own projects. Friends who replied that they hadn't seen the film expressed a desire to do so—rather, something close to insistence that I show it to them—or, in one case, embarrassment about not being able to claim the cachet of having seen it.

What all these anecdotes suggest is the multiplicity of personal meanings and sentimental values these tapes represent for their collectors. Although in most cases the root motivation for obtaining copies simply derives from wanting to see an obscure film or to possess a favorite text, *Superstar*'s out-of-distribution status complicates the tapes' value. The film's relative scarcity increases its worth and drives viewers to reproduce it when they finally have access to it; these actions suggest fear that they may not have access to seeing it again and dedication to maintaining their personal access. Because of the tapes' scarcity, higher-resolution dupes—those fewer generations removed from a master and displaying less distortion—become longed-for objects, and eBay entrepreneurs have made a point of advertising the high quality of their copies available for bidding. The bootlegging phenomenon, in effect, has created an amateur strategy to preserve the work and keep it in semipublic circulation through a wily and ultimately uncontainable network of tape sharing. As one e-mail survey respondent recalled, even early cassettes of the film were labeled with anticopy warnings, which were rarely abided:

> Sometime in the early '90s, a video copy circulated through Baltimore. The tape had a sticker on it that said something like "This film has been banned. . . . Watch this tape with your friends. Do not make copies of it. Then pass it on to someone else." A film teacher at my school took me to a small gathering at the home of a local movie theater owner, and we watched the tape three times. Of course, a copy was made of it before it was passed on to someone else, and from that copy, I'm sure many others were made.[51]

Obviously, no accurate census of *Superstar* dupes will ever be possible, as they have circulated and been reproduced, though the epidemic testifies to the grassroots potential of home taping.

My Own Private Collection

As I write this chapter, I own four videotape copies of *Superstar*: one duped from a friend in 1999, one that was a birthday gift in 2002, and two purchased from strangers via eBay auctions for "research" in 2004. (I also own digital versions on a CD-R with a QuickTime file version and on a DVD-R compilation from the *Illegal Art* exhibition.) Years before conceiving this research topic, I loaned my first copy to friends who complained about its warped image and sound; I have also used this tape for classroom and conference presentations, as well as the source for video grab images used in *Camera Obscura*. When preparing images for the journal article, I made an initial set of frame grabs, but I received complaints that the files were saved at a resolution too low for publication—even though the intention was to demonstrate analog video decay. When redoing video grabs at a different computer lab, I had to transfer the footage from my VHS dub to a mini-DV tape before importing the digital content into the computer. This extra step introduced a problem for high-fidelity images of bootleg distress, as the digitization process automatically "corrected" some of the analog faults. The particularities of specific videotapes' formal stress are thus difficult to document. As video is based on electronic signals rather than fixed images, even the same tape will exhibit some unique problems each time it is played back, and it may become more distorted with each repeated performance.

But each tape does demonstrate its own duplication specificity, along with unique labeling, packaging, and inscription. My first recording was dubbed on an old cassette I had used for timeshifting, and staticky remnants of an early *That '70s Show* episode appear for a few seconds at the head of the tape before *Superstar* begins—producing an accidental dialogue between two 1970s period pieces. My second tape begins with color bars, followed by a copyright warning, and then the identification tag "Video Data Bank Presents," which is abruptly cut off. This opening footage is curious, as VDB, one of two major video art distributors in the United States, never distributed *Superstar*—though, again, this coincidence of taping points back to the film's brief history as a video installation. It is unclear how or when this tag became part of the source recording; it seems that a prior bootlegger taped over a VDB tape and accidentally left the opening footage intact. In the footage that follows, the black leader is not a pure black but a buzzing rainbow of brightly colored flecks, and the opening black-and-white scene has a distinctly blue tint. Such discoloration suggests that the source tape had been reproduced many times over.

Opening with different but equally peculiar footage, my first auction tape begins with a DVD menu for the film, complete with a listing of chapter titles. It's unclear where the auctioneer obtained a DVD of the film or who created and named the chapters. The first chapter title is highlighted in pink and then flashes yellow-green, indicating when the bootlegger pressed the enter button on a DVD remote to start playback. This tape remediates and documents the phantom human interaction with a different, digital technology. The main *Superstar* footage, despite coming from a DVD, still looks at least one analog generation removed from a film-to-video transfer, and my specific recording is punctuated throughout by thin rolling lines of video tracking disturbance. The cassette arrived from Vancouver unlabeled and without a note. I sent a follow-up e-mail to the vendor asking about the dub's DVD source; the vendor succinctly responded that the recording was taped from a DVD but did not elaborate on his source.

A much more friendly correspondence arrived with my second auction tape. In a letter enclosed with my tape, the Mississippi-based auctioneer demonstrated southern hospitality—and up-selling—as he stressed the potential for personal contact, including his name, full address, phone number, and e-mail. He wrote:

> I try to maintain that personal aspect that I have come to love on eBay. . . . Let me know if you are looking for something special by dropping me an email. . . . If you are interested in rare videos, CD's or other items by The Carpenters, please email me for a complete list. I have many wonderful items that I have collected from all over the world.[52]

This vendor specialized in 1970s popular culture, not in cult films per se, and dealt in *Superstar* bootlegs as a Carpenters fan. The cassette came with computer-printed Avery labels on the spine and face, which demonstrate a certain level of professionalism, and arrived enclosed in a protective clear plastic snap-case. The tape's content begins with "PICTURE START" and the traditional film countdown leader, thereby reinforcing *Superstar*'s original film format and suggesting a direct film-to-video transfer—an effect that is reinforced as dark celluloid splotches sporadically appear. The image and sound are as crisp on this dupe as on any *Superstar* tape I've seen, but even on this copy, the outlines of sets and doll characters have fuzzy rather than sharp edges. Thus each tape presents a different version of the text. My most-used copies of *Superstar* have derived from personal relationships, whereas my anonymously purchased ones have suggested the potential for personal contact.

Mementos

While acknowledging that video collectors are motivated by a text's rarity or, conversely, sudden availability, Charles Tashiro has suggested that video collecting is predominantly based on irrational " 'emotional' reasons." He creates a hierarchy between acquisitions that are liked and those that are loved; liked ones are frequently viewed on tape—a format that inevitably wears out—while loved ones (or those that one should love and own) are often promoted to digital disc formats that sit on the shelf in pristine, unused condition.[53] The contradiction between like and love is also legible in bootleg proprietorship: the like impulse prompts the fan to watch and share the text as much as possible, whereas the love impulse makes preservation the priority. In love there is a fear of watching the text too much—and thereby risking physical wear and emotional inoculation, corporeally damaging the cassette and getting "sick" of its enclosed text. A video collection and its uses thereby reveal the owner's personality on the shelf. Indeed, as Jean Baudrillard states, "For it is invariably *oneself* that one collects."[54]

My first e-mail survey to friends basically confirmed my assumptions about the economics of the bootlegs' circulation, but what really struck me about the replies was that in every case, the respondents recalled the exact sources and circumstances of obtaining their copies.[55] Even if they didn't remember precise dates, they remembered who gave them the tapes, what their relationships were, and frequently specified whether they were connected through school, work, friends, relatives, or auction. Each individual cassette has been invested with a sentimental personal association or a quest narrative, such that it not only safeguards its owner's access to a favorite text but also records a personal history. A particularly affecting response came from Jim Hubbard, whose copy is a memento mori:

> I have a VHS copy (more a copy of a copy of a copy of Dior) that I inherited from a writer friend who died in November 1994. . . . To me it's more important as an object that belonged to my friend Dave than as Todd's film (which is rather poorly represented by this copy).[56]

Such sentimental value often does not transfer to extended users, however. Usually whenever a friend asks to borrow a copy of *Superstar*, he or she asks for my best copy—or specifies DVD-R upon learning that I have one. While this may contradict my claims for bootleg aesthetics' associative value, it does emphasize a general recognition of the degenerative materiality of videotape and the specificity of personal attachments.

As loans or presents, circulated from person to person, bootleg tapes operate within a gift economy, with the material wear and interpersonal resonances such forms of exchange suggest. A feminist reading of community building through garage sales reflects some of the bootlegging experience: "The commodities in garage sales have been preowned and broken in, so that something of the garage sale seller—whether stains, scratches, dents, personal sentiments, or a story about the object—is transferred with whatever item changes hands."[57] Reflecting on a very different example (Kwakiuti coppers), another scholar has suggested not only that gift economies connect the participants emotionally, but also that the objects transferred may exhibit their affective investments through physical alteration to the object exchanged. "At each transaction the concrete increase (the 'adornment') is a witness to the increase in feeling. . . . The mere passage of the gift, the act of donation, contains the feeling."[58] I return to the concept of the gift economy in the next chapter.

Bootleg tapes exist as souvenirs of specific periods in their collectors' lives, intimate and professional relationships, and searches for elusive objects. By virtue of its underground, bootleg-based circulation, *Superstar* has primarily and significantly been available through *personal* connections. The tapes, then, not only present an emotional narrative dependent on the viewers' nostalgic associations with the Carpenters' music and the "naive" pop culture of the early 1970s but also evoke memories of the tapes' sources.

After two decades of underground life, *Superstar* cannot be discussed outside the context of its distribution. Nor, I argue, can it be analyzed without looking at the meanings encoded onto the dub tapes. As a film in which the surface expresses the emotional and physical states of its main character as well as its political critique, it is perhaps fortuitous that the film has become primarily accessible in low-fidelity dubs. Bootleg aesthetics visually and acoustically replicate the psychological and physical trauma experienced by Karen in the story; these warbled tapes also record the cult audience's participation in remaking the text with each new duplicate produced and circulated. One of the great ironies of bootlegging is that it preserves *Superstar* in the public's possession as it progressively destroys the original work. Analog reproduction repeatedly renders the collective demise of the narrative subject, the author, and the format. Karen and Todd, we love you to death.

Tape Art

Various artists have explored magnetic tape specifically as a technology of distortion since it became popular.[1] The classic example is Alvin Lucier's *I Am Sitting in a Room*, an audio piece that was "composed" in 1969 and recorded in 1980. Lucier recorded a monologue and then made multiple, compounded recordings of it on magnetic audiotape. The work unfolds sequentially until, by the end of the work, the room tone and tape hiss distortion have completely engulfed his voice, which is no longer audible. Working in videotape, Jonathan Horowitz created a similar piece that visually degraded the media manufacturer Maxell's corporate image by repeatedly duplicating a ten-second shot of the word "Maxell." During the course of six minutes, the work, succinctly titled *Maxell* (1990), portrays the steady devolution of the brand name and its plain black background as it erupts into fits of gray streaks and scrambled video noise.

Two prominent feminist video artists have explored and used the specific properties of videotape as ways to suggest gendered communication and performance. Lynda Benglis, perhaps better known for her lavaesque sculptures (and her scandalous November 1974 ad in *Artforum* featuring herself in the nude with sunglasses and a double-headed dildo), emerged as one of the most important first-generation video artists. In particular, her works from 1972 and 1973, including *On-Screen, Noise, Document, Home Tape Revised, Mumble, Now*, and *Collage* all explored layers of video reproduction as tapes were reshot off playback monitors. In some cases, this strategy allowed for distanced commentary on the original footage, while in others she explored the aesthetics and breakdowns of fuzzy communication. A little more than a decade later, Pipilotti Rist emerged with *I'm Not the Girl Who Misses Much*

(1986), a takeoff from a line in John Lennon's song "Happiness Is a Warm Gun." Although often described as a "music video" (this was when MTV still played videos, mind you), this piece presents the artist as a young dancer whose movements are manipulated by adjusting the playback speed. Sepia segments show her movements slowed down, while standard color and blue sequences show her moving speedily; throughout, her body is prominently marked by streaks endemic to scanning in fast forward or reverse. Even more vibrantly portraying the colors and effects of analog video, Rist's *(Entlastungen) Pipilottis Fehler* (*[Absolution] Pipilotti's Mistakes*) (1988) percussively portrays a woman's and video technology's simultaneous breakdowns. Repeated short clips of Rist making faces or collapsing are skewed or stalled with video noise, cuts to color bars, and other interruptions. (An art critic has analyzed this video as portraying female hysteria.)[2] These works are all striking for the ways in which analog video—in particular its inherent technical flaws—allows for technologically specific representations of female experience.[3]

A couple more recent video art pieces exhibit intentional video decay, although their purpose is more conceptual and archaeological than formal or ideological. Ming-Yuen S. Ma's *Sniff* (1996) employs degeneration in addition to other video effects to suggest the fading and blurring of memories of various hookups; these fleeting moments of intimacy, disappointment, and perhaps even regret are recounted in voice-over as Ma appears crawling in circles on his bed and licking and smelling his sheets for the lingering traces of sex. Slater Bradley's video *Factory Archives* (2001) employs resolution loss from format shifting and generational duplication. Bradley shot original footage of an actor portraying Joy Division frontman Ian Curtis performing and then transferred the material from video to his computer and back and forth until it became so distressed and blurred that it could pass for an old, weathered tape and the actor with ultimately indistinguishable features could pass for the deceased musician. Bradley's tape offers a fascinating instance of video dropout and distortion that creates the text's nostalgic tone and simulates authenticity.

Appropriation video has been one of the predominant trends in video art since the 1980s. Although reformatting changes the resolution of the source material in all such work, decay is not always intended to be a focus of attention. One work that capitalizes on the effect of video transfers and manipulation is Jason Simon's deconstruction of TV advertisements, *Production Notes: Fast Food for Thought* (1986). While working at a commercial

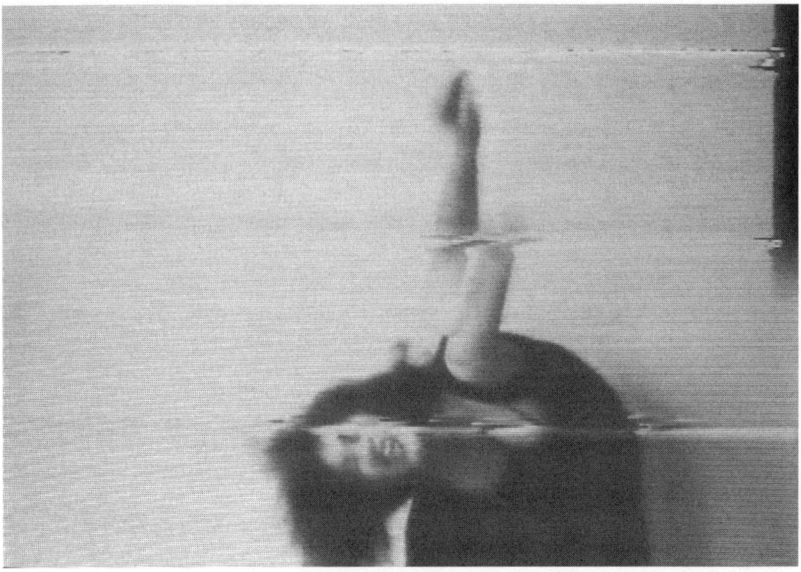

30. In Pipilotti Rist's video *I'm Not the Girl Who Misses Much* (1986), three horizontally skewed lines of interference alter the video image—and perhaps reflect the artist's distressed state. Video still courtesy of the artist and Lurhing Augustine, New York.

postproduction firm, Simon had access to spots for McDonald's, Mars bars, Schlitz Malt Liquor, Pepsi, and Pert Plus, all of which appear in the video. Each commercial plays through in full and is then repeated in slow motion with its budget superimposed over the image as Simon narrates the advertising agency's preproduction directives. These insider memos reveal the intentions and strategies motivating the images, making the tape popular for media studies classes. Yet the video also reveals one of the most common sites and sources for bootlegs: the workplace. For workers in media production, distribution, promotion, and exhibition, copying tapes is part of the job, and making take-home dupes on the side seems about as transgressive as making personal photocopies or using company e-mail for private correspondence.

The appropriation and exploitation of distressed video also function in Nguyen Tan Hoang's *KIP* (2001) to present a history of desire. Nguyen edited footage from old video store gay porn tapes starring Kip Knoll that had been stretched, distorted, and damaged by viewer abuse—presumably from pausing, slow-mo-ing, rewinding, and replaying the most intensely sexy moments. Nguyen taped the footage off a television monitor with his own reflection visible in the onscreen glare. This piece presents an archive of erotic consumption recorded (or, perhaps more appropriately, stripped) off the magnetic surface of the tapes themselves. Explicitly or implicitly, all these works comment on popular culture and the analog tape mediations that audiences recognize without typically reflecting on them.[4]

5. Joanie and Jackie and Everyone They Know: Video Chainletters as Feminist Community Network

In *The First Day of the Beginning of the End of the World* (Jenny Stark, 1995), a shy teenage girl slips an audiotape and a note into her math classmate Kathy's bag. The protagonist finds these presents just before the film's end, marking the denouement of this short set in suburban Antelope Valley, circa the mid-1980s. The note says, "Kathy, I don't know you, but you seem pretty smart right now. I don't have the nerve to talk to you, so I made you this. Hopefully we will be friends some day." Sitting in her room after a hard day, Kathy plays the mix tape, which begins with a new wave song that prompts her to smile and dance on her bed. The potential for a tape exchange to initiate interpersonal communication—and even friendship—coincidentally reflects the mission of the Joanie 4 Jackie video chainletter project, through which this short circulated on the *Me & My Chainletter* beginning in April 2002.

Founded by Miranda July under the banner of Big Miss Moviola in 1995 and later renamed Joanie 4 Jackie, these chainletters present a model of person-to-person videotape distribution.[1] (In fall 2003, July turned the project's reins over to Jacqueline Goss and interns in the film department at Bard College, where it continues.) Joanie 4 Jackie is an analog method of creating a community network in the truest sense of peer-to-peer exchange. The project works like this: female film and video makers send tapes to a specified address, along with five dollars and a personal statement, and their works are compiled onto videotape chainletter releases containing ten or twelve shorts and a zine made up of the artists' statements. The compilations are produced with introductory, interstitial, and closing content organized around a titular theme. Every submission gets included on tapes, thereby

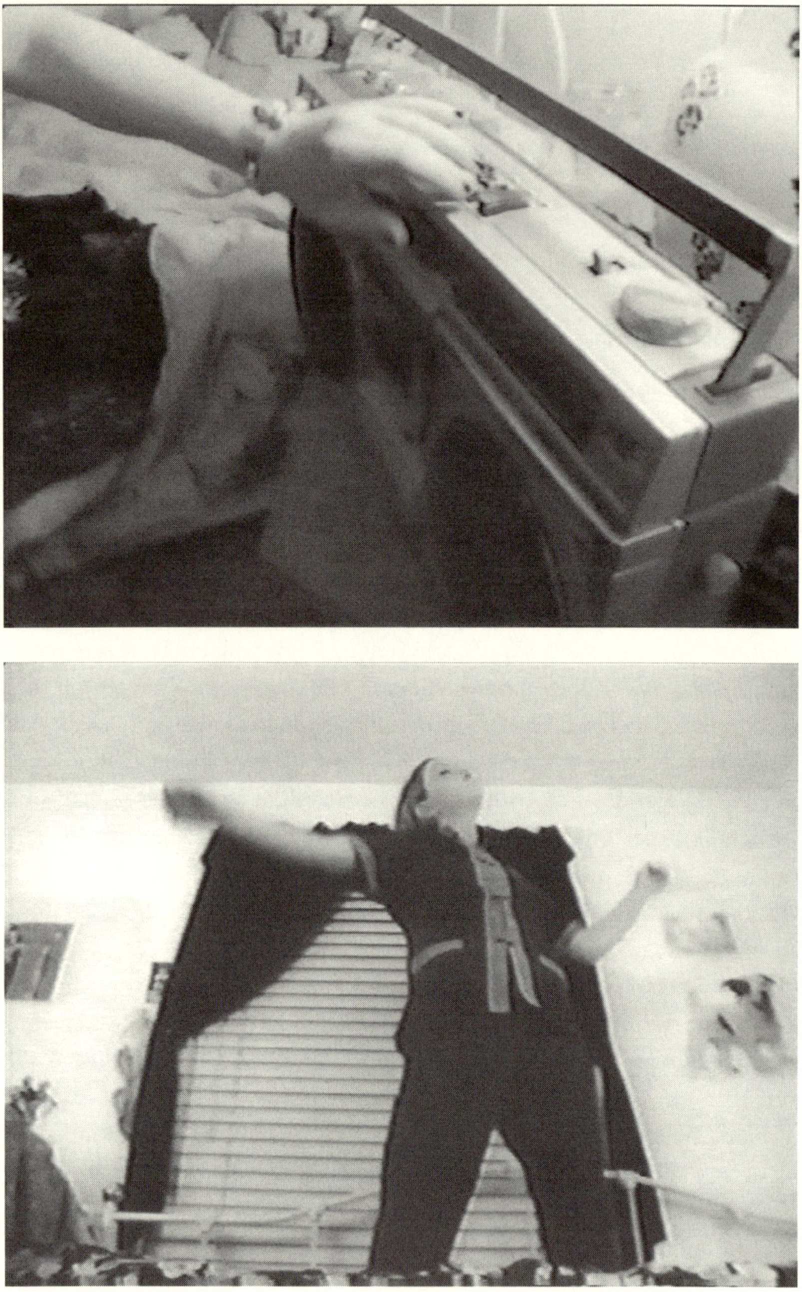

31a–b. The young protagonist plays a mix tape and dances on her bed in *The First Day of the Beginning of the End of the World.*

eliminating the risk of rejection or hierarchies of works and makers. The chainletters are mailed back to the contributors, screened publicly, and can also be purchased online at www.joanie4jackie.com. The project fosters interpersonal connections by including the makers' contact information in the zines and on the website. More along the lines of a mix tape, the term "chainletter" is something of a misnomer; once the content for each tape has been set, it is a completed compilation. Whereas written chainletters are open-ended exchanges that grow and survive through continued forwarding, these videos are an open-ended, serial project, and supplemental compilations are released when enough submissions have accumulated (typically one to three releases per year). By encouraging viewers to become future contributors, the Joanie 4 Jackie project keeps the cycle going.[2]

In chapter 4, I suggested that by reproducing and sharing copies of *Superstar*, audiences personalized the text and created new meanings by altering its images and sounds. Here I argue that the Joanie 4 Jackie chainletter distribution network has encouraged not only wholly new works but also new interpersonal connections between makers simultaneous with the popular boom of the World Wide Web in the mid- to late 1990s. These tapes created social networks before online "social networking." Chainletters present a model bootleg infrastructure that relies on analog technologies and distribution, draws from punk rock and feminist cultural models, and raises interconnected issues of autobiography and community.[3] As a process and project, the chainletters engage these methods, histories, and potentialities in specifically nondigital ways. As a scholar of new media asserted, "Video is a medium of intimacy, of close contact, encouraging interpersonal communication."[4] These homey, low-fi predecessors and alternatives to online content sharing facilitate bonds between makers and audiences through a form of gift exchange. This instance of bootlegging is explicitly interactive, as the project calls on its audience to become its participants.

Media Mail

The Joanie 4 Jackie video project operates as an analog, peer-to-peer video distribution model. It predates widespread amateur digital file or online video sharing, although the project has been more or less contemporaneous with popular uses of the World Wide Web. The chainletters' circulation by mail not only fosters a venue for female makers to share their work but also creates the potential for a nationwide network that ensures equal access, even for geographically isolated women. Through these dubbed and distributed videotapes, the Joanie 4 Jackie chainletters initiate contact between women of divergent sensibilities across regional divides. Video becomes a dually domestic medium in these exchanges, as the chainletters record private histories and map experiences across the country.

In analyzing the contents of some of these tapes, I suggest that these exchanges constitute a nationwide media network of first-person feminist videos in which the personal is the social as well as the political. The contributions to the video chainletters include art school projects, video diaries, homemade music videos, mondo film spoofs, cable access shows, and experimental projects. Some works have screened previously at film and video festivals, while some have circulated only by way of Joanie 4 Jackie. In some cases, the shorts were several years old before submission, so the chainletters present a revival for shorts with otherwise ephemeral public lives. After classroom crits and festival appearances, short works all too often disappear from view. This redistribution adds value to the short subject, a media form that has perhaps the most marginal existence in a culture that prioritizes feature films and TV-friendly half-hour and hour-long programming units. (This is beginning to change through YouTube and other Web-based video sites.) Since no submissions are rejected, the compilations do include a lot of work that would have been filtered out of programmed tapes or screenings (none of which I single out here).[5] Individual works are often poorly made, and the chainletters can be tedious to watch from beginning to end. But Joanie 4 Jackie provides a safe space for media makers to experiment, act out, and potentially make asses of themselves. The freedom of the mediated communication seen here could perhaps be equated to the (ambiguously) liberating anonymity of chat rooms and blogs.

Though it is now becoming obsolete, VHS was the first common home video distribution format. Joanie 4 Jackie relies on this shared format as essential for broad access, and the hard plastic cassettes are both sufficiently inexpensive to permit independent duplication and sturdy enough to allow distribution by mail. As of this writing, the project accepts submissions on VHS, MINI-DV, and DVD-R; master compilation tapes are produced on MINI-DV, though everything ends up on VHS for distribution. (A transition to digital delivery was under consideration as of 2005 to save on postage, though as far as I know, the shift hasn't taken place.)[6] The continued use of VHS suggests the economic and technological limitations of the project. But the low-fi tapes also suggest the aesthetic of access. The original works submitted to Joanie 4 Jackie reveal their amateur production resources, while the compilation tapes I've watched have compounded this aesthetic by displaying nearly every form of dubbing disaster, from soundtracks that cut out intermittently to flashes, static, and other video noise that mark clumsy transitions between tapes to degeneration of the shorts themselves from reproduction. The specific colorations, resolutions, and decay of consumer video production formats date and mediate viewers' experiences of the text as historically specific and as authentically indexical.[7] Thus the tapes demonstrate bootleg aesthetics by exhibiting their own assemblage and reproduction. As they appear on the chainletters, low-fi glitches self-reflexively add to the tapes' intimacy as unique person-to-person dubs.

In effect this bootleg aesthetic functions in the manner of photocopied, cut-and-paste, handwritten zines. As a breakthrough study of zines suggests, "The amateurism of the illustration reinforces the familiarity. Instead of emulating the slickness of the commercial mass media—which . . . constitutes an aesthetics of separation—the illustrations in zines are more reminiscent of the doodles and sketches in the margins of a personal letter: a style of intimate connection."[8] The adjectival choice of "amateurism" articulates both the informal aesthetic and the intense personal, emotional investment in the project. I also suggest that such productions are explicitly analog, offering a handmade aesthetic that cannot be replicated on the Internet or through other digital technologies.

Although Joanie 4 Jackie maintains a website, the digital interface directs the user to personal exchanges of tangible objects, much like eBay. The project is neither anonymous nor immaterial like online peer-to-peer file sharing. Tapes have to be sent to a personal address, and orders are customized. In my experiences, even the website's purchasing links ("I Want It") were dead, necessitating that I write e-mails directly to the project's offices and request materials personally rather than clicking through an online order form. I also had to pay the analog way—personal check—rather than by PayPal or credit card.

The Joanie 4 Jackie project's reliance on the postal system likewise contributes to the participant's experience as much as it functions logistically. Unlike cable access or microcinema screenings that may feature similarly personal, idiosyncratic, or undistributed content, there is no preset schedule for when the tapes are produced or arrive. And unlike downloads or streaming video, real-time waiting becomes part of the process. New compilations are produced only after enough submissions have trickled in and the interns have gotten around to producing a tape. Even orders placed for back titles take an indeterminate time to fill. These orders are sent by media mail, for which the delivery speed varies wildly and inexplicably; the postal service seems to deliver media mail packages whenever it feels the whim. Service can range from two days to three weeks, with nary an explanation why. So waiting by the mailbox—or, conversely, forgetting all about the order—can become part of the experience. Mail delivery introduces the element of the unexpected: Wow! They're already here! Or more likely: Will the tapes ever arrive? As one scholar has suggested, the wait for mail-order deliveries can induce forgetting, so that by the time a package arrives, it's as if it were a gift.[9] But mail order also introduces the pleasurable tangibility of durable goods packaged and sent from afar. There is a distinct epistolary joy at getting *real* mail in an age when electronic correspondence has left mailboxes cluttered with little other than credit card offers and bills. And for multitape orders there can be the curiosity of region-specific packing materials, such as local newspapers or grocery store bags—cultural detritus from elsewhere crumpled and stuffed into a box that offers clues about the tapes' geographic histories.

On a minor scale, Joanie 4 Jackie has facilitated national distribution for locally produced and regionally specific media. To a limited extent, cable access has allowed for exhibition of amateur video work and offered the potential to do—locally, at least—what the chainletters sought to achieve.[10] Unfortunately, as cable was deregulated and increasingly owned by national corporate conglomerates, the infrastructure and promise of the cable access outlet became less viable—and the frequently banal content more of a joke. Despite the increasingly national ownership of cable systems, such industrial structures have not facilitated national distribution for independent video. By using tapes and the postal service rather than public broadcast waves or private cables, the chainletters can go anywhere.

The postal distribution of the chainletters recalls early, perhaps now forgotten, modes of video distribution to private viewers: mail-order clubs, such as Video Club of America and the more pervasive video offshoot of the Columbia House record and tape club.[11] Before affordable sell-through titles were available at stores, mail-order clubs were the primary venues for purchasing prerecorded videos. In 1984 the Home Film Festival worked as an art film club that mailed "specialized" classic, foreign, and independent videos to viewers in the "hinterlands."[12] More recently, Netflix has returned video rental to its postal roots through online membership management and mail-delivery DVD service; it provides broad selection from a network of national warehouses and sends the discs to users in return-postage-paid envelopes. To a limited extent, Netflix also facilitates intimate communities of "friends" who allow each other access to their queues, ratings, and suggestions. Yet the Joanie 4 Jackie feminist network functions more like an actual social club—a site for shared identities and social connections, although no formal membership is required.

Perhaps even more directly influential on Joanie 4 Jackie than the video clubs was a decades-old art practice that used the postal service. Mail art, also called correspondence art, communications art, or networking, developed as a practice in the 1960s. Like conceptual art, the focus was on process rather than product, and like the contemporaneous art movement Fluxus, it blurred the boundaries between private and public, art and life. It was, originally, a way for artists to communicate and correspond among themselves and later became a broader forum for artists to communicate with the public. One writer in the mid-1990s observed a shift of focus for mail art during this period to emphasize values also central to the Joanie 4 Jackie project: "The stress on spiritual values and human relations, on community and contact suggests a dramatic shift of concerns for the mail art network."[13] Mail order and mail art suggest a kind of tangibly indexical bond between sender and recipient, maker and audience. But the unpredictability of arrival introduces an element of surprise and delight. These chainletters arrive as mysterious packages with unknown contents that create affective and intellectual bonds—like gifts, a connotation to which I return at the end of the chapter. The postal system was originally a forum for public information dissemination and belatedly became a mode of private, one-to-one correspondence through the introduction of sealed envelopes, stamps, and drop boxes.[14] It also served as "a network in the most modern sense" that fostered "a new culture of national . . . connectedness."[15] To some extent, the Joanie 4 Jackie chainletters re-create the now defunct postal purpose as a public communications network. Proposing that desire is central to the epistolary impulse, one that can be channeled toward a feminist project, one scholar queries, "Is it a second-wave feminist desire for a homogenous community or a third-wave feminist desire to connect through recognition of racial, ethnic, class, sex, and gendered differences?"[16] In the case of Joanie 4 Jackie, the chainletter project is both and combines 1970s and 1990s feminist strategies.

Making Grrrl Media Communities

Despite celebrations in the 1990s of independent cinema, Miranda July was concerned that no low-fi, personal cinema scene had emerged for filmmaking as it had with punk music and zines—perhaps because production costs remained prohibitive or because few venues existed for short subjects. July started her own alternative distribution system for projects made with relatively accessible resources such as camcorders and VCRs; she dubbed chainletter tapes onto used cassettes that she found at thrift shops, and mailed tapes at the discount media mail rate. A five-dollar submission fee—comparable to a punk show cover—financed the tapes and photocopied booklets for each compilation.

Joanie 4 Jackie developed during the height of riot grrrl culture and shared many of its principles of do-it-yourself (DIY) art and community building. Riot grrrl, which has been called "punk rock feminism," was an angry, youth-based third-wave feminist phenomenon of the 1990s, which was later mainstreamed (and marketed to younger girls) as "girl power" pop culture, such as the Spice Girls and the Powerpuff Girls.[17] Emerging in the early 1990s out of music scenes in Washington, D.C., and Olympia, Washington, riot grrrl culture was promoted through rock 'n' roll and zines, offering a female alternative to the machismo of the D.C. punk or Seattle grunge scenes. The angry edge to riot grrrl distinguishes it from prior feminist forms; whereas second-wave feminism had its roots in hippiedom and the sexual revolution, riot grrrl came out of punk.[18]

At its base, the Joanie 4 Jackie project has less to do with anger, however, than with love and providing a supportive way for female media makers to find a support system:[19]

> To most girls, Riot Grrrl means a community and emotional support. . . . While other feminist movements have been geared toward political action, Riot Grrrl, although remaining staunchly political, also pays attention to the personal and the everyday. It focuses more on the individual and the emotional than on marches, legislation, and public policy. This creates a community in which girls are able to speak about what is bothering them or write about what happened that day.[20]

In a discussion of riot grrrl, one participant suggested the significance of circulated print productions for girls living in isolation: "If you live in a town and don't have [Internet] access, zines are a way to interact with people who [feel] the same way. It keeps your sanity; it's therapeutic." She describes the positive effects for the DIY producers: "Putting it on paper is making it real. Someone will read this and make it real. People can revalidate you."[21] Riot grrrl's progressive politics perhaps had less to do with specific issues than with method and ethics: communication was grassroots, and cultural productions were shared rather than sold (or, if sold, sold at a reasonable, barely break-even rate). For riot grrrl zines and music, as well as the Joanie 4 Jackie tapes, media networks and intimate self-expression became the basis of community building.

Academic attention to the Joanie 4 Jackie project has located its origins in riot grrrl culture; the chainletters' connection to riot grrrl, however, is incidental. The project emerged from the same milieu and was probably inspired by its energy and ethos, but Joanie 4 Jackie was not explicitly a riot grrrl effort. (In fact, July originally intended for the chainletter contributors to be only young girls or senior women rather than twentysomethings; these marginalized groups, however, proved difficult to reach and could not sustain an ongoing video exchange.) Prefacing an interview with July, one writer connects Joanie 4 Jackie with the DIY aesthetics of punk and the politics of feminism.[22] Categorizing the video chainletters as a new cultural production "beyond Riot Grrrl," another presents the Big Miss Moviola project as modeled on girl punk zines and music.[23] A third author similarly suggests that the riot grrrl movement has created more venues for girl-made media and likewise references the Big Miss Moviola project as an extension of this trend for distribution.[24] Scholarly articles scarcely discuss what is actually *on* the tapes, an oversight I attempt to partially remedy in this chapter.

That the project has so consistently been related to punk aesthetics and values may perhaps be surprising to viewers. Relatively few of the tapes contain explicitly feminist works, and even fewer convey a punk sensibility. The project, then, may be punk in its conception of a distribution network and its valorization of anything-goes production values, but the girls and women who contribute to the project do not predominantly appear to explore or claim punk identities.

In a spin on riot grrrl, the filmmaker Sarah Kennedy is more biker chick than punk rock girl despite her dreadlocks in *Dirty Fingernails* (included on the *U-matic chainletter*, July 1997). She refuses to perform conventional femininity, except in an ironic fantasy sequence when, dressed in a wedding gown, she runs across a field toward her betrothed motorcycle—this to an altered version of the Carpenter's "Close to You," no less. Later Kennedy stages a typically insulting exchange with an auto parts store clerk, and in retort she offers time-lapse footage of herself dismantling and skillfully reassembling a motorcycle. Speaking in voiceover, she asserts, "For me, this bike project has been about . . . women having to struggle to do what they want to do and [then] doing it." That said, she speeds into the horizon, and the Carpenters' "We've Only Just Begun" plays into the credits.

The connection between the chainletter tapes and riot grrrl zines is more directly articulated through the inclusion of Kara Herold's *Grrlyshow*, a short documentary about girl zines, on Joanie 4 Jackie's *2001: a chainletter* (January 2001). Herold's short, like the zines it explores, is assembled with a collage aesthetic, alternating between ironic appropriation and sincere personal accounts by zine producers. The tape begins with close-ups of black-and-white ink sketches about zine production. Interviews with the female editors of *Bust*, *Bamboo Girl*, *Plotz*, *Hues*, *Pagan's Head*, *Bitch*, and *Java Turtle* are framed by parodic re-creations of educational films, complete with friendly yet authoritative male voice-over narration, chirpy scores, retro reenactments, and found footage.[25] In this documentary, Debbie Stoller, founder of *Bust*—perhaps the best known (and most mainstream) of these zines—argues that riot grrrl reclaimed certain feminine roles and pop culture pleasures that had been frowned on by second-wave feminism. According to her artist's statement, Herold discovered the zine anthology *A Girl's Guide to Taking over the World* in 1996, and the tape offers a similar introductory address to the viewer, which combines excerpts from breakthrough zines with the implicit encouragement for viewers to start their own print projects. This also describes the chainletters' mode of address, which attempts to stimulate audience participation and to encourage women to make their own cultural productions.

Feminist Video, Wave after Wave

Feminist video has a rich history that predates the Joanie 4 Jackie project. Probably more by coincidence than by conscious reference, the chainletters connect feminist strategies of both second-wave early video and third-wave revisions and mediations. Creating video letters was an early feminist video practice and a method of exploring the medium.[26] In one such art project, Lynda Benglis collaborated with Robert Morris on *Mumble* (1972) and *Exchange* (1973), which were composed as epistolary video experiments in which each artist rescanned (reshot the image off a playback monitor) and commented on the other's prior message—that is, in *Exchange* Morris responded to Benglis's *Mumble*. With each successive tape, the image became progressively fuzzier—as did the layers of meaning and interpretation.

Influenced by the women's movement and various community video access projects, a separate national feminist news network called International Videoletters was developed in 1975. This collective of thirteen organizations in nine cities across the United States produced bimonthly half-hour tapes profiling individual women and social issues; the tapes circulated for public screenings, and feedback sessions would be recorded and added to the end of the tapes. These chainletters, like their counterparts two decades later, relied on the rerecordability and compilation capabilities of video—functions that distinguish the technology from film. The project began as a result of discussions and strategic planning at the Conference of Feminist Film and Video Organizations in New York City and the Feminist Eye (both in early 1975). Although the political mission of International Videoletters was more explicit and its infrastructure more elaborate than that of Joanie 4 Jackie, the stated hopes were strikingly similar:

> Videoletters serve several different purposes: to increase awareness of what is happening throughout the country; to develop a feeling of closeness among women in different cities; to encourage the growth and participation of an interested audience; and to preserve and record women's history and culture.[27]

The project was supported through various feminist media collectives and screened in social spaces.[28] The videoletters of the 1970s strove not only for collective understanding but also for collective viewing experiences and reciprocity. The International Videoletters have become a fairly obscure bit of feminist video history, so it is unclear—even unlikely—that Miranda July knew of them.[29] A phenomenon of the *home* video age, Joanie 4 Jackie, in contrast, imagines that its female artists often work alone and that its viewers watch tapes in the privacy of their bedrooms; here the "community" is imagined or, at least, mediated.[30]

After two decades of experimentation, feminist video art in the 1990s was perhaps less preoccupied with formal concerns or community reporting, but it did return to the second wave's emphasis on body consciousness-raising. Alexandra Juhasz has pointed to this reclamation of explicit female sexuality and self-representation of female bodies. This trend returned to some of the strategies of early 1970s feminism, while informed by the poststructuralist feminist theory of the late 1970s and 1980s and the identity politics of the 1990s. "These images help us to see that while it is through our bodies that we access pleasure, political identity, pain and oppression, it is through video images of our bodies that we explore, re-make, and challenge the dominant cultural constructions of who and what our bodies define us as."[31] A corresponding turn toward autobiography also permitted sensual expressions and pleasures.

The Joanie 4 Jackie project has a similar, though more ambiguous, relationship to feminism. It is predicated on gender identity—submissions are made by (and implicitly for) female media makers—yet the tapes are not necessarily or explicitly feminist, nor in autobiographical tapes are their makers' identities primarily constructed in relation to gender. As a late-wave feminist project, the tapes I survey in this chapter suggest the multiplicity of factors that complicate female experience, including place (*Long after the Thrill*), sexual orientation (*All That I Can Be*), family (*A Wild Horse Rider*), age (*How the Miracle of Masturbation Saved Me from Becoming a Teenage Space Alien*), ethnicity (*Stories from the Black Asian Planet*), interests (*Dirty Fingernails*), and creative production (*A Girl's Guide to Taking over the World*).

The first Joanie 4 Jackie chainletter release, the *Velvet chainletter* (April 1996), speaks to a spectrum of personal and feminist issues; it may, in fact, be the most socially relevant and diverse of all the chainletters. Perhaps not surprisingly, this initial release includes tapes only from major urban centers, with a majority sent from the West Coast, where July was based. The collection begins with Tammy Rae Carland's *Dear Mom*, in which the maker rehearses coming out to her mother. The tape foregrounds the mediation of this private performance, as it is shot off a television console, with accentuated pixel lines, rainbow video flares, and rolling stripes on the cathode-ray tube monitor. Approaching a different set of issues around the intersections of intergenerational relationships and sexuality, Tana J. Johnson's *My Breasts Are My Children* investigates her mother's and stepmother's decisions to have breast implants. Mary Billyou's *Woman's Punk ArtMaking Party* features a young woman's empowered account of working as a stripper; the tape suggests that she has come to own and exploit her own to-be-looked-at-ness, to borrow Laura Mulvey's famous phrase.[32] Pat Baum, in contrast, sought a different type of visibility for women. Her short *The Cleansing Machine* portrays two semihomeless, possibly abused women; although it looks like a documentary, the maker refers to the two women as "characters" who represent "this voiceless, 'invisible class' of women."

The contents of other Joanie 4 Jackie chainletters likewise address female-specific experiences of sexuality and body issues—at times through comedic, inappropriate displays and gender performance. For instance, *Hans: Object of Desire* (*Me and My Chainletter*, March 2002) implies female sex play with humor as it shows a Dachshund gnawing away at a strap-on dildo as if it were a chew toy. In *The Yodeling Lesson*, by Vanessa Renwick (*2001: a chainletter*), a young woman bikes up a hill in Portland; a series of takes shows the ride to be arduously steep, and the exertion quickly becomes tiring for the viewer as well. But after a cut, we suddenly see the woman cycle-streaking as she glides down the other side of the hill stripped nude. What's more, she rides hands free throughout the long take, suggesting a *joie de vivre* and bodily release that contrasts with the overcast sky and desolate industrial location. Dulcie Clarkson's *How the Miracle of Masturbation Saved Me from Becoming a Teenage Space Alien* (*Cherry Cherry chainletter*, July 1998, also featured on the curated *Joanie 4 Jackie 4ever* co-star tape) presents a faux video diary about a pubescent girl growing up in a commune. One day in downtown Santa Fe, a punk boy calls the young protagonist an alien. For a year afterward, she confuses her sense of unbelonging with being an extraterrestrial, and she waits for a spaceship to take her back. Her fantasies of alien communion—at root, her mischanneled desire to fit in and feel at home—eventually cease to consume her when she finally becomes comfortable in her own skin by discovering masturbation. This far-fetched but compelling tape hybridizes two of the most prevalent modes on the chainletters—video diaries and B movie genre parodies.

For all the goofs on genre and gender, there are as many autobiographical submissions—works that are often the standouts on these compilations. First-person accounts are prevalent in classic and contemporary feminist video, as their makers give voice to their experiences and attempt to articulate their identities. Autobiography has become a major mode of documentary in the past few decades as well, marking a generic turn toward subjectivity. The documentary scholar Catherine Russell has recognized the implications of the homemade video aesthetic in how we watch and understand such works. "Autoethnography in film and video is always mediated by technology, and so unlike its written forms, identity will be an effect not only of history and culture but also of the history and culture of technologies of reproduction."[33]

First-person video production exploded during the same period as area studies and attention to autobiography as a topic of academic analysis—an era when self-expressions were validated as political acts, revisionist histories, and cultural productions.[34] Keep in mind, this is also the period when camcorders made amateur home video productions more affordable, easier to use, and culturally pervasive. Correspondingly, since the 1980s, autobiography has been a site of feminist theory and revisionist criticism. At times, these critical works have engaged in essentialism, as they have tried to define the gender gap between male and female autobiographical modes; perhaps the most common assertions have been that women, unlike men, foreground expressions of emotion and construct their identities through

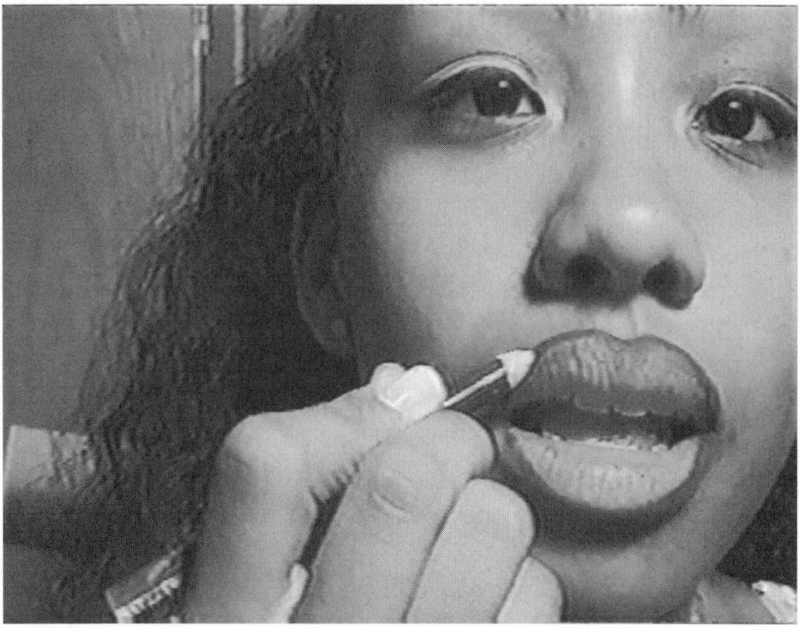

32. Wendy M. Thompson in *Stories from the Black Asian Planet.*

a series of personal relationships—in contrast to men's tendencies to create teleological narratives of their professional lives while playing down domestic relationships.[35]

Many of the chainletter tapes focus on their makers' relationships to their families, and parent-daughter tension is a pervasive theme. One example is *Stories from the Black Asian Planet* (*Me & My Chainletter*), which is one of the few accounts of a young woman's identity negotiation that focuses on nonwhite experiences. In this video, Wendy M. Thompson, a mixed-race Asian African American student at the University of California, Santa Barbara, takes a bus home to San Jose to visit her mother and grandmother. With her mother acting as translator, Wendy interviews her grandmother about fleeing Burma to move to Taiwan; her mother, born in Burma and educated in Taiwan, emigrated to San Francisco and eventually brought the grandmother to the United States. The young woman further reflects on her parents' tumultuous relationship and the familial rejection her mother faced for becoming romantically involved with a black man; first she was disowned and kicked out of her family's house, then her father left her mother for another woman. This homecoming trip is clearly Thompson's attempt to understand her complicated heritage, despite not speaking her "native" tongue and having an absentee father. We watch her spend the weekend avoiding having an important heart-to-heart with her mother until finally she can't not do it; time is running out, and the whole purpose of the trip is to ameliorate their rocky relationship. Young women's diaries and retold familial traumas constitute a sizable share of the chainletter submissions, and they are typically the most poignant works—especially in cases where the girls are doubly "othered" by sexuality, race, or religion, as well as gender. But their identities are also prevalently articulated in relation to their specific geographic locations.

Places in the Art

Among Joanie 4 Jackie's accomplishments is that submissions have come from all over the country, representing experiences far removed, geographically and culturally, from the cosmopolitan cultural hubs on the coasts. Through the chainletters, girls and women from suburban sprawls, forgotten midsize cities, and rural towns have a venue for sharing their experiences, potentially creating a greater understanding of the range of experiences across the United States. The TV scholar Victoria Johnson has suggested that the American heartland has long served as an imagined ideal and a regulated (and exploitable) market; indeed, the Midwest, both as an actual place and as a fictionalized setting, is more central to broadcasting content and history than most scholars have acknowledged. Yet relatively few TV shows "about" the all-American middle are actually from such places or suggest the complexity of life there.[36] The imagined ideal is precisely that—imagined. In Joanie 4 Jackie submissions from the Great Plains and the Southwest, young women witness rampant alcoholism, patriarchy, sexual alienation, and, in spite of everything, self-actualization. Throughout, the makers' identities are explicitly considered in relation to place: where they're from more than where they're going. This emphasis on place also suggests the geographic origins of the submitted tapes and traces the complex and compound circulatory histories for the compiled chainletters. Although some of the tapes I have singled out may confirm negative stereotypes about American cultures, they come from the perspectives of people who have lived in each of the places represented.

These media makers claim individual identities yet situate their experiences in relation to nationalist myths or regionally specific cultures. In effect, they perform what Russell has called "autoethnography": a form of first-person film and video making that stages the maker's subjectivity as performed and socially and historically situated.[37] Such works often take up diaristic or essayistic structures that explore their makers' experiences and identities in development. At the same time, the artists also recognize that their identities have been formed in relationship to families and friends—personal histories that are made public through chainletter reproduction and distribution. By circulating these stories on video to other women across the country, the makers both participate in forging a national network of alternative media and suggest a desire for an intimate community.

Themes of long-distance communication and travel pervade the chainletter tapes. Wynne Ryan's *1,2,3 This Is Me* (the *Cherry Cherry Chainletter*, July 1998) explores telephonic communication and masquerade, suggesting a longing for personal connections in a time of virtual media. The tape begins with a young woman's recollections of her fascination with "telephonic transport" and her childhood habit of taking apart her family's receiver in order to see where the voices came from. For the bulk of the video, the artist wears a long black wig and tarty make-up, acting as a psychic telephone operator answering calls with "1,2,3. This is me." Communication, she pensively comments, requires someone on the other end: "Most of all, you need someone, somewhere to reach, to call." On the same chainletter compilation, *This Red Envelope* by the native of Lubbock, Texas, K8 Hardy, who studied at Smith College and later moved to Brooklyn, explores long-distance desire inspired by an old, rediscovered letter. Shots of the letter evoke communication, while shots of freeways and exit signs (common throughout chainletter tapes) spur notions of both long hauls and homecomings.

Like communication and travel, escape is a recurring theme in the chainletter tapes and their sister co-star collections. Numerous urban contributors reflect on the isolated places where they grew up. For instance, in *The Slow Escape* (*Ball and Chainletter*, 1998), New York-based Sativa Peterson begins with the voice-over, "Let me tell you about the place that I'm from." Her small hometown of Winslow, Arizona, lies along Route 66 and houses a state prison; it's a transitory space and yet, she claims, was a nice place to grow up. A documentary mystery, the video is infused with shades of noir and horror, and Peterson remains haunted by the disappearance of a young waitress in her hometown and her troubled cousin's possible connection to her murder. Peterson never knew the victim yet reaches out to her and her memory through this tape. She escaped, but this stranger never will.[38]

Articulating the intersections of autobiography and Americana, gender identities and kinship, Dulcie Clarkson (based in Silver City, New Mexico) creates a feminist demythologization of iconic Old West cowboys and southern good old boys in her tape *A Wild Horse Rider* (*The U-Matic Chainletter*, July 1997). This video presents a complex, pained, and personal critique of father-daughter relationships. Contrasting the myth with a man, her father, Clarkson portrays lone rangers as selfish bastards. The tape begins with recollections of her parents' divorce and custody battle when she was five years old. In court, her father portrayed her mother as a hippy, lesbian, and unfit mother; her mother painted her father as an abusive, alcoholic, and unfit father. But, Clarkson explains, in Kentucky in the 1970s, single mothers were frowned upon, and her father had already found a new wife. So her father won custody, but soon thereafter her mother abducted Clarkson and drove west, where they moved around and changed names. Clarkson offers voice-over testimony of her relationship to her father:

> In my head, I built up a larger-than-life image of him. He became the symbol for all the irresponsible things in the world. He was the cowboy in the movies who led the West to waste and then rode off into the sunset to be made a hero. I took great pride in being able to say, with cool detachment, "My father is a red-neck bigot." It felt so good to hate him.

But this image was complicated when her father became ill with heart cancer. After he underwent a round of treatments, they took a road trip together, and all her grievances against him were confirmed. He wouldn't even let her drive, despite his condition, because that would mean admitting some vulnerability. In voice-over Clarkson explains that the road trip prompted her to make *A Wild Horse Rider* as a way of dealing with these issues:

> I wanted to expose the icon of the American cowboy that my father seemed to aspire to for the glorified selfishness and irresponsibility that it is. Not only does the Western mythology glorify racist violence, attempted genocide, and environmental destruction, but it also fosters the polarization of male dominance and female submission. I wanted to use my camera to expose my father for the bigot he was. I wanted to prove that there was nothing that he had ever had to offer me as a father figure. And I wanted to finally express my anger and outrage to him—and in the process prove my own adulthood.

Clarkson's monologue offers a revisionist feminist critique of the Western genre, but its deeply personal ties ground her claims in emotional experience. The tape features several clips from Westerns shot off TV monitors,

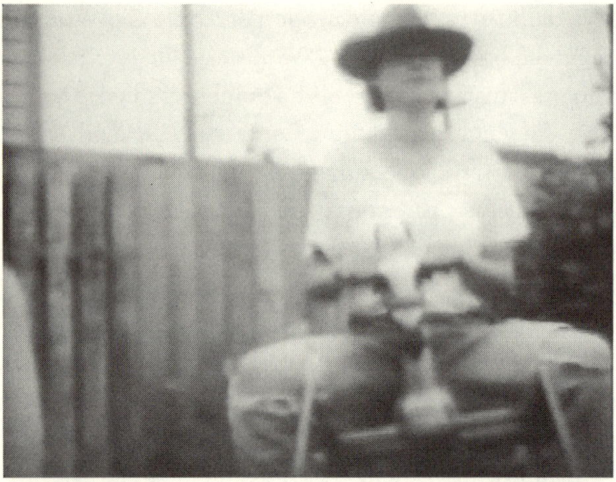

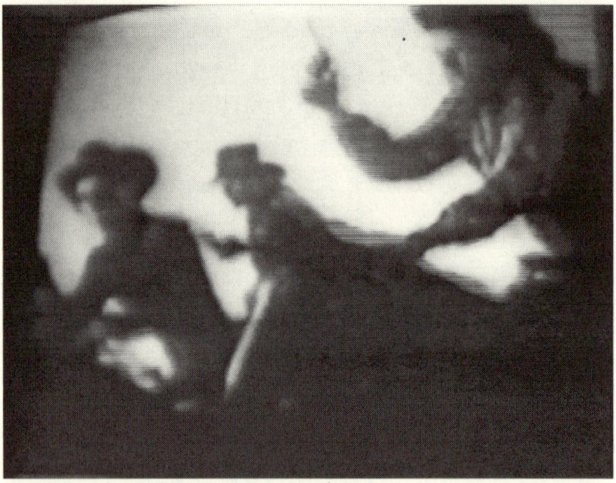

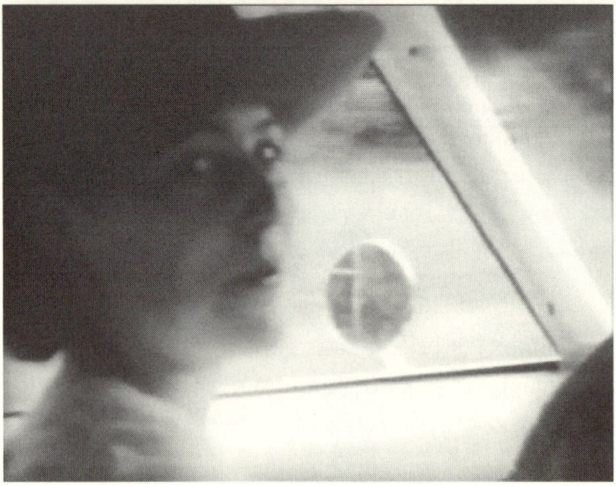

explicitly making connections between heroic icons of American culture and brutal masculinity. As in *Superstar*, discussed in chapter 4, the pixeled texture of the footage reinforces its status as mediated images rather than fragments of actuality. These cowboy shots are intercut with murky black-and-white filmed images of the maker riding a toddler's spring-mounted horsy ride—signaling, perhaps, the way that so many of us regress when we visit family—and shots of her driving a car down a back road. Color enters the video only through home video footage, first of her frail and bed-bound father, then of her older brother singing a song with an acoustic guitar. After the road trip, her father looked helpless and expressed his regrets and sentimental feelings for her; Clarkson says she could not refuse him reconciliation or forgiveness. But even in death, he maintained an image of cowboy virility. At his funeral, his friends took turns swigging from a bottle of Wild Turkey and eulogized him as "a fucker, a fighter, a wild horse rider." They even said that her father had taught them how to be men. This tape offers a powerful, personal, feminist response to arrogant American masculinity, at once intimate and sweepingly historical.

As I have already suggested, many of the tapes that circulate via Joanie 4 Jackie articulate personal experiences in relation to specific places. Exemplifying this tendency, *Long after the Thrill: A Christmas Story* (the *Newborn chainletter*, September 2004) records Erika Robo's reflections on returning to her hometown, Sioux Falls, South Dakota, during winter break from an unnamed California college. With approximately 140,000 residents, Sioux Falls is the largest city in the Northern Plains and has recently become one of the fastest-growing cities in the country. But with a surfeit of chain restaurants, ever-expanding and expensive housing developments, and little distinctive local color, the city resembles a giant suburb without metropolitan cultural life or diversity. It is the all-American nowhere—one I know all too well. (I grew up sixty miles north in the smaller college town of Brookings, and my parents moved to Sioux Falls immediately after I graduated from high school.) For me the place is deeply familiar and yet not "home." Although I can't imagine moving back, it undeniably contributed to who I am. Robo is just beginning to recognize a similar relationship for herself.

The tape expresses her ambivalence about her relationships to her friends from home: on the one hand, she is clearly relieved she got away, while on the other hand, she seems to feel an undercurrent of guilt that

---

33a–c. Dulcie Clarkson and a TV Western in *A Wild Horse Rider.*

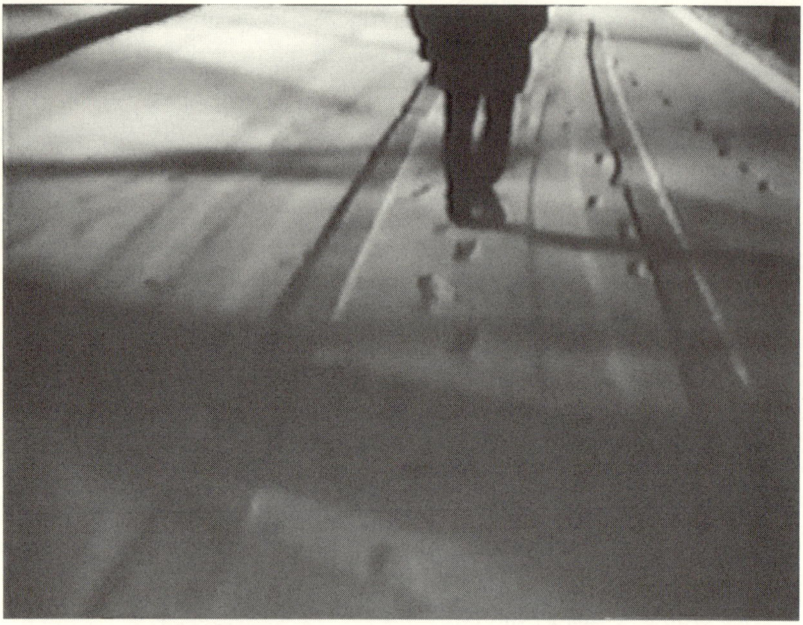

34. Bitter cold and loneliness in *Long after the Thrill.*

she left. Robo's tape opens with snow flurries, illuminated by a streetlight, against a black sky. It's a cold snap, the kind of midwestern "coldness West Coast kids can't understand." She describes the depressing experience of returning home to find that her friends lead such dreary lives; they have stayed in a town with few opportunities or cultural outlets, so all they do is drink themselves numb. Early in the tape, we see footage of friends at home as a young man sings along to "Sweet Transvestite" from *The Rocky Horror Picture Show*; the image alternates with shots of a lone man walking down a snowy road at night. The narrator recalls a night when she was drinking late with friends and a guy called on his cell phone from a bridge, saying that he was going to jump off. The people at the party were too drunk to deal with the intensity of the call, so they passed the phone from person to person, trying to minimize the situation and deny he would commit suicide. But he did jump, breaking his wrist and some ribs in the fall but not dying immediately; instead, she says, he crawled out of the river and slowly froze. A truck driver picked him up, but he died of hypothermia in the hospital nine hours after his jump. Pointing to the divisions between fantasy and reality, Robo comments later that she watched *The Royal Tenenbaums* (Wes

Anderson, 2001) while she was back, and it made her cry because it was more beautiful than life could ever be.

In voice-over Robo remarks on the pervasive alcoholism and substance abuse, teen pregnancy, and premature marriage among her classmates. By the time she was nineteen, she knew ten friends who had gotten pregnant. She comments on the impossibility of suggesting abortion to them, comparing having children too young to the bad juvenile judgment in getting a lousy tattoo. "Once someone got a shitty tattoo, you couldn't tell them it was hideous." She also includes footage of a conversation with two inebriated guys in the backseat of a car bragging about how much they love the wives or girlfriends they knocked up. Throughout the video, almost everyone onscreen is demonstrably under the influence of alcohol or other substances, including the filmmaker when a male friend interviews her in a bar at the end. She comments that she's getting a degree but she doesn't know how she'll use it. The implication, however, is that school was her escape. Her ambivalence is most powerfully conveyed during a monologue near the end of the tape. The image alternates between Robo performing a karaoke version of John Cougar Mellencamp's "Jack and Diane" ("Oh yeah, life goes on / Long after the thrill of living is gone . . .") and shots taken from the window of an airplane during takeoff. She narrates:

> It was a time in my life when everything just seemed kind of horrible and broken. Especially my hometown—this frozen, barren, prairie wasteland where nobody moved away, nobody went to college, everybody just got shitty service jobs and had kids and got fucked up all the time. This is when I'd just come back from *California*, from some fancy college where everyone was supposed to be so liberal and so politicized and so aware. And then I came back, and I saw what was going on, and it all just seemed so tragic and backwards and doomed. It was also because we were just getting to an age where everyone just realized they aren't going to live out all their dreams, no matter how hard they work at it. That nobody was going to be what they wanted. Nobody was going to be anything. It was like some shitty classic rock song—John Mellencamp or Bob Seger talking about the thrill of life dying away while you just had to keep plodding along.

This sequence suggests that her epiphanies about her identity and her relationship to her hometown are brought about by the altered state of drunkenness and by the physical transition of flying. The voice-over was

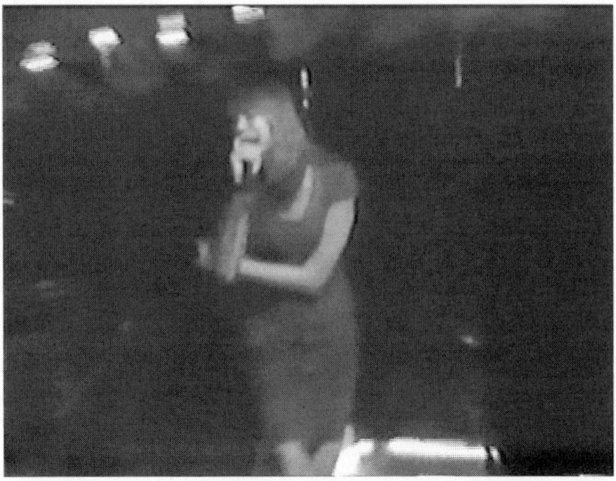

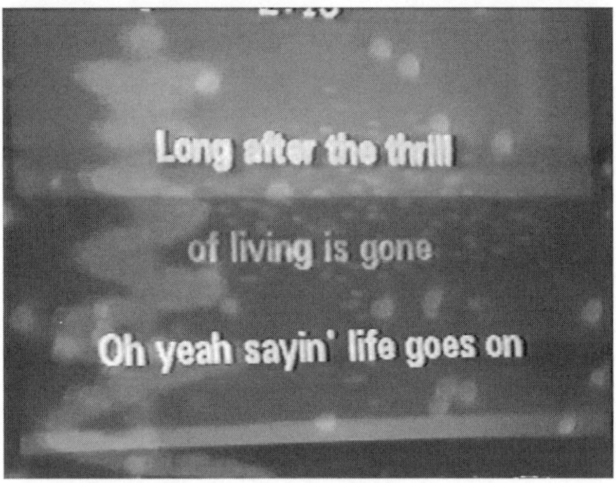
Long after the thrill
of living is gone
Oh yeah sayin' life goes on

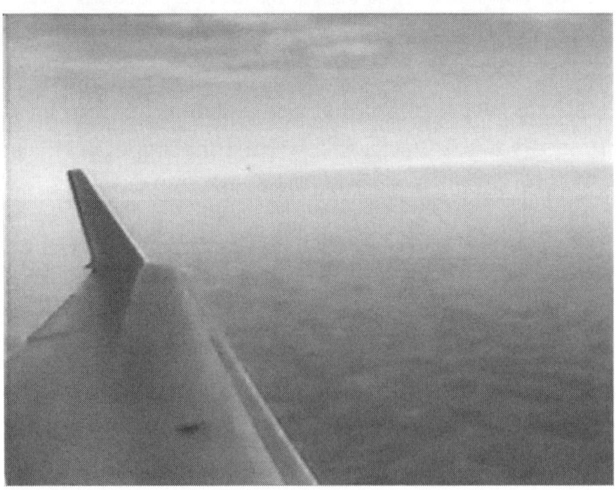

presumably written in postproduction, and these observations are mediated and revised through video recording and editing. Yet they retain a sort of candid immediacy.

When I showed this video to a class of undergraduates in New York, most of whom had also grown up someplace other than where they were attending school, they commented that her reflections hit home for them as well. Now that I'm in California, too, Sioux Falls seems both so similar and so distant. Orange County's chain stores, overdeveloped "ticky-tacky houses," and rightward political leanings are more or less the same as those in Sioux Falls, but the levels of privilege and sense of opportunity clearly are not. Whereas the "social problems" of alcoholism, teen pregnancy, and underemployment have typically been portrayed as attributes of inner-city existence, Robo presents them as facts of life in the heartland. In contrast to many of the other tapes I analyze, Robo does not comment on her own family life, just the bleak new domestic formations among her peers.

Peterson, Clarkson, and Robo offer personal narratives and ethnographies that function as closure for their makers; they uneasily come to terms with the people and places from which they came. In documenting and reflecting on private lives in frequently ignored locations, these tapes demonstrate the importance of videotape as an access format, both in terms of production and in terms of distribution. Bootlegging by mail allows for alternative media to speak of experiences in the Southwest and South Dakota, not only in New York and San Francisco. Furthermore, I would argue that it is precisely in these places where video access fills a greater need and potentially has the greater affective impact on participants who seek a sense of community.

Sharing Is Caring

As systematized self-distribution, Joanie 4 Jackie constructs a community of maker-viewers who express their most intimate histories. In a work on female biography, one scholar aligned the future of feminism with such community building through affection and sharing. "It is this love, I am certain, this sense of identification with women alone, not as fellow sufferers but as fellow achievers and fighters in the *public domain*, upon which the success of the current feminist movement depends."[39] Joanie 4 Jackie productively

35a–c. Erika Robo singing a karaoke version of John Cougar Mellencamp's "Jack and Diane," a dissolve between the dreary lyrics of "Jack and Diane" and a snowy shot of Christmas lights, and escaping Sioux Falls in *Long after the Thrill.*

conflates the concepts of a women's public domain (as in public sphere) with the sharing of media works and personal narratives—that is, it fuses feminist community building and progressive intellectual property principles.

For a chainletter to work, it must be recirculated. In this way, the Joanie 4 Jackie videos not only operate as a method of communication but also circulate through gift exchanges. Rejecting modes of distribution that rely on and enforce exclusive intellectual property rights, chainletter submissions adhere to an ethic of sharing that in the digital age has become known as peer production, open source, wikis, or Creative Commons.[40] Tapes are submitted without contracts and distributed without royalties; demanding creative control or profit would be antithetical to the project. A popular saying among public-domain advocates suggests, "information wants to be free." As a latter-day instance of women's liberation, this seems to be how the chainletter contributors view their own work, by sending it out into the world as gifts to others. In the seminal study of gifts, Marcel Mauss writes, "To give something is to give a part of oneself . . . while to receive is to receive part of someone's spiritual essence."[41] As should be clear from descriptions of the work that circulates on the chainletter tapes, the makers often give parts of themselves, through autobiographical accounts that share their experiences, identities, traumas, and creativity.

As Mauss observed, gift economies necessitate three types of actions: to give, to receive, and to reciprocate. A later scholar has extended this principle to observe that, in many cultures, a gift must also constantly be passed on. "While gifts are marked by motion and momentum at the level of the individual, gift exchanges at the level of the group offer equilibrium and coherence, a kind of anarchist stability."[42] Unlike the *Superstar* bootlegs studied in the previous chapter, which involve private person-to-person giving, the chainletter structure is person-to-public and creates a community through sharing. Joanie 4 Jackie creates an infrastructure for bootlegs like a gift economy, although it operates more like a community than an economy, since the desire to forge a social and creative network supersedes any intention of making the project profitable or indefinitely sustainable.

Through these chainletters, video becomes the medium for producing a networked female media community. Responding to the British bootlegger Emma Hedditch's "And I Will Do" project and to Joanie 4 Jackie, two critics hail the "joys of bootlegging" and the creativity endemic to such projects. These methods of exchange create polyamorous communities of affinity and creative exchanges that extend beyond the typical art world insiders and outside profit-driven market forces:

> There is something appealingly romantic about this way of creating, sharing and exchanging, and while it is a highly aestheticized position, this practice is far from utopian detachment. . . . The network of bootlegging is a way of relating to collaborators, audiences and guests that is as constitutive of the participants as it is a means to distribute artwork.[43]

These art critics observe how the recipients of chainletters become crucial to the creative process as bonds are forged via dupes and padded envelopes. Taking the rhetoric of gift theory, this form of self-distribution in effect distributes the self.

Since every contributor is ultimately also a recipient of the chainletters, every maker is also an audience member, and the compilations recontextualize their solo contributions as part of a video collection. The project strives to produce interactive viewers; the cardboard sleeves for each cassette proclaim the project as "a challenge and a promise" wherein every audience member is a potential contributor. Astonishingly, Miranda July began this distribution network before she even made her first video short, *Atlanta* (1996). Based in Portland at the time, she initiated the project to produce a sense of community for herself and to motivate her own video work. Already a musician and performance artist, July solicited work by word of mouth and flyers that she handed out at concerts. Within a year she had enough submissions to produce the first chainletter.[44] Likewise, making unlikely interpersonal connections has been a theme of July's own work, in particular her video *Nest of Tens* (2000) and her wondrous debut feature film, *Me and You and Everyone We Know* (2005). In 2002, as her tenure running Joanie 4 Jackie was winding down, July developed a series of participatory crafting projects online, called Learning to Love You More (www.learningtoloveyoumore.com), with Harrell Fletcher. From the beginning, the chainletters were not merely a means of distribution but were also conceived as ways of reaching out, of making contact. To borrow an infamous phrase from July's feature, these chainletters suggested the potential for video exchanges "Back and Forth. Forever."

These chainletter shorts are intimations in the hopes of finding a sympathetic viewer, missives seeking out a long-distance community. For the Joanie 4 Jackie project, sharing suggests a therapeutic potential. As a final example, I turn to the heartbreaking *All I Can Be (2001: a chainletter)*, in which Erica Hill, a teenager from Norman, Oklahoma, confides to her video

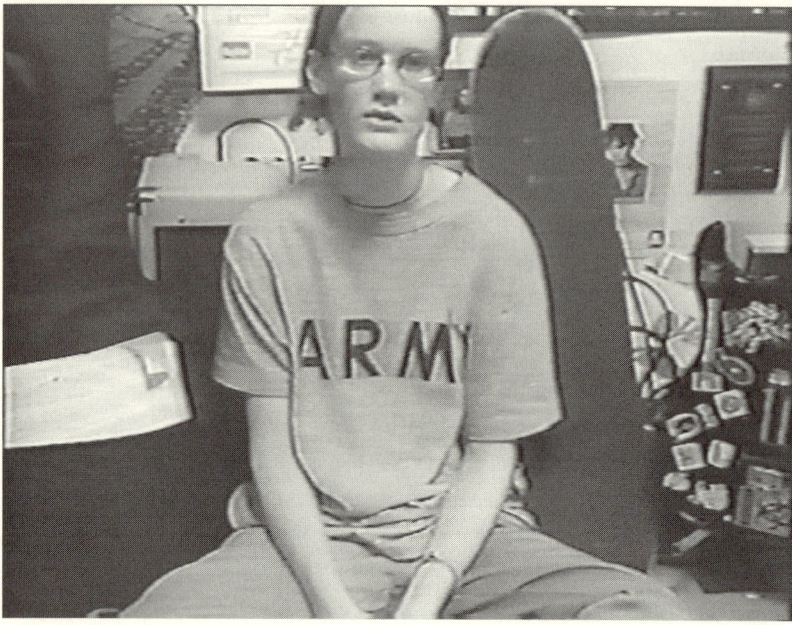

36. Erica Hill in *All I Can Be.*

camera her experiences with homophobia and domestic strife. Shot in fixed medium shot and interspersed with cuts to black and jump-cuts, this diary was apparently shot in a single evening. The maker is a lanky seventeen-year-old girl with a pale complexion who wears oval wire-frame glasses and a gray army T-shirt (hence the title); she sits cross-legged on the floor of her bedroom in front of a guitar amp, a Heart LP, a skateboard, and the various stickers and torn-out magazine images that plaster her stuff and walls.[45] Hill's intimations begin with recalling one night around one a.m. after a drag show in Oklahoma City's "gay ghetto." Like so many teenagers from smaller towns, Hill apparently drove to the closest city to seek refuge in the urban queer spaces. (This likewise holds for arty youths who must travel to experience museums, movies, or concerts.) Yet even there she and her friends were harassed with shouts of "queers" and pelted with eggs by guys in a passing truck. "It's the kind of stuff that happens here," she says matter-of-factly.

With a cut, she transitions to a discussion of her home life—a domestic scene that seems no less harsh. Her parents put her in therapy when she was fifteen, she says, and projected their marital problems onto her:

> They put me in therapy—because apparently I'm a bad child. . . . I just don't like going and being told how *I'm* the one with all the problems. How *I'm* the one that's responsible for this family falling apart when it's my father who's the one cheating on his wife and, you know, drinking himself into an oblivion every night. It's my fault. I'm the one to blame for my parents getting a divorce or whatever.

Hill clearly knows that it's *not* her fault, although on some level she can't help internalizing her father's words. Continuing her commentary on her father after a cut to black, she says:

> Then there was the time he called me a dirty little whore, told me to suck dicks on the street for a living, get out of his house, and never come back. But of course I came back. I mean, where else am I going to go? I was fifteen. What are you going to do when you're fifteen?

After a beat, she quietly reassures the camera, "I don't hate my father. I don't hate him." Or is she reassuring herself?

Eventually she turns to the topic that seems to have motivated the video confession: coming out. More so than her prior testimonies, however, she visibly has trouble articulating her sexuality. She avoids eye contact with the camera, and an increased rate of jump-cuts suggests that she repeatedly started and stopped the camera until she could muster to courage to explain herself. "When I was fourteen, I realized that . . . It's hard to say it out loud because if someone finds this, I could die." Then, quietly, she gets it off her chest: "I realized I like girls. And that shouldn't be hard to say, but it is." Reconsidering what she has just revealed, she says, "Someone could find this and kill me. . . . I know a lot of people who would. I'm friends with a lot of people who would." With a sense of hopelessness, she asks, "How do you change that?" In a couple of subsequent shots, she is speechless, lowering her head between her arms, then fidgeting with a ring. "It's just something in me, I guess," she concludes.

Of all the Joanie 4 Jackie contributions I've seen, *All I Can Be* is the closest to a call for help from an isolated female youth. The recording leaves Hill's intentions ambiguous. Was it originally a private diary or created with the chainletters in mind? Was it "merely" an act of autobiography or meant to help other girls like her? Are her stories even true, or is this a highly convincing fabrication? Frustrating communication at the same time she seems to desire it, Hill's e-mail address does not appear on the Joanie 4 Jackie website—perhaps for fear that someone she knows would discover it . . . and her. But her artist statement indicates that she wanted to reveal her town for what it was. "It's like where I live, people watch everything you do. You're being monitored every second of every day, and by documenting my life, I decide what you see." Her tape ends with a similar assertion of actuality and address to her unknown viewer: "Don't confuse this with art. This isn't art. This is my life. It scares me." Part of what is so striking about *All I Can Be* is its intense direct address to the viewer. It seems as if she is speaking directly to and for us, and her closing statement refuses artifice or aesthetic distance. Thus it is exemplary of the communicative potential—and longing—of the chainletter project.

While in the process of revising this book, I embarked on a road trip that took me through some of the places represented in these tapes, such as Arizona, New Mexico, and Oklahoma. The drive was not a spiritual quest, nor would I claim that my passing tourist glances gave me any deep insights into the places I visited. But driving alone through the western and plains states did remind me that distinct local cultures continue to exist, even if so much of popular culture is the same nationally (indeed, globally). Almost every day, I experienced striking juxtapositions of dissonant places in the same day: Los Angeles and the Grand Canyon, the largest cross in the Western Hemisphere (in Groom, Texas) and a startlingly cruisy gay "resort" (in Oklahoma City), the Enchanted World Doll Museum and Deadwood (both in South Dakota), Salt Lake City and Las Vegas. I had also never realized how far apart we really are. Almost every state was more expansive than I had anticipated, and getting from place to place was wearying. Media and mail do help people feel connected in a way that is impervious to the empty spaces, desert heat, and prairie winds. I know it's clichéd, but the road trip intensified both my love and my fear of America, my feelings of being from here and being out of place. The chainletter videos were frequently on my mind and mediated my experiences of some of these places, though I hope being in these spaces also enriched my readings of the tapes. Maybe it's that most of my friends are women or that I've spent so much time watching videos alone, but I feel an attachment to these video makers. Maybe this reflection is an indulgent way to end a case study, but these videos call out for this kind of self-reflection, openness, and sharing.

Admittedly, the submissions that I have described tend toward the depressing rather than the kick-ass-have-fun riot grrrl mode. Yet I have emphasized these tapes because they fulfill the chainletter project's original mission of connecting distant voices and potentially offering therapeutic communication by sharing their makers' private lives and personal testimonies. As July has remarked in an interview, "I only cared about people who were in some ways isolated. . . . At the time when I started Joanie 4 Jackie, I could barely see outside of the room I was in, and it and my work as a whole—the CDs and early videos—were like a message in a bottle."[46] Videotapes mediate not only communication but also potential communities. These bootleg chainletters are an amateur endeavor that is distinctively analog in its accessibility, aesthetics, and affect. The potential for written responses or for seriality in terms of the video submissions, however, may go unfulfilled; these tapes may remain messages in a bottle rather than answered letters. In this respect, at least, online video sharing—the subject of my epilogue—may more readily facilitate comment posting and responsive or parodic video posts.

Epilogue: YouTube: Where Cultural Memory and Copyright Converge

Let's begin this epilogue with a clip: William Shatner's infamous *Saturday Night Live* sketch in 1986 when he told a convention of Trekkies to "get a life." This scene signaled a defining moment in media reflexivity and public awareness of fan cultures, as well as inspired the opening of Henry Jenkins's book *Textual Poachers* (1992). The first time I presented some of the material that follows as a talk, I used a clip of the Shatner sketch as an illustration of content uploaded to YouTube that reflects and replays pop-cultural memory. But by the time I reworked my presentation for a conference about a month later, the clip had disappeared. Periodically I search for this clip again; sometimes it has been reposted by different users, and sometimes there aren't any hits. Perhaps something like this has happened to you, too.

YouTube has become the go-to website for finding topical and obscure streaming video clips, but everyday experiences also indicate how fleeting such access can be. Both casual viewers and academics have quickly come to treat the site as an informal archive of television texts. Even though YouTube and sites like it expand access to a rich spectrum of such material and suggest the potential for democratization of media memories and flows, they also introduce new ways to regulate and deny access to content under the guise of enforcing copyright protection. YouTube presents a model of digital bootlegging that reiterates many of the issues I've been discussing for analog media—except on a scale millions of times more popular. This new form of self-syndication raises major problems of technology, intellectual property, and postbroadcast networking. Amateur, grassroots, and timely clips have been important to YouTube's appeal. This epilogue, however, focuses on its controversial uses to access unauthorized content.

Web Video

At the forefront of web video, YouTube has been called "viral," "revolutionary," and a "phenomenon." Within a few months of the streaming video website's public launch in December 2005, tens of millions of visitors daily used the site to access television clips online and, in many cases, to post some of their own. Rather than being promoted by multi-million-dollar branding campaigns by major networks or tech firms, YouTube became popular by word of mouth—which in the Internet era means forwarded e-mail links, blogs, and MySpace profiles. (Or, for those older than the "Me Media" generation, articles in the *New York Times* or elsewhere.) The videos available on YouTube include home videos and remixes, up-to-the-minute television excerpts, music videos, trailers, commercials, and highlights from television history posted by users—and increasingly by producers and the networks themselves.

Despite all the hype surrounding the speed of YouTube's popularity, television-computer convergence had been a long-anticipated prospect. In the mid-1990s, tech companies, networks, and Internet service providers were already speculating about their future merger and the resulting potential for exact target marketing.[1] As Lisa Parks observes, "Industry leaders have identified the age of postbroadcasting as the era of 'personal television.' "[2] As conceived by corporate marketers, such "personal" television meant developing algorithms and tracking mechanisms to automatically program content according to users' tastes by matching their viewing habits and ratings—much the way Amazon, Netflix, and TiVo make suggestions to users as a method for upselling. Microsoft purchased WebTV in 1996 but failed to capture a media monopoly to complement its software empire. In the intervening decade, digital developments such as DVDs, DVRs (digital video recorders, such as TiVo), video-on-demand services, peer-to-peer (P2P) file-sharing networks, iTunes, and hulu.com have contributed to changes in how viewers receive and watch television. The digital video recorder TiVo has been perhaps the most successful televisual technology that has integrated broadcast content with a digital hard drive and user interface. Yet despite the enthusiasm of its adopters, TiVo has managed only minor market penetration compared to VCRs and has remained the addictive plaything of only the most privileged or voracious television consumers. It turns out that what Parks has termed "flexible microcasting" in relation to much of this speculative rhetoric even more aptly describes a boom of Web-based video sharing that appeared years after the dot.com bubble burst.

With the expansion of high-speed connections and growing computer memory capacities, Internet video distribution—from BitTorrent downloading to short-form streaming—has at long last become viable on a massive scale. Yet when the promise of television online finally became palpable, it was not in the way that corporations and the digerati had predicted in the 1990s. Indeed, if the histories of communications technologies have taught us anything, audiences rarely adopt and use media in the ways they were originally envisioned. YouTube, like popular P2Ps before it, was developed by a couple of young guys who wrote the basic programming code and millions of home users who developed its uses.[3]

YouTube's success has been attributed in part to its user-friendliness. Users do not need to log in to view clips, and videos start streaming as soon as the web page loads, so there is no need to worry about software compatibility, downloading files, or even clicking the "play" button. In the YouTube interface, videos appear with a scrollable sidebar of other videos that search results have concluded are of related interest, so users can click through from one clip to another without doing multiple searches. (Videos embedded on blogs or other sites lose these paratextual links until the video ends and additional video options appear over the darkened frame.) This mode of hyperlinking effectively replicates channel-surfing and introduces non-narrative seriality to the viewing experience. Frequently, as well, searches for an iconic or controversial moment of television will yield multiple clips of the same content, with minor variations in image quality, running time, titling, keywords, or spellings. Deciding which clip among the batch to view may depend on clues such as the thumbnail image or running time (to get the most complete or, conversely, the most efficient clip) or simply by rules of peer-review popularity (users give clips star ratings, and the number of times each clip has been viewed is also tracked for users' ready reference). Beyond YouTube's ease of use, however, its vast collection seems to be the primary draw.

YouTube and similar sites offer new and remediating relationships to texts that indicate changes in, and acceleration of, spectatorial consumption. In short, YouTube has contributed to a culture of the clip. The specific moments a viewer wants to see can now be searched and accessed without the hassles of watching live broadcasts, making recordings, or waiting through narrative exposition and commercial breaks. In the process, the clip fosters a new temporality of immediate gratification for audiences. As soon as the red bar across the bottom of the playback frame indicates how much of the streaming video is ready to view, users can actually drag the cursor to scan

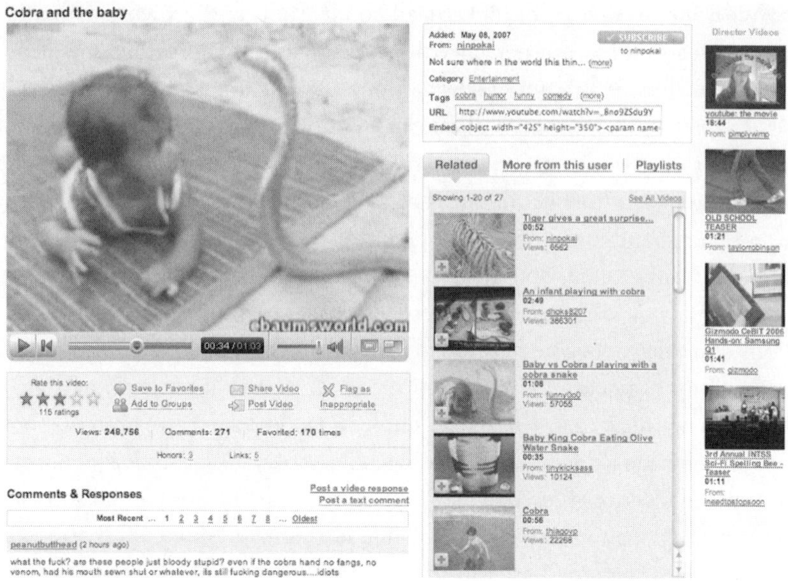

37. The YouTube interface allows users to control playback (left), provides spaces for user ratings and comments (bottom left), lists related clips with thumbnail images and hotlinks (right), and promotes featured clips (far right). Baby and animal clips are prevalent, though usually for cuteness rather than shock value.

ahead and arrive at the moment they seek even more quickly. Suddenly three minutes can seem like a life-sucking eternity, and I, for one, am prone to skipping ahead or moving on before a clip finishes if it's the least bit tedious. Frankly, I also find the site's design for immediate and automatic play irritating, especially if the instant blare of sound competes with other auditory multitasking or if the clip plays before it is fully loaded, which frequently means that it will stall to continue loading midway through the clip. According to the *Wired* profile "Things That Suck!" YouTube and other web video sites "use 1995-era video-encoding algorithms" that demand excessive bandwidth and are often intentionally streamed at inadequate speeds, since many users do not watch clips in their entireties in any case.[4]

The intervention of home video recording opened up the possibility for home audiences to catch up on live broadcasts that they had missed or to reexperience vintage moments. Videotape created audience expectations for access—whether for home video releases of theatrical feature films approximately six months after their debuts or for film classics, video art, or television shows that someone somewhere must have recorded. The Internet, Google, and YouTube have accelerated and exaggerated these expectations for availability. But YouTube reminds audiences that such content, once in their grasp, can still be temporary. The novelty and glee at finding an unexpected clip soon gives way to frustration and disbelief when searches for something else come up matchless—or, increasingly, when a desired clip has been deactivated because of copyright violation. All recording media have some degree of fallibility and ephemerality despite marketing claims to durability or permanence, and Web-based media are especially vulnerable to disappearance by way of deactivation. Perhaps more than at any time before, audiences and users seem to reject the content industry's proprietary claims, complaining when a video goes offline or even reposting new versions of formerly disabled clips. Expectations for access have developed into a sense of access entitlement.

As a forum for self-syndication and postbroadcast networking, YouTube has elicited discourses of "community" and "sharing." Cofounder Chad Hurley has commented, "People like to share experiences. . . . We started it with the idea of solving a problem—how to share video online with your friends."[5] A market analyst was quoted in the *New York Times* as saying, " 'YouTube figured out what Google and Yahoo and Microsoft and all the others in the marketplace didn't,' she said. 'It's not about the video. It's about creating a community around the video.' "[6] As its slogan "Broadcast Yourself" suggests, YouTube fosters exhibitionistic and narcissistic amateur video streams; it's tempting to suggest that user-generated content on YouTube is more about promoting oneself than about exchanging ideas with others.[7]

If YouTube can be said to facilitate communication, it's in ways that emphasize video over epistolary exchange. Friends, family, and coworkers can easily e-mail hotlinks for already-posted videos of cute critters or comical blasts from the past to each other and typically do so with minimal if any written explanations; forwarding YouTube videos can sustain e-mail contact between people with preestablished relationships without the effort of writing personal narratives.[8] In terms of forging new connections, two prevalent types of user-generated posts have emerged: first, talking-head webcam videos of users spouting extemporaneous rants in response to the clips they watch and, second, more elaborate parodies of popular videos. Despite designated spaces on the YouTube interface for descriptions about videos and for feedback from viewers, the potential for written communication via the site seems to be mostly unrealized. Browsing the posted user comments reveals a lot of plugs for posters' own clips, spam, chainletters, and xenophobic flames (insults). When users do make comments, they are typically brief and not terribly enlightening, along the lines of "lol. very funny!!!!!!" Written dialogue remains the domain of blogs and chat rooms.

YouTube, as a mishmash of poached and performed videos, promises a kind of potential totality, wherein every moment of video history or personal post can be searched and streamed. Perceptions of its popularity have had a snowball effect on YouTube's predominance for both uploads and streaming, thus making it the de facto repository for video clips—at least until they are deactivated. YouTube is only the most famous of the proliferating Web video sites, but as the best known, it has become a centralized repository and probably the first place users search for content. It has not only become the default site but is also becoming the generic term for cultural references to Web video clips and sharing—much the way Barbie, Xerox, Kleenex, and Coke can be used to describe a type of product beyond a specific brand name. As the catch-all streaming video site, YouTube can accommodate different kinds of uses, and I suspect the variety of uses may be partially generational. With the exception of the most popular viral videos, I probably have different interests than my students do; I am far more likely to watch excerpts from established television programs (new or old), whereas younger users seem more engaged by amateur video and media reedits.

As I have suggested with analog video, users typically begin to see "new" media as having histories only in the wake of their obsolescence, failures, losses, decay, and omissions. Historicizing the Web means historicizing the present, because so much of electronic media will not last long enough to serve as documents for future researchers. The swiftness with which the stakes surrounding YouTube changed in its first year and a half demonstrates just how difficult it is to rigorously assess cultural and technological developments in their present moment. For instance, an otherwise insightful book about "the transition from network to networked TV" published in 2006 completely missed the YouTube phenomenon.[9] The new media scholar Lisa Gitelman has written about the problems—and potential—of historicizing the Internet, with its surplus of information, inherent difficulties for long-term access, and sloppiness of record keeping between the short life spans of web pages, irregularities of dating, and changes in browser versions.[10] When media are new, users may not worry about long-term access and preservation, but all too quickly they may come to recognize that both content and technology are ephemeral when a link takes them to an "Error 404: File

Not Found" page or a blog has been suspended owing to lack of payment or a video has been disabled because of copyright violation. Sisyphean efforts to archive the Internet, such as the Wayback Machine at www.archive.org, while necessary, inevitably only partially capture the Web as it was. Hyperlinks are often dead, and images may no longer load, not to mention that the interface may be different simply because the user is anachronistically accessing the site through the latest version of Firefox or Internet Explorer instead of via an early form of Netscape.

Despite many unrealized promises for digital media in the past decade or so, a surprising number of advocates and scholars of digital technology remain celebratory in their rhetoric that technology has profoundly changed our culture, and continue to claim that in the near future, all content will be digital, interactive, and shared. As a reporter for *Wired* magazine asserted, "Without being overly simplistic or melodramatic, the state of the Old Commercial Broadcasting Model can be summarized like this: a spiraling vortex of ruin."[11] I'm far more skeptical. For mass audiences, broadcast, cable, and satellite television still dominates (not least because of class issues such as the digital divide—that is, uneven access to technology—or even the bourgeois pleasures of narrative structures and slick production values), and network content will continue to feed these streams. And I suspect that for many audiences, network content—new or old—still drives users to YouTube, and amateur content is discovered along the way, through suggested links, alternate search results, and forwarded e-mails.

Although some cultural critics have predicted that YouTube will displace the established corporate media, YouTube's popularity relies at least in part on recirculated selections of mainstream media.[12] As has been historically apparent with entertainment technologies, novelty often gives way to familiar content. Convergence usually means content redundancy across platforms, and YouTube perhaps relies more on mainstream media for source material than it threatens to displace it.[13] In some cases, the mainstream media have even been quick to appropriate YouTube's cachet. The traditional news media—print and broadcast—have paid considerable attention to the YouTube phenomenon, reporting on seemingly every technological development and business deal, as well as referencing clips as human-interest stories. The press has contributed to the site's hype and made it even more culturally central than it otherwise might have been. For print and television news alike, embracing YouTube may be a strategy the networks use to compete with amateur bloggers.

YouTube has become part of our cultural vernacular, so references creep into entertainment content as well. To offer just one example, the second episode of NBC's self-reflexive sitcom *30 Rock* (aired October 18, 2006) begins with a character watching a clip of an actress throwing a cat against a wall from the series pilot on YouTube; this moment both portrays a common use of the technology to watch outrageous TV moments and contributes to the show's knowing sensibility. Unauthorized fan videos from the show, however, have been taken down. Because of perceived audience drift to YouTube, NBC and other networks have begun posting free streaming episodes on their own websites for viewing on-demand with limited commercial interruptions. Given this situation, the conflict becomes not only about what media audiences watch but also about who can control and profit from it.

Cultural Memory

YouTube has given renewed public lives to thousands or even millions of now classic moments from television and offers access to a rich spectrum of important footage of history-shaping events and otherwise unavailable and obscure nuggets of popular culture. YouTube clips allow access to national traumas, such as CNN's coverage of the *Challenger* space shuttle explosion (1986), and epoch-defining events, such as footage of Los Angeles police beating Rodney King (1991). Such historically significant videos intermingle with innumerable, decidedly less important but nonetheless fascinating curiosities, from the Disney-animated *The Story of Menstruation* (1946) to Crispin Glover playing up his eccentricities on *Late Night with David Letterman* (1987). In cases such as commercials and talk show highlights, significant but small-scale ephemera have historically been the hardest content for fans and even historians to track down and reexperience. This Internet library has fed scholarly as well as nostalgic uses.

Culled from users' personal collections of recordings and productions, the site's videos and its search engine offer some evidence of what material from television's past now constitutes our cultural memory. Like memory (cultural or personal), YouTube is dynamic. It is an ever-changing clutter of stuff from users' pasts, some of which disappears and some of which remains overlooked, while new material is constantly being accrued and new associations or (literally, hypertext) links are being made.[14] The images are often hazy but may suffice to induce recall or to fill in where we could only previously imagine how things were from written or word-of-mouth accounts.

One of the dangers of seeing once-formative content on YouTube is being underwhelmed in the present; such disillusioning effects are probably only enhanced by the low resolution of the video stream. But these disappointments of history alternate with delightful rediscoveries.

YouTube introduces a new model of media access and amateur historiography that, while the images are imperfect and the links are impermanent, nonetheless realizes much of the Internet's potential to circulate rare, ephemeral, and elusive texts. YouTube extends the cultural logic of peer-to-peer file sharing and of blogs, suggesting that popular entertainment content and personal missives belong in the commons. But YouTube does not operate as an archive in the proper sense of the word. As documents, the low-resolution and often temporary postings to YouTube fall far short of archival preservation, and excerption changes the flow and format of broadcast and cable TV content. Archivists on the Association of Moving Image Archivists Listserv have criticized YouTube not only for circulating low-resolution copies of unauthorized content but also for skewing general perceptions that sites such as YouTube may render traditional archives irrelevant and are introducing unrealistic demands for access.

YouTube functions both as a portal of cultural memory and as a concept, and it reflects what has been observed happening in archives: assemblages of quotidian fragments, such that almost every detail potentially comes to stand as some kind of historical document. With the rise of electronic media, networked computers, and the Internet, the potential for the production and preservation of still more cultural fragments exponentially grows—as do the questions of ownership rights.[15] One archive theorist points to Jorge Luis Borges's short story "The Aleph" (1949) as an imagined early metaphor and model for the World Wide Web, which "offers speed, flexibility and mobility of images, along with completeness and effortlessness of access."[16] This description could just as well prefigure YouTube.

Memory media are mediated—and look it, as old video clips seem to exhibit a surface haze of worn old video. The YouTube recordings further remediate content and inscribe its sources onto the recordings. The homemade status of many television clips is marked by station identification logos in the corner of the frame and, in the cases of older recordings, VHS artifacts such as rainbows of discoloration and signal dropout. Such artifacts and alterations signal the videos' sources and demonstrate bootleg aesthetics. Clips that circulate beyond YouTube, as embedded videos on other websites, likewise feature branded YouTube logo watermarks. The identities of uploaders and comment posters are also inscribed on the interface, so that there is some record of where the footage came from and where it has gone.

Perhaps even more so than VHS bootlegs, streaming clips on YouTube reflect the aesthetics of access. In a word, YouTube clips look (and sound) terrible. Off-air recordings get compressed, source webcams and camera phone images look blocky and jerky from the moment of creation, and various filter options on DV cameras and postproduction software may also add layers of mediation to the image. Delays in streaming exacerbate all these effects. Videos that may look acceptable in miniature reveal low resolution if blown up to full-screen view. And digitization of analog source recordings takes color saturation down a few notches while introducing pixelation. I'm struck by the historical coincidence that YouTube, with its crummy image and sound quality, exploded simultaneously with the push by electronics firms, studios, and retailers for high-definition television and video. Although web video will surely increase in resolution over time, the popularity of YouTube suggests that access, for many viewers, is more important than aesthetics.

In the first chapter, I stressed the distinctions between the VCR, the cassette, and the tape that contribute to and make up analog video. YouTube clips come from many types of technology—old off-air tapes, ripped DVDs, mini-DV camcorders, cell phones—and traces of the source format may remain visible after clips are uploaded to YouTube. Yet distinctions between content and delivery device are simultaneously flattened as the clips appear embedded within web pages. Video loses much of its tactility when reduced to code, though the interface maintains interactivity through mouse clicks and keystrokes. Even the "Tube" in YouTube's name is anachronistic slang for TV, from the cathode-ray tube; today, for most Web users, the tube monitor has been replaced by a flat LCD screen.

Although I am making a claim for the site's centrality in accessing historical clips, instantaneity is one of its primary virtues. Users post television clips almost as soon as they have been broadcast, which allows viewers who missed a politician's faux pas or bits of incisive satire to see the relevant material in time to participate in water cooler conversations. Of course, rights owners can and do insist that such popular clips be taken down almost as quickly. It has become common for blog readers to click through an embedded clip from the previous night's television broadcast only to find that the footage has been taken offline in the few hours that elapsed between the post and the reader's attempted playback. This has become so common that bloggers even signal the likelihood of this outcome by suggesting readers click through while they can. Even newsworthy public events are not immune. Perhaps the most publicized and outrageous single takedown notice to date came when the public affairs network C-SPAN ordered the removal of Stephen Colbert's satirical speech at the White House Correspondents' Association dinner in May 2006, which had been watched 2.7 million times within forty-eight hours on YouTube and clearly satirized the state of political journalism.[17] This viewership statistic suggests that more viewers saw the speech on YouTube than during its original transmission and that, as outrageous as it seems, even governmental events can be subject to restrictive copyright claims. On the flip side, YouTube has also been used as a vehicle for grassroots alternative media to expose political gaffes, corporate exploitation, police violence, and the realities of the battlefront in Iraq. Once publicized on YouTube, events and issues at times get taken up by the mainstream press. In many cases, this feeds the greater good, though at other times, a few seconds of video can cause such a scandal that they can ruin a campaign or damage an entire political career. And rather than diversifying what audiences see, topical viral videos (viral in the sense of epidemic distribution, but also sometimes stealth in the sense of a computer virus) reinforce the cultural dominance of a few specific media clips.

The high viewership of short-lived clips—such as those mentioned in blogs or even reported in the traditional press—reintroduces the dialectic of ubiquity and ephemerality that has historically been the model of much of popular culture, especially broadcasting. Whether footage of major current events or seemingly random curiosities that have made the leap from obscurity, specific clips will routinely proliferate across blogs to become the clip of the moment. For example, for about a month in summer 2007, it seemed that everyone I knew either forwarded links or talked about a clip featuring hundreds of Filipino prisoners performing an amazingly synchronized dance routine to Michael Jackson's "Thriller."[18] Typically, however, such spotlighting lasts about a day or two, until saturation or something new prompts web surfers to move on. While some clips are short-lived only in the sense of waning public interest, many face immediate deactivation and actually disappear because of claims of copyright infringement. Clips that excerpt controversial footage or that revive texts from TV's past indicate users' desires to reclaim, reproduce, and recirculate fragments of a shared cultural memory. And, of course, these are the clips most at risk of being taken offline by their rights owners.

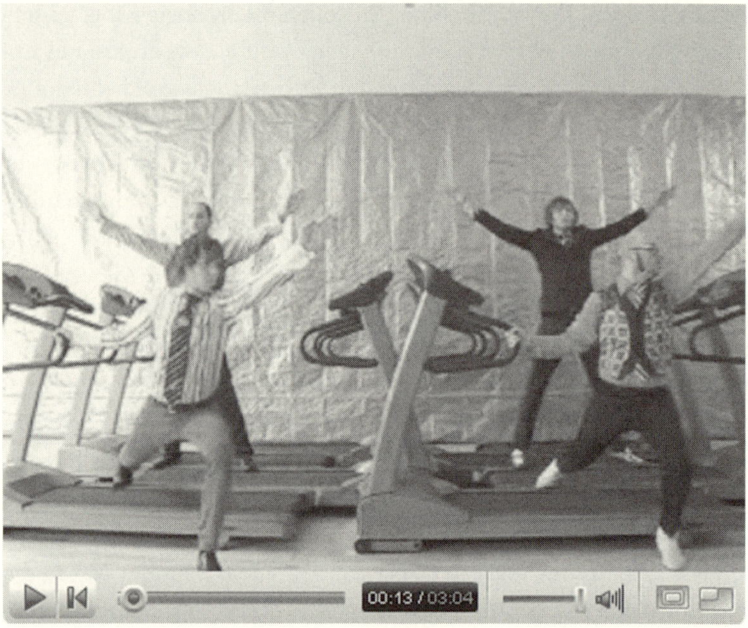

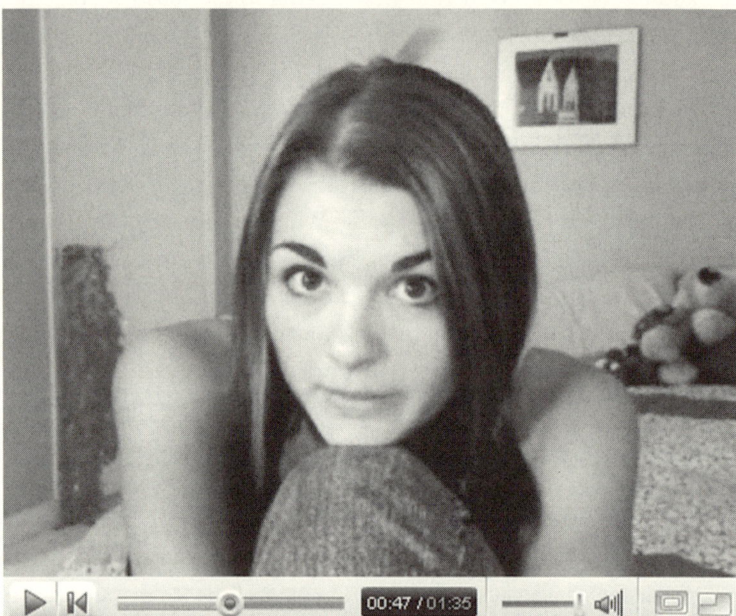

38a–d. Viral videos on YouTube: OK Go's music video "Here It Goes Again"; the first YouTube star (and fraud), lonelygirl15; one of many stunt experiments mixing partially chewed Mentos with two-liter bottles of Diet Coke to create fountains (pictured here) or rockets; and the Filipino prisoner performance of "Thriller."

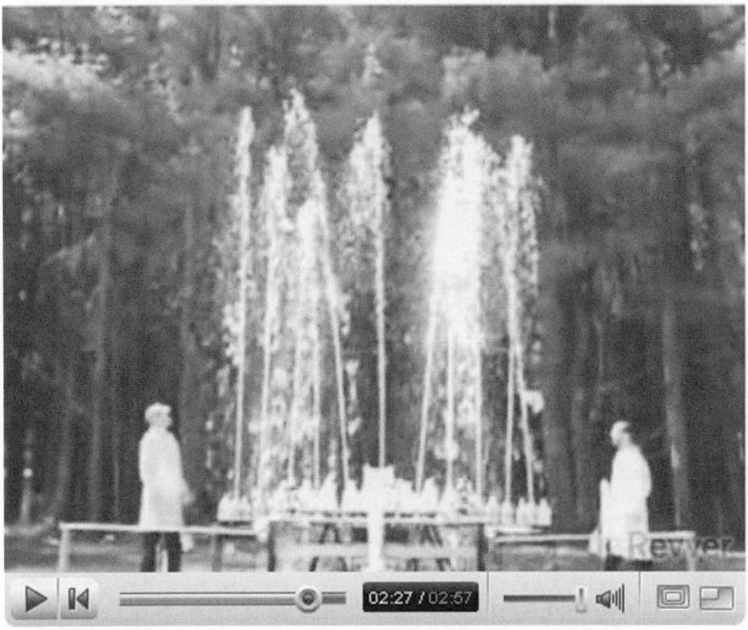

Revver
02:27 / 02:57

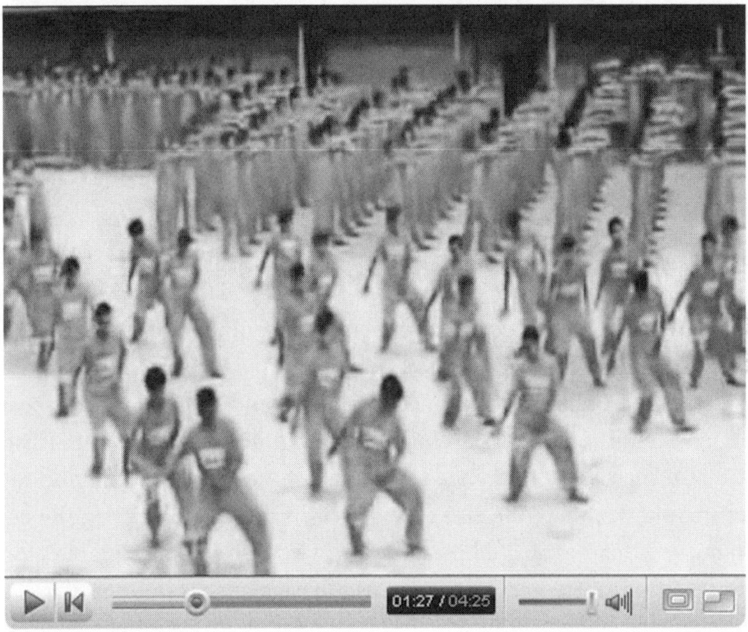

01:27 / 04:25

Copyright

Copyright has been at the center of public attention to YouTube, and it sets the terms on which much of personal (and scholarly) access to media texts will be available. It is also the major question that has shrouded YouTube's success. How long can YouTube survive in an age of aggressive antipiracy campaigns and lawsuits—content industry movements that have largely been supported by Congress and the courts? Google purchased YouTube for $1.6 billion in October 2006, undeniably making it *worth* suing.[19] Videos can easily be found through keyword searches on the site or simply through a general Web search on Google. In this sense, its design as a search engine matched Google's business model (free search results are underwritten by advertising) and allowed for integration with Google's own fledgling video databases when the company acquired YouTube. But it might be difficult to assert how Google's purchase of YouTube, which in effect corporatized it, might benefit users. The transaction, predictably, increased internal regulation of copyright-infringing clips.[20] In fact, Google even set aside $200 million for legal expenses in anticipation of a major copyright infringement case when it acquired YouTube.[21]

With all the attention YouTube has received as the central portal of Web video clips, it has seemed inevitable that some media conglomerate or other would sue YouTube for copyright infringement. If anything, it actually took longer than one might have expected. In March 2007, Viacom (parent company for Paramount Pictures, CBS, Comedy Central, MTV, VH1, BET, and King World) sued YouTube and its parent company, Google, for $1 billion.[22] The lawsuit followed Viacom's failed attempts to negotiate a cooperative deal (negotiations reportedly continue concurrently with litigation) and hundreds of thousands of requests for YouTube to disable clips of Viacom properties such as *The Daily Show*, *The Colbert Report*, and *South Park*. (Advocates of digital content sharing and remixing have pointed out the irony that Stephen Colbert repeatedly referenced and encouraged YouTube clips and remixes on his show.) Since the rise of content sharing through P2PS, the content industries have protested piracy and have received considerable attention for their purported economic losses. These claims mimic similar alarmist campaigns against audiocassette players and VCRS from the late 1970s and early 1980s; eventually the industries learned how to profit through new business models, just as the economics of web video will eventually yield viable business opportunities. Furthermore, litigation—whether based on a legitimate legal claim or merely a scare tactic and form of economic intimidation—can have inhibiting effects far more sweeping than the specific rule of law. Whether or not Viacom sees any financial reward for its litigation, this is the type of case that seems bound for the Supreme Court, to follow in the wake of its major precedents, *Sony v. Universal* (1984, aka "the Betamax case") and *MGM v. Grokster* (2005, which shut down the Kazaa-like P2P network Grokster for enabling unauthorized music sharing).

YouTube does not promote willy-nilly piracy so much as it enables access to culturally significant texts that would otherwise be elusive and the ability to repurpose videos in the creation of new derivative works. In other words, the site and its users (and I) advocate for what copyright is supposed to do. Copyright law was developed to stimulate publication of new works for the edification of culture. At base, copyright allows rights owners the right of publication and, in exchange for offering cultural works for public consumption, of profiting from such publication. This form of legal regulation was intended to foster a vibrant and continuing stream of new cultural works, though legislation and court rulings have increasingly favored rights owners over their audiences.

The same basic issues are at stake, if complicated, in the era of digital networks when peer sharing and video streaming are more or less indistinguishable from publication. (For analog media, content owners have considerable control in deciding how tangible content will enter the marketplace.) In many cases, rights owners request to have streaming YouTube videos disabled not necessarily because they are competing with owners' own residual marketing but because they want to maintain some kind of control over what is publicly accessible and how it is distributed. Digital technologies and policies have facilitated rapid and drastic methods of disabling the documents that feed cultural memories and enable scholarship. Hardware is now regularly engineered to prevent copying and to disable unauthorized uses, and the 1998 Digital Millennium Copyright Act (DMCA) forbids users to hack encryption technologies and allows offended parties to demand that online content be taken offline without due process to prove infringement. As Lawrence Lessig has suggested, in such situations, the layers of "code"—the hardware, the software, and the content—are typically all commercially designed and regulated.[23]

In the Preface, I suggested that this book's case studies, spanning the analog video and fair-use era from the 1970s to the 1990s, demonstrate shifting user attitudes toward copyright, from legal engagement to civil disobedience to defining their own terms. All of these predate the passage of the DMCA, but all remain at play in video postings to YouTube. When access is restricted or forbidden, not only do viewers lose out, but so do students when key texts simply aren't available to be studied or taught. I will go so far as to suggest that YouTube has had a major impact on how media history can be taught by opening up access to a wealth of clips that professors may have longed for but have been unable to locate; furthermore, students are now prone to making peer-produced curriculum by forwarding relevant links to their instructors and classmates. The copyrighted content is likely what is of most interest to scholars, and this content is the most vulnerable to infringement assertions and deactivation. YouTube searches and clips are sorry substitutes for archival research in cases of in-depth study, but the site is incredibly useful for spontaneous illustration in the classroom—or for reference, just as the Internet Movie Database and Wikipedia, despite (overblown) criticisms of their accuracy, conveniently fill in information such as credits, dates, and historical events.

In terms of copyright, the user-uploaded content streamed via YouTube falls into roughly three categories: copied, appropriative, and original. All three categories are prevalent, including original content, which helps bolster the claim that the site can and is used for substantial noninfringing uses. The copied texts derive primarily from users' television recordings, clipped into bite-sized portions without intended alteration of the source material other than excerpting. In some cases, such reproduction of public affairs programming or satire clearly serves the public interest, and such excerpting could arguably be defended as fair use. Appropriative clips include copyrighted music or footage used in the service of new derivative works; such uses range from amateur music videos as users dance and lip-sync to popular songs in their bedrooms to complex fan, slash, or culturejamming reedits of footage. Original content comprises any video footage that does not incorporate previously copyrighted works, such as home movies, video diaries, and small-scale productions. Although I have focused on vintage and current corporate clips, YouTube also provides a space for a broad spectrum of "original programming," documentation, and innumerable home videos, blogs, and remixes. Much of this content holds little appeal beyond the uploader's social circle, but some makers have found surprisingly broad and devoted audiences. There are also innumerable versions, imitations, and parodies of both corporate and amateur content. In many cases, what appears to be the same clip has been uploaded by different users, thus blurring distinctions between authorship, ownership, and distribution rights; these postings reflect the ethics of the cultural (and creative) commons.

In the Betamax case, which legalized home recording with VCRs, the Supreme Court came to three significant conclusions: first, that home video recorders must be allowed because of their potential for noninfringing uses; second, that the dominant uses of the machines were for timeshifting, which the Supreme Court considered fair use; and third, that Sony could not be held liable for its customers' misuses of the machines. The Court's Betamax ruling expanded the domain of fair use beyond orthodox interpretations, thus setting a curious but progressive precedent that imaginatively opened up the law to protect the audience's rights of access to television content. The failure of the Betamax precedent to save the P2Ps should not be seen to limit its viability for YouTube.

Judicial perceptions that Napster and Grokster did not have significant noninfringing uses and that the network managers could have intervened to disable infringing content were central their undoing. Because of the indisputable volume of material that in no way infringes copyright and can be argued to reflect the experiences and ideas of a generation and possibly even a whole cultural moment, YouTube cannot be completely shut down. Further distinguishing YouTube from peer-to-peer networks, YouTube regulates uses of the site. At the time of the Google purchase, YouTube was portrayed as a "good corporate citizen," one that may actually serve the content industry's interests.[24] YouTube has demonstrated such self-regulations as disabling clips that have been the subject of takedown requests from copyright owners in compliance with the DMCA or that have been deemed obscene by users. The site's inability—or refusal, depending on one's point of view—to stringently and preemptively monitor copyrighted content has led to criticism that it willingly hosts infringing content to boost its bottom line. Nearly a year after YouTube publicized a promise to develop an automated system to identify and disable infringing clips, Google announced a proprietary system that would track digital "fingerprints" in clips; the reaction from the content industry was mixed, however, as rights owners would need to give Google copies of all content to be banned for the sake of comparison.[25] From a user's perspective, such automation presents yet another example of technology policing access without due process to consider fair use and also introduces the risk of false positives that would disable noninfringing clips. Meanwhile YouTube's relatively stringent policies have spawned a proliferation of knockoff sites that use similar technologies and interfaces to provide access to illicit content. This trend reflects an existing pattern: the rise of alternative peer-to-peer services when popular ones face legal trouble. In fact, killing off YouTube may do more damage to the content industry than good, if doing so eliminates an industry-friendly site.

In contrast to Viacom, some record labels, studios, and networks have made limited attempts to use YouTube as a promotional platform by uploading previews and pilots through branded "channels" or through paid placement on the website's front page.[26] A handful, including Viacom-owned CBS, have even struck licensing or small-stake ownership agreements with the site. For a time, it seemed that industry licensing agreements and the Google purchase might have signaled a decisive shift in the content industry's war against so-called piracy and ensured the site's survival. YouTube has popularized online video viewing generally and very likely has driven traffic to other sites, including the networks' own. The mainstreaming of consumption patterns and collaboration with the entertainment industry invariably entail some compromises, but YouTube might have been part of achieving an access equilibrium—and maybe it still will be. Maybe the site has introduced a new paradigm for online digital video sharing that builds on the Betamax decision's protections in a way that can be reconciled with the DMCA. But to negotiate these seemingly opposed policies, it must do so in ways as complex, even imaginative, as both the Betamax decision and digital copyright laws. If YouTube and online video streaming continue to be embraced by the industry, a court ruling may find a way within copyright to protect the site's survival as a way to protect commerce—just as it did for VCRs at the time of an exploding video rental market.

Although YouTube may superficially resemble the peer-to-peer networks as a means of unauthorized content redistribution, I suggest that all the judicial reasons that ultimately protected VCRs can and should reasonably apply to YouTube. When the copyright question arises, YouTube representatives have cited the DMCA's safe-harbor provision for Internet service providers, which shields companies that provide technical infrastructure from liability for users' infringements. But the site's inability to build significant revenues—a familiar problem throughout the history of Internet start-ups—and the Viacom lawsuit may drive the site into financial ruin regardless of the lawsuit's outcome. The content industry's interests in the site may suffice to maintain its architecture—and, by extension, to sustain a space for amateur and bootleg media flows. Even if YouTube itself implodes, the technology for video sharing remains available, and viewer desire seems sufficient to drive video sharing to alternative venues. Bootlegging in the near future will continue as personal interventions and subversive streams within and through the copyright miasma of licensing agreements, commons, and fair uses.

In a technological, legal, and business sphere that has so far undone most utopian predictions about new media, my initial optimism about YouTube has given way to ambivalence. The site may not be a perfect or perpetual way to preserve content, but it has incredibly expanded access. Ultimately a commercial endeavor, the site is not—and probably never has been—inherently utopian or radical. Whatever YouTube's future, its meteoric rise to popularity and its role at the center of speculation about the near future of video technology make it historically significant. It should also alert media scholars and audiences to the ways that copyright can regulate video access and, by extension, erase media memory.

VHS and other analog formats have allowed users to own texts and to make texts their own: to keep them, study them, rework them, copy them, and share them with friends. For many film and television viewers who became users of videotape, these new modes of access, aesthetics, and affect contributed to who we are and how we have defined ourselves. Fair use—and the implied rights of personal use—enabled us to do this. Since 1998, technological copyguards and the DMCA's anticircumvention law have been understood to trump such exempted fair-use or archival reproductive rights. The implicit call for policy reform within this book's history is simple: these priorities must be shifted so that the public good is placed before market protection, by way of making fair and archival uses override such copy-prevention strategies.

Timeline

1909	•	U.S. copyright code revised.
1934	•	Magnetic tape first manufactured in Germany.
1944	•	3M begins experimenting with magnetic tape in United States.
1945	•	German magnetic tape recorders captured by U.S. military.
1946	•	Television sets on sale in United States.
	•	John T. Mullin demonstrates magnetic tape to Institute of Radio Engineers.
1947	•	Bing Crosby begins prerecording his radio programs on magnetic tape.
1948	•	Kinescopes introduced.
Late 1940s–early 1960s	•	Audio recording emerges as an office technology and as an amateur hobby.
1951	•	RCA and Ampex begin developing videotape.
1956	•	Ampex demonstrates 2-inch Quadruplex video tape recorder.
1962–64	•	Philips audiocassette format introduced (dates vary by source).
1964	•	8-track tapes introduced.
	•	First copyright bill including fair-use provision introduced to Congress.
1965	•	Sony develops 1/2-inch helical scan videotape.

1967 • The Paley Foundation initiates a TV archive study, continuing through 1971.

1968 • Paul Simpson begins pilot news taping project, which will become the Vanderbilt Television News Archive (VTNA); the archive uses 1-inch Type A videotape until 1979.
- Sony Portapak introduced.
- Protests and police violence at Democratic National Convention in Chicago.
- Richard Nixon elected U.S. president.

1969 • Senator Howard Baker makes first congressional statement for television news collection at Library of Congress.
- Library of Congress conducts TV archive feasibility study.
- VTNA screening at Executive Office Building at request of Senator Baker.
- Vice President Spiro T. Agnew gives speech on media bias.
- Supreme Court ruling on *Red Lion v. FCC* redefines fairness doctrine in terms of audience access to information.
- *TV as a Creative Medium* shows at Howard Wise Gallery.

1970 • First Baker Senate bill for national TV news archive; Richard Fulton proposes similar legislation in the House of Representatives.
- The Carpenters release "(They Long to Be) Close to You."

1971 • Sony 3/4-inch U-matic videocassette format introduced; it will become a broadcasting and professional standard format.
- Baker reintroduces bill for national TV news archive in the Senate; Spark Matsunaga introduces similar bill in the House.
- Republican National Convention requests VTNA screening of news coverage of Laos incursion.
- James Pilkington joins VTNA staff and begins indexing collection.
- CBS Reports' *The Selling of the Pentagon* aired and investigated.

1972 • VTNA begins publishing *Television News Index and Abstracts.*
- First Watergate reports; Nixon reelected.

1973 • Baker reintroduces bill for national TV news archive in the Senate; Matsunaga reintroduces similar bill in the House.
- CBS begins registering its *Evening News* for copyright as "motion picture . . . not reproduced for sale."
- CBS begins litigation against VTNA.
- Watergate investigations begin; White House audiotapes revealed; Agnew resigns; oil embargo begins.

1974
- Baker proposes copyright amendment protecting off-air news taping.
- CBS trial agreements with National Archives and Records Services and school licenses.
- Nixon resigns.

1975
- Sony Betamax introduced.
- General copyright revision bill reintroduced; final copyright code revision hearings with testimonies from CBS and VTNA representatives.
- CBS begins registering its *Evening News* for copyright as "published works."
- Home Box Office (HBO) debuts.
- Atari debuts home game system for Pong.

1976
- VHS introduced.
- Mandate for Library of Congress TV archive integrated into copyright law.
- Comprehensive U.S. copyright code passed, along with fair-use and off-air recording exemptions for libraries and archives.
- Universal and Disney initiate litigation against Sony, thus beginning "the Betamax case."
- CBS dismisses lawsuit against VTNA.
- Museum of Broadcasting opens; Peabody Award archive established; UCLA Film Archive adds "Television" to its name.
- U.S. bicentennial.

1977
- 12-inch laserdisc format introduced; it will become a high-end collectors' format in the early 1990s.
- International Federation of Television Archives (FIAT/IFTA) established.
- Atari debuts 2600 VCS, first interchangeable-cartridge home video game system.

1978
- Revised copyright code goes into effect.
- VHS begins to outsell Betamax.
- Television News Study Center established at George Washington University.

1979
- District court rules timeshifting is fair use in first decision of the Betamax case.
- Video rental stores begin to flourish.
- Reports begin that pornography's share of home video market is declining.

	• VTNA adopts 3/4-inch U-matic as master recording format. • Sony introduces the Walkman.
1979–81	• Hollywood studios form home video divisions.
1981	• Circuit court overturns district court Betamax ruling. • Columbia House begins video club.
1982	• VCRS surpass 5 percent penetration of U.S. TV households. • Jane Fonda's *Workout* released. • Professional-format Betacam introduced. • Compact cassettes outsell 8-tracks. • Philips introduces compact discs.
1983	• *Raiders of the Lost Ark* released as priced-to-own title; preorders outsell all previous releases. • *Videodrome*, a film conflating Betamax cassettes, altered consciousness, and sexual fetishism, released.
1984	• U.S. Supreme Court Betamax decision finds VCR timeshifting to be fair use. • VCRS surpass 10 percent penetration of U.S. TV households. • *Time* and *Newsweek* proclaim the "video revolution." • *Consumer Reports* begins reviewing blank videocassette quality.
1985	• VCRS surpass 25 percent penetration of U.S. TV households. • Forty thousand titles available as prerecorded videotapes. • Nintendo debuts home video game system.
1986	• Sony begins manufacturing VHS; professional- and archival-format Betacam SP introduced.
1987	• VCRS surpass 50 percent penetration of U.S. TV households. • *Superstar: The Karen Carpenter Story* premieres. • Sony acquires CBS records.
1988	• First Rob Lowe sex tape.
1989	• Hi8 consumer miniature camcorder format introduced. • VTNA begins taping CNN. • *Superstar* withdrawn from official distribution. • Sony acquires Columbia Pictures. • *sex, lies, and videotape* released. • Nintendo portable Game Boy debuts.
1992	• VCRS surpass 75 percent penetration of U.S. TV households. • Audio Home Recordings Act passed.

1994
- VTNA begins online publication of index and abstracts.

1995
- DV (digital video) and MINI-DV formats introduced.
- Digital copyright white paper published.
- *The Lion King* becomes the best-selling videotape of all time.
- Big Miss Moviola video chain letter project begins (later renamed Joanie 4 Jackie).
- Federal Antidilution Act for trademarks.
- World Wide Web debuts.
- Sony debuts PlayStation home video game system.

1996
- FCC Telecommunications Act.
- Microsoft acquires WebTV.

1997
- DVD consumer format introduced to U.S. market.
- *Pam and Tommy Lee: Hardcore and Uncensored* released, becomes best-selling adult title of all time.
- No Electronic Theft Act.

1998
- Digital Millennium Copyright Act passed.
- Copyright Term Extension Act (CTEA) passed.
- *Ringu*, Japanese horror film about killer videotapes in which only bootleggers survive, released.

1999
- Napster peer-to-peer file-sharing network debuts.
- TiVo debuts.
- Lawrence Lessig publishes *Code and Other Laws of Cyberspace*.

2001
- Napster shut down following copyright lawsuit and injunction from record companies.
- Apple debuts iPod.
- Microsoft debuts Xbox video game system.
- Lessig publishes *The Future of Ideas*; Jessica Litman publishes *Digital Copyright*; Siva Vaidhyanathan publishes *Copyrights and Copywrongs*.

2002
- Creative Commons copyright licenses introduced.
- Sony ceases manufacturing Betamax decks.
- *The Ring*, an American remake of *Ringu*, released and becomes a hit.

2003
- DVD rentals surpass VHS; major retailers phase VHS out of inventory.
- U.S. Supreme Court upholds the CTEA in *Eldred v. Ashcroft* ruling.
- VTNA begins digital off-air recording.

2004
- Induce Act threatens to override the Betamax decision and make time- and spaceshifting technologies illegal; a grassroots campaign opposes and stops the legislation.
- *Empire* declares VHS dead.

2005
- Supreme Court rules that operators of file-sharing systems are liable for contributory infringement in *MGM v. Grokster*.
- YouTube debuts.
- VTNA completes digital reformatting of its nightly news collections.
- *Washington Post* declares VHS dead.
- *The Ring Two* released; VHS cassettes still deadly.
- Video iPod debuts.

2006
- *Variety* declares VHS dead.
- You named *Time*'s Person of the Year.
- AFI names VHS's demise and the rise of YouTube among year's significant moments.
- Copyright office introduces exception allowing professors to hack DVDs for classroom clips.
- HD-DVD and Blu-ray debut.
- Sony acquires MGM.

2007
- Viacom begins litigation against YouTube.

2008
- Blue-ray wins format war; Toshiba discontinues HD DVD.
- *Be Kind, Rewind* and *Son of Rambow* prominently feature VHS camcorders, suggest technological nostalgia.
- *Wall-E* focuses on an endearing robot that fetishizes a videocassette of *Hello, Dolly!* and plays it with an iPod.
- JVC, inventor of VHS, stops manufacturing VCRs.
- Last remaining distributor of VHS cassettes ships final order.

2009
- Analog television broadcasting ends; digital-only broadcasting mandated by FCC.

Notes

Preface

1 A minor publishing industry of nostalgic picture books of classical Hollywood films and stars may have helped establish a collector's market for such films. One of the early distributors of classic films on video was called the Nostalgia Merchant. On nostalgia in the 1970s, see, for instance, Lasch, "The Politics of Nostalgia"; and Jameson, *Postmodernism*.

2 Moran, *There's No Place Like Home Video*, 55.

3 See, for instance, Armes, *On Video*; Cubitt, *Timeshift* and *Videography*; and Gray, *Video Playtime*; Jameson, *Postmodernism*, 67–96; and Berko, "Video: In Search of a Discourse." This work tends to conflate early industrial development, video art, broadcast programming, music videos, and home video under the reductively homogenizing category of "video."

4 See Levy, ed., *The VCR Age: Home Video and Mass Communication*; Dobrow, ed., *Social and Cultural Aspects of VCR Use*; and Gray, *Video Playtime*.

5 See Lardner, *Fast Forward*; Marlow and Secunda, *Shifting Time and Space*; Wasko, *Hollywood in the Information Age*; Prince, *A New Pot of Gold*, 90–141; Wasser, *Veni, Vidi, Video*; Greenberg, *From Betamax to Blockbuster*; and McDonald, *Video and DVD Industries*.

6 A disciplinary task force viewed the use of videotape in film studies classrooms as a "reluctant necessity" and asserted, "The Society for Cinema Studies believes that the integrity of the discipline is threatened by the increased use of video instead of film in the classroom." Society, "Statement," 3 and 5. For comparisons between celluloid and video transfers, see also Tashiro, "Videophilia," and Prince, *A New Pot of Gold*, 123–32. Important collections of work on video art include Handhardt, ed., *Video Culture*; Hall and Fifer, *Illuminating Video*; and Renov and Suderberg, *Resolutions*. See also more recent monographs, Rush, *Video Art*, and Spielman, *Video*.

7 See Laura U. Marks, *The Skin of the Film* and *Touch*. I admire her work, and it surely informed my early thinking for this project in ways that became so internalized that I thought that some of her ideas were my own. But I researched and wrote this book without relying too closely upon hers in order that I wouldn't reproduce what she had already suggested with such a distinctive perspective.

8 See, for instance, Bolter and Grusin, *Remediation*; Thorburn and Jenkins, eds., *Rethinking Media Change*; Gitelman and Pingree, eds., *New Media: 1740–1915*; Rabinovitz and Geil, eds., *Memory Bytes*; Evens, *Sound Ideas*; Chun and Keenan, eds., *New Media, Old Media*; and Gitelman, *Always Already New*. Although the collection *Technological Visions* also demonstrates some of these tendencies, it offers a more complicated and critical analysis of "the rhetoric of the new." Sturken, Thomas, and Ball-Rokeach, eds., *Technological Visions*. Prior to this wave of work, Carolyn Marvin played upon the concept of new media with her *When Old Technologies Were New*.

9 Numerous magazine and newspaper articles over the years have chronicled popular and cult films that were never (or only subsequently) released on video. Thus writers and audiences seemed to expect total access to cinema's past, whatever a film's marketability or whoever owns its rights. See, for instance, Hajdu, "Why Some of Your Favorite Movies Aren't on Cassette Yet"; Bernard, "Untaped Favorites"; Cerone, "Video Magic Is Rare"; and King, "A Trip Down Celluloid Lane."

10 Charles Acland, channeling Raymond Williams, uses the term "residual." See Acland, ed., *Residual Media*; and Williams, *Marxism and Literature*, 121–27. On storage and disposal of technological waste, see Slade, *Made to Break*; Sterne, "Out with the Trash: On the Future of New Media"; and Parks, "Falling Apart: Electronics Salvaging and the Global Media Economy." On resilient technologies, in the digital age, see Freedman, "Internet Transformations."

11 Kompare, *Rerun Nation*, 206.

12 Thorburn and Jenkins, Introduction, 1–16.

13 See Zielinski's *Deep Time of the Media*.

14 I previously worked through issues of progressive nostalgia and video technology in "Retroactivism." I subsequently discovered Stuart Tannock's article "Nostalgia Critique," which similarly argues for the potential of productive nostalgia.

15 On television and cultural memory, see also Lipsitz, *Time Passages*; Spigel, "From the Dark Ages"; and Spigel and Jenkins, "Same Bat Channel."

16 Sturken, "Politics of Video Memory," 4. See also Sturken, *Tangled Memories*.

Introduction: The Aesthetics of Access

1 Garret, "VHS, 30, Dies of Loneliness."

2 *Time*, December 25, 2006. Among its Person of the Year features, see Cloud, "The YouTube Gurus," 66–74. Also at the end of that year, the American Film Institute concurred with this transition from analog tape to Internet home video by ranking "VHS is dead, long live the digital future" and "YouTube Redefines 'The Tube' " among the year's "Moments of Significance." See McNary, "AFI Announces."

3 Public panic around so-called video nasties, which feature graphic violence and sex, can be seen as another of the early ways in which video technology was defined as degenerate. The UK's Video Recordings Act of 1984 required all releases to be approved and rated by the British Board of Film Classification. On the VRA and related scandal, see Becker, *The Video Nasties.*

4 Adam Smith, "In Loving Memory: R.I.P. VHS," 107–15. In late August 2005, the *Washington Post* likewise mourned VHS's death. Although neither as comprehensive nor as idiosyncratic as the *Empire* dossier, the *Post* tempered snide remarks with a certain cynical sentimentality. "It passed away peacefully after a long illness caused by chronic technological insignificance. . . . Still, even with its perversions, its personality quirks, you have to feel some love for the VHS tape." Chaney, "Parting Words." Some of my examples are also referenced in Lim, "Instant Nostalgia?" Popular press morbidity reports for VHS continued throughout 2008.

5 Lardner, *Fast Forward*, 9.

6 I suggest that access functions as a kind of preservation—circulation of texts enables cultural interactions and (re)produces cultural memories. It also changes the meaning and aesthetics of the texts. My attention to videotape's materiality and to issues of intellectual property was largely formed in relation to issues of archiving and the tensions between preservation and access.

7 I encountered this concept while reading Nicholson Baker's polemic against so-called preservation policies that have sacrificed so many still-functional (though space-hogging) physical newspapers, journals, and books for reproduction and replacement by inferior microfilm copies and digital scans. See Baker, *Double Fold.*

8 After developing this argument through this manuscript, I belatedly discovered a similar argument in Ernst, "Between Real Time."

9 The first videodisc formats, introduced in 1980, were nonrecordable, like subsequent laserdiscs and early DVDs. Wasko, *Hollywood in the Information Age*, 121.

10 For work on this history, see Patricia Mellencamp, "Video and the Counterculture"; William Boddy, "Alternative Television in the United States"; Deirdre Boyle, *Subject to Change*; Kenneth Rogers, "LA Freewaves' *Too Much Freedom?*: Alternative Video and Internet Distribution"; and various essays in Doug Hall and Sally Jo Fifer, eds., *Illuminating Video* and Kate Horsfield and Lucas Hilderbrand, eds., *Feedback*.

11 Tom O'Regan, "From Piracy to Sovereignty."

12 Corrigan, *A Cinema without Walls*, 28–29; Friedberg, "The End of Cinema"; Klinger, *Beyond the Multiplex*, 43, 46, 56.

13 On the issue of control and its relation to policy, see Foner, "Crypto Regs," 14.

14 For overviews of this work, see, for instance, Levy and Windahl, "Audience Activity and Gratifications"; and Morley, "Changing Paradigms." Also arguing against spectatorship theories that have presumed apathetic and receptive television audiences, John Caldwell notes, "The television viewer in practice has never been passive—nor even typically theorized as passive by the industry. Broadcasters from the start did not see the viewer as a couch potato, but as an active buyer and discriminating consumer." Caldwell, *Televisuality*, 250.

15 Information theorists have commented that "documents are not indifferent to the information they carry. They help shape it and, in the process, help shape its readership." J. Brown and Duguid, *Social Life of Information*, 185.

16 The archive has become a popular concept in critical theory and cultural studies, one that reflects a turn toward historical evidence but also increasingly describes the ways that everyday objects embody the past and that even institutional repositories can reveal alternative histories. Although Jacques Derrida may have catalyzed such work, the theoretical move can be traced back to Michel Foucault, who redefined the archive as enunciations. See Foucault, *Archaeology of Knowledge*; Derrida, *Archive Fever*; Steedman, *Dust*; Cvetkovich, *An Archive of Feelings*; D. Taylor, *Archive and the Repertoire*; Arondekar, "Without a Trace"; Burton, *Archive Stories*; Merewether, *The Archive*; and Featherstone, *Archiving Cultures*.

17 B. Mitchell, "The New American Library," n.p.

18 See Benjamin, "The Work of Art in the Age of Mechanical Reproduction," in *Illuminations*, 217–52.

19 Copyright has historically pertained to expressions in a "fixed form"—literally, embodied in a medium. Electronic media, which some scholars have suggested lack "presence" and exist in a virtual realm, complicate this issue. The New York–based U.S. Second Circuit Court of Appeals judge Learned Hand's ruling in *Nichols v. Universal Pictures Corp* (1930) helped to introduce one of the major principles of copyright law (or at least its interpretation), the dichotomy of ideas versus expression, arguing that ideas cannot be

protected but that only expressions can. See Vaidhyanathan, *Copyrights and Copywrongs*, 105–16.

20 Lessig distinguishes scarce and nonscarce types of properties in his discussion of commons in *The Future of Ideas*, 19–23.

21 Gillespie, *Wired Shut*, 15.

22 *Red Lion Broadcasting Co. v. FCC*, 395 U.S. 367, 390 (1969).

23 Liebman, "Brief of Media Studies Professors as Amici Curiae in Support of Respondents," *MGM v. Grokster*, filed before the Supreme Court, March 2005, 5.

24 Howard Besser made this observation. See U.S. Copyright Office, "Section 108 Study Group, Public Roundtable Transcripts, No. 3, Topic 3: New Preservation-Only Exception," Washington, March 16, 2006, http://www.loc.gov/section108 (accessed April 29, 2006), 23. This is not only a problem of preservation; as Lenny Foner has suggested, encrypted devices are technologically designed without any recognition of the possibility of public domain uses. Foner, "Crypto Regs," 27.

25 *Klute* (Alan J. Pakula, 1971), *The Conversation* (Francis Ford Coppola, 1974), and the later *Blow Out* (Brian De Palma, 1981) dramatized uses of tape recording to secretly bug and uncover murderous plots.

26 See Lessig, *Code and Other Laws*, *The Future of Ideas*, and *Code: Version 2.0*.

27 Gillespie, *Wired Shut*, 61.

28 I make this argument not as a neo-Luddite but out of recognition that both adapting and resisting new technologies are compromised positions. For more discussion of this, see the introduction to Jones, *Against Technology*.

29 On digital aesthetics of failure, see Sobchack, "Nostalgia for a Digital Object"; and White, *Body and the Screen*, 85–114.

30 Lisa Gitelman and Geoffrey Pingree pose transparency and immediacy as one of the myths of new media in "What's New about New Media?" their introduction to *New Media: 1740–1915*, xiii–xiv.

31 Section 108 Study Group, "Information for the March 2006 Public Roundtables and Request for Written Comments," February 10, 2006, 11, http://www.loc.gov/section108 (accessed April 27, 2006). In testimonies at the March roundtables, multiple participants used the phrase "inherently unstable" or comparable terms to describe digital formats. Transcripts are available at the same web address.

32 Benkler, *The Wealth of Networks*, 410.

33 Although videotape allows the potential for activist recording, I am not claiming that all bootlegging is progressive or radical. For the creativity argument, see Vaidhyanathan, *Copyrights and Copywrongs*; Lessig, *Free Culture*; and McLeod, *Freedom of Expression®*. This argument and these books have been enormously effective in mobilizing interest in the stakes of digital copyright codes. See also Zimmermann, "Pirates of the New World Image

Orders," in *States of Emergency*; and Rappaport, "Notes on *Rock Hudson's Home Movies*."

34 Scarry, *On Beauty and Being Just*, 93.

35 The term "bootleg" derives from the literal place of contraband circulation: alcohol and, later, audio recording devices were purportedly smuggled inside the legs of boots. The term is an Americanism for illicit liquor possession that, according to the *Oxford English Dictionary*, dates back to 1889, though the term is more popularly associated with Prohibition-era practices. As described by B. W. Starbuck, by 1930 the term's meaning had expanded to include "anything of an inferior quality smuggled into use. . . . The use of 'bootleg' as a verb for occupations of questionable character also appears." B. W. Starbuck, "Bootleg," 156.

36 Lee Marshall offers a more specific taxonomy of terms for music duplication, including counterfeiting, pirating, bootlegging, tape trading, home taping, and file sharing. Marshall, *Bootlegging*, 110–11. Majid Yar calls "piracy" a "social construction" in "The Global 'Epidemic.'"

37 Tarleton Gillespie, "Industry-Sponsored Anti-Piracy Campaigns," conference presentation, Problematizing Piracy panel, "Media in Transition 5," Massachusetts Institute of Technology, April 28, 2007. See also his chapter about Jack Valenti and his rhetoric in *Wired Shut*, 105–35.

38 Jessica Litman, "Sharing and Stealing," 18–20, quoted in Gillespie, *Wired Shut*, 114.

39 This is not to belittle the importance of these studies; it is merely to recognize the potential risks of Orientalism in this field if similar studies are not undertaken of U.S.-specific contexts. Useful studies of transnational video piracy include Boyd et al., *Videocassette Recorders*; O'Regan, "From Piracy to Sovereignty"; Wang, "Recontextualizing Copyright" and *Framing Piracy*; Larkin, "Degraded Images, Distorted Sounds" and "Piracy"; Pang, "Piracy/Privacy"; Yar, "The Global 'Epidemic'"; and Mertha, *The Politics of Piracy*. On international copyright issues related to media, see the chapter "Hollywood's Global Rights" in Miller et al., *Global Hollywood*.

40 See Ganley and Ganley, *Global Political Fallout*.

41 Significantly, work on "developing nation" and diasporic videos has emphasized the relatively outdated video technologies at use. "Low-rent globalization," as Sirida Srisombati calls it, has introduced media circulation practices ranging from personal interventions to increasingly systematized "transnational mobility created through a network of relatively inexpensive technologies not considered 'new.'" Srisombati, "Always Almost."

42 Marks, *Skin of the Film*, 172.

43 Neumann and Simpson, "Smuggled Sound," 321–22, 336.

44 Marshall, *Bootlegging*, 148.

45 Heylin, *Bootleg*, 6.
46 Lessig, Foreword, ix–x.

Video Clip 1: Diasporic Asian Video Markets

1 When I visited a similar video store in the basement of a Koreatown grocery in New York City, such in-house reproduction was more visible: there were fifty-four patched VCRs in a hallway between the stairs and the video shelves.
2 For an excellent study of Thai imports and bootlegs in Los Angeles, see Sirida Srisombati, "Always Almost."

Chapter 1: Be Kind, Rewind

1 Bensinger, *The Home Video Handbook*, 178.
2 Geist, "About New York," B3.
3 A few additional examples: another early sourcebook for home video users played up the reproductive connotations of the technology by describing videotape as "*impregnated* with a substance on which you can record video signals." In 1984 *Newsweek* quoted a nine-month-pregnant video store customer: " 'I can't say the VCR has changed my life, unless you count the night we rented *An Officer and a Gentleman*,' she says, patting her swollen stomach. 'If we hadn't stayed up late to watch Richard Gere, I might not be in this condition.' " (The reporter doesn't reveal if it was Gere who also got the baby's father in the mood.) An academic history of home video asserted that "many early adopters found themselves *infatuated* with the machine and what it could do." See Utz, *Complete Home Video Book*, 70; Gelman et al., "The Video Revolution," 50; and Greenberg, *From Betamax to Blockbuster*, 18 (italics mine). In film and television representations, videotapes have likewise served as storage devices for perverse fantasies (in David Cronenberg's *Videodrome*, 1983) and, inexplicably, a teenage girl's hidden birth control pills (in a season three episode of *Desperate Housewives*, "Not While I'm Around," 2007).
4 Benson-Allott, "VCR Autopsy," 180. The author also makes a striking (if a bit far-fetched) comparison between a VCR's face and Gustave Courbet's famous painting of a woman's genitals, *The Origin of the World* (1866).
5 Quoted in Davis, "X-Rated Video," 33.
6 Michael Chanan refers to this concept as "technical linkage" in *Repeated Takes*, 32–33.
7 The year 1975 is referenced in Zielinski, *Audiovisions*, 184. "The Wonderful World of Home Video" special advertising section in the October 30, 1978,

issue of *Time* features advertisements and text about tie-in devices and services such as video cameras, video games, Fotomat home movie-to-video transfers, the Video Club of America mail-order rental service, Time-Life prerecorded videos, blank tapes, and HBO subscription cable service.

8 These statistics appear in Wasser, *Veni, Vidi, Video*, 68, table 2.1.

9 See Alvarado, *Video World-Wide*, the UNESCO report on international video adoption. The Kuwait statistic is so high in part because there were already numerous multiple-VCR households.

10 The primary formats are NTSC (National Television Standards Committee), with 525 horizontal lines of resolution that flash 30 times per second, in the Americas and East Asia; PAL (Phase Alternation Line), with 625-line resolution at 25 flashes per second in most of Europe, central and southern Asia, the Middle East, and parts of Africa; and SECAM (Sequential Couleur avec Memoire), also with 625/25 resolution, in France, Russia, Greece, and parts of Africa. DVDs are similarly encoded according to six regions: Region 1 (North America), Region 2 (Japan, Europe, South Africa, Middle East), Region 3 (South Korea, Taiwan, Hong Kong, and parts of Southeast Asia), Region 4 (Latin America, Australia, and New Zealand), Region 5 (Eastern Europe, Russia, India, and Africa), and Region 6 (Mainland China). Videotapes and DVDs can be played only in decks programmed according to the corresponding regions, though some multiregion decks are manufactured for professional and educational uses, and some home users have figured out how to hack their systems to play all regions (which is a violation of copyright law).

11 One can clearly retrace similar dynamics between other audio and audiovisual technologies as well: in analog media, television developed out of radio, and this pattern was reiterated as DVDs mimicked CDs, and cell phones and iPods have added image and video options onto what were primarily audio devices. The major exception to this pattern of audio before video, of course, is film, where silent projected images (typically with live accompaniment) preceded movies with synchronous soundtracks.

12 Belton, "Looking through Video," 62, 63.

13 See Armes, *On Video*, chapters 7 and 8.

14 See, for example, Sterne, *The Audible Past*, 25.

15 Ibid.

16 In the United States, 3M (Minnesota Mining and Manufacturing) began experimenting with the magnetic recording technology on its own in 1944 but had not matched the German engineering.

17 Transcription discs preceded magnetic tape as a format for prerecording and syndicating radio programming. William Lafferty notes, "The 'ideology of live' had been promulgated by the radio networks as the essence of broadcasting, but in essence which served to maintain the network as the primary

distributors of programming and monopolizers of prime-time." Lafferty, "New Era in TV Programming," 408. On liveness, see Feuer, "Concept of Live Television"; and Boddy, *Fifties Television*. For a prior argument against "the ideology of liveness myth," see Caldwell, *Televisuality*, 27–31.

18 Karin Bijsterveld has written of a small international (though, it seems, predominantly European) hobbyist movement of "sound hunters" who used tape recorders to document everyday noises and to create sound effects during the 1950s and early 1960s; in Bijsterveld's history, such uses gave way to artists' uses of editable reel-to-reel tape and to consumers' uses of portable music recording on cassette tapes. See Bijsterveld, "What Do I Do."

19 Morton, *Off the Record*, 141.

20 Ibid., 155.

21 Zak, *The Poetics of Rock*, 13.

22 According to Zak, the popular precedent was set with the Beatles' "Strawberry Fields Forever" in 1967. As early as World War II, the Parisian radio engineer Pierre Schaeffer began scratching records to make *musique concrète* (found sound art) derived from the audio technology rather than recorded from an exterior source.

23 See Meikle, *American Plastic*.

24 This audiocassette history is summarized from Millard, *America on Record*, 315–19; Coleman, *Playback*; Produce, "Short History of the Cassette"; and Jones, "The Cassette Underground." Microcassettes (1969) were also marketed and widely used for dictation and interviews.

25 Russ Forster documented the 8-track collector community of the early 1990s in the film *So Wrong They're Right* (1995).

26 M. Fishbein, S. Middlestadt, and M. Kapp, *A Consumer Survey: Home Taping* (Warner Communications, 1980), quoted in McCleod, *Freedom of Expression®*, 279.

27 See Moore, *Mix Tape*.

28 See Stille, "War of Words: Oral Poetry, Writing, and Tape Cassettes in Somalia," in *Future of the Past*, 182–206; Hirschkind, "The Ethics of Listening"; and Manuel, *Cassette Culture*.

29 Chanan, *Repeated Takes*, 173.

30 Utz, *Complete Home Video Book*, 116.

31 Sugaya, "Consumer Video Recorders," 182.

32 *Variety* published "Glossary of Homevideo Terms" in 1983, 1984, and 1985, and Morton D. Dubin's "Videotape Glossary" was a recurring feature in *Backstage* during the early-to-mid-1980s. See Tony Seidman, "Glossary of Homevideo Terms," *Variety*, September 28, 1983, 42; May 4, 1984, 476; May 1, 1985, 440.

33 As William Lafferty observes, local stations provided a sizable market as well. See "New Era in TV Programming."

34 Zielinski, *Audiovisions*, 238.

35 Reels of two-inch Quadruplex videotape were erased and reused up to one hundred times. Martin, "The Dawn of Tape," 57.

36 Alvarado, *Video World-Wide*, 1.

37 Lachenbruch, "Sorry, We Missed It," 12–14.

38 *Life*, October 15, 1965, 120–21. The fine print in the ad's upper-left corner notes that the term "videorecorder" is a registered trademark of the Sony Corporation.

39 See, for instance, Edson, "Lone Inventor," 29, 80–87; and Kern, "Good Revolution," 47–52.

40 Doan, "Revolution Has Been Postponed," 6. See also Lachenbruch, "Videotape Era," 6–10; Lachenbruch, "The Big 'But,' " 23–29; and Jeffreys and Jeffreys, "Saturday Night," 12–13.

41 Library of Congress, *Report of the Librarian of Congress*, vol. 1, 32.

42 "The Video Revolution: How the VCR Is Changing What You Watch," *Newsweek*, August 6, 1984; and "VCRS: Santa's Hottest Gift; The Magic Box That Is Creating a Video Revolution," *Time*, December 24, 1984.

43 This is confirmed by early publicity for VCRS. An article in *TV Guide* from 1977 makes repeated comparisons to audiotape, and a 1978 advertising supplement to *Time* magazine promises, "If you're among the millions who already own an audio cassette recorder, you already know how to operate a VCR." See Lachenbruch, "Great Time-Shift Machine Experiment," 5; and Gerson, "Wonderful World of Home Video," n.p.

44 Viewed through YouTube but now offline.

45 See, for example, Utz, *Complete Home Video Book*, 72.

46 Some audiotape recorders had this feature as well, though it was not standard.

47 For more on Sony's specific corporate research, development, and intentions, see Lardner, *Fast Forward.*

48 I do not focus on the engineering or technical specifications of video. For detailed explanations and graphs on how the technology functions, see Inglis, *Video Engineering*; and Robinson, *The Video Primer*.

49 On bootleg and pirate tape covers, see Stine and Sacher-Masoch, *Trashfiend's Guide*, 6. Examining a very different context, Brian Larkin's study of Nigerian pirate tapes suggests that printed packaging sleeves have become the markers of authenticity rather than the image or sound quality of the videos' content. Larkin, "Degraded Images."

50 In *The Trashfiend's Guide to Collecting Videotapes*, the authors identify and illustrate multiple packaging formats, including studio sleeve, studio sleeve with gatefold cover, display box, display box with gatefold cover, display box with sliding tray, studio clamshell, display clamshell, display clamshell with

sealed inserts, and printed display clamshell. Stine and Sacher-Masoch, *Trashfiend's Guide*, 10–11.

51 See Spigel, *Make Room for TV*, 24, 29.

52 Roberts, *Video Cassettes*, 21.

53 Cusamano et al., "Strategic Maneuvering," 59–60.

54 One of Sony's objections to VHS was its size, which Sony developers felt was too bulky. VHS cassettes measure seven and one-half inches by four inches by one inch in dimension and weigh about eight ounces. For this history, see Lardner, *Fast Forward*, 91. Sony later introduced Hi8, an 8 mm video format approximately the size of audiocassettes, and MINI-DV (digital video), approximately the size of micro-audiocassettes; both maintained video's black casing. These two later formats' diminutive sizes have made for more comfortable portability in camcorder productions, though neither has become a major playback format.

55 A useful chart compares Betamax and VHS production between 1975 and 1988 in Cusamano et al., "Strategic Maneuvering," 54.

56 Greenberg, *From Betamax to Blockbuster*, 44.

57 Ibid., 77.

58 See the International Video Club advertisement reproduced in Heimann, *All-American Ads: 70s*, 209.

59 Enticknap, *Moving Image Technology*, 179–81, 185.

60 History condensed from Marlow and Secunda, *Shifting Time and Space*; Lardner, *Fast Forward*; and Cusamano et al., "Strategic Maneuvering." Whereas many sources tend to portray this history as a battle between U.S. and Japanese industries, Cusamano et al. recognize the importance of the European market in standardizing home video formats. It remains unclear what impact an American Supreme Court ruling against the Sony Betamax, which would have been a major setback for home video exploitation in the United States, would have had for home video manufacturing and policy in Europe or other continents.

61 DivX was a short-lived, low-price DVD format that operated on a licensing basis. Consumers had forty-eight hours to view the disc, which could be played only once. After viewing, users could either dispose of the disc or license it for further plays. See Gross, "Betamax Wars," 35.

62 See, for instance, Casey, "Apple and the Betamax Complex," F19; and T. Gray, "V-Chip," 30.

63 See, for instance, Mayes, "Technostalgia: Betamax," n.p.; and Taninecz, "Famous Flops," 46.

64 Bloom, "Bye-Bye, Beta," 7. An earlier profile suggested amazement that the format was still being manufactured. Crowe, "Despite All Odds," F1. Beta SP and Digital Betacam, high-fidelity derivatives of Betamax, remain popular

professional formats for broadcasting, replacing 3/4-inch U-matic as the standard archival formats.

65 See Richtel and Taub, "Taps for HD DVD," and Fackler, "Toshiba Concedes Defeat."

66 Zacks, "Are You Renting?" 28.

67 Greenberg, *From Betamax to Blockbuster*, 86–87.

68 Ibid., 77.

69 Arnie Saltzman, quoted in Robert Lindsey, "Sex Films," B15. See also "Vidtape Machines Boom," 2, 122; and Warner, "Top Vid-Cassettes."

70 Figures appear in Davis, "X-Rated Video," 33.

71 Cieply, "Risque Business," 80.

72 Seideman, "Explosion," 40A–41.

73 See the Fotomat two-page spread in *Hollywood Reporter*, August 3, 1979, n.p.; Linck, "Theatres Get a Crack," 16–17; "Video Rental Rooms Fought"; Schrage, "Popcorn and Movies," E1; Dobuler, "Time-Life Sets New Video Club," 1, 17; "CBS to Inaugurate Videocassette Club"; "Phoenix Company," 14; John Sippel, "Cassette Vending Machines Tested"; Young, "Get Your Red-Hot Cassettes-to-Go," B1; Ross, "Group 1, Diebold Debut," 67; Matthews, "Automated Video Tellers."

74 Greenberg, *From Betamax to Blockbuster*, 66–72.

75 "Videotapes: A Crowded Field," 31.

76 "Majors Plan to Enter Video Rental Biz," 55. See also "Film Biz Wary," 1, 44.

77 Pollack, "Battle over Video Cassettes," D1; Harris, "Hollywood Battle," F1; Landro, "Movie Studios' Cut," 33.

78 Quoted phrase from comment by Columbia Pictures senior vice president Lawrence Hilford in Warner, "Home Videocassette Distrib'n Business," n.p.

79 Knoll, "Majors Mulling," 1, 15. On the further development of this pricing system, see Wasser, *Veni, Vidi, Video*.

80 For a more comprehensive industrial history of video stores, see Greenberg, *From Betamax to Blockbuster*; and Wasser, *Veni, Vidi, Video*.

81 Bierbaum, "Off-Air Recording," 1, 10.

82 "The Video Revolution," *Newsweek*, August 6, 1984. The top ten, in descending order, were *All My Children*, *General Hospital*, *Days of Our Lives*, *As the World Turns*, *Guiding Light*, *One Life to Live*, *Hill Street Blues*, *Dallas*, *The Young and the Restless*, and (tied for tenth place) *Dynasty* and *Cheers*.

83 Bierbaum, "Macrovision Says."

84 See "Valenti Pledges," 1, 19; Melanson, "Go-Video Says," 1, 41; "Dual-Deck VCR Hits Fast Forward," 1, 29.

85 Vanessa Russell suggests that the potential to avert such body shame by working out at home was undone by intimidatingly perfect-looking instructors and overly difficult routines for beginners. V. Russell, "Make Me a Celebrity," 67–68.

86 Figure stated in Kleinhans, "Change from Film," 157.

87 See Canby, "A Revolution Reshapes Movies," H1; Nichols, "Movie Rentals Fade," 1; King, "Movies You Can't Just Rent"; Kronke, "Filmland's New Ploy"; Brass, "Playing a Title Role"; Sweeting, "Sell-Through or Rental?"

88 The original French meaning of "amateur" is referenced in Eisenberg, *The Recording Angel*, 177. Stephen Duncombe also traces the etymology of "amateur"—to the Latin *amator*—in his study of fanzines, using this meaning as defining that form of underground cultural production. *Notes from Underground*, 14. Patricia Zimmermann cites the Latin *amare* as the root word in *Reel Families*, 1.

89 Cowan, *Social History*, 208.

90 Zak, *The Poetics of Rock*, 115, previously cited in Oliver Read and Walter L. Welch, *From Tin Foil to Stereo: The Evolution of the Phonograph* (Indianapolis: Howard W. Sams, 1959), 385–86.

91 Greenberg, *From Betamax to Blockbuster*, 23–26.

92 For instance, the first FAQ entry at the Super Happy Fun website offers a standard indemnity response and then lampoons it: "Q: Is SuperHappyFun an illegal pirate operation? A: The section of American copyright law known as 'The Berne Act' clearly states: films unreleased in the United States, including original version of films altered and/or edited for release in the United States, are not protected by American copyright; thus, they are considered public domain. The entire purpose of our company is to provide (otherwise unavailable) films to the serious video collector. We do not offer videos owned by American releasing companies. If a film should become available domestically, or if another seller should offer a better copy, we immediately stop offering it to our clients. As the old saying goes: All titles on superhappyfun.com are believed to be in the public domain. No rights are given or implied. All titles are sold purely for research purposes. No entertainment should be gained from any title on this site. If you enjoy anything purchased at SuperHappyFun.com, destroy it immediately." FAQS, http://www.superhappyfun.com/content.htm (accessed April 15, 2006). For guides to bootleg dealers, see Atkinson, "Obscure Objects," 86; Atkinson, "Das Bootlegs," 61; and Hawkins, *Cutting Edge*, 33–49. For how-to and ratings guides, see "Dark Waters Tape Trading FAQ"; www.innermind.com/myguides/misc/faqtrade.htm (accessed January 10, 2006); and Stine and Sacher-Masoch, *Trashfiend's Guide*.

93 Tashiro, "Contradictions of Video Collecting," 11–18. See also Uma Dinsmore, "Chaos, Order," 315–26.

94 Bjarkman, "To Have and to Hold," 217–46.

95 P. Hall, "The Bootleg Files," http://www.filmthreat.com.

96 Hawkins, *Cutting Edge*, 45, 47.

97 Ganley and Ganley, *Global Political Fallout*, 54. On the aesthetics of global piracy, see also Brian Larkin's previously cited essays.

98 Kadrey, "Director's Cuts," 64–65.

99 Marks, *Touch*, 11, 13.

100 Price, *Video-Visions*, 216.

101 Since the mid-1990s, both professional and amateur pornography has also proliferated as pervasive and profitable content for the Internet, and pornography has been prominent amid the rise of shared streaming video in the middle of the present decade—as well as smut-oriented and celebrity gossip blogs. Whereas YouTube (discussed in more depth in the epilogue) deactivates any content deemed obscene by users, knockoff sites such as PornoTube and XTube feature an array of content, professional and personal, commercial and shared.

102 See Z. Patterson, "Going On-Line," 110–11.

103 In *There's No Place Like Home Video*, James Moran offers the most comprehensive academic study of camcorders, yet he ignores amateur pornography.

104 Hillyer, "Sex in the Suburban," 53, 66.

105 Kleinhans, "Pamela Anderson," 297–98.

106 Waugh, *Out/Lines*, 40.

Video Clip 2: Chiller Theatre Expo

1 The event has been held at various hotels in East Rutherford and Secaucus, New Jersey. For a study of the 1979 Video Collectors of Ohio Convention and early videophile culture, see Joshua Greenberg, *From Betamax to Blockbuster*, 17–19.

Chapter 2: The Fairest of Them All?

1 Lessig, *The Future of Ideas*, 23–25. See also Lessig, *Code: Version 2.0*.

2 My thinking here is informed by Lessig's refutation of "activist" Supreme Courts. See Lessig, *Code: Version 2.0*, 315.

3 U.S. Constitution, Article I, Section 8.

4 L. Patterson and Lindberg, *The Nature of Copyright*.

5 Litman, "Lawful Personal Use," 1879. She continues: "Some subset of personal use will be lawful, some subset will be infringing, and . . . the legality of some personal uses will be controversial" (1894).

6 Deborah Tussey, "From Fan Sites to Filesharing: Personal Use in Cyberspace," *Georgia Law Review* 35 (2001): 1129, 1134, quoted in Litman, "Lawful Personal Use," 1894n134.

7 As almost all the critical studies on copyright reiterate, the U.S.'s copyright code was modeled on the British system and legislated from the beginning of American law. For the standard history of U.S. copyright law before 1976, see L. Patterson, *Copyright in Historical Perspective.*

8 The 1976 revision introduced belated participation in the rules of the Berne Convention for the Protection of Literary and Artistic Works, an international agreement (largely adhering to the European copyright paradigm) dating back to 1890. As part of the Berne Convention, countries offer international copyright reciprocity; if a work is protected in one of the member countries, it receives copyright protections in all the other countries and according to the other countries' copyright codes. More recent U.S. copyright legislations have conformed to policies advocated by the World Intellectual Property Organization and the World Trade Organization; although both agencies are part of the United Nations, they initiate different and often overlapping international agreements.

9 Creative Commons was established by Lawrence Lessig and James Boyle. For more information, see www.creativecommons.org.

10 The closest equivalent to fair use in another country is Canada's "fair dealing," which provides for reasonable licensing.

11 Justice Harry Blackmun, Dissenting Opinion, *Sony Corporation of America, Inc., v. Universal City Studios, Inc.*, 464 U.S. 417 (1984), 475. (Hereafter abbreviated as *Sony v. Universal.*)

12 Ibid., 466–67.

13 Oler, "Copyright Law," 269, 270.

14 Copyright Law of the United States, Section 107.

15 Patry and Posner, "Fair Use," 1644. Subsequent attempts to clarify fair use have led to drawn-out debates that imploded, such as the infamous mid-1990s Conference on Fair Use (CONFU) that failed to achieve policy consensus, or the Technology, Education, and Copyright Harmonization (TEACH) Act, which established conservative minimum "safe" uses rather than progressive "best practices" guidelines. See Heins and Beckles, *Will Fair Use Survive*, 6.

16 However, this position could interfere with instances of critical repurposing; rights owners may not be willing to license works to be ridiculed.

17 Taking a different position, Register of Copyrights Marybeth Peters commented in 2004 that with its fair-use defense, "the *Sony* [*v. Universal*] precedent continues to be an impediment to obtaining effective relief" against infringement. The Intentional Inducement of Copyright Infringements Act of 2004: Hearing on S. 2560 before the U.S. Senate Committee on the Judiciary, 108th Cong. (2004), quoted in Trope and Upchurch, "Staple Article," 436.

18 Oler, "Copyright Law," 271.

19 H.R. *Report* no. 1476, n. 15, p. 66, quoted in Oler, "Copyright Law," 272.

20 Lessig, *Free Culture*, 187.

21 Lawrence Lessig, "The Current State of Fair Use," keynote address at the Comedies of Fair Use conference, New York University, April 28, 2006.

22 Litman, "Lawful Personal Use," 1902–3.

23 Liebman, "Brief of Media Studies Professors," 4.

24 There had long been an exception to the deposit requirements for audiovisual works, especially for limited-run publications, obscure films, or ephemeral broadcasts. This poses a major problem for researchers and historians, since such works may not be collected or preserved anywhere else and may disappear from the public record.

25 There has been a movement to liberate orphan films from the clutches of unknown copyright owners and to limit terms for commercially neglected content; these activists (including many librarians and scholars) argue that the Sonny Bono Copyright Term Extension Act (1998) eroded the growth of the public domain by prolonging copyright protections by twenty years as well as unconstitutionally violating the concept of "limited" copyright terms. The movement faced a major defeat when the Supreme Court ruled against this argument in *Eldred v. Ashcroft* (2003). Lessig argued this case before the Court and recounts his experience and the shortcomings of his argumentation in *Free Culture*, 213–56. The U.S. Copyright Office subsequently issued a *Report on Orphan Works*.

26 *Universal City Studios, Inc., v. Sony Corporation of America, Inc.*, 480 F. Supp. 429 (C.D. Cal. 1979); and *Sony Corporation of America, Inc., v. Universal City Studios, Inc.*, 659 F.2d 962 (9th Cir. 1981).

27 *CBS Evening News*, May 18, 1977.

28 Lardner, *Fast Forward*, 21.

29 Quoted in Roberts, *Video Cassettes*, 2.

30 Gelman et al., "The Video Revolution," 50.

31 "The Wonderful World of Home Video" (special advertising section), *Time*, October 30, 1978, n.p.

32 Lachenbruch, "Great Time-Shift Machine Experiment," 5, 6.

33 Justice Blackmun, Dissenting Opinion, *Sony v. Universal*, 458n1 and 492n42. Justice Blackmun's lengthy dissent, cosigned by Justices Thurgood Marshall, Lewis Powell, and William Rehnquist, was originally drafted in the anticipation of being the majority opinion, and it was through a series of memorandums, discussions, and a rehearing that Blackmun's opinion was modified and became the minority interpretation of the case.

34 *CBS Evening News*, January 17, 1984.

35 Bettig, *Copyrighting Culture*, 160.

36 Ibid.

37 Justice Stevens, Opinion of the Court, *Sony v. Universal*, 425; Bettig, *Copyrighting Culture*, 164–65.

38 Quoted in Lardner, *Fast Forward*, 134.

39 Band and McLaughlin, "The Marshall Papers," 436.

40 Opinion of the Court, *Sony v. Universal*, 417.

41 Ibid., 455–56n40.

42 Through a series of memos, negotiations, and reversals of individual justices' positions, Stevens's opinion incorporated the concept of contributory infringement from patent law and fair use from the 1976 copyright code (with significant input from Justices William Brennan, Byron White, and Sandra Day O'Connor). Band and McLaughlin, "The Marshall Papers," 427, 450. In her study of the case's history and subsequent influence, Litman observes that the justices initially had varied positions on if and how fair use might apply in this case and ultimately compromised for the two opinions. Litman also suggests that copyright lawyers and scholars thought that the ultimate decision "had no real historical foundation." See Litman, "Story of *Sony v. Universal Studios*," 8, 31, 21.

43 This, of course, raises the question whether television broadcasts are "sold" to audiences. Recordings from subscription television, such as cable and satellite services, potentially undermine or contradict this principle. The Court did not rule on the distinctions between recordings from broadcast and pay television.

44 Litman, "Story of *Sony v. Universal Studios*."

45 Justice Blackmun, Dissenting Opinion, *Sony v. Universal*, 480–81.

46 Ibid., 465.

47 Patterson and Lindberg, *The Nature of Copyright*, 194 (italics in original).

48 Ibid., 103.

49 Band and McLaughlin, "The Marshall Papers," 432.

50 For analysis of the case, see Bettig's chapter "The Law of Intellectual Property: The Videocassette Recorder and the Control of Copyrights," in *Copyrighting Culture*; Band and McLaughlin, "The Marshall Papers"; and, perhaps most obviously and insightfully, the Supreme Court's published opinion and dissent.

51 *Husbands and Wives* (Woody Allen, 1992).

52 That has yet to happen, though different bills have attempted to do this. In 2004 Senator Orin Hatch proposed the Intentional Inducement of Copyright Infringement Act, colloquially known as the "Induce Act," which would have effectively nullified the Supreme Court's Betamax decision and threatened to make now-common and taken-for-granted devices such as photocopiers, VCRs, and iPods illegal.

53 Opinion of the Court, *Sony v. Universal*, 430–31.

54 Blackmun, Dissenting Opinion, *Sony v. Universal*, 457–58.

55 This analysis was suggested in *CBS Evening News*, January 17, 1984.

56 See Febrikant, "Curtain Drops," D1; and Griffin and Masters, *Hit and Run*, 70, 184.

57 Benkler, *The Wealth of Networks*, 278.

58 Litman, *Digital Copyright*, 59–60.

59 Benkler, *The Wealth of Networks*, 383.

60 Ibid., 441–42.

61 Committee on Intellectual Property Rights and the Emerging Information Infrastructure/National Research Council, *The Digital Dilemma*, 200. (Hereafter cited as CIPREII/NRC.)

62 Gillespie, *Wired Shut*, 36–38.

63 CIPREII/NRC, *The Digital Dilemma*, 201–2.

64 Vaidhyanathan, *Copyrights and Copywrongs*, 152.

65 CIPREII/NRC, *The Digital Dilemma*, 141.

66 Ibid., 143. The report also points out that analog reproduction is a willful act: photocopying a book is done with full self-awareness of the process (whether or not the user understands copyright law), whereas many computer users may not realize they are making a copy with each mouse click (141–42).

67 Recent scholarship on copyright reflects another decisive shift—from cultural analysis to policy advocacy—that responds to the introduction of the DMCA and the CTEA in 1998. When James Boyle argued for the importance of intellectual property in the information age in *Software, Shamans, and Spleens* (1996), he was conceptually and politically avant-garde. Ronald Bettig's *Copyrighting Culture* (1996) and Rosemary Coombe's *The Cultural Life of Intellectual Property* (1998) likewise offered rigorous, even leftist, analyses of the structures and ideologies behind copyright codes, yet they were clearly written before these major policies of the late 1990s. In the wake of restrictive laws that favor rights holders and content owners, more polemical publications on copyright by Lessig, Litman, Vaidhyanathan, Pamela Samuelson, Kembrew McLeod, and the Electronic Frontier Foundation, among others, have flourished and focused on revising new policies as well as paradigms. These scholars are enthusiastic about the potential of digital media for information sharing and creative production, but they see the DMCA as a policy that counteracts much of what digital technologies and networking make possible. One common rhetorical strategy that emerges in these works is to stress that copyright was originally intended to benefit the public good by fostering creative production; this goal has been whittled away to the point where corporate distributors, rather than artists, are the primary beneficiaries. Additionally, old works are protected at the expense of new, derivative works, and the foundational concept of "limited-term" copyrights has been extended to the point that copyright monopolies are nearly perpetual.

68 1201 (a)(1)(A), 210. This section does, however, reference exceptions for noncommercial public use in libraries.

69 Vaidhyanathan, *Copyrights and Copywrongs*, 175.

70 Ibid., 177.

71 A narrow exemption under Section 1201 was renewed in 2006, pertaining to "computer programs and video games distributed in formats that have become obsolete and that require the original media or hardware as a condition of access, when circumvention is accomplished for the purpose of preservation or archival reproduction of published digital works by a library or archive. A format shall be considered obsolete if the machine or system necessary to render perceptible a work stored in that format is no longer manufactured or is no longer reasonably available in the commercial marketplace." http://www.copyright.gov/1201.

72 See Decherney, "From Fair Use to Exemption," 122–23.

73 Lessig, *Free Culture*, 180.

74 In a study of Section 1201 written just before the 2006 rules were made public, Bill D. Herman and Oscar H. Gandy Jr. argue: "We conclude that the rulemaking is best conceptualized as a vehicle for reducing the role of the courts—and of fair use—in the digital millennium. . . . The rulemaking procedure does not appear to be an earnest attempt to provide meaningful relief to adversely affected noninfringing users." Herman and Gandy, "Catch 1201," 124.

75 The exact exemption pertains to "audiovisual works included in the educational library of a college or university's film or media studies department, when circumvention is accomplished for the purpose of making compilations of portions of those works for educational use in the classroom by media studies or film professors." Section 1201(a)(1) title 17, United States Code.

76 A report with recommendations from the Copyright Office's Section 108 Study Group for legislative revision was released in March 2008. For more information, see http://www.section108.gov.

77 See Vaidhyanathan, *Anarchist in the Library*, 43–50.

78 *A & M Records, Inc., v. Napster, Inc.*, 114 F. Supp. 2d 896 (N.D. Cal. 2000); 239 F.3d 1004 (9th Cir. 2001).

79 Ginsburg, "Copyright and Control over New Technologies of Dissemination," 1640.

80 Opinion, *Metro-Goldwyn-Mayer Studios, Inc., et al., v. Grokster, Ltd., et al.* (04–0480), 545 U.S. 125 S. Ct. 2764 (2005) (referred to hereafter as *MGM v. Grokster*), 5.

81 The justices who remained on the Supreme Court from the 1984 decision retained their prior positions: dissenter Rehnquist signed Ruth Bader Ginsburg's concurring opinion that argued against *Betamax*, while Stevens and O'Connor maintained their support for the precedent in a concurring opinion written by Stephen Breyer. (Justice Anthony Kennedy was the third cosigner of the Ginsburg opinion.)

82 Justice Ruth Bader Ginsburg, Concurring Opinion, *MGM v. Grokster*, 5.

83 Justice Breyer, Concurring Opinion, *MGM v. Grokster*, 7, 4.

84 Despite his concurring opinion, Justice Breyer seems not so much to rule against Grokster as to suggest that the lower court should give more careful and thorough consideration to the Betamax precedent.

85 Justice Breyer, Concurring Opinion, *MGM v. Grokster*, 10.

86 Lessig, *Code: Version 2.0*, 147.

87 Benkler, *The Wealth of Networks*, 469–70.

88 Litman, *Digital Copyright*, 112.

89 See, for example, Lunney, "The Death of Copyright," 907.

Chapter 3: The Revolution Was Recorded

1 This chapter condenses two chapters of my dissertation; for more detailed accounts of the VTNA's history, workflow, and legal history, see dissertation chapters 3 and 4.

2 For overviews of opinion poll results, see Hallin, *The "Uncensored War,"* and Huntington, "The United States."

3 Simpson, *Network Television News*, 16–17.

4 Ibid., 8. Kinescopes, films shot off of television monitors, were introduced in 1948 as the first method of recording television broadcasts off-air, and the practice continued into the 1970s.

5 As persuasive as this argument may seem, the analogy that the VTNA is to CBS News as microfilm is to the *New York Times* presents a false correlation. The source for the *New York Times* on microfilm, Microfilming Corporation of America (MCA), is a subsidiary of the New York Times Company that capitalizes on a major ancillary library market for its print publications. MCA also later published CBS's microfilm transcripts. On the aesthetics of microfilm, see Baker, *Double Fold*.

6 Norman T. Hatch, Audiovisual Division chief, Directorate for Defense Information, unpublished correspondence to Fanette Singer, July 11, 1977; and William T. Murphy, chief of Motion Picture and Sound Recording Branch, National Archives and Records Service, unpublished correspondence to Fanette Singer, August 5, 1977. Unless otherwise noted, unpublished correspondence and documents cited in this chapter are housed in the VTNA files at the Vanderbilt University Archives.

7 A summer 1968 *U.S. News and World Report* article conveyed this belief through an example that would later be repeated by both Simpson and media critics: "One man who often speaks for the Administration on matters of national policy says: ' . . . Even a raised eyebrow, or the inflection of a voice, or a caustic remark dropped into the middle of a news broadcast can create doubt.' " "Television Comes Under Fire," 37.

8 Unpublished correspondence to Mumford signed by Baker, Brock, Fulton, and Gore (March 5, 1969); unpublished correspondence from Mumford to network presidents (May 28, 1969); unpublished report by Paul L. Berry, director of Reference Department at the Library of Congress (June 16, 1969). All on file at the Library of Congress Division of Motion Picture, Broadcasting, and Recorded Sound.

9 Paul Berry, director of Reference Department, and Alan Fern, assistant chief, Prints and Photographs Division, both Library of Congress, unpublished report, April 25, 1969. Unpublished correspondence, Mumford to Martin A. Jackson (June 2, 1971). The various reports, proposals, and bills that followed, especially in 1972 and 1973, were predominantly prospective budgets for operations. All reports at the Library of Congress.

10 Davidson and Lukow, *Administration of Television Newsfilm*, 172.

11 Schreibman, "Succinct History," 93.

12 Remarks about recent usage based on interview with VTNA staff compiler Lara Ray, January 12, 2005.

13 Duggan, *The Twilight of Equality*, 9.

14 A useful review of the literature on television news, dating up to the early 1980s, appears in Nimmo and Combs, *Nightly Horrors*, 5–9.

15 Colson "had a reputation as a 'hit man' " for the press and later served seven months in prison for Obstruction of Justice due to his role in the Watergate affair. Donovan and Sherer, *Unsilent Revolution*, 123. See also Paley, *As It Happened*, 323.

16 Simpson, *Network Television News*, 23.

17 Ibid., 24.

18 "Southern Eye Fixed on the Networks," 52. The article refers to a source that identified Simpson as a conservative.

19 Witcover, *White Knight*, 310–16.

20 Simpson's connection to the speech was more prominently reported in the Nashville press. The conservative *Nashville Banner* ran three articles above the fold on its front page: an editorial, "The Greeks Have a Word for It—Spiro T. (for Tiger)," which was placed top and center, an Associated Press wire report, "Agnew's TV Blast Lauded," and local coverage by Weldon Grimsley, "Local Man Aided TV Attack." The more moderate *Nashville Tennessean* also carried a less-prominent story, "Agnew Link Not Political, Says VU Man."

21 Michie, "GOP Marks," 1.

22 "Bill Would Give," 38, 60.

23 Donovan and Sherer, *Unsilent Revolution*, 111.

24 See, in particular, Halberstam, *The Powers That Be*, 596; and Paley, *As It Happened*, 313, 317. For clips and commentary on Nixon's use of television and

the news media up until his first presidential term, see Emile de Antonio's *Millhouse* (1971).

25 Charles Colson, memos to H. R. Haldeman, October 23, 1970, and July 23, 1971, published in Oudes, *From: The President*, 165, 301.

26 Colson, memo to Dwight Chapin, February 11, 1971, in Oudes, *From: The President*, 216–17.

27 CBS representatives included Paley, Stanton, Salant, executive vice president John Schneider, Broadcast Group president Richard W. Jencks, and CBS-TV president Bob Wood. Colson, memo to "The President's File," March 15, 1971, and Colson, memo to Haldeman, November 17, 1970, in Oudes, *From: The President*, 230–34, 171–72. See also Colson's memos dated July 22, 1971 (298–99), and October 20, 1971 (329–30).

28 Schorr, *Clearing the Air*, 44.

29 Colson, memo to Ken Clawson, May 1, 1972, in Oudes, *From: The President*, 436.

30 My dissertation includes a significantly longer account of the Nixon administration's attention to the news and of studies of news bias during this time.

31 Borrowers listed on document 16(a)-1 of Vanderbilt's answers to CBS's interrogatories, *Columbia Broadcasting System, Inc., v. Vanderbilt University* (6th Cir., Middle District of TN, Civil Action no. 7336, 1973), filed April 25, 1974. Additional names among notes in Vanderbilt University Archives.

32 *Congressional Record–Senate*, December 1, 1969, 36192–93. See also "Does Uncle Want to Become Big Brother?" 62. The article makes the connection between Baker and Vanderbilt explicit.

33 *Congressional Record–Senate*, April 15, 1970, 11794.

34 Unpublished correspondence, Rob Downey, executive secretary RTNDA, to senators, October 26, 1970.

35 *Congressional Record–Senate*, March 10, 1971, 2784–85; and *Congressional Record–Senate*, September 27, 1973, 11108.

36 *Congressional Record–Senate*, March 10, 1971, 2784.

37 Alan Fern (initials), handwritten comment on "Routing and Transmittal Slip," March 15, 1971, at the Library of Congress. The entertainment industry's trade press coverage of the 1971 bill likewise linked the bill to Republican responses to news coverage.

38 Numerous other senators cosponsored these bills after Senator Baker introduced them.

39 *Congressional Record–House of Representatives*, April 15, 1970, 11941.

40 *Congressional Record–House of Representatives*, January 22, 1971, 172, and January 24, 1973, 2149. According to Matsunaga's assistant, "A 1970 handout from the News Broadcasters Association sparked Congressman Matsunaga's interest in television archives." Notes from American Film Institute (AFI)

meeting "concerning coordination of television archival activities," March 8, 1974, p. 3, at the Library of Congress.

41 Nor was Baker alone in calling the Senate's attention to the VTNA. Senator Clifford Hansen (R-Wyoming), who had sponsored the 1971 screening of NBC's and CBS's coverage of Laos, reminded his fellow legislators of the Senate Office Building event on March 30, 1972. Two years later, at the beginning of the CBS litigation against Vanderbilt, Senator Hansen introduced into the *Congressional Record* the *Wall Street Journal* editorial "CBS and Its Tapes," which was reprinted in full. *Congressional Record–Senate*, March 4, 1974, S2688. See also "CBS and Its Tapes," 18.

42 *Congressional Record–Senate*, September 9, 1974, 28498.

43 *Congressional Record–Senate*, August 15, 1974, 28498.

44 At a meeting on television archives, Ringer's statements were summarized as "the most important thing to do is preserve, all else is secondary." Senator Ward White indicated that Baker was in talks with Ringer to incorporate his bill into copyright. Notes from AFI meeting, March 8, 1974, 6, 8, at the Library of Congress.

45 Testimony of Robert V. Evans, *Hearings before the Subcommittee on Courts, Civil Liberties, and the Administration of Justice of the Committee of the Judiciary*, House of Representatives, 49th session, HR 2223, June 12, 1975, 684.

46 Testimony of Barbara Ringer, *Hearings*, October 9, 1975, 1794.

47 Ibid., 1802.

48 Ibid.

49 Ringer, *Second Supplementary Report of the Register of Copyrights on the General Revision of the U.S. Copyright Law: 1975 Revision Bill*, 44.

50 "Markup of Copyright," 5; see also Frank Van Der Linden, "CBS vs. Vandy News Archive," n.p.; and "News Briefs," *Broadcasting*, April 12, 1976, n.p.

51 "Kastenmeier," n.p.

52 Chronology appears in Patry, "Copyright Law and Practice."

53 In 1977 Erik Barnouw was hired as a consultant to the Library of Congress to establish policies for the new collection; in 1978 he established the library's Motion Picture, Broadcasting, and Recorded Sound Division and served as its chief until 1981. Barnouw and the ATRA signed a cooperative agreement with the VTNA for the Vanderbilt archive to supply the library with its hard news collection in 1980. Supplemental copies also became part of the Library of Congress collection through the network's own copyright deposits, though NBC and CNN did not regularly contribute.

54 *Red Lion Broadcasting Co. v. FCC*, 395 U.S. 367, 390 (1969), quoted in Brief in Support of Defendant's First Motion to Dismiss, *CBS v. VU*, March 25, 1974, 7–8.

55 The Fairness Doctrine, a Federal Communications Commission regulation from 1949 to 1987, "was thrown out by the Reagan-era FCC [and] has been

passed in legislative version twice by Congress only to be vetoed by Presidents Bush and Reagan." Streeter, *Selling the Air*, 128, 130.

56 Various correspondence, mostly from 1971, is on file at the Vanderbilt University Archives.

57 Unpublished correspondence from Robert Evans, CBS vice president and general counsel, to Pilkington, April 4, 1972.

58 Note, signed by J. Pilkington, "9-6-1972 Visit to CBS," July 12, 1973; and Simpson, *Network Television News*, 85.

59 Unpublished correspondence from Val Sanford of Guillett, Steele, Sanford, Robinson and Merritt Law Offices to chancellor Alexander Heard, July 9, 1973.

60 Unpublished correspondence from Leslie C. Waffen, Audiovisual Archives Division, NARS (no addressee or date listed, written after February 16, 1975). "CBS Gives Federal Archive Go-Ahead," 56. The NARS agreement was also reported in the *New York Times*, *Wall Street Journal*, *Variety*, and *Village Voice*. The revised agreement received press coverage in the *Washington Post* and *Wall Street Journal*. School licenses were established statewide in Utah, Idaho, and Minnesota public schools; locally in Dublin, Georgia, and in Chatham, New York; and at the University of North Carolina, Chapel Hill; University of Nebraska, Lincoln; Forest Park Community College in St. Louis; and the U.S. Air Force Academy.

61 Carr, unpublished correspondence to Sanford, August 13, 1973.

62 Sanford to Carr, October 15, 1973.

63 Carr to Sanford, August 13, 1973; Sanford to Carr, September 10, 1973; Carr to Sanford, September 14, 1973; Sanford to Carr, September 18, 1973; Carr to Sanford, October 8, 1973; and Carr to Sanford, November 13, 1973.

64 CBS press release, "CBS Sues Vanderbilt University," December 21, 1973.

65 Complaint, *CBS v. VU*, December 21, 1973, 5.

66 The term "landmark" appears in "Editor's Notes" in the journalist fraternity paper the *Quill*, 3.

67 Brief in Support of Defendant's First Motion to Dismiss, *CBS v. VU*, March 25, 1974, 8. Italics in the original.

68 Ibid, 6–7.

69 Ibid., 11. CBS challenged the relevance of Vanderbilt's references to the *Red Lion* and *Teleprompter* cases in Reply Brief of Plaintiff to Defendant's Motion to Dismiss or for Summary Judgment, *CBS v. VU*, June 17, 1974, 54–56.

70 See Meyer, "TV Cassettes," 23–24, notes 24 and 26.

71 Report of the Senate Committee on the Judiciary, report no. 92–72, April 20, 1970, quoted in Meyer, "TV Cassettes," 21.

72 Reply Brief of Plaintiff, 30–40.

73 Defendant's Rebuttal, 43–45.

74 Defendant's Rebuttal, 47, 49.

75 The CBS News archive kept all film and video materials shot for news programs, along with edited segments and outtakes. Time-lapse video recordings were begun for each program beginning January 23, 1973 (presumably for copyright deposit of images). Three-quarter-inch color videocassette recordings, made during broadcast, for each entire episode of the nightly news began in mid-January 1974. Audiotapes of each broadcast were also made for transcription purposes; complete transcripts were made, and the audiotapes were kept for one year. Two-inch tapes of programs were typically erased after fifteen days. Occasionally redundant raw material and outtakes are de-accessioned from the archive. In 1973 the network also developed a computer-based searchable database of transcripts and indexes. See Reply Brief of Plaintiff, 6–8.

76 Reply Brief of Plaintiff, 9–10.

77 Memorandum Response of CBS to Vanderbilt's Rebuttal Brief, *CBS v. VU*, August 13, 1974, 4.

78 Ibid., 7.

79 Ibid., 10–14.

80 L. Patterson and Lindberg, *The Nature of Copyright*, 134.

81 Amended and Supplemental Complaint, *CBS v. VU*, June 19, 1975, 3.

82 Motion of Plaintiff to Strike Defendant's Motions to Dismiss and Briefs or to Exclude Matters outside the Complaint and Deny Motions to Dismiss, *CBS v. VU*, December 8, 1975; and Defendant's Brief in Response to Plaintiff's Motion to Strike Defendant's Motions to Dismiss and Briefs or to Exclude Matters outside the Complaint and Deny Motions to Dismiss, *CBS v. VU*, December 19, 1975.

83 Order, *CBS v. VU*, March 31, 1976.

84 Kies, "The CBS-Vanderbilt Litigation," 118.

85 Sanford, unpublished correspondence to Carr, August 5, 1976.

86 Sanford to Carr, December 8, 1976.

87 The lawsuit received regular coverage in the industry periodical *Broadcasting*, recurring reporting in the *New York Times* and *Variety*, substantial stories in the *Columbia Journalism Review*, the *Chronicle of Higher Education*, and the *Videoplay Report*, and various reprinted wire reports in local newspapers across the country.

88 Sargent, "CBS v. Vanderbilt Case," 9.

89 Cockburn, "Press Clips," March 7, 1974, 12; "CBS and Its Tapes," 18.

90 On the cultural significance of Nixon's Oval Office tapes—and the eighteen-and-a-half-minute gap on a recording made three days after the Watergate break-in—see Killen, *1973 Nervous Breakdown*, 227.

91 Kompare, *Rerun Nation*, 102.

92 Mann, "Evolution," 1.

93 Barnouw, *Tube of Plenty*, 467.

94 The earliest developments in television preservation were initiated by the industry. In 1965 the earliest nonnetwork television archive was established by the Academy of Television Arts and Sciences Foundation as a consortium between the University of California, Los Angeles, Columbia University, and American University. (The collection was later consolidated at UCLA.) This was not a video collection but a repository of film materials produced for television. Library of Congress, *Report of the Librarian of Congress*, vol. 1, *Report*, 156. The continued lack of comprehensive archives for television continues to be seen as a crisis, and digital technologies have introduced as many complications as they have raised hopes.

95 From 1990 to 2007, the institution had been called the Museum of Television and Radio; in 1996 a West Coast location opened in Beverly Hills. In 2007 the museum was renamed the Paley Center for Media.

96 On TV museums, see Kramp, "Changing Role."

97 Trotsky, "Networks Try," 17.

98 See Library of Congress, *Report of the Librarian of Congress*. Additional archives were later established and continue at the University of Wisconsin, Madison, the Museum of Broadcast Communications in Chicago, and the C-SPAN public affairs collection at Purdue University in Lafayette, Indiana.

99 Fay Schreibman McGrew, submission in Library of Congress, *Report of the Librarian of Congress*, vol. 5, *Submissions*, 190.

100 Schreibman, "Television News Archives," 104–6.

Video Clip 3: Experimental Film on Video

1 Telecine devices, which date back to 1938, transfer film prints to video signals and adapt film's rate of twenty-four frames per second to television's thirty frames per second. As videotape technology developed, the telecine process output signals to tape. Such telecine devices both enabled broadcast and video releases of film programming and were used by universities, archives, and film exhibitors to make study copies of rare film prints.

2 On this debate, see Enticknap, "Have Digital Technologies," 10–20.

Chapter 4: Grainy Days and Mondays

1 Throughout this chapter, I reference historical persons by their full names and the doll characters in the film by first name only—except in the final moment, when the two are conflated.

2 Bal et al., "Top 50 Cult Movies," 38; P. Hall, "The Bootleg Files." The following year, *EW* listed *Superstar* among twenty-four infamously "lost" projects by musicians, directors, and actors, most of which were suppressed by the artists themselves. See Pastorek, "Buried Treasure." The *Shock Cinema*

entry concludes, "Underground brilliance, though difficult to locate since surviving-shitheel Richard Carpenter sued Haynes for using their tunes without permission." Puchalski, *Shock Cinema*, 9.

3 Whitburn, *Billboard Book*, 109–10.

4 In "The Sleazy Pedigree of Todd Haynes," Joan Hawkins offers a reading of generic play, especially in relation to B movies, in Haynes's work.

5 Haynes refers to Sally Potter's *Thriller* (1979) as a particular influence. Haynes, telephone interview with author, August 12, 2003.

6 Kruger, "Into Thin Air," 108.

7 The art critic Dave Hickey ranked Karen Carpenter among the twentieth century's great tragic American vocalists. "[Chet] Baker knew what all songwriters know, what singers like Judy Garland and Patsy Cline and Karen Carpenter knew most profoundly, that *all songs are sad songs*." Hickey, *Air Guitar*, 75.

8 Dyer, "Judy Garland and Gay Men," 155.

9 This is J. Hoberman's phrasing in "Valley of the Dolls," 67.

10 Fusco, "Regimes of Normalcy," 18.

11 *Superstar* and *Goldmine* cover approximately the same period of popular culture (from 1969 to 1983 in *Superstar* and from the early 1970s to 1984 in *Goldmine*), but the two modes of music are worlds apart: *Goldmine*'s glam rock persona Maxwell Demon purports to bring an extraterrestrial polysexuality to earth. And yet the films' parallel pop universes present similar narratives of entertainment's escapist fantasies. The Carpenters presented a wholesome, TV-ready version of all-American normalcy that was virtually impossible to live up to but was also visible in *The Brady Bunch*, *The Partridge Family*, and *The Osmonds*. The glam scene portrayed in *Goldmine* may have been cloudy outside, but inside nightclubs and teen bedrooms it was a utopian alternative public (and private) sphere of surface glitter. Ultimately, both fantasies met their ends by the early 1980s with Karen Carpenter's death in 1983 and with the 1984 tenth anniversary of Maxwell Demon's staged death, triggering recognition of unfulfilled dreams.

12 This chapter condenses the more detailed history included in the earlier version published in *Camera Obscura*, no. 57 (December 2004): 61–70.

13 Haynes, press release, July 1987.

14 Lieberman, "Todd Haynes's *Superstar*"; and Koch, "Andy Warhol, 1928–1987," 93–94. Speaking of Warhol, he demonstrated that analog reproduction via silk screens may produce similar images from a master source, but each print reveals its own streaks and blotches, sometimes with the paint gummed up or running thin. There's a beauty to the imperfect serial reproduction; and I would claim that the same holds for tape-to-tape dupes.

15 Exhibition history reconstructed from interview with Haynes, as well as reviews and listings in relevant publications and e-mail survey responses.

16 Haynes, e-mail correspondence, September 30, 2003.

17 This number is only an estimate. Haynes duped batches of ten tapes for the store, but there were fewer than ten batches made. Haynes, interview and e-mail correspondence.

18 Haynes started the film while in an MFA program at Bard College.

19 Haynes, press release.

20 Echols, "Low-Impact Horror," n.p.

21 This narrative is based on Haynes's recollection during the interview.

22 Haynes, interview.

23 Information about *The Distorted Barbie*, as well as reproductions of the October 10, 1997, letter Mattel sent to Napier's website host, can be found at http://users.rcn.com/napier.interport/barbie/barbie.html or at http://chillingeffects.org (both accessed May 16, 2006). Images of *Food Chain Barbie* can be seen on Forsyth's website at www.tomforsythe.com (accessed May 16, 2006). Mattel sued Forsythe in 1999; on December 29, 2003, the Ninth Circuit Court of Appeals ruled against Mattel. The video artist Joe Gibbons has also made a name for himself with Barbie-titled shorts, including *Barbie's Audition* (1995) and *Multiple Barbie* (1998).

24 On "genericide," see Coombe, *Cultural Life*, 79–82.

25 Erica Rand offers a similar but far more extensive analysis of tensions between Barbie's marketed biography and children's imaginations, though she asserts, "Mattel has always wanted to direct children to fantasy play that would be abetted by buying specific additional Barbie products." Rand, *Barbie's Queer Accessories*, 41.

26 Notably, the published screenplay includes reprint permission notices for lyrics to all of the Carpenters' songs in the film except the Richard Carpenter–composed "Top of the World." Todd Haynes, *Three Screenplays*, n.p.

27 *Superstar* presents Richard as an uptight nag who pressures Karen to perform; Karen refers to Richard's secret life, which could be a covert reference to his prescription drug addiction. Between her shrill voice and monstrously molded face, it is the siblings' overbearing mother, however, who gets the least flattering portrayal.

28 In terms of its legal infringement of music rights, *Superstar*'s withdrawal from authorized public viewing preceded the similar case of John Greyson's *The Making of Monsters* (1991). This video featurette playfully dramatizes the aesthetics debate between Georg Lukács and Bertolt Brecht (played by a catfish) as they make a film, *Monsters*, about the gay bashing of a Toronto high school teacher. Greyson offered to pay the Kurt Weill estate to use the tune of "Mack the Knife" for the parodic song "I Hate Straights," but his request was denied. Although Greyson's film also exists in bootleg forms that are occasionally screened (predominantly, it seems, in university courses), it has not earned the cult following or notoriety of *Superstar*. Its hybrid structure,

however, is strikingly similar, though its content is more pedantically theoretical. Ironically, Greyson stated that he was not concerned about copyright issues in an interview shortly before the film's removal from circulation. See McGann, "A Kiss Is Not a Kiss," 10–13.

29 Richard Carpenter states in the notes for the final track, "Karen's Theme," "We all make mistakes, and one of my biggest was allowing myself to be persuaded into authorizing, and participating in, the making of *The Karen Carpenter Story*, approximately 90 minutes of creative license that gives biopics, in general, a dubious name." Carpenter, liner notes, *Carpenters: Gold* (A&M RECORDS, 2004).

30 See http://illegal-art.org/video (accessed June 7, 2003).

31 Anonymous e-mail survey respondent, October 28, 2004.

32 From http://www.blindinglight.com/prog.asp (June 7, 2003). The venue closed in July 2003 after five years as a full-time micro-cinema. An e-mail survey respondent recalled that Blinding Light "showed the thing at *least* 15 times or more while the theater was running in its 4 year run. The crowds were just *nuts* for the show, full houses every time we'd show it." Bill Taylor, e-mail correspondence, October 28, 2004. Blinding Light typically screened *Superstar* with vintage Barbie commercials. The venue screened the film numerous times, calling it "the ol' BL mainstay and rent-payer" in an August 6, 2000, posting on the Frameworks Listserv. Frameworks archive, http://www.hi-beam.net/fw/fw14/0551.html (accessed October 26, 2004).

33 In our interview, Haynes recalled manipulating the color levels of the playback monitors.

34 Quoted in A. Glenn Mandeville, "The Many Cases of Barbie," *Barbie Bazaar* 2 (January–February 1990): 12, cited in Rand, *Barbie's Queer Accessories*, 40.

35 Intentionally or not, *Superstar* fulfills all of Peter Wollen's criteria of "counter-cinema": narrative interruptions, estrangement, medium foregrounding, multiple diegeses, intertextuality, provocation, and breakdown of representational "truth." See Wollen, "Godard and Counter-Cinema," 79–91.

36 Burdette, "Queer Readings/Queer Cinema," 75.

37 Stephens, "Gentlemen Prefer Haynes," 77.

38 Altman, "Material Heterogeneity," 26, 30.

39 See Tanselle, "Reproductions and Scholarship" (1989), in *Literature and Artifacts*; and Garvey, "Scissoring and Scrapbooks," 211.

40 Barthes, "Death of the Author," in *Image/Music/Text*, 146.

41 Marshall McLuhan suggested as much (though not, perhaps, considering such an extreme example) when he argued that television was a "cool" low-resolution medium that required the mental and perceptual participation of the audience. McLuhan, *Understanding Media*, 22–23.

42 On vision and blindness, see Elkins, *Object Stares Back*, 201–2. On listening and "audile technique," see Sterne, *The Audible Past*, 112–13.

43 Metz, *The Imaginary Signifier*, 45–49. Oddly enough, Patrice Petro has suggested that the influence of 1970s psychoanalytic and feminist film theory has degenerated over time like video copies, and the article that inspired her disciplinary metaphor drew similar parallels between video degeneration and inferior celebrity biopics. See Petro, *Aftershocks of the New*, 157; and MacGregor, "Copying Copies," 1.

44 Metz, *The Imaginary Signifier*, 52.

45 Marks, *Touch*, 97.

46 Sterne also discusses the separation of the senses through practices of reception in relation to audio recording. Sterne, *The Audible Past*, 62. Metz, *The Imaginary Signifier*, 59. Marks briefly notes Metz's division of the senses in *Skin of the Film*, 210–11. Marks also explains her use of "haptic vision" in this book, xi, 162–64.

47 Metz, *The Imaginary Signifier*, 57. Marks presents fetishes primarily in an anthropological sense of cultural appropriation and the international circulation of commodities. Her reading is done through a dialogue between William Pietz and Walter Benjamin. Marks, *Skin of the Film*, 85–94.

48 On fetishism, see Pietz, "Fetishism and Materialism," 119–51; and Stallybrass, "Marx's Coat," 183–207. On souvenirs, see Stewart, *On Longing*; and Olalquiaga, *The Artificial Kingdom.*

49 Michel de Certeau writes of the search for primary evidence, "The history of its diffusion will thus be the history of a progressive degradation. . . . [H]istorians never apprehend origins, but only successive stages of their loss." de Certeau, *The Writing of History*, 22.

50 I'm not using the phrase in quite the way Cvetkovich does. See her *An Archive of Feelings.*

51 "Skizz Cyzyk," e-mail correspondence, October 27, 2004.

52 "Perksplace," enclosure with videocassette, June 23, 2004.

53 Tashiro, "Contradictions of Video Collecting," 12.

54 Baudrillard, "The System of Collecting," 12.

55 To clarify a distinction: respondents did not always remember how they first saw the film, but those who possess personal copies did recall their tapes' origins.

56 Hubbard, e-mail correspondence, September 8, 2003.

57 Herrmann, "Women's Exchange," 710.

58 Hyde, *The Gift*, 34.

Video Clip 4: Tape Art

1 Early video art, however, more often emphasized the technological and engineering properties of the medium, approaching video as a specifically electronic art form in which artists played with signals, image processors,

and synthesizers. In addition, in Nam June Paik's work, the monitor became a sculptural element, while his manipulation of the image was specifically magnetic and analog. The classic early survey of video art is Gene Youngblood's *Expanded Cinema*, especially chapter 5.

2 *(Entlastungen) Pipilottis Fehler* is extensively illustrated in Phelan, Obrist, and Bronfen, *Pipilotti Rist.*

3 Joan Jonas's *Vertical Roll* (1972) and Dara Birnbaum's *Technology/Transformation: Wonder Woman* (1978–79) are also among the seminal feminist works that engage with the technology's properties and potential—although in ways that differ from the ones I have focused on.

4 Video Data Bank distributes work by Lynda Benglis, Jason Simon, Joan Jonas, and Dara Birnbaum. Electronic Arts Intermix distributes work by Pipilotti Rist, Benglis, Jonas, and Birnbaum. Other videos described in this video clip are either represented by galleries or self-distributed by the artists.

Chapter 5: Joanie, Jackie, Everyone They Know

1 The company J&R FILM/Moviola Digital demanded that July cease using the trademarked term "Moviola" in the project's name and web address. See Alissa Quart, "Cultural Sabotage," G10.

2 For more about the project's history, see Shauna McGarry's short documentary *Joanie 4 Jackie: A Quick Overview*, created (alongside a retrospective curated by McGarry and Miranda July) for the exhibition *The Way That We Rhyme: Women, Art & Politics* at the Yerba Buena Center for the Arts in San Francisco, March 29–June 29, 2008.

3 I do not problematize the concept of community in depth in this chapter. For insightful analysis and critiques of this topic, see Joseph, *Against the Romance of Community.*

4 Kluszczynski, "From Film to Interactive Art," 214.

5 Guest-curated Co-Star compilation tapes are also available. To date the Co-Star tapes include *Joanie 4 Jackie 4 Ever* (curated by July and apparently the first use of "Joanie 4 Jackie"), *I Saw Bones* (curated by Rita Gonzalez), and *Some Kind of Loving* (curated by Astria Suparak and Jane Gang).

6 Charlotte Greville, Joanie 4 Jackie intern, e-mail correspondence, November 7, 2005.

7 I previously suggested this argument in a different context in "Retroactivism," 301–15.

8 Duncombe, *Notes from Underground*, 98.

9 Simon, *Mail-Orders*, 209.

10 See Rogers, "LA Freewaves." As Victoria Johnson has pointed out to me, nonurban local cable companies and PBS stations based at land grant universities

are perhaps more likely to allow local access to production resources and airtime than those in major metropolitan areas.

11 On Video Club of America, see Lardner, *Fast Forward*, 173–74.

12 C. Taylor, "Mail Art," W26.

13 K. Friedman, "Foreword," xvii.

14 John Peters, *Speaking into the Air*, 165–67.

15 Henkin, *The Postage Age*, 5, 8.

16 Simon, *Mail-Orders*, x.

17 Rosenberg and Garofalo, "Riot Grrrl," 809.

18 This "anger" was most clearly manifest in the screamed vocals and rough guitars of riot grrrl music. Klein, "Duality and Redefinition," 219. For an excellent account that situates riot grrrl popular culture in relation to prior feminist waves and representations of female sexuality, see Buszek, *Pin-Up Grrrls*, 341–54.

19 July commented in an interview, "Joanie 4 Jackie was really built to help me create a space for myself, for other women too, but most urgently for myself, that was filled with warmth. I needed that warm space in order to take massive risks in my life." Bryan-Wilson, "Some Kind of Grace," 188.

20 Rosenberg and Garofalo, "Riot Grrrl," 810.

21 Erin A. McCarley, quoted in Rosenberg and Garofalo, "Riot Grrrl," 823.

22 Bryan-Wilson, "Some Kind of Grace," 182.

23 J. Smith, "Doin' It for the Ladies," 230–32.

24 Kearney, "Girls Make Movies," 31.

25 One of the critiques of riot grrrl communities has been their racial (white) homogeneity—a criticism that could also be made of the Joanie 4 Jackie contents. Some of these zines do address specific ethnic identities and experiences: *Bamboo Girl* (Asian American), *Plotz* (Jewish), *Hues* (women of color), and *Java Turtle* (African American).

26 Boyle, "Brief History," 62.

27 "International Videoletters," listing in Grimstad and Rennie, *New Woman's Survival Sourcebook*, 171. Curiously, the project is included in the "arts" section of the book with other film and video art resources rather than in the "communication" section with print publications.

28 *The New Woman's Survival Sourcebook* lists contact information for the following venues: Feminist Studio Workshops in Hollywood and San Diego; L.A. Access Feminist Access Project; Santa Cruz Media Collective; Just Us Video Collective in Berkeley; Tucson Feminist Media Collective; Kartemquin LTD in Chicago; Rochester Women's Video Collective; Spectra Feminist Media Project in Washington, D.C.; and Open Video, Video Commune, Women Make Movies, and Women's Interart Center in New York City. An article on the New York conference indicates that initial plans for the project included a site in Cleveland and—making the project international—Sydney, Austra-

lia, and somewhere in Alberta, Canada; the same article also stated that the project was tried out for a six-month pilot. See *TeleVISIONS Magazine* 3, no. 1 (January–February 1975): 9. See also Milano, "Women's Media," 25.

29 Video letters have also been conceptualized more recently as an art practice (by Yau Ching) and as a mode of communication (by geographically dispersed relatives). See, respectively, Marks, *Skin of the Film*, 176; and Kolar-Panov, *Video, War, and the Diasporic Imagination*, 57–62.

30 Benedict Anderson has traced the origins of nationalism—and its affective sense of fraternity and patriotism—to the creation of "imagined communities" via the rise of standardized vernacular languages and, in tandem, common experiences of consuming novels and newspapers. This form of "horizontal comradeship" is imagined precisely because the community members may never know each other, yet they imagine common identities. See Anderson, *Imagined Communities*. In a reformulation of Anderson's work, Peter Coviello has introduced the concept of an "affect-nation" to describe the emotional bonds implicit in identifying with an anonymous community. Coviello, *Intimacy in America*, 4. Joanie 4 Jackie's remarkable revision of the virtual nation does not merely imagine a community of strangers but rather imagines that the strangers can actually form a sisterly network and communicate.

31 Juhasz, "Our Auto-Bodies, Ourselves," 14. For histories of feminist video art, see also Straayer, "I Say I Am"; Gever, "The Feminism Factor"; and V. Green, "Vertical Hold."

32 See Mulvey, "Visual Pleasure," 6–18. The artist's statement says, "I studied film theory at school but I wasn't really ever that great at speaking the language. . . . I believe in fucking it up from the inside."

33 C. Russell, *Experimental Ethnography*, 281. See also Renov, *The Subject of Documentary*; Lesage, "Women's Fragmented Consciousness"; and Lane, *Autobiographical Documentary.*

34 See Olney, "Autobiography and the Cultural Moment," 13.

35 Scholars have suggested that women's autobiographies that focus on personal experiences and relationships do not conform to masculinist values and have thus been marginalized in literary studies: "This emphasis by women on the personal, especially on other people, rather than their work life, their professional successes, or their connectedness to current political or intellectual history clearly contradicts the established criterion about the content of autobiography." Jelinek, "Introduction," 10. Taking on one of the founding fathers of autobiography studies, a feminist literary scholar argues, "The very sense[s] of *identification*, *interdependence*, and *community* that [Georges] Gusdorf dismisses from autobiographical selves are key elements in the development of a woman's identity." S. Friedman, "Women's Autobiographical Selves," 34, 38. Yet Domna C. Stanton has suggested that

even the conception of feminine identity constructed through relationships reflects continued patriarchal ideology. "Some feminist critics defined the personal in women's autobiographies as a primary emphasis on the relation of self to others. However, this relatedness was traced to the dependence imposed on women by the patriarchal system, or then it was upheld as a fundamental female quality." Stanton, "Autogynography."

36 See Johnson, *Heartland TV* and "Welcome Home?"

37 C. Russell, *Experimental Ethnography*, 277.

38 Another failed escape appears in the enigmatically perverse puppet play *There's No Place Like Home, Parts 1 & 2* by Baltimore-based Karen Yasinski (*Some Kind of Loving* co-star tape, 2000). In this video a pair of legs taps the heels of its ruby slippers but never gets magically whisked away from the dreary world it inhabits; instead, the mute legs become embroiled in a troubling erotic relationship with a man and a domestic psychodrama with a woman.

39 Heilbrun, *Writing a Woman's Life*, 72 (italics mine).

40 Creative Commons is a licensing system in which artists define what rights they grant to users in order to foster a thriving public domain. See creative commons.org. The concept of the commons has been written about by Lawrence Lessig, the cofounder of Creative Commons, in *The Future of Ideas* and *Free Culture*.

41 Mauss, *The Gift*, 10. Along the same lines, Lewis Hyde writes, "It is the cardinal difference between gift and commodity exchange that a gift establishes a feeling-bond between two people, while the sale of a commodity leaves no necessary connection." Hyde, *The Gift*, 56.

42 Hyde, *The Gift*, 74–75.

43 Grant and Nadim, "Working Things Out Together," 52.

44 The project received its first mainstream attention in 1996, when July was featured in *Sassy*, the now-defunct young women's magazine. "She's Way Sassy," 24.

45 This teen dyke's bedroom confession may elicit comparisons to Sadie Benning's Pixelvision video diaries that were so celebrated a decade prior, but Hill's tape is far less performative. Considering her situation as a teenager in Oklahoma, it's highly unlikely she knew of Benning's work. Benning's video diaries were shot with a Fisher Price Pixelvision camera, which makes black-and-white video recordings on audiotape cassettes. She typically talked about sexuality, pop culture, agoraphobia, and cutting class. Her work was celebrated as a youth video component of the hailed New Queer Cinema that appeared on the Sundance Film Festival scene in the early 1990s; her work also screened at the Whitney Museum of American Art and prestigious venues across the country and has been the subject of several academic essays. It seems that her prominence has prompted broader interest and mate-

rial support of (queer) youth media. Video Data Bank distributes her video work.

46 Bryan-Wilson, "Some Kind of Grace," 188–89.

Epilogue

1 See Seiter, *Television and New Media*, 115–30.

2 Parks, "Flexible Microcasting," 135.

3 YouTube was created by three PayPal alumni still in their twenties: Steve Chen, Chad Hurley, and Jawed Karim, who left the company to attend grad school before PayPal hit big.

4 Paul Boutin, "Web Video," part of "Why Things Suck!" *Wired*, February 2008, 112.

5 Quoted in McManis, "It's You. It's YouTube," n.p.

6 Charlene Li, quoted in Ross Sorkin and Edmonston, "Google Is Said." As John McMurria has observed, the "community" rhetoric was rampant and open to dispute following the sale of YouTube to Google. See McMurria, "The YouTube Community."

7 In this way YouTube recalls Rosalind Krauss's seminal assertion that video art indulged a pervasive "aesthetics of narcissism." Krauss, "Video."

8 This practice has surprisingly old roots; in the mid-nineteenth century forwarding newspapers by mail became a common, cheap, and lazy way to sustain contact with distant relative and friends without having to write a letter. Henkin, *The Postal Age*, 43–47, 50–51.

9 Palmer, *Television Disrupted*.

10 Gitelman, *Always Already New*, 123–50.

11 Garfield, "YouTube vs. Boob Tube."

12 See Baumer, "YouTube vs. Main Stream." The conventional wisdom that infringing clips are the most popular has been challenged by the tracking service Vidmeter, which found that clips subject to takedown requests made up less than 10 percent of content and only slightly more than 5 percent of the page views. D. Mitchell, "YouTube's Favorite Clips."

13 See Jenkins, *Convergence Culture*, 13–16.

14 Peter Krapp examines connections between hypertext, archives, and cultural memory in *Déjà Vu*, 119–42.

15 Featherstone, "Archiving Cultures," 169–70.

16 Ibid., 165.

17 C-SPAN later requested the takedown of a clip from Speaker of the House Nancy Pelosi's blog nine months later. See Cohen, "Which Videos Are Protected?"

18 In the article version of this epilogue, I profiled a dozen of the most popular YouTube videos, including the "inspirational comedian" Judson Laipply's

"Evolution of Dance," lonelygirl15's pseudo-confessions, OK Go's music video "Here It Goes Again," explosive experiments in mixing Mentos and Diet Coke, a piano-playing cat, slash/parody trailers, lip-sync videos, and culturejamming election ads. See Hilderbrand, "The Clip Canon."

19 Even during the economic resurgence of the so-called Web 2.0, this price reflects market deflation compared to the $5.7 billion Yahoo paid for the short-lived broadcast.com.

20 Of course, Google has famously pushed the boundaries of copyright, librarianship, and exclusivity with its controversial Google Book project, which strives to become an online Library of Alexandria with searchable and complete digital scans of nearly every available book—scans that may drastically reduce purchases of actual books and are not accessible to other search engines, thus making the project commercially competitive and proprietary if at the same time expanding some methods of access to printed texts.

21 Fred Vogelstein, interview with Eric Schmidt, *Wired*, May 2007, 173.

22 See Learmonth, "Viacom Sues YouTube, Google"; and J. Peters, "Viacom Sues Google."

23 Lessig, *The Future of Ideas*, 23–25. On "code," see also Lessig, *Code: Version 2.0*.

24 The description in quotation marks appears in a statement by a representative of the Motion Picture Association of America in Wallenstein, "Catch YouTube."

25 See Kirsner, "YouTube's New Tools"; and Helft, "Google Takes Step."

26 H. Green, "Waiting for the Payoff," 56.

Bibliography

A & M Records, Inc., v. Napster, Inc., 114 F. Supp. 2d 896 (N.D. Cal. 2000), 239 F.3d 1004 (9th Cir. 2001).

Abramson, Albert. "Video Recording: 1922 to 1959." *Video–Apparat/Medium, Kunst, Kultur*, ed. Siegfried Zielinski, 35–45. Frankfurt am Main: Peter Lang, 1992.

Acland, Charles R., ed. *Residual Media*. Minneapolis: University of Minnesota Press, 2007.

"Agnew Link Not Political, Says VU Man." *Nashville Tennessean*, November 16, 1969, 5A.

"Agnew's TV Blast Lauded." *Nashville Banner*, November 15, 1969, 1.

Altman, Rick. "The Material Heterogeneity of Recorded Sound." In *Sound Theory, Sound Practice*, ed. Rick Altman, 15–31. New York: Routledge, 1992.

Alvarado, Manuel, ed. *Video World-Wide: An International Study*. Paris: United Nations Educational, Scientific, and Cultural Organization, 1988.

Anderson, Benedict. *Imagined Communities: Reflections on the Origin and Spread of Nationalism*. Rev. ed. New York: Verso, 1991.

Armes, Roy. *On Video*. New York: Routledge, 1988.

Arondekar, Anjali. "Without a Trace: Sexuality and the Colonial Archive." *Journal of the History of Sexuality* 14, nos. 1–2 (January–April 2005): 10–27.

Atkinson, Michael. "Das Bootlegs: Hunting Down Verboten DVDs and Videos on the Internet." *Village Voice*, June 30, 2004, 61.

———. "Obscure Objects: Satisfying Cinephiliac Lusts." *Village Voice*, April 22, 1997, 86.

Baker, Nicholson. *Double Fold: Libraries and the Assault on Paper*. New York: Random House, 2001.

Bal, Sumeet, et al. "The Top 50 Cult Movies." *Entertainment Weekly*, May 23, 2003, 38.

Band, Jonathan, and Andrew J. McLaughlin. "The Marshall Papers: A Peek behind the Scenes at the Making of *Sony v. Universal*." *Columbia-VLA Journal of Law and the Arts* 17, no. 4 (summer 1993): 427–51.

Barnouw, Erik. *Tube of Plenty: The Evolution of American Television*. 2nd rev. ed. New York: Oxford University Press, 1990.

Barthes, Roland. *Image/Music/Text*. Trans. Stephen Heath. New York: Noonday Press, 1977.

Baudrillard, Jean. "The System of Collecting." Trans. Roger Cardinal. In *Cultures of Collecting*, ed. John Elsner and Roger Cardinal, 7–24. Cambridge: Harvard University Press, 1994.

Baumer, Sonja. "YouTube vs. Main Stream Media: Kissing Cousins or Feuding Siblings?" *Flow* 5, no. 9 (March 2007).

Becker, Martin, ed. *The Video Nasties: Freedom and Censorship in the Media*. London: Pluto Press, 1984.

Belson, Ken. "In Sony's Stumble, the Ghost of Betamax." *New York Times*, February 26, 2006.

Belton, John. "Looking through Video: The Psychology of Video and Film." In *Resolutions: Contemporary Video Practices*, ed. Michael Renov and Erika Suderberg, 61–72. Minneapolis: University of Minnesota Press, 1996.

Benjamin, Walter. *Illuminations: Essays and Reflections*. Ed. Hannah Arendt, trans. Harry Zohn. New York: Schocken Books, 1969.

Benkler, Yochai. *The Wealth of Networks: How Social Production Transforms Markets and Freedom*. New Haven, Conn.: Yale University Press, 2006.

Bensinger, Charles. *The Home Video Handbook*. 2nd ed. Santa Barbara: Video-Info Publications, 1981.

Benson-Allott, Caetlin. "VCR Autopsy." *Journal of Visual Culture* 6, no. 2 (2007): 175–81.

Berko, Lili. "Video: In Search of a Discourse." *Quarterly Review of Film Studies* 10 (1989): 289–307.

Bernard, Jami. "Untaped Favorites." *New York Post*, August 1, 1988, 23, 26.

Bettig, Ronald V. *Copyrighting Culture: The Political Economy of Intellectual Property*. Boulder, Colo.: Westview Press, 1996.

Bierbaum, Tom. "Macrovision Says It's Not Integral Part of Homevid." *Variety*, May 5, 1987.

———. "Off-Air Recording Is the Dominant VCR Use; Tape Rents Grow, Buying Last." *Variety*, August 28, 1984, 1, 10.

Bijsterveld, Karin. " 'What Do I Do with My Tape Recorder . . . ?': Sound Hunting and the Sounds of Everyday Dutch Life in the 1950s and 1960s." *Historical Journal of Film, Radio, and Television* 24, no. 4 (2004): 613–34.

"Bill Would Give Library of Congress Vanderbilt U.'s Store of Web's News." *Variety*, March 17, 1971, 38, 60.

Billson, Murray. "Vanderbilt U. Sued by CBS on Sale of Cronkite Tapes." *New York Times*, December 22, 1973, 48.
Bjarkman, Kim. "To Have and to Hold: The Video Collector's Relationship to an Ethereal Medium." *Television and New Media* 5, no. 3 (August 2004): 217–46.
Bloom, David. "Bye-Bye, Beta: Sony's Also-Ran Format Ends Its 27-Year Run." *Variety*, September 2–8, 2002, 7.
Boddy, William. "Alternative Television in the United States." *Screen* 31, no. 1 (1990): 91–101.
———. *Fifties Television*. Urbana: University of Illinois Press, 1990.
Bolter, Jay David, and Richard Grusin. *Remediation: Understanding New Media*. Cambridge: MIT Press, 1999.
Boutin, Paul. "Web Video," in "Why Things Suck!" *Wired*, February 2008, 112.
Boyd, Douglas A., Joseph D. Straubhaar, and John A. Lent. *Videocassette Recorders in the Third World*. New York: Longman, 1989.
Boyle, Deirdre. "A Brief History of American Documentary Video." In *Illuminating Video: An Essential Guide to Video Art*, ed. Doug Hall and Sally Jo Fifer, 51–69. New York: Aperture, 1990.
———. *Subject to Change: Guerrilla Television Revisited*. New York: Oxford University Press, 1997.
Boyle, James. *Shamans, Software, and Spleens: Law and the Construction of the Information Society*. Cambridge: Harvard University Press, 1996.
Brass, Kevin. "Playing a Title Role." *Los Angeles Times*, October 18, 1996.
Brown, John Seely, and Paul Duguid. *The Social Life of Information*. Cambridge: Harvard Business School Press, 2000.
Brown, Les. "CBS Cites 'Misuse' in Archive Case." *New York Times*, February 26, 1974, 75.
———. "CBS Gives News-Taping Right to National Archives Service." *New York Times*, April 3, 1974, 87.
———. "Nixon's Charge of 'Vicious' Reporting on TV to Be Studied by News Council." *New York Times*, October 31, 1973, 22.
———. "Vanderbilt U. Acts to End Suit by CBS against News Archive." *New York Times*, March 30, 1974, 63.
Bryan-Wilson, Julia. "Some Kind of Grace: An Interview with Miranda July." *Camera Obscura*, no. 55 (2004): 181–97.
Burdette, K. "Queer Readings/Queer Cinema: An Examination of the Early Work of Todd Haynes." *Velvet Light Trap*, no. 41 (spring 1998): 68–80.
Burton, Antoinette, ed. *Archive Stories: Facts, Fictions, and the Writing of History*. Durham: Duke University Press, 2006.
Buszek, Maria Elena. *Pin-Up Grrrls: Feminism, Sexuality, Popular Culture*. Durham: Duke University Press, 2006.

Caldwell, John. *Televisuality: Style, Crisis, and Authority in American Television*. New Brunswick, N.J.: Rutgers University Press, 1994.

Canby, Vincent. "A Revolution Reshapes Movies." *New York Times*, January 7, 1990, H1.

Carmody, John. "To Preserve a Legacy of News." *Washington Post*, November 15, 1974, B1.

Casey, William. "Apple and the Betamax Complex." *Washington Post*, October 17, 1994, F19.

"CBS and Its Tapes." *Wall Street Journal*, February 20, 1974, 18.

"CBS Gives Federal Archive Go-Ahead to Tape and Preserve Walter Cronkite, Other News Shows." *Broadcasting*, April 8, 1974, 56.

"CBS Inc. Broadens Agreement on Use of News Broadcasts." *Wall Street Journal*, November 15, 1974, 36.

"CBS Inc. versus Vanderbilt University: Copy-'Right or Wrong.' " *Videoplay Report* 4, no. 11 (May 20, 1974): 1–6.

"CBS to Inaugurate Videocassette Club." *Variety*, March 4, 1981.

Cerone, Daniel. "Video Magic Is Rare: Classic Woes for Buffs." *New York Post*, January 7, 1992, 21.

Chafe, William H. *The Unfinished Journey: America since World War II*. 6th ed. New York: Oxford University Press, 2007.

Chanan, Michael. *Repeated Takes: A Short History of Recording and Its Effects on Music*. New York: Verso, 1995.

Chaney, Jen. "Parting Words for VHS Tapes, Soon to Be Gone with the Rewind." *Washington Post*, August 28, 2005.

Chun, Wendy Hui Kyong, and Thomas W. Keenan, eds. *New Media, Old Media: A History and Theory Reader*. New York: Routledge, 2006.

Cieply, Michael. "Risque Business: Video Outlets Face Mounting Pressure to Stop Carrying X-Rated Cassettes." *Wall Street Journal*, April 21, 1986, 80.

Cloud, John. "The YouTube Gurus: How a Couple of Regular Guys Built a Company That Changed the Way We See Ourselves." *Time*, December 25, 2006, 66–74.

Cockburn, Alexander. "Press Clips." *Village Voice*, March 7, 1974, 12.

———. "Press Clips." *Village Voice*, April 11, 1974, 11.

Cohen, Noam. "Which Videos Are Protected? Lawmakers Get a Lesson." *New York Times*, February 26, 2006.

Coleman, Mark. *Playback: From the Victrola to MP3; 100 Years of Music, Machines, and Money*. New York: Da Capo Press, 2004.

Columbia Broadcasting System, Inc., vs. Vanderbilt University, 6th Cir., Middle District of Tennessee, Civil Action No. 7336, 1973.

Committee on Intellectual Property Rights and the Emerging Information Infrastructure/National Research Council. *The Digital Dilemma: Intellectual Property in the Information Age*. Washington: National Academy Press, 2000.

Coombe, Rosemary J. *The Cultural Life of Intellectual Properties: Authorship, Appropriation, and the Law*. Durham: Duke University Press, 1998.

Corrigan, Timothy. *A Cinema without Walls: Movies and Culture after Vietnam*. New Brunswick, N.J.: Rutgers University Press, 1991.

Coviello, Peter. *Intimacy in America: Dreams of Affiliation in Antebellum Literature*. Minneapolis: University of Minnesota Press, 2005.

Cowan, Ruth Schwartz. *A Social History of American Technology*. New York: Oxford University Press, 1997.

Crowe, Jerry. "Despite All Odds, Sony's Beta Format Still Lives." *Los Angeles Times*, May 29, 1995, F1.

Cubitt, Sean. *Timeshift: On Video Culture*. New York: Routledge, 1991.

———. *Videography: Video Media as Art and Culture*. New York: St. Martin's Press, 1993.

Cummings, Neil, and Marysia Lewandowska. "From Enthusiasm to Creative Commons: Interview with Anthony Spira." In *The Archive*, ed. Charles Merewether. Cambridge: MIT Press, 2006.

Cusamano, Michael A., Yiorgos Mylondais, and Richard S. Rosenbloom. "Strategic Maneuvering and Mass-Market Dynamics: The Triumph of VHS over Beta." *Business History Review* 66, no. 1 (spring 1992): 51–94.

Cvetkovich, Ann. *An Archive of Feelings: Trauma, Sexuality, and Lesbian Public Cultures*. Durham: Duke University Press, 2003.

Davidson, Steven, and Gregory Lukow, eds. *The Administration of Television Newsfilm and Videotape Collections: A Curatorial Manual*. Los Angeles: American Film Institute, 1997.

Davis, Bob. "X-Rated Video Losing Share of Tape Sales." *Wall Street Journal*, January 19, 1984, 33.

de Certeau, Michel. *The Writing of History*. Trans. Tom Conley. New York: Columbia University Press, 1988.

Decherney, Peter. *Hollywood and the Culture Elite: How the Movies Became American*. New York: Columbia University Press, 2005.

———. "From Fair Use to Exemption." *Cinema Journal* 46, no. 2 (winter 2007): 120–27.

de la Peña, Carolyn. " 'Slow and Low Progress,' or Why American Studies Should Do Technology." *American Quarterly* 58, no. 3 (September 2006): 915–42.

Derrida, Jacques. *Archive Fever: A Freudian Impression*. Trans. Eric Prenowitz. Chicago: University of Chicago Press, 1996.

Dinsmore, Uma. "Chaos, Order, and Plastic Boxes: The Significance of Videotapes for the People Who Collect Them." In *The Television Studies Book*, ed. Christine Gregory and David Lusted, 315–26. New York: Arnold, 1998.

Doan, Richard K. "The Revolution Has Been Postponed." *TV Guide*, June 3, 1972, 6.

Dobrow, Julia R., ed. *Social and Cultural Aspects of VCR Use*. Hillsdale, N.J.: Lawrence Erlbaum Associates, 1990.

Dobuler, Sharon Lee. "Time-Life Sets New Video Club for Home Market." *Hollywood Reporter*, October 3, 1979, 1, 17.

"Does Uncle Want to Become Big Brother?" *Broadcasting*, December 8, 1969, 62.

Donovan, Robert J., and Ray Sherer. *Unsilent Revolution: Television News and American Public Life*. New York: Cambridge University Press, 1992.

"Dual-Deck VCR Hits Fast Forward." *Variety*, March 2, 1989, 1, 29.

Duggan, Lisa. *The Twilight of Equality? Neoliberalism, Cultural Politics, and the Attack on Democracy*. Boston: Beacon Press, 2003.

Duncombe, Stephen. *Notes from Underground: Zines and the Politics of Alternative Culture*. New York: Verso, 1997.

Dyer, Richard, "Judy Garland and Gay Men." In *Heavenly Bodies: Film Stars and Society*. New York: St. Martin's Press, 1986.

Echols, Alice. "Low-Impact Horror: Todd Haynes Talks about His New Movie, *Safe*." *LA Weekly*, June 30–July 6, 1995.

"Editor's Notes." *Quill*, February 1974, 3.

Edson, Lee. "Lone Inventor with a Genie Complex." *New York Times Magazine*, December 17, 1967, 29, 80–87.

Efron, Edith. *How CBS Tried to Kill a Book*. Los Angeles: Nash, 1972.

———. *The News Twisters*. Los Angeles: Nash, 1971.

Eisenberg, Evan. *The Recording Angel: Explorations in Phonography*. New York: McGraw-Hill, 1987.

Elkins, James. *The Object Stares Back: On the Nature of Seeing*. New York: Simon and Schuster, 1996.

Enticknap, Leo. "Have Digital Technologies Reopened the Lindgren/Langlois Debate?" *Spectator* 27, no. 1 (spring 2007): 10–20.

———. *Moving Image Technology: From Zoetrope to Digital*. London: Wallflower, 2005.

Epstein, Edward Jay. *News from Nowhere: Television and the News*. New York: Random House, 1973.

Ernst, Wolfgang. "Between Real Time and Memory on Demand: Reflections on/of Television." *South Atlantic Quarterly* 101, no. 3 (summer 2002): 625–37.

Evens, Aden. *Sound Ideas: Music, Machines, and Experience*. Minneapolis: University of Minnesota Press, 2005.

Fackler, Martin. "Toshiba Concedes Defeat in the DVD Battle." *New York Times*, Feruary 20, 2008.

Featherstone, Mike. "Archiving Cultures." *British Journal of Sociology* 51, no. 1 (January–March 2000): 161–84.

Febrikant, Geraldine. "The Curtain Drops on a Career at Sony." *New York Times*, December 6, 1995, D1.

Feuer, Jane. "The Concept of Live Television: Ontology as Ideology." In *Regarding Television*, ed. E. Ann Kaplan, 12–22. Los Angeles: American Film Institute, 1983.

"Film Biz Wary of Home Video Market: Interested, Yes, but Not Yet Ready to Plunge into It, Says Valenti at Tape Assn. Sesh." *Variety*, October 20, 1978, 1, 44.

Foner, Lenny. "Crypto Regs: Fear, Greed, and the Destruction of the Digital Commons." In *Global Currents: Media and Technology Now*, ed. Tasha G. Oren and Patrice Petro, 13–41. New Brunswick, N.J.: Rutgers University Press, 2000.

Foucault, Michel. *The Archaeology of Knowledge and the Discourse on Language*. Trans. A. M. Sheridan Smith. New York: Pantheon, 1972.

Freedman, Des. "Internet Transformations: 'Old' Media Resilience in the 'New Media' Revolution." In *Media and Cultural Theory*, ed. James Curran and David Morley, 275–90. New York: Routledge, 2006.

Friedberg, Anne. "The End of Cinema: Multimedia and Technological Change." In *Reinventing Film Studies*, ed. Christine Gledhill and Linda Williams, 438–52. New York: Oxford University Press, 2000.

Friedman, Ken. Foreword to *The Eternal Network: A Mail Art Anthology*, ed. Chuck Welch. Calgary: University of Calgary Press, 1995.

Friedman, Susan Stanford. "Women's Autobiographical Selves." In *The Private Self: Theory and Practice of Women's Autobiographical Writings*, ed. Shari Benstock, 34–62. Chapel Hill: University of North Carolina Press, 1988.

Friendly, Fred. *Due to Circumstances beyond Our Control . . .* New York: Random House, 1967.

Frith, Simon. *Sound Effects: Youth, Leisure, and the Politics of Rock 'n' Roll*. New York: Pantheon, 1981.

Fusco, Coco. "Regimes of Normalcy." *Afterimage* 16, no. 1 (summer 1988): 18.

Gaines, Jane M. *Contested Culture: The Image, the Voice, and the Law*. Chapel Hill: University of North Carolina Press, 1991.

Ganley, Gladys D., and Oswald H. Ganley. *Global Political Fallout: The First Decade of the VCR, 1976–1985*. Norwood, N.J.: Ablex Publishing; Cambridge: Harvard University Program on Information Resources Policy, 1987.

Garfield, Bob. "YouTube vs. Boob Tube." *Wired*, December 2006.

Garret, Diane. "VHS, 30, Dies of Loneliness." *Variety*, November 14, 2006.

Garvey, Ellen Gruber. "Scissoring and Scrapbooks: Nineteenth-Century Reading, Remaking, and Recirculating." In *New Media, 1740–1915*, ed. Lisa Gitelman and Geoffrey B. Pingree, 207–27. Cambridge: MIT Press, 2003.

Geist, William E. "About New York: The Invasion of the VCR Owner." *New York Times*, January 9, 1985, B3.

Gelman, Eric, Janet Huck, Connie Leslie, Carolyn Friday, Pamela Abramson, and Michael Reese. "The Video Revolution." *Newsweek*, August 6, 1984, 50–57.

Gerson, Robert E. "The Wonderful World of Home Video." Special advertising section. *Time*, October 30, 1978.

Gever, Martha. "The Feminism Factor: Video and Its Relation to Feminism." In *Illuminating Video: An Essential Guide to Video Art*, ed. Doug Hall and Sally Jo Fifer, 226–41. New York: Aperture, 1990.

———. “Pressure Points: Video in the Public Sphere.” *Art Journal* 45, no. 3 (autumn 1985): 238–43.

Gillespie, Tarleton. *Wired Shut: Copyright and the Shape of Digital Culture*. Cambridge: MIT Press, 2007.

Ginsburg, Jane C. “Copyright and Control over New Technologies of Dissemination.” *Columbia Law Review* 101, no. 7 (November 2001): 1613–47.

Gitelman, Lisa. *Always Already New: Media, History, and the Data of Culture*. Cambridge: MIT Press, 2006.

Gitelman, Lisa, and Geoffrey B. Pingree, eds. *New Media: 1740–1915*. Cambridge: MIT Press, 2003.

Gould, Jack. “Movies on Tape Expected in 1956.” *New York Times*, July 5, 1955, 31, 49.

Grant, Catherine, and Tahani Nadim. “ ‘Working Things Out Together’: The Joys of Bootlegging, Bartering, and Collectivity.” *Parachute*, July–September 2003, 52–57.

Gray, Ann. *Video Playtime: The Gendering of a Leisure Technology*. New York: Routledge, 1992.

Gray, Timothy E. “V-Chip: The Betamax of the ’90s.” *Broadcasting and Cable*, April 15, 1996, 30.

“The Greeks Have a Word for It—Spiro T. (for Tiger).” *Nashville Banner*, November 15, 1969, 1.

Green, Heather. “Waiting for the Payoff: The Video-Sharing Web Site Is a Runaway Success—Everywhere but on the Bottom Line.” *Business Week*, September 18, 2006, 56.

Green, Vanalyne. “Vertical Hold: A History of Women’s Video Art.” In *Feedback: The Video Data Bank Catalog of Video Art and Artist Interviews*, ed. Kate Horsfield and Lucas Hilderbrand, 23–29. Philadelphia, Pa.: Temple University Press, 2006.

Greenberg, Joshua M. *From Betamax to Blockbuster: Video Stores and the Invention of Movies on Video*. Cambridge: MIT Press, 2008.

Griffin, Nancy, and Kim Masters. *Hit and Run: How Jon Peters and Peter Guber Took Sony for a Ride in Hollywood*. New York: Simon and Schuster, 1996.

Grimsley, Weldon. “Local Man Aided TV Attack.” *Nashville Banner*, November 15, 1969, 1.

Grimstad, Kirsten, and Susan Rennie. *The New Woman’s Survival Sourcebook*. New York: Knopf, 1975.

Gross, Neil. “Betamax Wars All Over Again? Digital Videodisks Are on the Way—in Rival Formats.” *Business Week*, September 29, 1997, 35.

Hajdu, David. “Why Some of Your Favorite Movies Aren’t on Cassette Yet.” *TV Guide*, May 23, 1987, 39–40.

Halberstam, David. *The Powers That Be*. New York: Knopf, 1979.

Hall, Doug, and Sally Jo Fifer, eds. *Illuminating Video: An Essential Guide to Video Art*. New York: Aperture, 1990.

Hallin, Daniel C. *The "Uncensored War": The Media and Vietnam*. New York: Oxford University Press, 1986.

Hanhardt, John, ed. *Video Culture: A Critical Investigation*, Rochester, N.Y.: Visual Studies Workshop Press, 1986.

Harris, Kathryn. "Hollywood Battle over Videocassette Rentals." *Los Angeles Times*, October 17, 1982, F1.

Hawkins, Joan. *Cutting Edge: Art-Horror and the Horrific Avant-Garde*. Minneapolis: University of Minnesota Press, 2000.

———. "The Sleazy Pedigree of Todd Haynes." In *Sleaze Artists: Cinema at the Margins of Taste, Style, and Politics*, ed. Jeffrey Sconce. Durham: Duke University Press, 2007.

Haynes, Todd. *Three Screenplays*. New York: Grove Press, 2003.

Heilbroner, Robert L. "Do Machines Make History?" *Technology and Culture* 8 (July 1967): 335–45.

Heilbrun, Carolyn G. *Writing a Woman's Life*. New York: Ballantine Books, 1988.

Heimann, Jim, ed. *All-American Ads: 70s*. Cologne, Germany: Taschen, 2004.

———. *All-American Ads: 80s*. Cologne, Germany: Taschen, 2005.

Heins, Marjorie, and Tricia Beckles. *Will Fair Use Survive? Free Expression in the Age of Copyright Control*. Free Expression Policy Project report, 2005.

Helft, Miguel. "Google Takes Step on Video Copyrights." *New York Times*, October 16, 2007.

Henkin, David M. *The Postal Age: The Emergence of Modern Communications in Nineteenth-Century America*. Chicago: University of Chicago Press, 2006.

Henning, Michelle. "New Lamps for Old: Photography, Obsolescence, and Social Change." In *Residual Media*, ed. Charles R. Acland, 48–65. Minneapolis: University of Minnesota Press, 2007.

Herman, Bill D., and Oscar H. Gandy. "Catch 1201: A Legislative History and Content Analysis of the DMCA Exemptions Proceedings." *Cardozo Arts and Entertainment Law Journal* 24, no. 1 (2006): 121–90.

Herrmann, Gretchen M. "Women's Exchange in the U.S. Garage Sale: Giving Gifts and Creating Community." *Gender and Society* 10, no. 6 (December 1996): 703–28.

Heylin, Clinton. *Bootleg: The Secret History of the Other Recording Industry*. New York: St. Martin's Press, 1994.

Hickey, Dave. *Air Guitar: Essays on Art and Democracy*. Los Angeles: Art Issues Press, 1997.

Hilderbrand, Lucas. "The Clip Canon." *Film Quarterly* 61, no. 1 (fall 2007):51–53.

———. "Grainy Days and Mondays: *Superstar* and Bootleg Aesthetics." *Camera Obscura*, no. 57 (2004): 57–91.

———. "Retroactivism." *GLQ* 12, no. 2 (2006): 301–13.

Hillyer, Minette. "Sex in the Suburban: Porn, Home Movies, and the Live Action Performance of Love in *Pam and Tommy Lee: Hardcore and Uncensored.*" In *Porn Studies*, ed. Linda Williams, 50–76. Durham: Duke University Press, 2004.

Hirschkind, Charles. "The Ethics of Listening: Cassette-Sermon Audition in Contemporary Egypt." *American Ethnologist* 28, no. 3 (August 2001): 623–49.

Hoberman, J. "Valley of the Dolls." *Village Voice*, November 24, 1987, 67.

Horsfield, Kate, and Lucas Hilderbrand, eds. *Feedback: The Video Databank Catalog of Video Art and Artist Interviews.* Philadelphia: Temple University Press, 2006.

Hughes, Thomas P. "Technological Momentum." In *Does Technology Drive History? The Dilemma of Technological Determinism*, ed. Merritt Roe Smith and Leo Marx, 101–14. Cambridge: MIT Press, 1994.

Huntington, Samuel P. "The United States." In *The Crisis of Democracy: Report on the Governability of Democracies to the Trilateral Commission*, ed. Michel Crozier et al. New York: New York University Press, 1975.

Hyde, Lewis. *The Gift: Imagination and the Erotic Life of Property.* New York: Vintage, 1983.

Inglis, Andrew F. *Video Engineering.* New York: McGraw-Hill, 1993.

Jameson, Fredric. *Postmodernism; or, The Cultural Logic of Late Capitalism.* Durham: Duke University Press, 1991.

Jeffreys, June, and Allan Jeffreys. "Saturday Night with a Video Cassette." *TV Guide*, July 10, 1973, 12–13.

Jelinek, Estelle C. "Introduction: Women's Autobiography and the Male Tradition." In *Women's Autobiography: Essays in Criticism*, ed. Estelle C. Jelinek. Bloomington: Indiana University Press, 1980.

Jenkins, Henry. *Convergence Culture: When Old and New Media Collide.* New York: New York University Press, 2006.

———. *Textual Poachers: Television Fans and Participatory Culture.* New York: Routledge, 1992.

Johnson, Victoria E. *Heartland TV: Prime Time Television and the Struggle for U.S. Identity.* New York: New York University Press, 2007.

———. "Welcome Home? CBS, PAX-TV, and 'Heartland' Values in a Neo-network Era." In *The Television Studies Reader*, ed. Robert C. Allen and Annette Hill. New York: Routledge, 2004.

Jones, Steve. "The Cassette Underground." In *Cassette Mythos*, ed. Robin James. Brooklyn, N.Y.: Autonomedia, 1992.

Jones, Steven E. *Against Technology: From the Luddites to Neo-Luddism.* New York: Routledge, 2006.

Joseph, Miranda. *Against the Romance of Community.* Minneapolis: University of Minnesota Press, 2002.

Juhasz, Alexandra. "Our Auto-Bodies, Ourselves: Representing Real Women in Feminist Video." *Afterimage* 21, no. 7 (February 1994): 10–14.

Kadrey, Richard. "Director's Cuts." *World Art* 3 (1996): 64–65.

"Kastenmeier: Cable Will Not Be Shuffled out of Copyright Bill." *Broadcasting*, May 3, 1976.

Kearney, Mary Celeste. "Girls Make Movies." In *Youth Cultures: Texts, Images, and Identities*, ed. Kerry Mallan and Sharyn Pearce, 17–34. Westport, Conn.: Praeger, 2003.

Kellner, Douglas. "Television Research and Fair Use." In *Fair Use and Free Inquiry: Copyright Law and the New Media*, ed. John Shelton Lawrence and Bernard Timberg, 96–97. Norwood, N.J.: Ablex, 1980.

Kern, Edward. "A Good Revolution Goes on Sale: Cassette TV Lets the Viewer Pick His Own Show." *Life*, October 1970, 47–52.

Kies, Cosette. "The CBS-Vanderbilt Litigation: Taping the Evening News." In *Fair Use and Free Inquiry: Copyright Law and the New Media*, ed. John Shelton Lawrence and Bernard Timberg, 111–20. Norwood, N.J.: Ablex, 1980.

Killen, Andreas. *1973 Nervous Breakdown: Watergate, Warhol, and the Birth of Post-sixties America*. New York: Bloomsbury, 2006.

King, Susan. "Movies You Can't Just Rent." *Los Angeles Times*, March 21, 1994.

———. "A Trip down Celluloid Lane." *Los Angeles Times*, November 13, 1994, 92, 94.

Kirsner, Scott. "YouTube's New Tools Axe Illicit Video." *Variety*, October 15, 2007.

Klein, Melissa. "Duality and Redefinition: Young Feminism and the Alternative Music Community." In *Third Wave Agenda: Being Feminist, Doing Feminism*, ed. Leslie Heywood and Jennifer Drake, 207–25. Minneapolis: University of Minnesota Press, 1997.

Kleinhans, Chuck. "The Change from Film to Video Pornography: Implications for Analysis." In *Pornography: Film and Culture*, ed. Peter Lehman, 154–67. New Brunswick, N.J.: Rutgers University Press, 2006.

———. "Pamela Anderson and the Slippery Slope." In *The End of Cinema as We Know It: American Film in the Nineties*, ed. Jon Lewis, 287–99. New York: New York University Press, 2001.

Klinger, Barbara. *Beyond the Multiplex: Cinema, New Technologies, and the Home*. Berkeley: University of California Press, 2006.

Kluszczynski, Ryszard W. "From Film to Interactive Art: Transformations in Media Arts." In *MediaArtHistories*, ed. Oliver Grau. Cambridge: MIT Press, 2007.

Knoll, Steve. "Majors Mulling Rent-Sell Plans for Videocassettes." *Variety*, September 19, 1980, 1, 15.

Knowles, Jeffrey G. "The Debate over Sony-Betamax and Peer-to-Peer File Sharing: Will the Supreme Court Settle It in *MGM v. Grokster*?" *The Computer and Internet Lawyer* 22, no. 3 (March 2005): 1–10.

Koch, Stephen. "Andy Warhol, 1928–1987." *Artforum*, April 2003, 94.

Kolar-Panov, Dona. *Video, War, and the Diasporic Imagination*. New York: Routledge, 1997.

Kompare, Derek. *Rerun Nation: How Repeats Invented American Television*. New York: Routledge, 2005.

Kramp, Leif. "The Changing Role of Television in the Museum." *Spectator* 27, no. 1 (2007): 48–57.

Krapp, Peter. *Déja Vu: Aberrations of Cultural Memory*. Minneapolis: University of Minnesota Press, 2004.

Krauss, Rosalind. "Video: The Aesthetics of Narcissism" (1978). In *Video Culture: A Critical Investigation*, ed. John Hanhardt, 179–91. Rochester, N.Y.: Visual Studies Workshop Press, 1986.

Kronke, David. "Filmland's New Ploy: 'Sell-Through.' " *Los Angeles Times*, December 19, 1994, 1.

Kruger, Barbara. "Into Thin Air." *Artforum*, December 1987, 108.

Lachenbruch, David. "The Big 'But' That Clouds the Future." *TV Guide*, January 23, 1971, 23–29.

———. "The Great Time-Shift Machine Experiment." *TV Guide*, April 9, 1977, 5.

———. "Sorry, We Missed It." *TV Guide*, July 11, 1964, 12–14.

———. "The Videotape Era . . . May Be at Hand." *TV Guide*, January 16, 1971, 6–10.

Lafferty, William. " 'A New Era in TV Programming' Becomes 'Business as Usual': Videotape Technology, Local Stations, and Network Power, 1957–1961." *Quarterly Review of Film and Video* 16, nos. 3–4 (1999): 405–19.

Landro, Laura. "Movie Studios' Cut in Videocassette Prices Stir Battle with Retailers on Video Rentals." *Wall Street Journal*, September 23, 1983, 33.

Lane, Jim. *The Autobiographical Documentary in America*. Madison: University of Wisconsin Press, 2002.

Lardner, James. *Fast Forward: Hollywood, the Japanese, and the VCR Wars*. New York: Norton, 1987.

Larkin, Brian. "Degraded Images, Distorted Sounds: Nigerian Video and the Infrastructure of Piracy." *Public Culture* 16, no. 2 (May 2004): 289–314.

———. "Piracy, Infrastructure, and the Rise of a Nigerian Video Industry." In *Global Currents: Media and Technology Now*, ed. Tasha G. Oren and Patrice Petro, 159–70. New Brunswick, N.J.: Rutgers University Press, 2000.

Lasch, Christopher. "The Politics of Nostalgia." *Harper's*, November 1984, 65–70.

Lastra, James. *Sound Technology and American Cinema*. New York: Columbia University Press, 2000.

Learmonth, Michael. "Viacom Sues YouTube, Google." *Variety*, March 13, 2007.

Lesage, Julia. "Women's Fragmented Consciousness in Feminist Experimental Autobiographical Video." In *Feminism and Documentary*, ed. Diane Waldman and Janet Walker, 309–38. Minneapolis: University of Minnesota Press, 1999.

Lessig, Lawrence. *Code and Other Laws of Cyberspace*. New York: Basic Books, 1999.
———. *Code: Version 2.0*. New York: Basic Books, 2006.
———. "Foreword: An Ideal Lawyer-Citizen." In *Freedom of Expression: Resistance and Repression in the Age of Intellectual Property*, by Kembrew McLeod, ix–x. Minneapolis: University of Minnesota Press, 2007.
———. *Free Culture: How Big Media Uses Technology and the Law to Lock Down Culture and Control Creativity*. New York: Penguin, 2004.
———. *The Future of Ideas: The Fate of the Commons in a Connected World*. New York: Vintage, 2002.
Levy, Mark, ed. *The VCR Age: Home Video and Mass Communication*. Newbury Park, Calif.: Sage, 1989.
Levy, Mark R., and Sven Windahl. "Audience Activity and Gratifications." *Communication Research* 11, no. 1 (1984): 51–78.
Lichtman, Doug. "The Case against YouTube: Technology Has to Have Room to Grow, but Not at All Costs." *Los Angeles Times*, March 20, 2007.
Lieberman, Rhonda. "Todd Haynes's *Superstar*." *Artforum*, April 2003, 93.
Liebman, Roy I. "Brief of Media Studies Professors as Amici Curiae in Support of Respondents." *MGM v. Grokster*, filed before the Supreme Court, March 2005.
Lim, Dennis. "Instant Nostalgia? Let's Go to the Videotape." *New York Times*, January 27, 2008.
Linck, David. "Theatres Get a Crack at the Booming Video Rental Business." *Box Office*, July 15, 1982, 16–17.
Lindsey, Robert. "Sex Films Find Big Market in Home Video." *New York Times*, April 5, 1979, B15.
Lipsitz, George. *Time Passages: Collective Memory and American Popular Culture*. Minneapolis: University of Minnesota Press, 1990.
Litman, Jessica. "Copyright and Personal Copying: *Sony v. Universal City Studios* Twenty-one Years Later." The Law, Technology, and the Arts Symposium, Case Western Reserve University School of Law, February 25, 2005, http://www.law.wayne.edu/litman/papers (April 29, 2006).
———. *Digital Copyright: Protecting Intellectual Property on the Internet*. Amherst, N.Y.: Prometheus, 2001.
———. "The Exclusive Right to Read." *Cardozo Arts and Entertainment Law Journal* 13 (1994), http://www.law.wayne.edu/litman/papers (April 29, 2006).
———. "Lawful Personal Use." *Texas Law Review* 85 (2007): 1871–1920.
———. "Sharing and Stealing." *Hastings Communication and Entertainment Law Journal* 27 (2004).
———. "The Story of *Sony v. Universal Studios*: Mary Poppins Meets the Boston Strangler." In *Intellectual Property Stories*, ed. Jane C. Ginsburg and Rochelle C. Dreyfuss. Westbury, N.Y.: Foundation Press, 2005.

Lord, M. G. *Forever Barbie: The Unauthorized Biography of a Real Doll*. New York: Morrow, 1994.

Lunney, Glynn S., Jr. "The Death of Copyright: Digital Technology, Private Copying, and the Digital Millennium Copyright Act." *Virginia Law Review* 87, no. 5 (September 2001): 813–920.

Lynch, John. "Vanderbilt Television News Archive." *Historical Journal of Film, Radio, and Television* 16, no. 1 (1996): 81–83.

MacGregor, Jeff. "Copying Copies: The Sad Slide from Stardom to Celebrity." *New York Times*, March 19, 2000, Arts and Leisure, 1.

MacNeil, Robert. *The People Machine: The Influence of Television on American Politics*. New York: Harper and Row, 1968.

"Majors Plan to Enter Video Rental Biz." *Variety*, September 17, 1980, 55.

Mann, Sarah Ziebell. "The Evolution of Moving Image Preservation." *Moving Image* 1, no. 2 (fall 2001): 1–20.

Manuel, Peter. *Cassette Culture: Popular Music and Technology in North India*. Chicago: University of Chicago Press, 1993.

Marks, Laura U. *The Skin of the Film: Intercultural Cinema, Embodiment, and the Senses*. Durham: Duke University Press, 2000.

———. *Touch: Sensuous Theory and Multisensory Media*. Minneapolis: University of Minnesota Press, 2002.

"Markup of Copyright." *Television Digest* 16, no. 15 (April 12, 1976): 5.

Marlow, Eugene, and Eugene Secunda. *Shifting Time and Space: The Story of Videotape*. New York: Praeger, 1991.

Marshall, Lee. *Bootlegging: Romanticism and Copyright in the Music Industry*. London: Sage, 2005.

Martin, Jeff. "The Dawn of Tape: Transmission Device as Preservation Medium." *Moving Image* 5, no. 1 (spring 2005): 45–66.

Marvin, Carolyn. *When Old Technologies Were New: Thinking about Electric Communication in the Late Nineteenth Century*. New York: Oxford University Press, 1988.

Matthews, Jack. "Automated Video Tellers Take Movies to Markets." *Los Angeles Times*, n.d. [1986].

Mauss, Marcel. *The Gift: The Form and Reason for Exchange in Archaic Societies*. New York: Norton, 1967.

Mayes, Tessa. "Technostalgia: Betamax." *Guardian*, June 16, 1994.

McDonald, Paul. *Video and DVD Industries*. London: BFI, 2007.

McDonough, Yona Zeldis, ed. *The Barbie Chronicles*. New York: Touchstone, 1999.

McGann, Nadine L. "A Kiss Is Not a Kiss: An Interview with John Greyson." *Afterimage* 19, no. 4 (January 1992): 10–13.

McLeod, Kembrew. *Freedom of Expression®: Overzealous Copyright Bozos and Other Enemies of Creativity*. New York: Doubleday, 2005.

McLuhan, Marshall. *Understanding Media: The Extensions of Man* (1964). Cambridge: MIT Press, 1994.
McManis, Sam. "It's You. It's YouTube." *Sacramento Bee*, March 14, 2006.
McMurria, John. "The YouTube Community." *Flow* 5, no. 2 (2006).
McNary, Dave. "AFI Announces 'Moments of Significance' Awards." *Variety*, December 27, 2006.
Meikle, Jeffrey L. *American Plastic: A Cultural History*. New Brunswick, N.J.: Rutgers University Press, 1995.
Melanson, James. "Go-Video Says It's Ready to Intro Two-Deck Vidtape Machine, Tangle with MPAA." *Variety*, December 18, 1986, 1, 41.
Mellencamp, Patricia. "Video and the Counterculture." In *Global Television*, ed. Cynthia Schneider and Brian Wallis, 199–224. Cambridge: MIT Press, 1988.
Merewether, Charles, ed. *The Archive*. Cambridge: MIT Press, 2006.
Mertha, Andrew. *The Politics of Piracy: Intellectual Property in Contemporary China*. Ithaca, N.Y.: Cornell University Press, 2005.
Metro-Goldwyn-Mayer Studios, Inc., et al., v. Grokster, Ltd., et al (04-0480), 545 U.S. 125 S. Ct. 2764 (2005).
Metz, Christian. *The Imaginary Signifier: Psychoanalysis and Cinema*. Trans. Celia Britton, Annwyl Williams, Ben Brewster, and Alfred Guzzetti. Bloomington: Indiana University Press, 1982.
Meyer, Gerald. "TV Cassettes: A New Frontier for Pioneers and Pirates." *Bulletin, Copyright Society of the U.S.A.* 19, no. 1 (1971): 16–47.
Michie, Larry. "GOP Marks TV News Laos-Y: Senators Screen Tapes, Scream." *Variety*, March 17, 1971, 1.
Milano, Susan. "Women's Media: 9 Cities Share Videoletters." *TeleVISIONS Magazine* 3, no. 4 (October–November 1975): 25.
Millard, Andre. *America on Record: A History of Recorded Sound*. New York: Cambridge University Press, 1995.
Miller, Toby, Nitin Govil, John McMurria, and Richard Maxwell. *Global Hollywood*. London: British Film Institute, 2001.
Mitchell, Barry. "The New American Library: What Can You Say about a Culture Dedicated to Preserving 'My Mother, the Car'?" *New York Daily News*, July 13, 1980.
Mitchell, Dan. "YouTube's Favorite Clips." *New York Times*, April 7, 2007.
Moore, Thurston, ed. *Mix Tape: The Art of Cassette Culture*. New York: Universe/Rizzoli, 2004.
Moran, James M. *There's No Place Like Home Video*. Minneapolis: University of Minnesota Press, 2002.
Morley, David. "Changing Paradigms in Audience Studies." In *Remote Control: Television, Audiences, and Cultural Power*, ed. Ellen Seiter, Hans Borchers, Gabriele Kreutzner, and Eva-Maria Warth, 16–43. New York: Routledge, 1991.

Morton, David. *Off the Record: The Technology and Culture of Sound Recording in America*. New Brunswick, N.J.: Rutgers University Press, 2000.
Mulvey, Laura. "Visual Pleasure and Narrative Cinema." *Screen* 16, no. 3 (1975): 6–18.
"National Archives Is Given the Right to CBS TV Shows." *Wall Street Journal*, April 3, 1974, 16.
"National Archives, via Defense Dept., to Tape CBS News." *Variety*, April 10, 1974, 38.
Neumann, Mark, and Timothy A. Simpson. "Smuggled Sound: Bootleg Recording and the Pursuit of Popular Memory." *Symbolic Interaction* 20, no. 4 (1997): 319–41.
"News Briefs." *Broadcasting*, April 12, 1976, n.p.
Newitz, Annalee. "Television Is History." *AlterNet*, November 1, 2006, www.alternet.org (accessed November 2, 2006).
Nichols, Peter M. "Movie Rentals Fade, Forcing an Industry to Change Its Focus." *New York Times*, May 6, 1990, 1.
Nimmo, Dan, and James E. Combs. *Nightly Horrors: Crisis Coverage by Television Network News*. Knoxville: University of Tennessee Press, 1985.
Olalquiaga, Celeste. *The Artificial Kingdom: The Kitsch Experience*. Minneapolis: University of Minnesota Press, 2002.
Oler, Harriet L. "Copyright Law and the Fair Use of Visual Images." In *Fair Use and Free Inquiry: Copyright Law and the New Media*, ed. John Shelton Lawrence and Bernard Timberg. Norwood, N.J.: Ablex, 1980.
Olney, James. "Autobiography and the Cultural Moment." In *Autobiography: Essays Theoretical and Critical*, ed. James Olney, 3–27. Princeton, N.J.: Princeton University Press, 1980.
O'Regan, Tom. "From Piracy to Sovereignty: International VCR Trends." *Continuum* 4, no. 2 (1991): accessed online at www.mcc.murdoch.edu.au/ReadingRoom/4.2/oregon.html.
Oudes, Bruce, ed. *From: The President: Richard Nixon's Secret Files*. New York: Harper and Row, 1989.
Paley, William S. *As It Happened: A Memoir*. Garden City, N.Y.: Doubleday, 1979.
Palmer, Shelly. *Television Disrupted: The Transition from Network to Networked TV*. Burlington, Mass.: Focal Press, 2006.
Pang, Laikwan. "Piracy/Privacy: The Despair of Cinema and Collectivity in China." *Boundary 2* 31, no. 3 (2004): 101–24.
Parks, Lisa. "Falling Apart: Electronics Salvaging and the Global Media Economy." In *Residual Media*, ed. Charles R. Acland, 32–47. Minneapolis: University of Minnesota Press, 2007.
———. "Flexible Microcasting: Gender, Generation, and Television-Internet Convergence." In *Television after TV: Essays on a Medium in Transition*, ed. Lynn Spigel and Jan Olsson, 133–56. Durham: Duke University Press, 2004.

Pastorek, Whitney. "Buried Treasure." *Entertainment Weekly*, December 3, 2004, 46.

Patry, William F. "Copyright Law and Practice." Bureau of National Affairs, 2000, http://digital-law-online.info/patry/patry8.html#_ftn312 (accessed May 30, 2005).

Patry, William F., and Richard A. Posner. "Fair Use and Statutory Reform in the Wake of *Eldred*." *California Law Review* 92 (2004): 1639–61.

Patterson, L. Ray. *Copyright in Historical Perspective*. Nashville: Vanderbilt University Press, 1968.

Patterson, L. Ray, and Stanley W. Lindberg. *The Nature of Copyright: A Law of Users' Rights*. Athens: University of Georgia Press, 1991.

Patterson, Zabet. "Going On-Line: Consuming Pornography in the Digital Era." In *Porn Studies*, ed. Linda Williams, 104–24. Durham: Duke University Press, 2004.

"Person of the Year: You." *Time*, December 25, 2006.

Peters, Jeremy W. "Viacom Sues Google over YouTube Video Clips." *New York Times*, March 14, 2007.

Peters, John Durham. *Speaking into the Air: A History of the Idea of Communication*. Chicago: University of Chicago Press, 1999.

Petro, Patrice. *Aftershocks of the New: Feminism and Film History*. New Brunswick, N.J.: Rutgers University Press, 2002.

Phelan, Peggy, Hans Ulrich Obrist, and Elisabeth Bronfen. *Pipilotti Rist*. New York: Phaidon, 2001.

"Phoenix Company Introducing Portavideo Rental Concept." *Variety*, October 29, 1982, 14.

Pietz, William. "Fetishism and Materialism: The Limits of Theory in Marx." In *Fetishism as Cultural Discourse*, ed. Emily Apter and William Pietz, 119–51. Ithaca, N.Y.: Cornell University Press, 1993.

Pollack, Andrew. "A Battle over Video Cassettes: Millions in Tape Rentals Are at Stake." *New York Times*, December 11, 1981, D1, D15.

Price, Jonathan. *Video-Visions: A Medium Discovers Itself*. New York: Plume, 1977.

Pride, Richard A. "The Medium versus the Message: The Issue of Access to TV News." *P.S.* 9, no. 3 (summer 1976): 270–73.

Prince, Stephen. *A New Pot of Gold: Hollywood under the Electronic Rainbow, 1980–1989*. Berkeley: University of California Press, 2000.

Produce, A. "A Short History of the Cassette." In *Cassette Mythos*, ed. Robin James. Brooklyn, N.Y.: Autonomedia, 1992.

Puchalski, Steve. Review of *Superstar: The Karen Carpenter Story*. *Shock Cinema* no. 6 (1994):9.

Quart, Alissa. "Cultural Sabotage Waged in Cyberspace." *New York Times*, August 17, 2000, G10.

Rabinovitz, Lauren, and Abraham Geil, eds. *Memory Bytes: History, Technology, and Digital Culture*. Durham: Duke University Press, 2004.

Rand, Erika. *Barbie's Queer Accessories*. Durham: Duke University Press, 1995.

Rappaport, Mark. "Mark Rappaport's Notes on *Rock Hudson's Home Movies*." *Film Quarterly* 49, no. 4 (summer 1996): 16–22.

"Rare Vid Recorder Donated to UCLA." *Hollywood Reporter*, April 24, 1987.

Rawley-Saldich, Anne. "Access to Television's Past." *Columbia Journalism Review* (November–December 1976): 46–48.

Red Lion Broadcasting Co. v. FCC, 395 U.S. 367, 390 (1969).

Renov, Michael. *The Subject of Documentary*. Minneapolis: University of Minnesota Press, 2005.

———. "Toward a Poetics of Documentary." In *Theorizing Documentary*, ed. Michael Renov, 12–36. New York: Routledge, 1993.

Renov, Michael, and Erika Suderberg, eds. *Resolutions: Contemporary Video Practices*. Minneapolis: University of Minnesota Press, 1996.

Richtel, Matt, and Eric A. Taub. "Taps for HD DVD as Wal-Mart Backs Blu-Ray." *New York Times*, February 16, 2008.

Report of the Librarian of Congress: Television and Video Preservation 1997. Washington: Library of Congress, 1997.

Roberts, Martin. *Video Cassettes: The Systems, the Market, the Future*. Beverly Hills, Calif.: Martin Roberts and Associates, 1970.

Robinson, David. *The Video Primer: Equipment, Production, and Concepts*. 3rd ed. New York: Perigee, 1983.

Rogers, Kenneth. "LA Freewaves' *Too Much Freedom?* Alternative Video and Internet Distribution." *Spectator* 27, no. 1 (spring 2007): 58–68.

Rosenberg, Jessica, and Gitana Garofalo. "Riot Grrrl: Revolutions from Within." *Signs* 23, no. 3 (1998): 809–41.

Ross, Chuck. "Group 1, Diebold Debut Vid Vending." *Hollywood Reporter*, October 24, 1986, 1, 67.

Rush, Michael. *Video Art*, rev. ed. New York: Thames and Hudson, 2007.

Russell, Catherine. *Experimental Ethnography: The Work of Film in the Age of Video*. Durham: Duke University Press, 1999.

Russell, Vanessa. "Make Me a Celebrity: Celebrity Exercise Videos and the Origins of Makeover Television." In *Makeover Television: Realities Remodeled*, ed. Dana Heller, 67–78. New York: I. B. Tauris, 2007.

Sargent, Wayne. "CBS v. Vanderbilt Case Is a Lulu." *Nashville Banner*, February 11, 1974, 9.

Scarry, Elaine. *On Beauty and Being Just*. Princeton: Princeton University Press, 2001.

Schorr, Daniel. *Clearing the Air*. Boston: Houghton Mifflin, 1977.

Schrage, Michael. "Popcorn and Movies: One Stop at 7-Eleven." *Washington Post*, January 21, 1986, E1.

Schreibman, Fay C. "A Succinct History of American Television Archives." *Film and History* 21, nos. 2–3 (May–September 1991): 89–95.

———. "Television News Archives: A Guide to Major Collections." In *Television Network News: Issues in Content Research*, ed. William Adams and Fay Schreibman, 104–6. Washington: George Washington University, 1978.

Schulman, Bruce. *The Seventies: The Great Shift in American Culture, Society, and Politics*. New York: Da Capo, 2002.

Scully, Malcolm G. "CBS, Vanderbilt Battle over Taping News." *Chronicle of Higher Education*, September 30, 1974, 11.

Seideman, Tony. "Explosion in Number of Titles Available." *Billboard*, January 11, 1986, 40A–41.

Seiter, Ellen. *Television and New Media Audiences*. New York: Oxford University Press, 1999.

Shaw, D. L., and M. E. McCombs. *The Emergence of American Political Issues: The Agenda-Setting Function of the Press*. St. Paul, Minn.: West Publishing, 1971.

"She's Way Sassy." *Sassy*, April 1996, 24.

Simon, Sunka. *Mail-Orders: The Fiction of Letters in Postmodern Culture*. Albany: State University of New York Press, 2002.

Simpson, Paul C., with Patricia G. Lane and F. Lynne Bachleda. *Network Television News: Conviction, Controversy, and a Point of View*. Franklin, Tenn.: Legacy Communications, 1995.

Sippel, John. "Cassette Vending Machines Tested." *Billboard*, May 4, 1985.

Slade, Giles. *Made to Break: Technology and Obsolescence in America*. Cambridge: Harvard University Press, 2006.

Small, William. *To Kill a Messenger: Television News and the Real World*. New York: Hastings House, 1970.

Smith, Adam. "In Loving Memory: R.I.P. VHS." *Empire*, April 2004, 107–15.

Smith, Jen. "Doin' It for the Ladies—Youth Feminism: Cultural Productions/Cultural Activism." In *Third Wave Agenda: Being Feminist, Doing Feminism*, ed. Leslie Heywood and Jennifer Drake, 226–38. Minneapolis: University of Minnesota Press, 1997.

Smith, Merritt Roe. "Technological Determinism in American Culture." In *Does Technology Drive History? The Dilemma of Technological Determinism*, ed. Merritt Roe Smith and Leo Marx, 1–36. Cambridge: MIT Press, 1994.

Sobchack, Vivian. "Nostalgia for a Digital Object: Regrets on the Quickening of QuickTime." *Millennium Film Journal*, no. 34 (fall 1999): 4–23.

Society for Cinema Studies Task Force on Film Integrity. "Statement on the Use of Video in the Classroom." *Cinema Journal* 30, no. 4 (summer 1991): 3–6.

Sony Corporation of America, Inc., v. Universal City Studios, Inc., 464 U.S. 417 (1984).

Sorkin, Andrew Ross, and Peter Edmonston. "Google Is Said to Set Sights on YouTube." *New York Times*, October 7, 2006.

"Southern Eye Fixed on the Networks." *Broadcasting*, October 7, 1968, 52.

Spielmann, Yvonne. *Video: The Reflexive Medium*. Trans. Anja Welle and Stan Jones. Cambridge: MIT Press, 2008.

Spigel, Lynn. "From the Dark Ages to the Golden Age: Women's Memories and Television Reruns." In *Welcome to the Dreamhouse: Popular Media and Postwar Suburbs*, 357–80. Durham: Duke University Press, 2001.

———. *Make Room for TV*. Chicago: University of Chicago Press, 1992.

Spigel, Lynn, and Henry Jenkins. "Same Bat Channel, Different Bat Times: Mass Culture and Popular Memory." In *The Many Lives of the Batman: Critical Approaches to a Superhero and His Media*, ed. Roberta E. Pearson and William Uricchio, 117–46. New York: Routledge, 1991.

Srisombati, Sirida. "Always Almost: Thai Television and Not-Quite Transnationalism." Manuscript.

Stallybrass, Peter. "Marx's Coat." In *Border Fetishisms: Material Objects in Unstable Spaces*, ed. Patricia Spyer, 183–207. New York: Routledge, 1998.

Stanton, Domna C. "Autogynography: Is the Subject Different?" In *The Female Autograph: Theory and Practice of Autobiography from the Tenth to the Twentieth Century*, ed. Domna C. Stanton, 3–20. Chicago: University of Chicago Press, 1984.

Starbuck, B. W. "Bootleg." *American Speech* 6, no. 2 (December 1930): 156.

Steedman, Carolyn. *Dust: The Archive and Cultural History*. New Brunswick, N.J.: Rutgers University Press, 2002.

Stephens, Chuck. "Gentlemen Prefer Haynes: Of Dolls, Dioramas, and Disease; Todd Haynes' *Safe* Passage." *Film Comment*, July–August 1995, 76–81.

Sterne, Jonathan. *The Audible Past: Cultural Origins of Sound Reproduction*. Durham: Duke University Press, 2003.

———. "The MP3 as Cultural Artifact." *New Media and Society* 8, no. 5 (2006): 825–42.

———. "Out with the Trash: On the Future of New Media." In *Residual Media*, ed. Charles R. Acland, 16–31. Minneapolis: University of Minnesota Press, 2007.

Stewart, Susan. *On Longing: Narratives of the Miniature, the Gigantic, the Souvenir, the Collection*. Durham: Duke University Press, 1993.

Stille, Alexander. *The Future of the Past*. New York: Farrar, Straus and Giroux, 2002.

Stine, Scott Aaron, and Michael von Sacher-Masoch. *The Trashfiend's Guide to Collecting Videotapes*. Seattle, Wash.: Stigmata Press, 2003.

Straayer, Chris. "I Say I Am: Feminist Performance Video in the '70s." *Afterimage* 13, no. 4 (November 1985): 8–12.

Streeter, Thomas. *Selling the Air: A Critique of the Policy of Commercial Broadcasting in the United States*. Chicago: University of Chicago Press, 1996.

Sturken, Marita. "Paradox in the Evolution of an Art Form: Great Expectations and the Making of a History." In *Illuminating Video: An Essential Guide to Video Art*, ed. Doug Hall and Sally Jo Fifer, 101–21. New York: Aperture, 1990.

———. "The Politics of Video Memory: Electronic Erasures and Inscriptions." In *Resolutions: Contemporary Video Practices*, ed. Michael Renov and Erika Suderberg, 1–12. Minneapolis: University of Minnesota Press, 1996.

———. *Tangled Memories: The Vietnam War, the AIDS Epidemic, and the Politics of Remembering*. Berkeley: University of California Press, 1997.

Sturken, Marita, Douglas Thomas, and Sandra J. Ball-Rokeach, eds. *Technological Visions: The Hopes and Fears That Shape New Technologies*. Philadelphia, Pa.: Temple University Press, 2004.

Sugaya, Hiroshi. "Consumer Video Recorders." In *Magnetic Recording: The First 100 Years*, ed. Eric D. Daniel et al., 182–200. New York: Institute of Electrical and Electronics Engineers Press, 1999.

Sweeting, Paul. "Sell-Through or Rental? The Rules Have Changed." *Variety*, October 5, 1998, 14.

Taninecz, George. "Famous Flops." *Industry Week*, December 16, 1996, 46.

Tannock, Stuart. "Nostalgia Critique." *Cultural Studies* 9, no. 3 (1995): 453–64.

Tanselle, G. Thomas. *Literature and Artifacts*. Charlottesville: Bibliographic Society of the University of Virginia, 1998.

Tashiro, Charles. "The Contradictions of Video Collecting." *Film Quarterly* 50, no. 2 (winter 1996): 11–18.

———. "Videophilia: What Happens When You Wait for It on Video." *Film Quarterly* 45, no. 1 (autumn 1991): 7–17.

Taylor, Clark. "Mail Art." *Los Angeles Times*, December 2, 1984, W26.

Taylor, Diana. *The Archive and the Repertoire*. Durham: Duke University Press, 2003.

"Television Comes Under Fire." *U.S. News and World Report*, July 15, 1968, 37.

Thorburn, David, and Henry Jenkins, eds. *Rethinking Media Change: The Aesthetics of Transition*. Cambridge: MIT Press, 1999.

Trope, Ronald L., and Greg E. Upchurch. " 'Staple Article': In Defense of Betamax and Its Progeny." *Business Lawyer*, November 2004, 417–37.

Trotsky, Judith. "The Networks Try to Keep History on the Shelf." *Wall Street Journal*, March 7, 1980, 17.

Ubois, Jeff. "New Approaches to Television Archiving." *First Monday* 10, no. 3 (March 2005), www.firstmonday.org (accessed November 30, 2006).

Utz, Peter. *The Complete Home Video Book*. Englewood Cliffs, N.J.: Prentice-Hall, 1983.

Vaidhyanathan, Siva. *The Anarchist in the Library: How the Clash between Freedom and Control Is Leaving Cyberspace and Entering the Real World*. New York: Basic Books, 2004.

———. *Copyrights and Copywrongs: The Rise of Intellectual Property and How It Threatens Creativity*. New York: New York University Press, 2003.

"Valenti Pledges All-Out Fight against Double-Cassette VCR." *Variety*, January 31, 1985, 1, 19.

Van Der Linden, Frank. "CBS vs. the Vandy News Archive." *Nashville Banner*, April 21, 1976.

"Vanderbilt News Tapes Hit in New Attack by CBS' Taylor." *Variety*, February 27, 1974, 48.

"Vanderbilt TV News Tapes Are Hit by CBS Copyright Suit." *Variety*, December 26, 1973, 22.

"VCRs: Santa's Hottest Gift; The Magic Box That Is Creating a Video Revolution." *Time*, December 24, 1984.

"VHS Video Tapes." *Consumer Reports*, November 1984, 658–61.

"Video Rental Rooms Fought." *New York Times*, August 20, 1984, D1.

"The Video Revolution: How the VCR Is Changing What You Watch." *Newsweek*, August 6, 1984.

"Video Tapes." *Consumer Reports*, November 1986, 729–32.

"Videotapes." *Consumer Reports*, September 1988, 583–86.

"Videotapes." *Consumer Reports*, September 1990, 584–85.

"Videotapes: A Crowded Field." *New York Times*, February 13, 1982, 31.

"Vidtape Machines Boom but the Only Feature Is Porno." *Variety*, November 23, 1977, 2, 122.

Villarejo, Amy. *Lesbian Rule: Cultural Criticism and the Value of Desire*. Durham: Duke University Press, 2003.

Vogelstein, Fred. Interview with Eric Schmidt, *Wired*, May 2007.

Wallenstein, Andrew. "Catch YouTube If You Can." *Hollywood Reporter*, March 21, 2006.

Wang, Shujen. *Framing Piracy: Globalization and Film Distribution in Greater China*. Lanham, Md.: Rowman and Littlefield, 2003.

———. "Recontextualizing Copyright: Piracy, Hollywood, the State, and Globalization." *Cinema Journal* 43, no. 1 (fall 2003): 25–43.

Warner, Peter. "Home Videocassette Distrib'n Business Labeled 'Disaster.'" *Hollywood Reporter*, March 13, 1980.

———. "Top Vid-Cassettes Skewed toward Nonpornographic." *Hollywood Reporter*, June 5, 1979.

Wasko, Janet. *Hollywood in the Information Age*. Austin: University of Texas Press, 1995.

Wasser, Frederick. *Veni, Vidi, Video: The Hollywood Empire and the VCR*. Austin: University of Texas Press, 2001.

Waugh, Thomas. *Out/Lines: Underground Gay Graphics from before Stonewall*. Vancouver: Arsenal Pulp, 2002.

Whitburn, Joel. *The Billboard Book of Top 40 Hits*. 7th ed. New York: Billboard Books, 2000.
White, Michele. *The Body and the Screen: Theories of Internet Spectatorship*. Cambridge: MIT Press, 2006.
Williams, Raymond. *Marxism and Literature*. New York: Oxford University Press, 1977.
———. *Television: Technology and Cultural Form*. New York: Routledge, 2003.
Willinsky, John. *The Access Principle: The Case for Open Access to Research and Scholarship*. Cambridge: MIT Press, 2006.
Winston, Brian. *Media, Technology, and Society: A History; From the Telegraph to the Internet*. New York: Routledge, 1998.
Witcover, Jules. *White Knight: The Rise of Spiro Agnew*. New York: Random House, 1972.
Wollen, Peter. "Godard and Counter-Cinema: *Vent d'Est*." In *Readings and Writings: Semiotic Counter-Strategies*. New York: Verso, 1982.
Yar, Majid. "The Global 'Epidemic' of Movie 'Piracy': Crime-Wave or Social Construction?" *Media, Culture and Society* 27, no. 5 (2005): 677–96.
Young, Robert. "Get Your Red-Hot Cassettes-to-Go, Next to the TV Dinners." *Los Angeles Herald-Examiner*, April 19, 1986, B1.
Youngblood, Gene. *Expanded Cinema*. New York: E. P. Dutton, 1970.
Zacks, Richard. "Are You Renting? Are You Buying? Taping, Maybe?" *Daily News*, November 8, 1987, 28.
Zak, Albin J., III. *The Poetics of Rock: Cutting Tracks, Making Records*. Berkeley: University of California Press, 2001.
Zielinski, Siegfried. *Audiovisions: Cinema and Television as Entr'actes in History*. Trans. Gloria Custance. Amsterdam: University of Amsterdam Press, 1999.
———. *Deep Time of the Media: Toward an Archaeology of Hearing and Seeing by Technical Means*. Trans. Gloria Custance. Cambridge: MIT Press, 2006.
———, ed. *Video: Apparat/Medium, Kunst, Kultur*. Frankfurt am Main: Peter Lang, 1992.
Zimmermann, Patricia R. *States of Emergency: Documentaries, Wars, Democracies*. Minneapolis: University of Minnesota Press, 2000.
———. *Reel Families: A Social History of Amateur Film*. Bloomington: Indiana University Press, 1995.

Index

Lucas Hilderbrand is an assistant professor of film and media studies at the University of California, Irvine.

An earlier version of chapter 4 was published in *Camera Obscura*, no. 57 (December 2004): 57–92. A version of the epilogue was published in *Film Quarterly* 61, no. 1 (fall 2007): 48–57.

Library of Congress Cataloging-in-Publication Data
Hilderbrand, Lucas
Inherent vice: bootleg histories of videotape
and copyright / Lucas Hilderbrand.
p. cm.
Includes bibliographical references and index.
ISBN 978-0-8223-4353-0 (cloth: alk. paper)
ISBN 978-0-8223-4376-9 (pbk.: alk. paper)
1. Video recordings—Fair use (Copyright)—United States. 2. Copyright—Video recordings—United States. 3. Fair use (Copyright). 4. Piracy (Copyright). I. Title.
KF3030.4.H55 2009
346.7304'82—dc22 2008053652